RELIGIOUS TOLERANCE IN

WORLD RELIGIONS

RELIGIOUS TOLERANCE IN

WORLD RELIGIONS

EDITED BY JACOB NEUSNER

AND BRUCE CHILTON

TEMPLETON FOUNDATION PRESS

West Conshohocken, Pennsylvania

Templeton Foundation Press
300 Conshohocken State Road, Suite 670
West Conshohocken, PA 19428
www.templetonpress.org

*Templeton Foundation Press helps intellectual leaders and others learn about
science research on aspects of realities, invisible and intangible. Spiritual realities
include unlimited love, accelerating creativity, worship, and the benefits of
purpose in persons and in the cosmos.*

Designed and typeset by Kachergis Book Design

LIBRARY OF CONGRESS CATALOGING-IN-PUBLICATION DATA
Religious tolerance in world religions / edited by Jacob Neusner
and Bruce Chilton.
p. cm.
Includes bibliographical references and index.
ISBN-13: 978-1-59947-136-5 (pbk. : alk. paper)
ISBN-10: 1-59947-136-1 (pbk. : alk. paper)   1. Religions.   2. Religious
tolerance.   I. Neusner, Jacob, 1932–   II. Chilton, Bruce.
BL85.R3897 2008
201'.5—dc22
2007041443

Printed in the United States of America

08   09   10   11   12   13   10   9   8   7   6   5   4   3   2   1

CONTENTS

PREFACE

No one contests the proposition that religions bring about intolerance. But the mixed record of religious traditions also encompasses teachings that lead to the tolerance of specified peoples, behaviors, or beliefs. Through case studies covering a wide range of the major world religions, this book attempts to identify the components of religious systems—beliefs, practices, definitions of the social order—that yield attitudes of tolerance for or intolerance of other religious groups.

The contributors to this book frame the question of tolerance and intolerance as matters of public policy in the theory and practice of religious systems, past and present. We inquire into how a religious system in its political statement produces categories of tolerance that are to be explained in that system's logical context, emphasizing cases that generate tolerance in social and political situations. Through these examinations, we hope to show the importance to public policy of understanding world religions as they have been practiced in diverse places and historical periods, of finding that the "infidel" or nonbeliever may be accorded an honorable position within the social order defined by Islam or Christianity or Judaism or Buddhism or Hinduism.

The Question We Propose to Investigate
and Its Importance

Religions by their nature compete, for they present claims about matters of truth and value that conflict with the truths put forth by others. That is the reason religions have to learn how to live with competition. The question we propose to investigate is this: What ideas do religions advance that nurture toleration for competing religious traditions? What ideas does a given religion set forth to explain why it owes to the stranger in its midst the same rights of human dignity and respect that it accords to its own communicants?

In our current political atmosphere, people assume that religions feed intolerance and intergroup hatred. But there is a different record to examine, too.

Islam, for example, has produced Islamic states that located the foundations for tolerating the presence of Christians and Jews within the theology of Islam, most notably in Spain from the seventh century to the reconquest and in the Ottoman Empire. Christianity has a long record of coexisting with different faiths. Judaism, Buddhism, Hinduism, and the other world religions, likewise, have had to formulate, out of their own resources, an explanation of how the outsider, the nonbeliever, finds a legitimate place within the social order of humanity. Because today we hear more about the way in which religions condemn the outsider or the other, we feel that it is important to focus attention on the basis, in the world religions, for the opposite attitude.

An important clarification is in order. The word *tolerance* has more than the meaning "the capacity to live alongside a different religious tradition from one's own." It also refers to acceptance of attitudes and actions contrary to the morality to which one adheres, thus, tolerance of what is, from one's own perspective, deceit or deviancy. This second connotation is not the sense in which the conception is approached in this book. We mean by *tolerance* the capacity to live with religious difference and, by *toleration*, the theory that permits a majority religion to accommodate the presence of a minority religion. Along with the aforementioned example of Islamic tolerance in Spain and the Ottoman Empire, we need to look only at the efforts of the Roman Catholic Church in the Second Vatican Council (1962–1965) to provide a basis for a Catholic theology of toleration of other religions for a single Christian counterpart, among many. Indeed, the religious amity that characterizes American, Canadian, and British religious life draws its ideas from Christianity more than from any other religion. The power of religions to compete with one another—as they do—derives from a fundamental attitude that makes them able to live side by side with difference.

Acknowledgments

The conference at Bard College at which these papers were presented was a project of the Institute of Advanced Theology of Bard College and was supported by the National Endowment for the Humanities, with additional support coming from Bard College, the John Templeton Foundation, and the Institute for Research on Unlimited Love. Views, findings, conclusions, or recommendations expressed in these papers do not necessarily reflect those of the National Endowment for the Humanities, the John Templeton Foundation, or the Institute for Research on Unlimited Love.

Jacob Neusner
Bruce Chilton

PART 1

QUESTIONS ABOUT RELIGIOUS TOLERATION

1

THE "WHAT" AND "WHY"
OF RELIGIOUS TOLERATION

Some Questions to Consider

WILLIAM SCOTT GREEN

Diversity is now a ubiquitous fact of life. In the industrialized West and increasingly in less-developed parts of the world as well, people are deluged with information about and images and interpretations of people unlike themselves. The globalization of the film and television industries, to say nothing of the impact of the World Wide Web means that people from across the globe encounter one another as never before in history. For the world's religions, this is an important new condition. Not only do religions imagine one another in doctrine, in principle, and in theory, but they now experience and engage one another increasingly in practice. No religion, whatever its doctrine may say, can pretend that it is the only one here or even that it is the only one succeeding, at least in earthly terms.

The new environment of nearly instant communication sharpens the practical dimension of the enduring and important question of religious tolerance, the capacity of a religion to forbear another religion with which it disagrees. Since religious pluralism is now a practical reality of everyday life, the capacity of religions to tolerate one another in theory and in practice is a consequential issue of contemporary society.

To achieve a broad and preliminary perspective on this important question, the Department of Religion and Classics at the University of Rochester and Zogby International carried out a global religion poll in 2003.[1]

After developing questions in collaboration with Rochester's department, Zogby International conducted interviews of eleven religious communities in seven nations: 600 people each in India (Hindu, Muslim), Peru (Roman Catholic), Russia (Russian Orthodox), Saudi Arabia (Muslim), and South Korea (Buddhist, Christian); 593 in Israel (Jewish, Muslim, Druze); and 795 in the United States (Catholic, Protestant).[2] All interviews in India, Peru, Russia, Saudi Arabia, and South Korea were conducted face-to-face. All interviews in Israel and the Unites States were conducted over the telephone. All calls for the United States were made from Zogby International headquarters in Utica, New York. All interviews—face-to-face and telephone—were conducted from January through March of 2003. The margin of error for India, Peru, Russia, Saudi Arabia, South Korea, and Israel is +/−4 percent. The margin of error for the United States is +/−3.6 percent. Margins of error are higher in subgroups. The survey yielded comparative results for six different Christian communities, three different Muslim communities, and one each for Hinduism, Judaism, and Buddhism. It can, thus, serve as a useful empirical foundation upon which it is possible to frame questions about religious tolerance. Let us review pertinent results from the survey.

Religious Exclusivism

Respondents from the seven nations were asked which of three statements most closely reflects their religious beliefs. The statements were:

(1) My religion offers the one true path to God and success in the next life.

(2) Other religions that share beliefs similar to mine might also offer a path to God.

(3) My religion is but one of many paths to God and salvation; nearly all religious traditions also lead to God and salvation.

The graph on the following pages charts the results.

Table 1.1 does not demonstrate a correlation between discrete religions and an intolerance toward other religions. The responses of the six Christian communities vary significantly. American Roman Catholics and mainstream Protestants exhibit a high degree of acceptance of the efficacy of other religions. South Korean Christians are at the other end of the spectrum. A similar difference is evident among the Muslim communities. Israeli and Indian Muslims are considerably more accepting of the efficacy of other religions

TABLE 1.1. Evaluating the true path to God

Q 14	Christian					
	Christian	Catholic		Protestant		Orthodox
	S. Korea	Peru	U.S.	U.S. Main-stream	U.S. Born-again	Russia
My religion offers the one true path to God and success in the next life	65	23	15	16	41	24
Other religions which share beliefs similar to mine might also offer a path to God	7	45	18	16	23	26
My religion is but one of many paths to God and salvation; nearly all religious traditions also lead to God and salvation	7	21	63	61	31	41
Not sure	21	12	4	7	5	10

Q 14	Muslim			Hindu	Judaism	Buddhist
	India	Israel	Saudi Arabia	India	Israel	S. Korea
My religion offers the one true path to God and success in the next life	49	37	79	37	33	31
Other religions which share beliefs similar to mine might also offer a path to God	26	7	13	26	15	16
My religion is but one of many paths to God and salvation; nearly all religious traditions also lead to God and salvation	24	55	7	37	25	25
Not sure	1	1	1	0	27	29

than are Saudi Muslims. If the second and third responses are combined, the communities surveyed exhibit a strong degree of tolerance for other religions. Over two-thirds of Indian and Israeli Muslims, Peruvian and American Christians (all Protestants and Catholics), Israeli Jews, and Buddhists claim to hold nonexclusivist views about religion. They acknowledge the possibility of multiple paths to religious truth. South Korean Christians and Saudis are the reverse. American Catholics and mainstream Protestants are the most flexible and accepting on these measures. Sixty-three percent of Catholics and 61 percent of mainstream Protestants say their religion is but one of many paths to God.

Equality of Religious Practitioners

In another question, respondents were asked whether they considered people of other religious faiths to be equal to people of their own faith.

The pattern of table 1.1 is repeated in table 1.2. In all communities except South Korean Christians and Saudi Muslims, a majority regards people of other religions to be equal to themselves. Ninety-five percent of Catholics and 92 percent of mainstream Protestants hold that position.

Interfaith Marriage

In a third question, respondents polled in the seven countries were asked if they would approve or disapprove if their child were to marry someone from another religious tradition.

The views on religious exclusivism do not correlate with attitudes on interfaith marriage. A majority of South Korean Christians, Hindus, and Jews disapprove of marriage outside their religion. Muslims, following Islamic teaching, approve of it for sons but not for daughters. American Catholics and Protestants, and Peruvian Catholics massively approve of interfaith marriage. It appears that the acknowledgment of the equality of the practitioners of other religions does not necessarily translate into a willingness to have them in one's family.

Consequences of Disobedience to Religion

Finally, respondents in the seven countries were asked what they believe will happen if they disobey the teachings of their religions. The options presented were:

TABLE 1.2. Considering the equality of people of other religious faiths

Q 25	Christian					
	Christian	Catholic		Protestant		Orthodox
	S. Korea	Peru	U.S.	U.S. Main-stream	U.S. Born-again	Russia
Yes	35	81	95	92	83	65
No	56	15	3	3	10	18
Not sure	10	4	2	6	7	17

Q 25	Muslim			Hindu	Judaism	Buddhist
	India	Israel	Saudi Arabia	India	Israel	S. Korea
Yes	84	73	29	79	69	52
No	12	15	71	17	24	28
Not sure	4	12	1	4	8	21

TABLE 1.3. Approval of interfaith marriage

Q 26	Christian					
	Christian	Catholic		Protestant		Orthodox
	S. Korea	Peru	U.S.	U.S. Main-stream	U.S. Born-again	Russia
Approve	8	73	86	86	63	34
Disapprove	82	17	9	6	29	23
Not sure	10	11	5	8	8	44

Q 26	Muslim			Hindu	Judaism	Buddhist
	India	Israel	Saudi Arabia	India	Israel	S. Korea
Approve	26	28	32	34	25	35
Disapprove	70	69	68	61	67	35
Not sure	3	3	0	5	8	31

- I will be punished in this life.
- I will be punished after I die.
- I will suffer both in this life and in the next.
- There will be no consequences.

This table suggests that we should be cautious in correlating attitudes of religions' tolerance with conformity to religious teachings. Israeli and Saudi Muslims, for example, hold extremely similar views on the likelihood of their suffering or being punished for religious disobedience, but they hold very divergent views on the viability of other religions and the acceptance of practitioners of other religions as equals to themselves.

TABLE 1.4. Consequences of disobedience to faith

Q 28	Christian					
	Christian	Catholic		Protestant		Orthodox
	S. Korea	Peru	U.S.	U.S. Main-stream	U.S. Born-again	Russia
I will be punished in this life	19	27	15	18	17	19
I will be punished after I die	16	24	16	8	14	23
I will suffer both in this life and in the next	27	33	29	23	39	24
There will be no consequences	10	10	28	31	15	17
Not sure	26	6	12	21	16	18

Q 28	Muslim			Hindu	Judaism	Buddhist
	India	Israel	Saudi Arabia	India	Israel	S. Korea
I will be punished in this life	45	14	8	57	4	8
I will be punished after I die	34	15	14	7	10	14
I will suffer both in this life and in the next	17	67	76	18	18	21
There will be no consequences	1	—	1	13	40	25
Not sure	3	4	1	5	28	30

At the very least, the results of the Rochester/Zogby global religion survey suggest that it is unwise to see the religions of the world as monoliths. Within them, attitudes toward other religions and their practitioners can vary widely. In general, being religious does not correlate with, and therefore does not necessarily generate, attitudes of exclusivism, superiority, or intolerance. These results can help guide our collective reflection on the question of the religious sources of religious toleration.

Questions to Consider: Seeking Generalizations

Keeping the survey's results in mind, we might build the agenda for our work around the following questions:

(1) In the classical sources of the religion you study, what is the role of other religions?

(2) Are different religions acknowledged, rejected, merely endured, or religiously constructive? Are other religions treated generically or differentiated?

(3) How do your sources justify or account for the existence and persistence of other religions? Are the other religions seen as errors, accidents, the consequence of evil, a constructive part of reality, or some combination of variation of these options?

(4) Since we know that, within religions, there are divergent, sometimes opposed, views of other religions, what are the doctrinal fault lines within the religion that produce this divergence? Which teachings within the sources you study justify tolerance of other religions, and which justify intolerance?

(5) Are there historical, political, and/or behavioral factors that correlate with the expression of tolerance in the religion you study? With intolerance? How do you explain the choices made within the religion for tolerance and intolerance?

By working through these questions, it may be possible for us to develop a general model for religious tolerance and intolerance and the factors—both religious and nonreligious—that generate each.

Notes

1. The full results of the poll, which addressed a number of issues in addition to questions of tolerance, can be found at www.zogby.com.

2. The character of the sample groups are as follows:

India (New Delhi). The total sample size was specified to be six hundred interviews with questionnaires to be filled out in the capital, New Delhi, with the two main localities (i.e., religions) Hindu (70 percent) and Muslims (30 percent). The gender composition was based on that of the Indian population (above 15 years of age), with 52 percent males and 48 percent females, applied to each locality. Therefore, one can say that a stratified random sample selection was adopted with probability proportional to the size (PPS) of the population in case of selection of males and females.

The sample selection was based on a list of the electoral polls of the Delhi region provided by the census of the Office of the Registrar General India. To select the required number of subjects from the list, a systematic random sampling scheme was adopted.

Israel. The total sample size was specified to be six hundred adults from the general population interviewed nationwide by telephone. Telephone numbers were randomly selected. Israelis composed 90 percent of the sample, while Palestinians made up 10 percent of the sample. Interviews were conducted in Hebrew or Arabic. Calls were made from January 11 to January 16, 2003.

Peru (Lima). The total sample size was specified to be six hundred interviews with questionnaires to be filled out in the capital, Lima, interviewing only Catholic Christians.

Interviewers resorted to public places chosen from different social neighborhoods and workplaces, which may result in a "selection bias." The choice of interviewees in each coffee shop and workplace was random. As for the gender, it was controlled when choosing the interviewees to reflect the gender composition of Peru's population (above 15 years of age), with 50 percent males and 50 percent females.

It may be worth noting that there is a comparison limitation to this methodology because comparisons can only be applied to other countries' middle-class population, as it is a common behavior for middle-class people to go to coffee shops. Generally, the upper and lower social classes do not visit these public coffee shops.

Russia (Moscow). The total sample size was specified to be six hundred interviews with questionnaires to be filled out in the capital, Moscow, interviewing only Russian Orthodox.

Interviewers resorted to public places chosen from different social neighborhoods, such as coffee shops, which may result in a "selection bias." The choice of interviewees in each coffee shop was random, with not more than one person from each table. Gender was controlled when choosing the interviewees to reflect the gender composition of Russia's population (above 15 years of age), with 46 percent males and 54 percent females.

It may be worth noting there is a comparison limitation to this methodology because comparisons can only be applied to other countries' middle-class population, as it is a common behavior for middle-class people to go to coffee shops. Generally, the upper and lower social class people do not visit these public coffee shops.

Saudi Arabia (Riyadh/Jeddah). The total sample size was specified to be six hundred interviews with questionnaires to be filled out in both Riyadh and Jeddah, with a sample distributed as 60 percent and 40 percent, respectively, which was based on Information International's experience in Saudi Arabia and the population size of both cities. The main religion in Saudi Arabia is Muslim and, consequently, all the six hundred interviewees are Muslims. The gender composition of the sample was based on that of the Saudi population (above 15 years of age) with 59 percent males and 41 percent females. Consequently, and due to the lack of a population census, the sample was chosen based on a systematic random sampling scheme within the three different strata of economic social class, whereby certain starting points inside each stratum were specified (i.e., thirty-six starting points were chosen in

Riyadh and twenty-four in Jeddah) and ten random household interviews around each starting point were conducted.

Therefore, one can say that a stratified random sample selection was adopted with probability proportional to the size (PPS) of the population in case of selection of males and females.

South Korea (Seoul). The total sample size was specified to be six hundred interviews with questionnaires to be filled out in the capital, Seoul, with the two main localities (i.e., religions) Christian (50 percent) and Buddhist (50 percent). The gender composition of the sample was based on that of the Korean population (above 15 years of age), with 49 percent males and 51 percent females. Therefore, one can say that a stratified random sample selection was adopted with probability proportional to the size (PPS) of the population in case of selection of males and females.

The sample was selected based on a systematic random sampling scheme after specifying certain starting points (i.e., areas) for both Christian and Buddhist areas that also take into consideration the three different strata of economic social class.

United States. Zogby International conducted interviews of 795 adults chosen at random nationwide. All calls were made from Zogby International headquarters in Utica, New York, from February 19 to February 21, 2003. The margin of error is +/−3.7 percent. Slight weights were applied to age, gender, region, and religion to more accurately reflect the adult population. Margins of error are higher in subgroups.

PART 2

ANCIENT ISRAEL

2

TOLERANCE IN
ANCIENT ISRAELITE MONOTHEISM

BARUCH A. LEVINE

At a time in human history when there is so little religious toleration in many parts of the world, it is well to look to our respective traditions for insight and guidance. In so doing, we ought to be honest in evaluating our received religious teachings, in my case, those of the Hebrew Bible. I am aware that early Judaism reinterpreted the Hebrew Bible through a process that has never really ended and that the same is true of Christianity and, with some differences, also of Islam. Such developments are to be discussed by others; it is my challenge to remain in context by providing an analysis of the evidence preserved in the Hebrew Bible itself. In so doing, I will try to avoid eisegesis in favor of exegesis—to read out of the Hebrew Bible rather than reading into it.

Also to be avoided in biblical study is apologetic or, shall we say, tendentious selectivity, a process that highlights what we regard as good but obscures or downplays what we regard as bad, and then proceeds to evaluate what has been selected as representative of the whole. The apologist attempts to justify what is problematic instead of confronting it, thereby distorting the picture. There is, however, another kind of selectivity that is desirable, even indispensable. We can accept what we regard as representing the best of the Hebrew Bible's teachings but honestly question, and at times even disapprove of, that which severely troubles us. Believers are reluctant to do this, as we would expect, because to do so requires us to assign priority to our own judgment over the authority of the religious traditions themselves. And yet, I find the exercise of critical judgment to be indispensable in furthering religious toleration, as history moves along. Attempting to make religious traditions say what we want to hear is illusory; it lacks credibility.

Enlightened selectivity views the Hebrew Bible as speaking with a multiplicity of voices over a period of about a thousand years. We perceive that the Hebrew Bible registers an ongoing debate on the major issues that confronted the Israelite-Jewish societies. It variously speaks for heroes, kings and prophets, priests and scribes, and even at times for "everyman." It is precisely this dialectic that accounts for the continuing communicative power of the Hebrew Bible, as it addresses ever-present human concerns. I hasten to state that factoring in the passage of time is not tantamount to positivism. To do so does not imply that there is steady improvement over time. Indeed, in charting biblical thought, the graph shows diachronic ups and downs and, what is even more revealing, synchronic oppositions.

As an example, certain priestly writers believed that the God of Israel commanded the massacre of women and children at the battle of Jericho (see Josh. 6:17–21), and in the Midiante war of Num. 31. Other priestly writers who contributed significant content to the book of Genesis and who were not far removed in time continued to portray Abraham and his followers as peaceful settlers in Canaan, who entered into treaties with the inhabitants and purchased land from them legally. I cannot precisely identify when the respective groups of authors produced these multilayered narratives and when others compiled them in final form, but I see grounds for dating the finished products relatively late, in the Achemenid period, following the Babylonian exile. I assume that the priestly authors who recounted the battle of Jericho and the Midianite war of Num. 31 wrote at a time when relations with Canaanites and nearby peoples were extremely hostile. In contrast, those who depicted peaceful coexistence in configuring the earliest period of settlement in Canaan either had experienced a more favorable situation or wished for better times. It goes without saying that I am edified by the latter view, while being deeply troubled by the former. To react with hatred to the hatred of others is less than acceptable to me, but I must confess that it most certainly was acceptable, if not mandatory, in the view of some biblical authors.

Terms of Reference

Three terms of reference require clarification at the outset. The first is *toleration* (or *tolerance*), the second is the modifier *religious*, and the third is *monotheism*. It is generally recognized that the verb *to tolerate* bears a negative implication. To tolerate is to allow or permit—at the worst, to put up with; at the best, to accept as rightful. Toleration does not of itself connote an understanding of what or of whom one tolerates nor agreement with the beliefs or way of life of those who are the objects of toleration. It does, however, repudiate coercion and aggression and, if implemented, would enhance cooperation among individuals and peoples. Even in this minimal view, it needs to be stressed that the Hebrew Bible is hardly a paradigm of toleration! After all, waging war is the most intolerant of human acts, and the Hebrew Bible is replete with chronicles of warfare, some of them declared to be "holy wars."

As for the adjective *religious*, it is doubtful whether we can speak of religious toleration in antiquity apart from ethnicity and political identity (the same stricture appears to be true today!).When we discuss religious tolerance versus intolerance in biblical Israel, we are talking about a variety of Israelite attitudes toward other peoples who worship other gods and toward disloyal, fellow Israelites and their kings who join in such worship or who sponsor and sanction it. There is no evidence that in pre-Hellenistic times, conquering, ancient Near Eastern peoples sought to impose their religion on defeated enemies. Understandably, the winners proclaimed the supremacy of their standard-bearing deities; but, as far as we know, the Assyrians, for example, never required Israelites to worship their chief state deity, Aššur. While acting with extreme cruelty toward defeated enemies and annexing conquered territories, they were relatively tolerant in religious terms, strictly speaking. It is only in the book of Daniel and the Esther scroll, both composed in the Hellenistic period, though cast in earlier times, that we are first introduced to religious coercion directed at Jews and then only in exceptional circumstances.

This leads us to an observation that will occupy us again and again: there is an irony with respect to the development of universal monotheism in biblical Israel. Its exponents, primarily the prophets, proclaimed an absolute truth, whereas polytheists operated with the view that it was normal for different nations to worship different gods. As the ultimate logic of monotheism played out and its horizons broadened, this absolutism led to intolerance, both ideological and actual, as has been seen throughout history. In this connection, it must be understood that the term *monotheism* is often used inaccurately, as if to identify a static belief system, without taking into account the developmental phases of its history in biblical times. We can actually identify three principal phases in the process as regards ancient Israel:

(1) In the first phase, we observe that the patriarchs worshiped El Shadday and that the author(s) of the Balaam oracles speak additionally of the West-Semitic deity Elyon (Num. 23–24). Abram participated in the worship of El-

Elyon together with Abimelek, the petty Canaanite king of Shalem (Gen. 14:18–24). The Jahwist and Elohist, who gave us the earliest narratives of the Pentateuch, operated with this viewpoint. In such terms, Yahweh is regarded as the national God of the Israelites but not the only God that Israelites may legitimately worship, with the old West-Semitic, regional pantheon still recognized. We can say that this early outlook was at least implicitly tolerant.

(2) The second phase is epitomized by the statement of the Decalogue, "You shall have no other gods in my presence," echoed in the pronouncement, "Give heed, oh Israel. Yahweh is our God, Yahweh is (the only) one." (That is, by the way, what the Hebrew YHWH *ᵉḥḥād* means). This theology is usually referred to as *henotheism*. Contrary to the observable pattern in Iron Age Levant, the Israelites were now forbidden to do what they had been doing before. Henceforth, they must worship only Yahweh. The old pantheon is rejected, and the religious outlook becomes far less tolerant as a result. Ultimately, the resultant intolerance was realized in the policy known as *ḥērem*, "destruction, condemnation" (see, for example, Deut. 7). The exclusive worship of Yahweh became territorial, and a policy of iconoclasm went into practice. If the Israelites faithfully implement this policy, Yahweh will enable them to drive out the former inhabitants of the land, who worshiped "other gods." Failure to fulfill these commandments, as by entering into treaties with the native Canaanites or tolerating pagan worship, will lead to severe punishment, ultimately to exile.

At this point, nothing is being said about the worship of other gods on the part of other nations in their own lands. The existence of such deities is not denied. This is the mentality underlying the Egyptian saga: Yahweh defeated the gods of mighty Egypt, who indeed exist but who are surprisingly less powerful than the God of Israel (see Exod. 12:12). Historically, this phase in the development of monotheism coincides with the earlier period of Israelite hegemony in Canaan, when two kingdoms were established in that land. The message has changed: Yahweh is the sole deity who has granted these blessings, and continuing to venerate the regional pantheon is now seen as threatening the distinctiveness of Israelite religion and culture. We observe a process of separation, even of opposition, and a consequent diminution of tolerance.

(3) The third phase in the evolution of Israelite monotheism constituted a response to empire, a political statement on the subject of power. Specifically, First Isaiah of Jerusalem responded to the western conquests of the Late Assyrian Empire, which impacted Judah and Jerusalem most directly during the reign of Sennacherib at the close of the eighth century BCE. It was soon after the year 701, when Jerusalem had come under Assyrian blockade, that

Isaiah spoke of Assyria as the rod of Yahweh's wrath, an instrument empowered by the God of Israel to punish his own people. Judah's suffering was part of a divine plan for the entire world and for all nations (see Isa. 10 and 14:24–27). According to this plan, Assyria, too, would ultimately fall. The exceptional sparing of Jerusalem was taken as a sign of divine providence. Under Isaiah's guidance, Hezekiah, king of Judah, finally submitted to the yoke of Assyria, thereby enabling the now diminished kingdom of Judah to exist for another century. The doctrine of submission to empire is endorsed by Jeremiah a century later, and it was because Zedekiah, unlike Hezekiah, could not resist the urge to rebel against Babylonia that Jerusalem fell, the Temple was destroyed, and the exile began.

First Isaiah utterly denied the existence and power of the gods of other nations and did so in the face of the reality that, as the supreme deity of the Assyrians, the god Aššur headed the pantheon of a world empire. Precisely at the moment when Judah was weakest and Assyria strongest, he redefined the concept of power, removing it from the political sphere and divorcing it from military might. The henotheistic model would no longer work. Yahweh had enabled the Israelites to conquer the land of Canaan, to defeat neighboring nations like Moabites, Midianite, even Philistines from the Aegean, and Arameans from Syria by military means, but neither Judah nor the nations of western Asia could withstand the Assyrian onslaught. There could be no military victory, as the failed Syro-Ephraimite alliance had earlier demonstrated. It is only Yahweh, God of Israel, who will ultimately bring about the destruction of the Assyrians (Isa. 14:24–27).[1]

Two Visions of the Triumph of Universal Monotheism: The Catastrophic and the Spiritual

We are getting ahead of the story. We must consider more fully the negations implied by the universalist assertion that there is only one, true God. Most obvious is the judgment that the deities venerated by other nations and empires are no gods at all, notwithstanding the earthly power exercised in their names. This is a way of expressing the conviction that terrestrial power is transient and that, consequently, those pagan empires that threatened Israel will be destroyed. There is zero tolerance for other religions because, in the first instance, they were associated with the imperial enemies of Israel. Denying their existence is not merely a theological imperative; it is a statement on the subject of Israelite-Jewish survival and security.

This raises the all-important question as to how the sovereignty of the God

of Israel, now proclaimed to be the only true God, is to be manifested throughout the world. Was it now the duty of the Israelites to attempt to eliminate the
worship of false gods on the part of others, to use power to destroy paganism in
other lands, as they were commanded to do in their own land? How does Israel's unfolding destiny, characterized by powerlessness, correlate with the concept of a sole, universal God? We can say at the outset that no biblical tradition,
from the time of First Isaiah on, envisioned that Israel, as a force, would sub-
due other nations, certainly not world empires. Inevitably, this would be God's
work. We accordingly observe two lines of ideological development in biblical literature, which we may call the *catastrophic* and the *spiritual*, respectively.
These most often interact and are both part of the larger scheme of things; but,
for purposes of their clarification, it would be best to address each separately in
the first instance.

The catastrophic vision is more distinct than the spiritual, and it was both
more ancient and more enduring. In fact, it gained emphasis with time, reaching its climax in apocalyptic literature, as exemplified by the book of Daniel.
Ultimately, it derives from the literature of theophany, more precisely, of theo-
machy, the wars between gods in ancient mythology. Poetic resonances of such
thunderous theophanies are to be found in Deut. 33:2, in the Song of Deborah, Judg. 5:4, in Hab. 3:3–5, and in Ps. 68:8–9, which similarly describe the
awesome approach of the God of Israel, who arrives on the scene to assure victory to his people. In a curious way, the same catastrophic vision informs the
account of Yahweh's revelation to Elijah on the Mountain of God at Horeb
(1 Kgs. 8:11–13):

Behold, as Yahweh passed by, there was a great and mighty wind, splitting mountains
and shattering rocks in advance of Yahweh; but Yahweh was not in the wind. After the
wind—an earthquake; but Yahweh was not in the earthquake. After the earthquake—
fire; but Yahweh was not in the fire. But after the fire—a still, small voice [or "a soft
murmuring sound"]. When Elijah heard it, he wrapped his mantle over his face, and
went out and stood at the entrance of the cave. Then a voice addressed him: "Why are
you here, Elijah?"

This passage conveys the clear expectation by the prophet of a catastrophic
revelation, expressed in words that recall the poetic theophanies. But the Elijah encounter remains cryptic; we are at a loss to interpret precisely what the
"still, small voice" means. Might it not constitute a rejection of the catastrophic
vision in favor of the spiritual, providing an exceptional insight into an alternate concept of divine intervention, according to which humans must strain to
hear the almost inaudible voice of God amid the tumult of human events? (See
further.)

The Elijah encounter is exceptional, however. For the most part, it is the catastrophic vision that gains strength with time, as it projects cataclysmic battles on an international scale. These are waged by the God of Israel against the nations of the world who would seek to destroy his resettled people after the Babylonian exile and who would attack Israel's land, coming from the corners of the earth. These encounters are variously dramatized as natural disasters or, in contrast, as miraculous transformations in nature to the benefit of God's people and his land. We have already mentioned the prediction of Assyrian defeat at the hands of Yahweh announced in Isa. 14:24–27. The most dramatic of the catastrophic projections is known as "the War of Gog and Magog," preserved in Ezek. 38–39. Woven through these texts are repeated references to the acknowledgment of the God of Israel by all nations, a thought expressed by forms of the verb *yādaʿ* "to know, acknowledge." God will draw Gog, commander of the coalition of nations, into a trap on the hills of Israel, and then destroy him. Thus, we have Ezek. 38:16, where Yahweh addresses Gog directly:

You shall advance against my people, Israel, like a cloud covering the earth. This shall happen on that distant day: I will bring you to my land, that the nations may know me, when before their eyes, I manifest my holiness through you, Gog.

Yahweh's victory over the nations assembled will demonstrate beyond contradiction that he is the only true God, the only real power, and that he is guardian over Israel. (For similar thoughts, see Isa. 49:25–26; Ezek. 21:6–10; and especially Ezek. 36.). Zechariah 14, the conclusion of what we refer to as II Zechariah, composed later in the postexilic period, makes a similar statement in a manner close to apocalyptic. In future days, Yahweh will assemble all the nations to Jerusalem to do battle, only to destroy them, causing even the natural order to be altered:

Yahweh shall become king over all the earth. On that day, Yahweh shall be the only one, and his name the only one. (Zech. 14:9)

Resonating with the Deuteronomic cry "Give heed, oh Israel," the Hebrew construction YHWH *ᵓeḥḥād* now means that Yahweh is the sole deity sovereign over all nations, not merely the only deity to be worshiped by Israelites. A petitionary statement to similar effect occurs in Ps. 79:6:

Pour out your wrath upon the nations who do not know you, and upon the kingdoms that have not called upon your name.

The Spiritual Vision of Universal Monotheism

So much for the scheme of the catastrophic vision, which declares that only through utter defeat will the nations of the world be compelled to know the God of Israel. But, as already anticipated in the discussion of the Elijah encounter, there is another vision, expressed as the hope, even the prediction, that all humans may become sufficiently enlightened so as to know the truth that there is only one God. This awareness is most eloquently expressed in the vision of world peace enunciated by First Isaiah and paralleled in Micah. It is important to note, however, that the vision of Isa. 2 is presented in a different context from that of Mic. 4, although they are contemporary. It remains uncertain as to which is the primary source. We had best examine each of these pivotal texts in turn.

In Isa. 2:14, the vision of world peace is presented as a part of a larger prophecy of the universal sovereignty of the God of Israel. The context is overtly international, and belongs with the spiritual ideology.

> In the days to come, the mount of Yahweh's house
> Shall stand firm above the mountains, and tower above the hills;
> And all the nations shall gaze upon it with joy.
> And the many peoples shall go and say:
> "Come, let us go up to the mount of Yahweh,
> To the house of the God of Jacob.
> That he may instruct us in his ways,
> And that we may walk in his paths."
> For instruction shall come forth from Zion,
> The word of Yahweh from Jerusalem.
> Thus he will judge among the nations.
> And arbitrate for the many peoples.
> And they shall beat their swords into plowshares,
> And their spears into pruning hooks.
> Nation shall not take up sword against nation,
> They shall never again train for warfare.

This is followed in verses 5–9 by a call to the people of Israel to be guided by God's light, which narrows the horizon, as the Israelites are reminded of their own past faithlessness and, what is more important, forewarned of Yahweh's terror in bringing them low. Proceeding to verses 10–22, we observe the horizon broadening again, becoming international. Here we are introduced to a major theme in biblical prophecy, yôm YHWH, "the day of Yahweh," which exhibits both national and global perspectives. There is an admitted ambiguity, stemming from the connotation in various contexts of such terms as

Hebrew *'eres*, "earth," which can also mean a particular "land." And yet, the tone of the prophecy is best taken as global. Humankind will be humbled by God's awesome power. This prophecy contrasts dramatically with the spiritual tone of Isa. 2:1–4, where there had been no mention of terror or destruction because the nations had come to understand the power of God's word.

And so it is that a most beautiful prophecy on world peace is followed by a prediction of catastrophy. One may compare a similar sequence in Joel 3 and 4, where the prophecies open with the prediction that all flesh will be endowed by God's spirit but quickly continue by predicting the manifestation of God's awesome power, turning day into night and dimming the heavenly bodies. It is remarkable, therefore, that in Mic. 4:1–4, the spiritual vision of world peace, paralleling that of Isa. 2, does not similarly lead into a catastrophic vision involving the manifestation of Yahweh's awful power. For the most part, prophets held on to the catastrophic ideology, even while portraying international peace, which, on the human level, meant the resolution of international disputes without recourse to war.

I regret that the dramatic impact of Isa. 2 and of other spiritual visions of redemption is inevitably diminished by contextual analysis, but it does no good to ignore context. The spiritual vision was emergent, part of a uniquely Israelite response to Assyrian world domination, an alternative to *pax Assyriana*, if you will. Instead of an earthly power imposing law and order, we are introduced to the notion of God's kingdom, a world instructed by God's revealed word, coming forth from Zion. The earlier catastrophic traditions are never fully superseded, however, certainly not during the biblical period. Furthermore, the spiritual vision, even in its purest form, will be realized only through the total rejection of paganism, and the universal acknowledgment of Israel's God as the only true divinity.[2]

Further Expressions of the Spiritual Vision

If we fast-forward to the exilic and early postexilic periods, we find in Deutero-Isaiah, specifically in chapter 45, the application of First Isaiah's catastrophic projection in reverse. In contrast to the kings of Assyria who, as Yahweh's instruments, had ravaged northern Israel and Judah and in contrast to the Babylonian conqueror Nebuchdnezzar II, who destroyed Judah and Jerusalem a century later, acting as Yahweh's "servant" (Jer. 25:9, et passim), Cyrus the Great, ruler of the Persian empire, was commissioned by Yahweh to restore his people and rebuild the Temple of Jerusalem; and for this purpose, he was granted victory (see Isa. 41:1–7). He is actually called *mešîhî*, "my anointed one."

Such is the conceptual framework of universal monotheism. According to Isa. 45, it is not expected that Cyrus, or any other earthly ruler, first acknowledge the sovereignty of the God of Israel before being granted victory. This is the point of the repeated emphasis in Isa. 45 that Yahweh called Cyrus by name and empowered him, although the latter did not "know" him. This also marks the beginning of another process by which Cyrus will ultimately come to "know" the God of Israel as the power behind his victories, whose purpose it was to come to the aid of his people, Israel. Although Cyrus' conquests were catastrophic in themselves, his role in Israel's restoration belongs with the spiritual vision. Such is the other side of the coin, most clearly stated in I Zechariah: "This is the word of Yahweh to Zerubabel: Not by military might and not by force, but rather by My spirit, says Yahweh of hosts" (Zech. 4:6). The God of Israel had restored his people and had enabled them to rebuild the temple in Jerusalem without their having to exercise military might, as had been the case in the earlier conquest and settlement of Canaan. The God of Israel had rearranged world politics and redistributed imperial power so as to prepare a highway for his people, Israel.

It would be well to examine other biblical sources that incorporate the spiritual ideology, all of which are late in the literary sequence, authored in the postexilic period. An interesting text of this sort is the late addition to Solomon's prayer, preserved in 1 Kgs. 8:22–53, especially verses 41–43:

And as well for the foreigner who is not of your people, Israel, should he arrive from a distant land, for the sake of your name—for they shall hear of your great name, and your mighty hand, and your outstretched arm—and he comes to pray at this temple: Oh, hear in your heavenly abode, and grant all that the foreigner asks of you. Thereby all the peoples of the earth will know your name and revere you, as does your people, Israel; and they will recognize that your name has been invoked on this temple which I have built.

Isaiah 19:19–25, a late prophecy (compare the language of Trito-Isaiah 56:6–7), projects the conversion of the Egyptians and their acknowledgment (once again, the Hebrew verb *yādaᶜ*) of Israel's God as supreme. Although not devoid of the catastrophic element, this prophecy progressively engages the spiritual vision:

In that day there shall be a highway from Egypt to Assyria. The Assyrians shall join with the Egyptians, and the Egyptians shall join with the Assyrians, and then the Egyptians together with the Assyrians shall serve [Yahweh]. In that day, Israel shall be the third partner with Egypt and Assyria as a blessing on earth, for Yahweh of hosts will bless them as follows: "Blessed be my people, Egypt; my handiwork, Assyria; and my own possession, Israel." (Isa. 19:23–25)

International peace was traditionally conceived as requiring cooperation between the two principal foci of political power in the ancient Near East, Egypt and Mesopotamia, where the zenith of power is associated with Assyria. Here, Israel is elevated far beyond its political importance and given equal footing with the great empires by virtue of the truth of its religion, which will ultimately be acknowledged universally.

And then, there is the book of Jonah, a relatively late parable on repentance and divine compassion. I now realize why it was cast in Nineveh, Sennacherib's Assyrian capital: it revives the national memory of a bygone crisis. The tale of Jonah is to be seen as a late resonance of the historic Assyrian threat, once again linking Israel's destiny to the fate of empires. It resonates with Isa. 19, where Assyria is blessed and characterized as Yahweh's handiwork. Compare "my handiwork, Assyria" of Isa. 19: 25 with Jon. 4:10–11: "You cared about the plant which you did not toil over and which you did not grow, and should I not care about Nineveh." The God of Israel cares for all of his creatures, even the most wicked of them, once they repent.

Jonah is also an epitome of toleration and a tale of religious conversion. Chapter 1 is set in the ship en route to Tarshish, when it was caught in an awful storm. Each man prayed to his god, but after being trapped by lot, Jonah admitted that he had offended the God whom he worshiped: "I am a Hebrew, and I worship Yahweh, God of the heavens, who made the sea and the dry land" (Jon. 1:9). Whereupon the men on the ship were overtaken by great fear, as they tried valiantly to reach the shore, beseeching Yahweh to spare them from taking a human life. Amazingly, they refer to Jonah as an innocent person, even though his guilt had been clearly established. What is more, they acknowledged that Jonah's God had caused the storm, in true storm-god tradition. "The men feared Yahweh greatly; they offered a meal offering to Yahweh and pronounced vows" (Jon. 1:14). As the story unfolds, the king of Nineveh and his people heed the admonition of an Israelite prophet of Yahweh and are spared. I would classify the perspective of the Jonah tale as near-catastrophic, and yet it also bespeaks enlightenment, expressed by the readiness of different peoples to acknowledge religious truth, their ability to learn the truth from experiencing crisis. Ironically, this tale also alludes to the upside of polytheism, which accepts the reality of many gods, worshiped by many nations, rather than insisting on the absolute exclusivity of one deity. And yet, in the final analysis, it is the God of Israel who created the natural world and who rules over heaven and earth and the deep.

Summary and Conclusions

As we enter the Hellenistic period, the catastrophic vision reasserts itself in the form of apocalyptic, exemplified by the book of Daniel. The doctrine of submission to empires that are instruments of Israel's God shifts to the Ptolemies and Seleucids, in a layered configuration of cryptic, ghastly visions referring to successive empires in panoramic perspective, covering eons of time. The kingdom of God is being translocated to the heavenly spheres, in what was as a theology of despair, a wisdom-like reaction to the seemingly endless succession of world empires. The principal vision is catastrophic from the word *go*, as a perusal of Dan. 11 demonstrates. It reads like a replay of the war of Gog and Magog. There is little in Daniel to suggest that redemption will ever come about through the enlightened conversion of the gentiles to a belief in the one, true God. A new world order will have to be imposed forcefully and dramatically from on high.

Indeed, the Hebrew Bible speaks of the spiritual vision with "a still, small voice," in contrast to its emphasis on the catastrophic vision. For a period of time, the future of the Israelite-Jewish people looked fairly hopeful, after surviving the Assyrian threat of 701 BCE and after the restoration to Zion during the Achemenid period. But it didn't take very long for life under imperial domination to drown out any hope for predictable relief. As the biblical period closes in the Hellenistic period, we see an otherworldly mentality assuming control, whereby only God in all his power will establish justice in the world.

Is the engagement of biblical traditions on the subject of religious toleration, as charted above, at all relevant to the present human condition and, if so, how? Permit me to suggest several factors:

1. Religious toleration is always and everywhere a function of sociopolitical realities, wherein power is a constant factor.

2. The development of Israelite monotheism correlates with the phases of national existence in antiquity and in its most developed form constitutes a response first to Assyrian, then to Babylonian, then to Persian imperial domination. As the Hebrew Bible closes, we discover a last response to the realities of life under the Seleucids.

3. Universal monotheism is innately absolutist; such is its ultimate logic. Even the most spiritual version of prophetic universalism requires an end to paganism. The most that can be said is that monotheists ought to be patient in their expectations and await the enlightened acceptance of Israel's God by all peoples, showing toleration in the protracted interim.

4. If there is in the traditions of the Hebrew Bible a springboard for inter-religious dialogue, it rests in the spiritual vision of international peace, even with the just stated limitation. As already noted, war and its concomitants represent the most extreme expressions of human intolerance, and failure to establish a peaceful world order will doom to failure any international effort to promote religious toleration. To hope for a cataclysmic end to injustice is, in my humble opinion, to invite cataclysm without achieving justice.

5. Ultimately, those of us who pray for a tolerant world will be called upon to reinterpret our respective theologies so as to accommodate the sincerity of the search for religious truth among members of all religious communions, whether theistic or not, whether monotheistic or not. In Job 28:28, part of an elegy on wisdom, we read:

Then he (=God) said to man: "Verily, fear of the LORD—that is wisdom, and turning away from evil—understanding."

The equation of goodness with religious faith suggests that we should direct our attention toward human behavior as the ultimate test of religious acceptability and away from an evaluation of our fellow man based on the acceptance of what we each choose to believe is religious truth.

Notes

1. The argument for identifying the here-outlined three phases in the development of Israelite monotheism is elaborated in Baruch A. Levine, "Assyrian Ideology and Israelite Monotheism," *Iraq* 67, no. 1 (2005): 411–427 [=*Recontre Assyriologique International* 48, no. 2 (2005)].

2. The Micah version of the prophecy of international peace (Mic. 4:1–4) is immediately followed by what is clearly a contradictory statement (Mic. 4:5): "For though all of the peoples 'walk,' each in the name of its god, we will 'walk' in the name of Yahweh, our God, forever." It is generally accepted that 4:5 bears the earmarks of a secondary interpolation. It picks up on the notion expressed in the original prophecy (4:2), of walking in the paths of Yahweh but reuses it or reapplies it in order to acknowledge the right of other peoples to follow the dictates of their gods. The original prophecy is unequivocal in its vision of all nations turning to the God of Israel for instruction. Apparently, someone was troubled by the universal vision, leaving us to wonder who it was and for whom that redactor spoke.

PART 3

THE PRE-CHRISTIAN WEST

3

GRECO-ROMAN LITERARY EXPRESSIONS OF RELIGIOUS TOLERANCE

CAROLYN DEWALD

If one were to order all mankind to choose the best set of rules in the world, each group would, after due consideration, choose its own customs; each group regards its own as being by far the best. So it is unlikely that anyone except a madman would laugh at [customs]. There is plenty of other evidence to support the idea that this opinion of one's own customs is universal, but here is one instance. During the reign of Darius, King of Persia, Darius invited some Greeks who were present to a conference, and asked them how much money it would take for them to be prepared to eat the corpses of their fathers; they replied that they would not do that for any amount of money. Next, Darius summoned some members of the Indian tribe known as Callatiae, who eat their parents, and asked them in the presence of the Greeks, with an interpreter present so that they could understand what was being said, how much money it would take for them to be willing to cremate their fathers' corpses; they cried out in horror and told him not to say such appalling things. So these practices have become enshrined as customs just as they are, and I think Pindar was right to have said in his poem that custom is king of all.

Herodotus, The Histories 3.38

"Vae, puto, deus fio" ("Oh dear, I think I'm becoming a god").

The Emperor Vespasian (on his deathbed), Suet. Vesp. 23

The ancient Greeks and Romans parsed religion and divinity quite differently from the way any modern religion does, and yet, for our Western civilization, they are important cultural ancestors. At least two of the three major monotheistic religions of today emerged from the crucible of the Greco-Roman world, as well as many of the civic habits underlying current Western assumptions about the nature and function of political community. So it is worth looking carefully at Greco-Roman ideas of religious tolerance. If Rodney King's question—"Can't we all just get along?"—is our question today, our cultural ancestors' successes and failures in this area will continue to be instructive to us in the search for answers.

We cannot, however, interview ancient Greeks and Romans for their attitudes about religious tolerance. What I can do here is survey a sampling of the Greco-Roman literary tradition, to tease out some of the cultural assumptions and habits of mind that underlie the evolving political and religious structures of the ancient world described by Robert Berchman and Kevin Corrigan [in this volume]. The literary evidence does not speak with one voice or in one language, but its medley gives expression to a variety of the attitudes underlying the cultural practices they describe.

A word of caution is in order, however. The works I look at here were culled from more than eight centuries of the lived experience of two complex and quite variegated cultures and were produced by people from places stretching from Spain to Syria and involving most of the Mediterranean world that lay in between. Moreover, all of them were men, from Homer, the oral poet of the archaic era (eighth century BCE), to Lucian, the clever sophist of the second sophistic (second century CE), and men either born into the educated upper class or accepted into it, often because of the recognition accorded to their literary gifts. We have no literary record expressing what the ordinary man-in-the-street (let alone the ordinary woman-in-the-house) thought about religious tolerance in the ancient classical world. Finally, the authors whose works we have extant were not directly addressing the issue of religious tolerance; their attitudes come through obliquely, embedded in texts that were written to entertain or instruct their audiences about quite different matters. In most instances, the attitudes toward what we would call religion exist as part of an unstressed, neutral background for the major plot line of the text. It is difficult, sometimes, to be sure that we are reading the tone of a given comment correctly. The imperial Roman author Juvenal, in his lengthy and snarling attack against the vices of women, mocks one Roman woman for consulting a series of fortune-tellers (6.542–47):

No sooner has that [Egyptian] fellow departed than a palsied Jewish woman, leaving her basket and hay, comes begging to her private ear; she is an interpreter of the laws of Jerusalem, a high priestess of the tree, a trustworthy go-between of highest heaven. She too fills her palm, but more sparingly, for a Jew will tell you dreams of any kind you please for a tiny coin.

Is it religious intolerance, ethnic slur, or just general and widespread misogyny or misanthropy that is in question here? Hard to tell.

On the other hand, some of these limitations are also, for our purposes, an advantage. The poets and prose writers were not editing their responses and attitudes to fit the expectations of an interview situation, but mostly took them for granted, as they expected their contemporary audiences to do as well. Many of the literary works considered here were already part of the ethnic heritage, the cultural capital, of the late antique men who comprised the elites governing the cities of the Greco-Roman world and who created the political tolerance described by Prof. Berchman in the Roman middle imperial period. The early epic and lyric poets, the Attic dramatists and orators, and the Greek and Roman philosophers, historians, orators, and later poets produced texts that educated Greek and Roman young men from powerful families had learned to recite and imitate in school and to read in their leisure hours; in their own literary productions and political speeches, they could refer to these texts allusively, expecting their audiences to understand their allusions. Greek, Roman, and imperial cities were adorned with art depicting scenes from these works—statues of gods and men and women favored by the Greco-Roman gods, paintings and mosaics depicting various mythic encounters of people with gods.

Before embarking directly on the questions about tolerance that William Scott Green in this volume, has asked (and very provocative questions they are), I want to sketch out some of the real distinctiveness of ancient Greek and Roman cultural assumptions regarding religion in general. Ancient Greek not only had no word for tolerance; it had no word for religion, either. Words connected to religion included *ta theia*, literally "things connected with the gods"; *theôn therapeia*, "worship"; *hosiotês*, "ritual purity"; or *eusebeia*, "piety, religiousness." Even in Latin, the word *religio* meant "fear of the gods" or "piety" or "religious scrupulousness" long before, in late Latin, it acquired the meaning of a system of religious belief that we give it today. (The Latin Dictionary of Lewis and Short ascribes this usage to Flavius Eutropius in the late fourth century CE and Ammianus Marcellinus a little later.)[1]

For the ancient pagans of the Mediterranean world, the stories shaping their thinking about religion were quite different from the kinds of stories that shape the identity of religions today. The human world and the first generation of gods emerged out of the same stuff, for the Greeks and then, mythically and literarily at least, the Romans who proceeded to build on Greek beginnings. According to Hesiod's *Theogony*, produced in the seventh century BCE, Chaos (the void), Gaia (earth), and Eros (desire) first arose, and then Gaia bore "starry Ouranos," or heaven, "to cover her all over" (*Theog.* 127). Earth and sky were forcibly separated from each other when one of their children, Cronos, castrated his father, threw the genitals into the sea, and Aphrodite, goddess of love, emerged from the foam on the island of Cyprus or Cythera. Cronos' children and grandchildren became the other Titans and the Olympian gods (*theoi*), twelve of whom lived atop Mount Olympus as a large clan, ruled over by Father Zeus (Greek) or Ju-Piter (Latin).

(Note: this version of the origin story, Hesiod's, was certainly heavily influenced by Near Eastern theogonies. In more ancient Indo-European myth, we do see some familiar gods named, for instance, the sky-father, Zeus or Jupiter, and the divine twins, the Dioscuri—compare the Asvins of Hindu theology—but the origin myths shaping the later Greco-Roman literary tradition were basically Hesiod's.)[2]

The gods, differently in different versions of the myth, shaped human beings out of earth and gave them sentience; the Titan Prometheus gave them fire and was punished for it because Zeus felt that, with such a gift, humans would become themselves too much like gods. The gods (and this meant not just the Olympian gods but also the chthonic gods beneath the earth, and the various divine beings that were more local in nature—nymphs, river gods, and so forth) had power over human beings and expected both regular acknowledgment, in ritual offerings and prayerful attention, and obedience on the humans' part to standards of behavior that reflected communal ethical norms. The gods themselves, at least in the early period, were not responsible for living up to the same ethical standards; in Homer, one distinguishing trait of divinity was that a god could do things human beings could not do and incur only temporary inconvenience for doing them.[3] In Homer and later literature as well, the gods plot against each other and even make war against each other, using human beings as their pawns, but because they are immortal, it doesn't ultimately matter very much what they do; Walter Burkert calls their final battle in the *Iliad* "a harmless farce."[4] However, both in the literature and in the popular beliefs of ordinary Greeks and Romans, when people either individually or collectively did not honor the obligation of ritual propitiation and ethical behavior, they might be punished by the gods with disease, failure of crops or herds, civic discord or loss in battle, natural disaster, or sudden death. The gods spoke their displeasure to men through such catastrophes; they could also communicate, if they chose, about the future, through dreams, portents, or oracles like those at Delphi, Dodona, or Cumae.

Put this way, it all looks to us rather primitive and strange. And yet, looked at another way, it is not. The myths or stories about the gods that figured heavily in the Greco-Roman literary consciousness did not define Greco-Roman religion in the way that the historical accounts of origins matter in many modern religions. The important thing was not the narratives about the gods, but the correct performance of religious practice. For ancient Greek and Roman people, the gods literally, even tautologically, were the various powers and forces to which human beings were vulnerable; hence, people had to propitiate these powers if they wanted to have a reasonably good life. The resources of nature and natural forces, physical or intellectual or artistic abilities displayed by some human beings, even physical beauty itself—all these were seen, again self-evidently, as gifts from the divine powers. Herodotus, the fifth-century historian, expressed the tautology well: the gods were called *theoi* because they set (the Greek root for the verb *set* is *the-*) the world in order (2.52). This might have been an incorrect etymology, but it expressed a religious truth.[5]

This state of things began to change with the writings of the Ionian philosophers in the sixth century BCE and the sophists and Athenian intellectuals of the fifth and fourth centuries, so that, for instance, in the later fifth century Aristophanes could in his comedy, *Clouds*, make fun of various notions of meteorological forces and their worship. Even here, however, the Clouds themselves turn out in the play to be Zeus' agents in enforcing civic good behavior, rather than the wispy, intellectual, amoral abstractions that the sophist Socrates in the play has assumed them to be. This shows another aspect of the difference between the Greco-Roman world and our own, already noted: the Greeks and Romans sharply differentiated religious practice, which had to be observed because it represented the contract between gods and men, from thoughts and words about the gods, which were accorded much more license—even what we would call enormous tolerance.[6] (More on this below, however, since Aristophanes' depiction of Socrates in *Clouds*, Plato later went on to argue, played a part in costing the real Socrates his life, several decades after the play was first performed.)

So, some of the basic ideas underlying ancient Greco-Roman literary depictions of religion seem very foreign to us today, some disconcertingly familiar, but they are still worth mapping out as a Western cultural background, within which the comments about tolerance that we will consider below arose. With these introductory thoughts, let us proceed to William Scott Green's five questions.

(1) In the classical sources of the religion you study, what is the role of other religions?

(2) Are different religions acknowledged, rejected, merely endured, or religiously constructive? Are other religions treated generically or differentiated?

(3) How do your sources justify or account for the existence and persistence of other religions? Are the other religions seen as errors, accidents, the consequence of evil, a constructive part of reality, or some combination of variation of these options?

(4) Since we know that, within religions, there are divergent, sometimes opposed, views of other religions, what are the doctrinal fault lines within the religion that produce this divergence? Which teachings within the sources you study justify tolerance of other religions, and which justify intolerance?

(5) Are there historical, political, and/or behavioral factors that correlate with the expression of tolerance in the religion you study? With intolerance? How do you explain the choices made within the religion for tolerance and intolerance?

I will structure the discussion into three roughly chronological stages, considering the particularly relevant parts of the five questions for each stage. Please note, however, that the stages are not easy to disentangle completely from each other. The first, and earliest, lasts in some respects throughout the Greco-Roman world, and the others are added to it; some of the advances we see in the later periods are already adumbrated or hinted at in some of the earliest texts as well.

A. Greco-Roman Literary and Cultural Paganism (eighth century BCE–third century CE)

1. What is the role of other religions?

In its most basic and enduring form, in Greco-Roman paganism, there are no other religions. There are only many, many gods with many names and forms. In Homer's *Iliad*, the same Olympian gods are prayed to, and work for or against, both Greeks and Trojans. As the poem opens, Zeus is off visiting the "blameless Aethiopians" (1.423), with whom the gods habitually dine. Later, Hector goes from the battlefield to Troy, to ask his mother to make special prayers to Athene (6.269), "but Pallas Athene turned her head from her" (6.311); she, of course, favored the Greeks in the Trojan War. But the Olympian gods are merely the tip of a much larger polytheistic iceberg, so to speak. "Catullus, Vergil, Tibullus, Ovid are instinct with the power of the divine in the countryside. . . . Trees were sacred: Pliny the elder has a long section on the subject."[7] Pliny the younger remarks on the source of the spring Clitumnus: "Near it there is an ancient and venerable temple. In it stands Clitumnus himself, clothed, and draped in a crimson-bordered robe: the oracular lots around him show that his divinity is present and can foretell coming events. Around this temple there are several smaller shrines, each with its own god."[8] Strabo describes the mouth of the Alpheus river, which flows past Olympia: "The whole tract is full of shrines of Artemis, Aphrodite, and the nymphs, in flowery groves, due mainly to the abundance of water; there are numerous herms on the road, and shrines of Poseidon on the headlands by the sea."[9]

In one's family, one revered with prayer and various offerings the particular ancestral divinities of one's home but also the powers that oversaw a particular function or transitional moment: birth, a child's maturity, the stages in the agricultural year. When one visited another city, even nearby, one took for granted that the ways of describing, honoring, or even thinking about the gods in that city differed somewhat from one's own familiar practices.[10] If one went further afield still, among people who did not speak Greek or Latin, one would expect that the gods would have different names and very different appearance and cult. Herodotus discusses the worship of Athene among the Ausees, a Libyan tribe: they celebrate "a festival to Athene once a year at which the unmarried young women of the tribe divide into two groups and fight one another with sticks and stones; the women say that this is how they fulfill their ancestral duties to their native goddess, the one we call Athene" (4.180). The ancients had a "habit of looking for numina," spirits, finding their proper names, and giving them their due, as a matter of course.[11]

> 2. Are different religions acknowledged, rejected, merely endured, or
> religiously constructive? Are other religions treated generically or differentiated?
>
> 3. How do your sources justify or account for the existence and
> persistence of other religions? Are the other religions seen as errors,
> accidents, the consequence of evil, a constructive part of reality,
> or some combination of variation of these options?

These questions do not really apply, then, until the Greeks and the Romans encountered religions that did not admit of syncretistic assimilation of the sort described above, in the Hellenistic period and especially in its later stage, in the Roman Empire. That does not mean that some of the reverberations of tolerance and intolerance were entirely absent in the earlier period; the way human sympathy and compassion for the stranger or the enemy appears in the early literary texts certainly contributes to the way religious tolerance was later thought about and articulated. Religion in this early period was largely a matter of following the practices of one's group; in Greece, this meant the clan and the *polis*, or city. And the same, of course, went for depictions of hatred and intolerance. So we will consider questions 4 and 5 below in these terms.

4. Which teachings justify tolerance, and which justify intolerance?

Even if Greek did not have a word for tolerance, per se, it was clear that the early Greeks knew, experienced, and valued the quality of fellow feeling for the foreign, the other, that would later develop into ethnic and religious tolerance. Most famously, in the *Iliad*, the early poem about the ten-year war in Troy, the Greeks are destined to destroy the city and most of its inhabitants. At almost the end of the epic, however, occurs one of the most moving passages in Greek literature, since it conveys the idea of a common humanity binding foreigners, even enemies, together. Achilles has killed Hector and is daily dragging his body around the city, behind his chariot, to outrage his corpse. The gods are offended, and Zeus sends Hermes to Priam, the aged and heartbroken king of Troy. Hermes guides Priam past enemy lines, to visit Achilles in the Achaean camp, and begs for the body of his son, Hector, kissing the hand of his enemy in supplication:

So [Priam] spoke, and stirred in the other a passion of grieving for his own father. [Achilleus] took the old man's hand and pushed him gently away, and the two remembered, as Priam sat huddled at the feet of Achilleus and wept close for manslaughtering Hektor and Achilleus wept now for his own father, now again for Patroklos. The sound of their mourning moved in the house. Then when great Achilleus had taken full satisfaction in sorrow and the passion for it had gone from his mind and body, thereafter he rose from his chair, and took the old man by the hand, and set him on his feet again, in pity for the grey head and the grey beard. . . . (*Il.* 24.507–516)

In the classical period of the Athenian fifth century, there is another famous formulation, this time of civic tolerance, in Pericles' funeral oration, describing for the Athenians why they are different in habit from other Greek cities:

And just as our political life is free and open, so is our day-to-day life in our relations with each other. We do not get into a state with our next-door neighbour if he enjoys himself in his own way, nor do we give him the kind of black looks which, though they do no real harm, still do hurt people's feelings. We [associate without offense] in our private lives; but in public affairs we keep to the law. (Thuc. 2.37)[12]

This is a vision first articulated in our extant sources by Solon, the great Athenian legislator of 594 BCE, who commented that he had averted *stasis*, or civic warfare, between the Athenian rich and poor by being "a strong shield for both." The theme of reconciliation among potential enemies was taken up by the fifth-century Athenian dramatists and extrapolated and extended as a civic habit, it was claimed, to foreigners, outcasts, and problematic strangers. Aeschylus in the last play of the *Oresteia* depicts Athene herself refusing to judge the Furies by their disgusting appearance and granting them a hearing and benefits at Athens that will eventually turn them into *Eumenides*, or well-wishers; Sophocles in the *Oedipus at Colonus* has King Theseus, and some ordinary Athenian citizens as well, articulate a generalized compassion for the polluted, cursed, blinded old king-beggar, Oedipus, at the end of his life. Clearly, a lot of what is in our notion of "tolerance" is something that Athens believed was intrinsic to its civic mores and identity, at the height of its fifth-century powers.[13]

Intolerance, when it appears, is often expressed by one god resentful of another's encroachment on his or her proper honors. In Euripides' *Hippolytus*, Aphrodite, goddess of love, comes on at the beginning of the play to announce that she will create deadly havoc because she has been denied her proper honors by the young man Hippolytus, who only honors Artemis, the virginal goddess of the hunt. In the *Bacchae*, Dionysus performs the same function. He dooms his human cousin Pentheus to be ripped apart by the maddened women of Thebes (his own mother included!) because Pentheus has denied Dionysus' divinity and denied Thebes the right to celebrate it. Human beings in the plays quarrel over the appropriate establishment and performance of cult; the young and intolerant king, Pentheus, in the Bacchae mocks his old grandfather, Cadmus, and the seer, Teiresias, for performing the rites of Dionysus. King Creon, in Sophocles' *Antigone*, refuses burial to Antigone's brother Polyneices because he has attacked the city, and he condemns Antigone to death for performing the ritual he has outlawed. Here, however, an unwritten divine law expressly takes precedence over human edicts since the prophet Teiresias tells Creon that Antigone is right not to refuse burial (998 ff.); the gods have backed up her compassion for the fallen enemy, her brother. Antigone herself says, of Creon's edict,

For me it was not Zeus who made that order./ Nor did that Justice who lives with the gods below/ mark out such laws to hold among mankind./ Nor did I think your orders were so strong/ that you, a mortal man, could over-run/ the gods' unwritten and unfailing laws./ Not now, nor yesterday's, they always live,/ and no one knows their origin in time." (*Ant.*, 450 ff.)

5. Are there historical, political, and/or behavioral factors that correlate with expressions of tolerance? With intolerance? How does one explain the choices made within the religion for tolerance and intolerance?

Presumably, the origins of Greek syncretism occurred back before the Greeks had really become Greek—as they brought their Indo-European gods and beliefs down into the Helladic peninsula in the early second millennium and met its "Pelasgian" inhabitants and their quite different sets of divinities.[14] Both "internal" and "contact" syncretism occurred at the outset of the Greek integration into the Mediterranean world; and, once habitual, they would occur again and again, among different Greek tribes, between Greeks and Romans, and among Greeks, Romans, and the other peoples they encountered. "*Interpretatio Graeca*" and "*interpretatio Romana*" are the names generally applied to the Greek and Roman habit of encountering some alien people's deity and assigning it a familiar Greek or Roman deity's name (compare Tacitus *Germ.* 43.3).

Aristophanes' freedom to generate ridiculous stories about the gods in comedy reminds us once more of the centrality of the correct performance of ritual; if one honored the deities of the city, the neighborhood, the family, and those divinities controlling important human moments of transition, one was not putting at risk the health of the community, and that was what counted above all. Evidence of religious intolerance, however, does occasionally emerge.[15] What bothered Greeks of the early period they sometimes called "atheism."[16] Already in the mid-400s BCE, the philosopher Anaxagoras (who thought Helios, the sun god, was a large incandescent rock) was put on trial in Athens for impiety and withdrew to Lampsacus; it is likely that his friendship with the powerful Athenian politician Pericles was more germane to the prosecution than his philosophical speculations. The poet Diagoras of Melos apparently mocked the Eleusinian mysteries and, condemned to death, fled Athens in the later years of the fifth century.[17] Alcibiades was forced to flee Athens or face prosecution in 415 BCE, ostensibly because he had mocked the mysteries of Eleusis and was believed to have defaced the statues of the guardian spirits that stood outside every Athenian house. Certainly Socrates' death sentence in 399 BCE in Athens had much more to do with the role some of his pupils had played in Athens' defeat in the Peloponnesian War (431–404 BCE) than it did with his heterodox religious ideas.

B. The Early Intellectuals: Ionian Philosophers, Sophists, Historians (Sixth Century BCE –Early Fourth Ccentury BCE)

1. What is the role of other religions?

Some cultural trends emerge in the literature of the late archaic and early classical period that begin to suggest the notion of "different religions," and play a part in the later development of Greco-Roman ideas of tolerance and intolerance.

(a) In the cities of the east Aegean, first of all, the practices and beliefs of Greek polytheism came under critical observation from the first group of intellectuals that we might call natural philosophers. As we have already seen, in Greco-Roman thought, the gods were shaped out of and closely identified with the natural world—they were believed to be a powerful and sentient part of that world, one that human beings could propitiate. The Milesian philosophers, about 500 BCE, began to question this concept, doubting the truth-value of both traditional religious myths and rituals, in the context of their efforts to understand the reality of the natural world and the elements that went into its composition. Without delving into the specifics of their various physical theories, we may note that their speculations in the realm of natural science also, therefore, called into question Greek religious ideas and that this sometimes led to fears on the part of Greek communities and consequent expressions of intolerance (see A.5, p. 40, above). This also led into a growing split between popular religion and philosophy.

Xenophanes of Colophon opined: "Homer and Hesiod have attributed to the gods everything that is a shame and reproach among men, stealing and committing adultery and deceiving each other" (frag. 169); "The Ethiopians say that their gods are snub-nosed and black, the Thracians that theirs have light blue eyes and red hair" (frag. 171); "One god, greatest among gods and men, in no way similar to mortals either in body or in thought" (frag. 173); "No man knows, or ever will know, the truth about the gods and about everything I speak of: for even if one chanced to say the complete truth, yet he himself does not know it . . ." (frag. 189). Heraclitus of Ephesus also declared: "To god all things are beautiful and good and just, but men have supposed some things to be unjust, others just" (frag. 209); "*Polemos* (war, strife) is the father of all and king of all, and some he shows as gods, others as men; some he makes slaves, other free" (frag. 215); "Man's character is his daimon" (frag. 250). Ideas like these would eventually lead to the ethical formulations of the great Hellenistic philosophical schools, whose differences from one another gave rise to occasional expressions of intolerance among themselves and toward the "superstitions" of traditional religion. Heraclitus already opined in about 500 BCE: "The learning of many things (*polumathiê*) does not teach intelligence; if so it would have taught Hesiod and Pythagoras, and again Xenophanes and Hecataeus" (frag. 260).

(b) There also grew up during the Greek archaic period a variety of what were later called by scholars "mystery religions." Some of these were home-grown, others came out of syncretistic connections with Egypt or the Near East, but they involved cults that cut across civic and ethnic lines, promising some form of special relation and favor for the devotee from the god in return for participation in particular rituals, usually open only to initiates. The most famous of these was the Eleusinian mysteries in Attica, a cult honoring Demeter and her daughter Persephone, in which slaves and free, men and women, could participate, although they had to be able to speak Greek to participate; the *Homeric Hymn to Demeter* gives the story connected to the cult. There were Bacchic and Orphic cults, cults of Cybele, the great mother-goddess of Anatolia, Mithraic cults, Isis cults (Apuleius' *Metamorphoses*, in the Roman period, conveys in its hymn to Isis [11.1–6] some of the religious impact of such a cult). The anxieties these sometimes raised in the larger culture are suggested in Euripides' *Bacchae*; Livy's account of the expulsion of the Bacchanalia from Rome in 186 BCE also remains a classic depiction of the fears "secret" rituals could arouse if a city felt threatened by them: charges were made in Rome of night meetings, promiscuity, initiations with debauchery and murder.[18] Aristophanes' *Frogs*, however, also shows their emotional value to the citizen of a classical *polis*, since mystery cults often promised something like a happy afterlife in the groves of the blessed for the initiate. In the Greek world, traveling priests promulgated Orphic-Bacchic initiations; initiates put in their graves gold leaves specifying their attendant eschatological beliefs; in the Roman period, one thinks of the depiction of Aeneas' father Anchises, in Vergil's *Aeneid*, book six, rejoicing in a green glen, as he contemplates the happy throng of his descendants to come.

Eighty-seven Orphic hymns are known from the Hellenistic world; it is remarkable, however, that the secrets of Eleusis were never fully revealed, even in the Christian period. Aeschylus, the fifth-century Athenian dramatist, was charged with revealing some of them but managed to persuade the jury that he was not an initiate (although he was from Eleusis) and so had only revealed something inadvertently.[19] Some philosophical sects also included overtones of secret initiatory ritual and knowledge, like the Pythagorean sect in southern Italy, from the sixth century BCE onward.

(c) In the second half of the fifth century BCE, Herodotus wrote the first narrative history. His plan was to describe the great conflict between the Greeks and the Persians that had occupied the generation before his own (499–494; 481–479 BCE). He begins his account with the rise of Persia and describes peoples conquered by the Persians, as each appears in turn in his account of the growth of the Persian Empire. He states in book two, about Egypt (2.3), "Because I believe that everyone is equal in terms of religious knowledge, I do not see any point in relating anything I was told about the gods, except their names alone. If I do refer to such matters, it will be because my account leaves me no choice." Herodotus himself seems to express the classic tolerance of Greek syncretism (see the quotation at the beginning of this essay), but his description of the peculiarities of many foreign rituals and myths also suggests how the later articulation of critical attitudes toward different religions arose. He shows, moreover, some influence of the sophists (see d below), when he comments (2.53), "After all, I think that Hesiod and Homer lived no more than four hundred years before my time, and they were the ones who created the gods' family trees for the Greek world, gave them their names, assigned them their honors and areas of expertise, and told us what they looked like." He thought that the Greeks got most of their ideas about the gods from Egypt (2.50)—this is not to say, however, that he doubted the role divinity played in helping the Greeks evade Persian conquest. The powers of the gods were real; what Herodotus doubted, like other thoughtful Greeks of his generation, was the possibility that human beings could understand or define them.

Thucydides, writing soon after Herodotus, ignores the gods and religion almost entirely, except to comment rather cynically on the superstition of the Athenians and their general Nicias in Syracuse (7.50); Nicias ("rather over-inclined to divination and such things") refused to leave Syracuse promptly with the Athenian fleet, because of an eclipse of the moon, and this decision ultimately cost the Athenians victory in the twenty-seven-year Peloponnesian War with Sparta. Thucydides has the Athenian generals who are ruthlessly about to destroy the city of Melos say, in response to a Melian plea that they remember the gods, "Our aims and our actions are perfectly consistent with the beliefs men hold about the gods and with the principles which govern their own conduct. Our opinion of the gods and our knowledge of men lead us to conclude that it is a general and necessary law of nature to rule whatever one can. This is not a law that we made ourselves, nor were we the first to act upon it when it was made. . . . We know that you or anybody else with the same power as ours would be acting in precisely the same way" (5.105). Other, later historians were more pious, but in Herodotus and Thucydides we first see religious practice and beliefs described as a part of a people's sociology— depicted primarily as one of the things that separates different people from each other, with the possibility of some religious habits and beliefs being better than others. Certainly in Thucydides' judgment, the Athenians were disastrously egged on by unscrupulous demagogues and succumbed to religious and political hysteria when they prosecuted Alcibiades for sacrilegious treatment of the mysteries and the desecration of the herms (6.53; see A.5, p. 40, above).

(d) Socrates, the Athenian philosopher, was considered by his contemporaries to be just one of the sophists, a group of intellectuals who came to Athens in the fifth century to teach the Athenian young, for money, the art of argument (something that would make them successful in a political career and in the law court). The sophists took the scientific arguments of the Ionians before them a step further, examining the nature of human society and the bonds that hold communities together, including religious ones. The most famous sophist, Protagoras, argued, "[M]an is the measure of all things, of existing things, that they exist, of non-existent things, that they do not exist . . ." (Diels-Kranz A14); he also said, "Concerning the gods I cannot say that they exist, by human reasoning. Many things impede knowledge: the absurdity of the question and the short span of human life" (D-K A1). In the dialogue *Protagoras* (337c6), Plato has the sophist Hippias state: "Gentlemen here present, I believe that you are all kin and relations and fellow citizens— by nature, not by convention: for things that are similar to one another are by nature kindred, but convention, which is a tyrant over human beings, forces many things to go against nature." Critias, a relative of Plato, had one of the speakers in his play *Sisyphus* say, after violent deeds were committed, "I believe some smart and clever man invented the gods for mortals, so that they might serve as a terror to the bad . . ." (D-K B25).

Euripides, the fifth-century playwright (and a possible author of the *Sisyphus*) was said to be a pupil of the sophists. In the *Hecuba* (969–990), Hecuba argues that Helen used the gods as an excuse for her own failings, claiming that Aphrodite made her fall in love with Paris: "All lust is Aphrodite for mortals." Although Plato goes out of his way to depict Socrates, his teacher, as a religious man, the dialogues also show him demanding that the Athenians hold up all their beliefs, including moral and religious ones, to rigorous examination (the *Apology*, the *Euthyphro*); in this, both Plato and his teacher were very much a part of the sophistic movement.

2. Are different religions acknowledged, rejected, merely endured, or religiously
constructive? Are other religions treated generically or differentiated?

3. How do your sources justify or account for the existence and persistence of other
religions? Are the other religions seen as errors, accidents, the consequence of evil, a
constructive part of reality, or some combination or variation of these options?

For many early intellectuals, in particular the natural philosophers and the
sophists, conventional mythic and religious answers to the basic questions of
human life seemed, all of them, to be wrong, though different thinkers saw
them as different kinds of error, with different kinds of complicity or blind-
ness involved, on the part of the human beings believing in them. They rarely
tried, however, to undo or even overtly attack their cities' cults in practice
or to differentiate among the various forms of popular religious expression
on the grounds that one was more erroneous than another. As members of a
civic community, they would generally engage in the worship demanded by
the *polis*; as intellectuals, speaking privately, they would dismiss the beliefs of
popular religion.[20]

For the devotees of the mysteries, their own special cults promised a kind
of personal blessedness unavailable elsewhere, but they do not seem to have
believed that other rituals or gods were wrong or unhelpful. As the charge
against Aeschylus showed, in fifth-century Athens, one could be an Athenian
citizen fully integrated into the rituals of the city and also an initiate of the
Eleusinian mysteries; in fact, one could be charged in the city with impiety
for revealing the secrets of the mysteries.

The attitude toward religion in general, and toward other religions
than their own in particular, taken by the fifth-century historians is somewhat more difficult to assess. Herodotus explicitly disapproves of some religious customs, like Babylonian ritual prostitution (1.199), and disbelieves
some religious narratives (1.182), but seems self-consciously tolerant in general: "[C]ustom is king of all" (3.38). He is impressed by the care with which
the Persians respect the customs, religious and otherwise, of all the people
they conquer (1.135, 6.97 and 118). He depicts religious intolerance as prevailing among the savage Scythians, who lived north of the Black Sea (4.76–80);
he tells how Scyles, a Scythian king, was killed by his brother for performing Greek rituals for Dionysus: "Now the Bacchic rites are one of the aspects
of Greek culture of which the Scythians disapprove, on the grounds that it
is unreasonable to seek out a god who drives people out of their minds. . . .
[His brother] Octamasades beheaded Scyles on the spot. The Scythians are
so protective of their own ways, then, that they punish people who adopt foreign ones" (4.79–80). As I have noted (B.1.c, p. 43, above), Thucydides on the

other hand, like the sophists, seems genuinely dismissive of religious beliefs, at least when they conflict with the findings of common sense (2.54, 7.50).

Of Plato and Socrates there is a little more to say. Although in his early and middle dialogues Plato depicts Socrates demanding that Athenians test all kinds of beliefs, he nonetheless stresses in the *Republic* and the *Laws* that respect for religion is fundamental in his ideal city: he demands that Delphi be, as was traditionally the case for Greek colonies, responsible for "establishment of temples, sacrifices, and other rites of gods, daimones, and heroes; burial of the dead and the various duties to those in the Beyond which are necessary to propitiate them" (*Republic* 4.427b–c); "[N]one of these provisions should be altered in the slightest degree by the lawgiver; to each district he must allot a god or a spirit or some hero . . . "(*Laws* 5.738 c–d). Plato, however, is intolerant of privately established religious cults:

[L]et this be the law: "Let no one possess shrines of the gods in a private house; if anyone is shown to possess and to worship before a shrine other than the public one, and if he has done no great wrong, let . . . it be reported to the guardians of the law . . . and let those who don't obey be punished until the shrines are taken away. If anyone is convicted of impiety . . . let him be punished with death for not sacrificing in a state of purity."

(*Laws* 10.910d)

Whether Plato's belief stemmed from the idea of real gods who would punish heterodoxy or simply from the conviction of the social utility of religious order in the state, the result was a hypothetical state of things very much like that found in a conventional fourth-century Greek *polis*, except under a tighter idealized control, exercised by the Platonic guardians in the *Republic* or, in the *Laws*, the *tyrannos* and his legislator, guided by the nocturnal council.

Demosthenes, the great fourth-century Attic orator, tried to excite popular prejudice against the management of a private cult, attacking his political rival Aeschines in his famous speech, *On the Crown* (258–260):

[W]hen you became a man you assisted your mother in her initiations, reading the service-book while she performed the ritual, and helping generally with the paraphernalia. At night it was your duty to mix the libations, to clothe the initiates in fawnskins, to wash and scour them with the loam and the bran . . . and you squeezed the fat-cheeked snakes, or brandished them above your head, now shouting your *Euoi Saboi!* now footing it to the measure of *Hyes Attes! Attes Hyes!*, saluted by the old women . . . and you would get as payment tipsy-cakes, and cracknels, and currant-buns. With such rewards who would not rejoice greatly, and account himself the favourite of fortune?

The scorn here, however, seems to have come from issues of class as well as those of religion per se.[21]

4. Which teachings justify tolerance, and which justify intolerance?
5. Are there historical, political, and/or behavioral factors that correlate with the expression of tolerance?

As we saw in A.5, p. 40, above, the early philosophers who articulated a system of belief that might lead to the neglect of cult were sometimes prosecuted in a Greek city, presumably because the citizens believed that a widespread following of their ideas would put the city at risk. This tended to happen, however, in times of political stress of other kinds. Intellectuals expressed intolerance of each other because, like believers in the later monotheistic religions, they felt that the truth-content of their narratives mattered, and they could not all be right in their various versions of the nature of reality. The sophists were blamed, after the Athenian defeat in the Peloponnesian War, by Plato and others for leading the young political elite into intellectual conceit and self-serving, shortsighted, godless ways. Plato dedicated much of his energy in his early dialogues to distinguishing Socrates, his teacher, from the other sophists, precisely because (he argued) Socrates had never acted except for the benefit of his city, Athens. Something very like popular religious intolerance, however, surely played a part in the Athenians' decision to convict Socrates in 399 BCE for "introducing new gods and corrupting the youth."[22]

On the whole, most significant in this period was the growing acknowledgment by thoughtful Greeks noted earlier, that one's private intellectual opinions and one's civic religious duties to the traditional gods did not necessarily stem from a single and coherent set of beliefs about the nature of the world and the role of human beings in it. This habit of mind, together with the earlier and more basic habits of syncretism, would allow the governing classes in the Hellenistic and Roman period to come to think of other religions as something to be accommodated, as long as they did not lead to civic disruption or threaten the political regime.

C. The Hellenistic World: Philosophical Schools and Ruler Cults

The trends sketched above take place in the world of the fifth- and fourth-century Greek *poleis*, which, during the classical period, were still face-to-face communities with relatively homogeneous populations and shared ancestral customs. A new stage in the Greek literary depictions of religion and religious tolerance began when the Macedonians of the north, Philip and his son, Alexander, conquered Athens and Thebes in 338 BCE, in the Battle of Chaeronea. Alexander promptly consolidated his father's victory and brought all of Greece under Macedonian rule. Leaving a regent to mind affairs there, he turned his highly trained Macedonian army in 334 toward the east, to combat the Persian Achaemenid empire, which had ruled Egypt and most of the Near East and Middle East since the sixth century BCE. He was perhaps inspired not just by a rich set of territories ripe for his picking but also by the Hellenism of his teacher, Aristotle, who is said to have exhorted him "to treat the Greeks as if he were their leader, and other people as if he were their master—and, while caring for Greeks as friends and kinsmen, to have the same attitude toward barbarians as to animals or plants."[23] Fourth-century Greek intellectuals like Isocrates, in his *Panegyricus*, had also urged a pan-Greek crusade directed against the barbarian East, as a way of escaping the dreary round of interstate rivalries and wars that was progressively exhausting the cities of fourth-century Greece.

Remarkably, in a little more than a decade, Alexander brought into the Greek world an empire that stretched through Asia Minor to the borders of India in the east and southwest into Egypt. Alexander himself died in Babylon in 323, still a young man, but some of his Macedonian generals went on to establish the Hellenistic kingdoms of the east Mediterranean world that would be ruled by the families and connections of these Diadochoi, "successors," down into the era of Roman conquest in the mid-second century BCE, and in some cases long thereafter. During the Hellenistic era, the Ptolemies ruled Egypt (yes, Cleopatra was a descendant of a Macedonian general); the Seleucids ruled the Fertile Crescent, the Attalids ruled northwest Asia Minor, and the Antigonids ruled Macedonia and kept a strong military eye on the city-states of the Hellenic peninsula.

The third and second centuries BCE were a period of great change, as economic habits, political powers, and personal living conditions were adjusting to a newly cosmopolitan Greek and then, increasingly, Greco-Roman, world; the world of the Greek city-states was finally conquered by the Romans at the Battle of Corinth in 146 BCE. The establishment of the great Greek philosophical schools is a crucial topic here because of its literary implications for the topic of religious tolerance. All Greek and Roman authors of the Hellenistic and Greco-Roman period were profoundly influenced by the way the Hellenistic philosophical schools hammered out the articulation of the major ethical issues concerning the rights and obligations of human beings in community to each other.

Plato began the process, in the mid-fourth century BCE. He was a member of an elite Athenian family (the hereditary ancient kingship of Athens, had it still existed, would have belonged to his elder brother), and so was able to own Athenian property. In the grove of the hero Academus, he established a school, the Academy, that ran continuously until the mid-first century BCE; philosophers of this school were called Academics. His pupil Aristotle, not Athenian by birth but the tutor of Alexander of Macedon and after Alexander's death under Macedonian protection, established another school in Athens in a grove and gymnasium, devoted to Apollo and called, after one of Apollo's cult names, the Lyceum. Its colonnades were famous places for intellectuals to walk and talk, and so Aristotle's school was named the Peripatos and its scholars were called Peripatetics. Although it was not tied to Athenian property (Aristotle, not a citizen, could not own land), Aristotle's school flourished in Athens until Sulla took Aristotle's library with him to Rome in 87 BCE; meanwhile under its inspiration the great Library in Alexandria was founded, under the Ptolemies.[24]

Other schools flourished in the Hellenistic period in Athens, most notably those of the Epicureans, following the teachings of Epicurus of Samos (341–270 BCE), and the Stoics, following Zeno of Citium, who had come from Cyprus to Athens to learn at its philosophical schools in 313 BCE. Also noteworthy for its later presence in Greco-Roman literature was the school, if it can be called that, of Diogenes the Cynic, who came to Athens in the mid-fourth century BCE from Sinope on the Black Sea and spent his life thereafter in an iconoclastic tweaking of Greek convention. Much later, Diogenes Laertius (6.54) comments that Plato called Diogenes a "mad Socrates"; Crates, the teacher of Zeno the Stoic, had been a follower of Diogenes, and so one charge leveled against some of Zeno's writings were that they were written "on the dog's tail."[25] Diogenes and his followers were called Cynics because, like dogs (*kunes*), they did everything "naturally," that is, in public, that men living by convention did in private. More important for our purposes was Diogenes' passionate cosmopolitanism; Diogenes rejected the idea of the Greek city-state and furiously propounded the notion that all human beings, of whatever race or ethnicity or sex, were alike in their natures. Stoicism was profoundly influenced by this aspect of Cynic philosophy.

Space does not permit an investigation of the philosophical doctrines discussed and defended in the schools, but we can briefly note some of their most basic differences, differences that would play a part in how literary men of the Hellenistic period thought and wrote about religious tolerance. One of Plato's most basic concerns was with justice, both the justice of a human community and justice within the human psyche. Throughout his life, he seems to have believed in a series of natural, innate divisions: men were superior to women, and men of a philosophical turn superior to men with a predominately energetic or appetitive nature. In the *Republic* (470c), he commented that Greeks and barbarians were natural enemies of each other.[26] Toward the end of his career, in the *Statesman*, he apparently rejected a view he had earlier held, of Greek superiority to barbarians, but he never questioned the justice of slavery, for instance, as an institution. Basic throughout his life was the Socratic belief that the universe had been well designed and that, in it, knowledge and virtue were inextricably connected: wrongdoing is always done through ignorance of the Good.[27]

Aristotle's tendencies, unlike those of his more metaphysically minded teacher, Plato, were those of a biologist and a cataloguer of phenomena that already existed, on earth. As H. C. Baldry notes,

On the one hand, he continues the scientific tradition, if it can be so called, with its emphasis on the unity of the human species . . . but Aristotle combines it—how systematically or completely, we cannot tell—with the idea of hierarchical gradation which we have seen in Isocrates and Plato; so that in many passages he only seems to be reformulating more definitely doctrines already stated or implied in Plato's dialogues . . . . [I]f he seems much more "reactionary" in his conclusions than even Plato, the possibility must not be forgotten that he reflects more closely the common assumptions and prejudices of his time.[28]

Among Aristotle's Peripatetic successors, little was made of Plato's distinction between the wise and the many, who are ignorant; Dicaearchus and Theophrastus seem to have emphasized the idea of a single human species, in which *phronêsis*, practical intelligence, is more important than *sophia*, the theoretical wisdom of a philosophical elite.

The Epicureans, Cynics, and Stoics held theoretically distinct views that are easy to distinguish superficially, although in practice many Hellenistic thinkers seem to have blended together beliefs of these schools. The Stoics seem to have taken from the early Cynics the idea of the unity of humankind, believing that the whole of the universe is governed by *logos*, a divine principle of rationality that can, therefore, be found in the soul of every human being. "In Cicero, Seneca and other later writers the concept is explicit enough: the world is now in fact a single community, in which the common gift of reason makes all men kin."[29] Zeno himself proposed the idea of a utopian community, inhabited by the wise, that lacked the biological family as an organizing principle. Men and women would dress alike, property would be held in common, and sexual intercourse would not be restricted. Later Stoic thinkers rejected these ideas and instead considered the state an appropriate framework in which human being might work out the virtuous life, embodying *oikeiôsis* or inclination to self-preservation as also leading ultimately to the appreciation of *logos* and submission to its law. In *De finibus* (62–63), Cicero has the Stoic Cato state "that nature implants in parents love for their children, and this is the beginning from which we eventually reach the common fellowship of mankind." Great stress was laid throughout the Stoic tradition on virtue rather than happiness as the desirable and attainable goal of every human being.

The Epicureans, unlike the Stoics, rejected the idea of productive engagement in the state. Metrodorus, a follower of Epicurus, announced, "There is no point in saving the Greeks"; "It is the individual's own pleasure that matters: mankind is to be seen as a conglomeration of individuals each concerned with his own good, just as the whole material universe is a collection of individual atoms."[30] Epicurean philosophers believed in living unobtrusively, separate from the world, but united in the delights of loving friendship; a sentence attributed later to Epicurus still holds its charm: "Friendship dances across the world calling on us to awake and praise our happy life." Epicureans admitted women and slaves to their philosophical circle but disapproved of unbridled sensuality and an active love life in particular, believing that it led to more pain than pleasure: "Don't you also see that those whom mutual pleasure overcomes are quite often tortured in common chains?" (Lucretius, *De rerum natura*, 4.1200–1202). They believed in the existence of the gods, using what looks like an early form of Anselm's argument—since people dream of gods and can visualize them, there must be a referent for these aspects of sense perception. But the Epicureans believed that the gods dwelt in a distant heaven, unconcerned with human cares, and that human beings completely ceased to exist when they died; if properly contemplated, this idea was a comfort that they believed should lead to a tranquil fearlessness.

Difference in ethnicity and religion was a topic that would increasingly come up in Hellenistic literature, as the Greco-Roman world strove to integrate in its new boundaries people from many different traditions. In an important change from the earlier classical period, Greek and Roman culture now had to confront other peoples not in the context of their own travels or immigration by foreigners to their own Greco-Roman cities (like Orlando Patterson's "natally alienated" slaves or emigrants, newly isolated in a foreign world),[31] but as local inhabitants, on their own turf, surrounded by their own religious architecture and deeply rooted traditional cultures. In Alexandria or Tarsus or Sardis, Susa, and Babylon, the Greco-Roman conquerors had to learn to apply their own ancient syncretistic religious habits to the new world they were governing. The Greco-Roman philosophical systems helped the young elite members of the governing class to engage in this process, by synthesizing and essentializing ideas about the nature of morality and public ethics, the divine and divine plans for humanity, and the purpose and point of human life in general.[32] The second-century CE Roman emperor, Marcus Aurelius, "in lonely vigils during campaigns in the Danube territory,"[33] wrote his famous *Meditations*; though he was a professed Stoic and pupil of Epictetus, his philosophy included elements drawn from Platonism, Epicureanism, and even late Academic skepticism. He argued basic questions out with himself as follows:

If the power of thought is common to us all, common also is reason (*logos*), through which we are rational beings. If so, that reason is also common which tells us what to do and what not to do. If so, law also is common. If so, we are citizens. If so, we are fellow-members of a community. If so, the universe is, as it were, a city. For of what other community can the whole human race be said to be fellow members? (*Med.* 4.4)

Although much of what I want to say about Greco-Roman religious tolerance and intolerance in the Hellenistic world has already been expressed, some additional important aspects emerge when we specifically consider William Scott Green's five questions.

1. What is the role of other religions?
2. Are different religions acknowledged, rejected, merely endured, or religiously constructive? Are other religions treated generically or differentiated?

A new kind of religion appeared in the Hellenistic period, as a result of Alexander's eastern adventures: ruler worship. "For half a millennium, from the dynasty of the Ptolemies to the dynasty of the Severi, ruler worship played a major role in achieving that integration of religion and politics which lay at the very heart of the ancient state."[34] Thinking of a ruler, particularly a defunct ruler, as a divinity was not unknown in the earlier Hellenic world; hero cults for half-divine beings like Herakles were among the earliest Greek religious rituals established, probably before the archaic age, and even Lysander, the Spartan general victorious in the Peloponnesian War in the fifth century, was granted divine honors in death. Alexander thought he was himself a descendant of Herakles, and in 331 he made a pilgrimage to the temple of Zeus Ammon at Siwa, was recognized as a form of the god (a customary treatment for Egyptian pharaohs), and thereafter proclaimed himself son of Zeus Ammon. Trouble came in 327 when he attempted to require *proskynêsis*, ritual prostration, not just of Persians and Egyptians, who expected it, but of Greeks, for whom bowing to a human being was anathema. Callisthenes,

Aristotle's nephew, had come along on Alexander's great journey as a propagandist and, refusing the practice, was executed; by this act, Alexander incurred the enmity of the Peripatetics, who often wrote of him thereafter as a megalomaniac tyrant. In 324, he demanded recognition of his deity by all of the Greek states; in Sparta, the required decree read, "Since Alexander wants to be a god, let him be a god."[35]

The Athenians flattered his Macedonian successor in Athens, Demetrius, calling him the only true god and giving him the Parthenon for his palace. Ptolemy took Alexander's body to Egypt and established an enduring cult for him; a cult of the reigning monarch, for the Greek Alexandrians as well as Egyptians, was established in Egypt by 270. The Romans later moved carefully into this eastern, Hellenized practice. Augustus at Rome called himself *divi filius*, son of the divinized Julius, although Horace's poems suggest apotheosis.[36] Megalomaniacs like Gaius (nicknamed Caligula), Nero, Domitian, and Commodus demanded worship in their lifetimes, though Tiberius refused "divine" for himself, remarking that a better title would be "laborious," and (as noted at the beginning of this essay) Vespasian sardonically remarked, on his deathbed in 79 CE, "Oh dear, I think I'm becoming a god." Ferguson acutely observes that the cities of the Asiatic provinces threw themselves into the lucrative business of housing imperial cults; Pergamum had a temple of Augustus and Roma, and such cults were particularly firmly established, because they were more necessary, in the newer, less secure provinces like Britain and Germany.[37] A variety of responses occurred to the establishment of ruler cult; it was out of this practice in particular, as well as civic cult in general that much of the conflict with Jews and, later, Christians in the eastern provinces arose.

3. How do your sources justify or account for the existence and persistence of other religions? Are the other religions seen as errors, accidents, the consequence of evil, a constructive part of reality, or some combination of variation of these options?

4. Since we know that within religions there are divergent, sometimes opposed, views of other religions, what are the doctrinal fault lines within the religion that produce this divergence? Which teachings justify tolerance, and which justify intolerance?

Enough has been said above about the various philosophical schools to make it clear that most educated Hellenistic Greeks and later Hellenized Romans thought of traditional pagan religion as part of their culture, rather than as a necessary vehicle for the expression of deep private belief about the nature of the world or of their obligations as human beings to it. Although the Hellenistic philosophical schools differed in the way they thought that life should be lived, many educated Greeks and later Romans took elements from a number of different schools, as it suited the conditions of their life, in order to reach for themselves the kind of personal coherence that Marcus Aurelius struggles to articulate in his *Meditations*.[38]

One error that the philosophers particularly disliked and even were on occasion intolerant toward, at least verbally, was religious superstition. The Peripatetic and pupil of Aristotle, Theophrastus, included in his *Characters* a portrait of the superstitious man (16):

[Superstition would simply seem to be cowardice with regard to the divine.] . . . The superstitious man . . . when he has a dream, visits not only dream-analysts but also seers and bird-watchers to ask which god or goddess he should pray to. He makes a monthly visit to the Orphic ritualists to take the sacrament, accompanied by his wife (or if she is busy, the nurse) and his children. . . . If he sees a madman or an epileptic he shudders and spits into his chest.[39]

This is a theme that the Epicureans took up, as part of their belief in *ataraxia*, tranquility of spirit, as the fundamental root quality leading to happiness. Lucretius, the Roman Epicurean poet of the first century BCE, is eloquent on the problems of superstition, and especially the superstitious fear of death (3.87–93):

> For just like children who tremble and fear everything
> in the dark night, so we are afraid in the light sometimes
> of things that ought to be no more feared than
> the things that children tremble at and imagine will happen.
> Therefore this fear and darkness of the mind must be shattered
> apart not by the rays of the sun and the clear shafts
> of the day but by the external appearance and inner law of nature.

In all of the philosophical schools, there is a clear inclination to see the ordinarily religious Greco-Roman citizen (in the sense of A.1, page 36 above) as a lesser being, unable to be consoled by the truths of philosophy and having therefore to take refuge in the superstitions of cult. Both foreign and domestic rituals are mocked by the poets, particularly satirists like Persius, Juvenal, Lucian, or even Horace.[40] Jews and Christians, in particular, were frequently mentioned; they were thought to be especially superstitious, precisely because they had not split their religious life in two, but considered cult and personal philosophy closely intertwined.[41]

*(5) Are there historical, political, and/or behavioral factors that correlate
with the expression of tolerance? Intolerance? How do you explain the
choices made within the religion for tolerance and intolerance?*

At this point, the narrative and analysis that I have delivered here largely join
up with Robert Berchman's narrative [in this collection], since the conditions
of the Hellenistic world merge into those of the Roman one, and the stresses
that were felt, as Greeks and Romans raised in the culture whose various fac-
ets are described here go out to the larger world of the Roman provinces, to
try to weave into their classical heritage communities of a very different sort.
It is a big story, with many fascinating twists and turns to it, in which the various strains in Greco-Roman literary culture played an important part. I have
tried to show here how Greco-Roman pagan religion made possible the development of the ethical sophistication of the Hellenistic philosophical schools,
and how they, in turn, developed the language out of which the political foundations of tolerance in the Roman period would come. I want to end with a
comment from Seneca's *Epistulae Morales* (95.51–53), where he quotes to excellent effect the comment of Terence, the Roman dramatist of the second century BCE, as the essential definition of *humanitas*:

There is one short rule that should regulate human relationships. All that you see,
both divine and human, is one. We are the parts of one great body. Nature created
us from the same source and to the same end. She imbued us with mutual affection
and sociability, she taught us to be fair and just, to suffer injury rather than to inflict
it. She bids us extend our hands to all in need of help. Let that well-known line be in
our hearts and on our lips: *homo sum, humani nihil a me alienum puto*—I am a human
being, I think nothing human foreign to me.[42]

Bibliography

Adkins, A. *Moral Values and Political Behavior in Ancient Greece: From Homer to the End of the
Fifth Century.* New York: W. W. Norton & Company, 1972.
Baldry, H.C. *The Unity of Mankind in Greek Thought.* Cambridge: Cambridge University
Press, 1965.
Bauman, R.A. *Human Rights in Ancient Rome.* London and New York: Routledge, 2000.
Benko, S. *Pagan Rome and the Early Christians.* Bloomington: Indiana University Press, 1984.
Boedeker, D. "Athenian Religion in the Age of Pericles." In *The Cambridge Companion to the
Age of Pericles,* edited by L. Samons, 46–69. Cambridge: Cambridge University Press,
2007.
Burkert, W. *Greek Religion.* Cambridge, MA: Harvard University Press, 1985.
Buxton, R. *Oxford Readings in Greek Religion.* Oxford: Oxford University Press, 2000.

Demosthenes. *De Corona; De Falsa Legatione XVIII, XIX*. Translated by C. Vince and J. Vince. Cambridge, MA, and London: Harvard University Press, 1939.

Diels, H., and W. Kranz. *Fragmente der Vorsokratiker*, 6th ed. 3 vols. Berlin: Weildmann, 1951–52.

Dillon, J. *Morality and Custom in Ancient Greece*. Bloomington: Indiana University Press, 2004.

Dodds, E. R. *The Ancient Concept of Progress and Other Essays on Greek Literature and Belief*. Oxford: Oxford University Press, 1973.

Dover, K. J. "The Freedom of the Intellectual in Greek Society," *Talenta* 7 (1976): 24–54.

Dudley, D. *Lucretius*. New York: Basic Books, 1965.

Fears, J. R. "Ruler Worship." In *Civilization of the Ancient Mediterranean: Greece and Rome*, 2:1009–1025. Edited by M. Grant and R. Kitzinger. New York: Scribner, 1988.

Ferguson, J. *The Religions of the Roman Empire*. Ithaca, NY: Cornell University Press, 1970.

———. "Roman Cults." In *Civilization of the Ancient Mediterranean*, 2:900–923. Edited by M. Grant and R. Kitzinger. New York: Scribner, 1988.

Francis, J. *Subversive Virtue: Asceticism and Authority in the Second-Century Pagan World*. University Park: Pennsylvania State University Press, 1995.

Grant, M., and R. Kitzinger. *Civilization of the Ancient Mediterranean: Greece and Rome*. 3 vols. New York: Scribner's, 1988.

Herodotus. *The Histories*. Translated by Robin Waterfield. With Introduction and Notes by Carolyn Dewald. Oxford: Oxford University Press, 1998.

Homer. *The Iliad*. Translated by R. Lattimore. Chicago and London: University of Chicago Press, 1961.

Horace. *Satires, Epistles and Ars Poetica*. Translated by H. Fairclough. Cambridge, MA, and London: Harvard University Press, 1929.

Hornblower, S., and A. Spawforth, eds.. *The Oxford Classical Dictionary*. Oxford: Oxford University Press, 1996.

Johnstone, S. *Disputes and Democracy: The Consequences of Litigation in Ancient Athens*. Austin: University of Texas Press, 1999.

Juvenal and Persius. *Satires*. Translated by G. Ramsay. Cambridge, MA, and London: Harvard University Press, 1940.

Kirk, G., and J. Raven. *The Presocratic Philosophers: A Critical History with a Selection of Texts*. Cambridge: Cambridge University Press, 1966.

Konstan, D. "Cosmopolitan Traditions." In *Blackwell Companion to Greek and Roman Political Thought*. Forthcoming.

Lesky, A. *A History of Greek Literature*. Translated by James Willis and Cornelis de Heer. London: Methuen, 1966.

———. *Greek Tragic Poetry*. Translated by Matthew Dillon. New Haven, CT: Yale University Press, 1972.

Lucretius. *On the Nature of Things*. Translated by W. Englert. Newburyport, MA: Focus Books, 2003.

Meijer, P. "Philosophers, Intellectuals and Religion in Hellas." In *Faith, Hope and Worship: Aspects of Religious Mentality in the Ancient World*, edited by H. Versnel. Leiden: Brill, 1981.

Most, G. "Anger and Pity in Homer's Iliad." In *Ancient Anger: Perspectives from Homer to Galen*, edited by S. Braund and G. Most, 32:50–75. Yale Classical Studies. New Haven, CT: Yale University Press, 2003.

Nock, A. D. *Conversion: The Old and New in Religion from Alexander the Great to Augustine of Hippo.* Oxford: Oxford University Press, 1965.

North, H. *Sophrosyne: Self-Knowledge and Self-Restraint in Greek Literature.* Ithaca, NY: Cornell University Press, 1966.

Ostwald, M. "Plato's Academy; Aristotle and the Peripatos." In *The Cambridge Ancient History*, 2nd ed., edited by D. Lewis, J. Boardman, S. Hornblower, and M. Ostwald, 6:602–633. Cambridge: Cambridge University Press, 1994.

Parker, R. "Atheism." In *The Oxford Classical Dictionary*, edited by S. Hornblower and A. Spawforth, 201. Oxford: Oxford University Press, 1996.

Patterson, O. *Slavery and Social Death: A Comparative Study.* Cambridge, MA: Harvard University Press, 1982.

Rice, D., and J. Stambaugh. *Sources for the Study of Greek Religion, for the Society of Biblical Literature.* SBL Sources for Biblical Study. Vol. 14. Atlanta: Scholars Press, 1979

Sophocles. *Antigone.* Translated by E. Wyckoff. In *The Complete Greek Tragedies*, edited by D. Grene and R. Lattimore. Chicago: University of Chicago Press. 1959.

Theophrastus. *Characters.* Translated and edited by J. Diggle. Cambridge Classical Texts and Commentaries. Cambridge: Cambridge University Press, 2004.

Thucydides. *History of the Peloponnesian War.* Translated by R. Warner. Harmondsworth, U.K.: Penguin Books, 1972.

Veyne, P. *Seneca: The Life of a Stoic.* Translated by David Sullivan. New York: Routledge, 2003.

Watkins, C., ed. *The American Heritage Dictionary of Indo-European Roots*, 2nd ed. Boston: Houghton Mifflin, 2000.

Notes

1. Watkins (90) notes for "tolerance" the Indo-European root *tele-*, "to lift, support, weigh"; with derivatives referring to measured weights and thence to money and payment. The specific Latin root means "bear, carry, endure"; other words from the same root include *toll, retaliate, talent* (from the Greek weight of gold or silver), and all the derivatives of the Latin perfect passive participle *(t)latus*, "carried, borne": *collate, dilatory, legislator, relate*, etc.

2. Burkert (15–19) discusses the marginalization of the earlier Indo-European gods in Greek myth. Hurrian, Hittite, Akkadian, and Babylonian elements can be found in Hesiod's poems; his father had come to Boeotia from Asia Minor.

3. See, for instance, the story of Aphrodite and Ares in Homer's *Odyssey*, book 8. According to Burkert (128), the late ancient mythographers counted up that Zeus sired children from 115 mortal women.

4. Burkert, 122.

5. Watkins (18–19) comments that Herodotus might have been right; the word *theos* might indeed come from the Indo-European root *dhê-*, "to put, set."

6. The mockery of Dionysus in Aristophanes' *Frogs* or of Poseidon, Herakles, and a savage foreign god in *Birds*, would not, *mutatis mutandis*, be tolerated today.

7. Ferguson, 66.

8. Pliny *Ep.* 8, 8, in Ferguson 66–67. Unless there is a bibliographic entry for the individual ancient author, all translations from Greek and Latin in this article are those found in the cited secondary sources.

9. Strabo 8, 343, in Ferguson 67.

10. Ferguson (Grant and Kitzinger, vol. 2, 856) mentions Cook's list of 250 known different cult titles for Zeus, at least 50 for Jupiter, 100 for Athene.

11. Ferguson, 72. Some anxiety attended this practice; Herodotus ends an exposition about the priority of the Egyptian Heracles to the Greek one with the plea, "That's all I have to say about this matter; may the gods and heroes look kindly on my words!" (2.45). Deborah Boedeker adds that, as early as Herodotus, for instance, the Greeks were very alert to differences in religious cult and belief and used these as important markers distinguishing different cultures.

12. Rex Warner, in the Penguin *Thucydides*, even translates the last sentence rather loosely, in order to drive home the point being made here. The Greek, "We associate without offense in our daily lives," becomes, in his translation into English, "we are free and tolerant in our private lives."

13. See Johnstone, 111, for the seriousness with which classical Athens took its reputation for fairness, tolerance, pity; in the law courts, defendants regularly sought pity from their juries. In the fifth-century agora, there was an altar to Pity, as a goddess (Johnstone, 113, n.17). But compare the citizenship law passed by Pericles in 451/0 BCE, denying Athenian citizenship to anyone who did not have two full-citizen parents. Theseus himself, although the mythic founder of the city, would have been disqualified as a citizen under Pericles' law.

14. Already in Homer the Pelasgoi were Trojan allies, probably from Thrace (*Il.*2.840); in the fifth century, Herodotus uses the term to signify all of the pre-Greek populations in the Hellenic peninsula and environs.

15. See, on Athenian intolerance in particular, the articles of Boedeker, Meijer, and Dover cited in the bibliography.

16. Parker, 201, notes: "The Greek word *atheos* can be applied to atheism (Plato *Ap.* 26c), but in the earliest instances it means "impious, vicious" or "hated, abandoned by the gods," and these senses persist along with the other; so too with *atheotês*. Thus Christians and pagans were to swap charges of *atheotês*, by which they meant "impious views about the divine."

17. Dillon, 157.

18. Livy 39.8–19; see Benko, 62–63.

19. Lesky, *Greek Tragic Poetry*, 37–38.

20. Some withdrew, like Pythagoras from Samos, and founded their own communities; Heraclitus is said to have refused the hereditary kingship of Ephesus. The Jewish and, later, Christian refusal to countenance the customary pagan divergence between private, personal belief and civic religious practice puzzled and offended upper-class Roman citizens like Celsus, who ridiculed various aspects of Christianity in the second century CE. By this time, the Greco-Roman educated elite had long been accustomed to a split between private thought and public cult.

21. Indirect testimony to the deep-seated acceptance of a variety of religious beliefs and practices comes from the rarity with which it emerges in the abuse directed at the speakers' opponents in the extant fourth-century Attic speeches, since Attic orators wrote speeches that regularly indulged in no-holds-barred attacks.

22. See n. 15 above.

23. Plutarch, *On the Fortunes of Alexander* (329A–C); this is an early, rhetorical work of Plutarch (late first and early second century CE), and the sentence as it stands is unlikely to

have been Aristotle's (fourth century BCE). Whatever Aristotle's charge to Alexander actually was, Alexander went on to practice an extreme form of assimilationism, requiring Macedonian and Greek men, for instance, to marry Persian women and giving a banquet at Opis for nine thousand leaders of deliberately mixed ethnic groups, probably in the belief that it would make his vast empire easier to rule.

24. Ptolemy I at the end of his reign founded the Museum; "[T]he library was designed by Ptolemy II Philadelphus with the intention of assembling Greek literature in its entirety: enthusiasm, foresight and a complete lack of scruple went into the amassing of 500,000 volumes, which must have risen to some 700,000 by the time of the disaster in 47 B.C." (Lesky, 3).

25. Diogenes Laertius, 8.4.

26. See White, 147, for a fuller discussion of Plato's prejudices against non-Greeks.

27. See Baldry, 72–87, for Platonic passages exemplifying these ideas. Necessarily omitted here is discussion of Platonic epistemology, especially the theory of forms.

28. Ibid., 88–89.

29. Ibid., 152.

30. Ibid., 147.

31. Patterson, 5–8.

32. White, 343, points out that, in this way, the Hellenistic philosophical schools, the Stoics and Epicureans in particular, took up the task of the systematization of ethics that pagan religion had renounced, showing how philosophical deliberation might settle basic conflicts between peoples.

33. Ferguson, 198.

34. Fears, 1018.

35. Ferguson, 89.

36. Ibid., 90–91; Horace Od. 3.3,9.

37. This whole discussion is dependent on Ferguson's chapter 6, "The Sacred Figure of the Emperor," 88–98.

38. Seneca, a devout Stoic, was exiled by Nero and during his exile became appreciative of Epicurean philosophy, in particular of its definition of withdrawal from public life as a spiritual benefit.

39. Diggle, 111–113.

40. For Lucian's complex attitude toward religious ascetics, see Francis, 53–81.

41. Horace mocks even a Stoic sage for rigidity in Sat. 1.3.133–142; in Sat. 1.9.67–74, he tells of being buttonholed by a bore. Hoping that a friend passing by would relieve him by demanding his presence, he says: "Surely you said there was something you wanted to tell me in private?" The friend replies: "I mind it well, but I'll tell you at a better time. Today is the thirtieth Sabbath. Would you affront the circumcised Jews?" "I have no scruples," say I. His friend retorts, "But I have. I'm a somewhat weaker brother, one of the many. You will pardon me; I'll talk another day." Horace is angry at his friend: "To think so black a sun as this has shone for me! The rascal runs away and leaves me under the knife."

42. Bauman, 1–9. I would like to thank Deborah Boedeker and David Konstan here for significant guidance in matters of fact and interpretation.

4

GRECO-ROMAN PAGANISM

The Political Foundations of Tolerance in the Greco-Roman Period

ROBERT M. BERCHMAN

Introduction

This chapter has as its goal a general definition of the political foundations of religious tolerance in Greco-Roman Paganism. Addressing this question should involve a comprehensive survey of political foundations of religious toleration in the Greco-Roman period. What I attempt here is much more modest. My purpose is, first, to throw some light on the Hellenistic and Roman political foundations of religious tolerance and intolerance; second, to offer examples underlying these practices; and third, to map the emergence of the political foundations of theological tolerance and intolerance at the end of Roman antiquity. Since the sources of religious and theological tolerance and intolerance are wide-ranging in the Greco-Roman period, focus is upon Judaism in the period of the Hellenistic kingdoms, Judaism and other foreign religions, and cults in the late Roman Republic and early Roman Empire. In the later Roman Empire, analysis shifts to Christianity. The study concludes with a consideration of the differences between ancient and modern theories of justice and tolerance.

Since there is no Greek word for tolerance, a consideration of tolerance in the Pre-Christian West must begin with the Latin word *tolerare*. Although the conventional translation of *tolerare* is "to tolerate," the term covers a wider range of meanings under the general rubric "to endure."[1] Tolerance refers to the civic and consensual obligations individuals and groups have to a polity and to the gods that maintain the state. Since maintenance of the state requires peace among the gods, tolerance is the obligation of the state and its religious communities to bear, to endure, to be patient of other religions and cults within a heterogeneous political community.

To say the least, the sheer range and detail of the evidence that faces the modern student of tolerance in Greco-Roman paganism are overwhelming. It is even difficult to distinguish cultural tolerance from religious tolerance since "religion" was a matter of ethnic community (*ethnos*) for the Greeks and obedience (*obediencia*) for the Romans. Nonetheless, cultural and religious tolerance existed in the Pre-Christian West however differently tolerance was parsed by the Greeks and Romans. In the Hellenistic kingdoms, tolerance was a political, legal, and religious sanction of ethnic communities and their deities. In the Roman Republic and Empire, tolerance also required the political obedience of foreign communities and their deities to the *pax deorum*. If the subjugated were obedient, Rome tolerated foreign peoples and their gods as a *religio licita*.

1. The Political Origins of Religious Tolerance in the Hellenistic Period

Jacob Neusner notes that the monotheistic religions—Judaism, Christianity, and Islam—find it difficult to tolerate one another but impossible to tolerate any religion beside themselves. Succinctly, he claims that "the logic of monotheism . . . yields little basis for tolerating other religions."[2] However, there are in Greco-Roman Paganism ample grounds for toleration of other religions and cults. So, while intolerance informs the Jewish, Christian, and Islamic monotheistic traditions, why does tolerance of other religions and cults characterize Greco-Roman polytheism and (inclusive) monotheism?[3]

In brief, pagan religious tolerance of others was a political, religious, and theological praxis that required state sanction. Within the Hellenistic kingdoms, colonies of peoples of foreign birth were not defined as outsiders by the ruling Greeks. As colonists (*katoikia*), foreign mercenaries in Ptolemaic Egypt and Seleucid Syria were citizens who acquired Greek names and customs and who strove after civic and legal rights. Once recognized as a political community (*politeuma*) by king or queen, these communities were acknowledged as autonomous organizations. They enjoyed special arrangements and privileges sanctioned by the state that placed communities within well-defined political and legal frameworks. Since it was common that every *politeuma* had a specific religious complexion, its deities and cults were also sanctioned by law.

This was the case in Ptolemaic Egypt with Jewish communities who had written constitutions.[4] Jews were not considered aliens or regarded as simple metics. Within Hellenistic cities ruled by divine kings, the Jewish people (*ethnos*) were a legally recognized community (*politeuma*).[5] Privileges included the right to live according to ancestral laws, which included the right to appoint rulers and maintain courts, educational facilities, and places of worship.[6] However, Jews did not assume the important liturgies of the city (*polis*) and community (*oikumene*), which included administering municipal posts, supplying the needs of the gymnasia, organizing athletic games, and building temples. They were also exempt from duties such as taxation, military service, and worship of the state and local deities. These activities were associated with the city, kingdom, and empire of which members of a *polituema* were not always a part.

However, such political tolerance of foreign communities was difficult for many Greeks to understand, and the consequences often led to cultural and religious intolerance of foreigners and their deities. Polybius reflects such animus. He claimed that the Jews' solemn oath was "*ut imicitatis contra Graecos haberent*"—to nurture hatred for the Greeks.[7] Josephus tells us that "contempt" of a community and its gods was associated by the Greeks with a Jewish hatred of *polis*, *paideia*, and the legacy of Alexander's *theokrasia*.[8] Consequently, Josephus reports that Greeks in Asia Minor attempted to prevent Jews from living in their cities and from observing Jewish customs and wanted the Jews "to honor the gods whom we honor."[9] He also notes that these disputes were settled legally in favor of the Jews who were allowed to maintain their legally sanctioned ancestral customs.[10]

In nuce, the political tolerance or intolerance of religions in the Hellenistic period rested on community and legal grounds, not behavioral ones. In a multi-ethnic and culturally diverse polity, tolerance rather than intolerance makes sound political sense. To answer William Scott Green's questions, posed in the first chapter of this collection: (1) the role of other religions in the Hellenistic kingdoms is defined in terms of *ethnos*; (2) religions are acknowledged and differentiated according to their *ethnos*; (3) once legally sanctioned, religions are justified as a constructive part of political and legal reality, not as errors, accidents, or the consequence of evil; (4) tolerance and intolerance of other religions rest on political and judicial fault lines; and (5) political and legal factors, not behavioral factors, correlate to the expression of tolerance or intolerance of a religion or cult.

2. The Political Origins of Tolerance in
the Roman Period

Hellenistic political tolerance of other religions and cults was adopted by the Romans. They also added several criteria that were centered on civic, religious, and theological obedience of foreign deities and peoples to *Dea Romana*, the Senate, and the people of Rome. Here the phenomena of sacred landscapes and the sacralization of the land illustrate how religious tolerance in Roman paganism was actually practiced.

In 201 CE, Roman legionaries built a military camp at Gholaia (Bu Njem, Libya) in Tripolitania. Their first act was to consecrate a place for divine beings. The first deity consecrated was the genius of Gholaia. The Romans then consecrated their own gods inside the camp, along with the genius of Gholaia. Outside the camp, they built a complex of temples dedicated to romanized African gods such as Juppiter Hammon, patron of caravan routers. Thus, for these Roman legionaries, it was a duty to honor not to offend divine beings who had power over a region. After the Romans departed in 260 CE, the locals desecrated the sacred spaces within the Roman camp and the cult statues consecrated to Victory and Fortune.[11]

How is Roman policy in Gholaia illustrative for our study of tolerance and intolerance in Roman paganism? The phenomenon of sacralization includes the dedication of something or somebody to a divine being. Space and time function as a place of divine and human interaction, a nodal point of communication that ensures divine benevolence over a region and its peoples through the organization of a religious calendar. Once such communication opens, humans are consecrated to divine beings and practice public and private rituals that bond diverse divinities and ethnicities together. Desacralization encompasses the return of sacred things, such as religious buildings and sacred writings, to profane use, or to desecration, which includes the defilement or destruction of religious shrines and sacrilege to holy texts.[12]

I would like to link the phenomena of sacralization and desacralization to those of tolerance and intolerance. Sacralization is a tolerance that provides an interactive place and time that allows communication among deities, regions, and peoples. Moreover, sacralization establishes a tolerance for others that offers a political opportunity for diverse gods, lands, and humanities to be consecrated to *Dea Romana* both in public ceremonies such as a dedication of a city and in small private offerings such as the burning of incense. Desacralization is an intolerance that restricts the public face of religions and cults that have fallen into political disrepute. Moreover, desacralization sets the boundaries of intolerance toward those who have breached the political rules of behavior with sacred things or persons consecrated to *Dea Romana*. Furthermore, sacralization and desacralization suggest two possible pagan attitudes toward divine beings: one is encompassing and accumulative; the other is a choice of one or more deities and the rejection of all others.[13] The Romans opted for the first, tolerance. African deities were incorporated into the Roman pantheon. The local inhabitants chose the second option, intolerance. Juppiter Hamon was worshiped, but the Libyans rejected those goddesses whose cult had been organized by Romans.

Why were the Romans tolerant and the Libyans intolerant of other (foreign) religions? Here another horizon beckons. Historians claim that religion in the pagan Roman world had a civic and consensual dimension. The religious skyline of town and city was dominated by the state and imperial cults. Participation in civic cults was necessary to preserve the *pax deorum* and to show political loyalty to the Senate and later Caesars. Ethical theorists argue there is also a "monistic" and "pluralistic" theory of goods in play. A monistic theory recognizes only one good; a pluralistic theory recognizes several goods. Pagan Roman notions of political tolerance of foreign religions suggests both a pluralistic and monistic theory of goods. First, there is tolerance and intolerance of more than one kind based on a tactical religious theory of goods. Second, there is only one strategic political good—the maintenance of the Roman state and its pantheon. The peace of the Roman state depends upon peace among all the gods. Consequently, if a foreign religion or cult is beneficial to the state, on the grounds of a pluralistic theory of goods, it would be tolerated. If it is not beneficial, on the basis of a monistic theory of goods, it cannot be tolerated.

3. The Politics of Tolerance

Roman political tolerance of foreign cults was driven by a concern for the maintenance of the Roman state and its deities. Since a tolerance of local deities ensured the maintenance of the *pax deorum* and *pax Romana*, it was the duty of the Roman state to tolerate, to honor, and not to offend divine beings who have power over a region. Since political stability was of utmost importance to the state's success, Roman authorities were faced with two alternatives when dealing with foreign religions and cults: either tolerance or intolerance.

The basis for decision one way or the other was primarily political and practical. As Rome expanded commercially and territorially, the state encompassed more and more foreigners. These peoples and their deities required appeasement, unification, and a sense of identity with the polity if Rome were to maintain political domination. Toleration and adoption of foreign religions and cults accomplished this, allowing various religious cults to coexist, to span social classes, geography, and local traditions.

Ultimately, toleration allowed social groups, fractured by distinct religious and ethnic traditions, to find unity within a state. *In nuce*, religions were tolerated because toleration mediated political and social control, thereby domesticating the possibility of long-term revolts against the polity and ensuring that possible enemies remain citizens and allies. Generally, religious toleration was given a legal basis when a religion was recognized as a *religio licita*. This fact is central as we address the political and religious ideas that produce a public policy of tolerance. Religious tolerance rests fundamentally on political and social foundations. In brief, maintenance of the *pax deorum* guarantees the continuance of the *res publica* and *imperium*.

Stoic political theory stands behind such a virtue. It is a paradigm of the world as it might be if humanity could be united not by artificial ties but by the recognition in each other of common values and purposes. In brief, the Stoic theory of the relation of the part to the whole drives Greco-Roman understandings of tolerance. Such a motive underlies later Platonic theory as well.[14] Diogenes Laertius puts it succinctly:

The virtue of the happy man and the well-running life consists in this: that all actions are based on the principle of harmony between his own spirit and the will of the director of the universe.[15]

A second-century CE contemporary of Diogenes Laertius, Marcus Aurelius, who employed the teaching of Panaetius passed on to him by Cicero, proclaims:

Man is the citizen of the supreme city in which the other cities are as it were houses.[16]

In what other universal constitution can the whole race of man have a share?[17]

For me as Antoninus my city and fatherland is Rome, but as man the world.[18]

In political terms, the *ratio* or reason that directs the polity is the Senate, its Princeps, and later its Emperor. Religious tolerance allows for groups to act in harmony with the aims of the state. Whether the Republic, where all peoples existed in a confederation in willing allegiance to Rome, or the Empire, where all peoples existed as citizens in a united world, Stoic principles govern. Thus, Marcus is not merely the first citizen of Rome but of the "Great State" of reason, the providentially guided controller of a unifying centralized Empire. In brief, religious toleration presupposes the existence of the state and its rulers. Once the state tolerates a religion, it can disapprove of it or even outlaw it again because toleration presumes a political authority that has a divine mandate to become coercive.

There is much to suggest that the political foundations of religious tolerance in the Roman period assist in answering the questions that Green raises in the introduction to this book:

(1) The role of all religions and cults are important to the state. The religious and theological criteria employed to define their roles are fluid but politically grounded.

(2) Different religions are acknowledged, rejected, or endured if they contribute to the maintenance of the polity. The religious and theological criteria employed to justify political tolerance or intolerance vary dependent upon political and social praxis. Foreign religions are differentiated from the state religion and are tolerated if they support the legitimacy of the *pax deorum*.

(3) All religions are justified if they are a constructive part of political reality, even if viewed as erroneous or accidental. Whether a religion is defined as evil is largely justified on political, social, and moral criteria.

(4) Although religions and cults hold divergent, sometimes opposed views, there is only one doctrinal fault line that ultimately matters. Religious and theological tolerance and intolerance are state concerns. Various religions, cults, or their adherents do not decide the criteria of religious tolerance.

(5) A variety of historical, political, and social factors correlate with an expression of state tolerance (or intolerance) of religions and cults. As "a part to the whole," the fundamental criterion of tolerance, intolerance, the legality, or the illegality of a religion or cult rests in its recognition of the political hegemony of the state in religious affairs.

4. Religious Tolerance

Romans maintained that their greatness was always dependent on the favor of divine *numina* and the maintenance of the *pax deorum*.[19] The fundamental question was how to maintain divine peace so Roman power could continue. Religious tolerance was an extension of political tolerance. In the words of Livy, it was Roman policy to turn recent foes into allies and citizens.[20] Thus, among the policies that maintained peace and prosperity was religious tolerance. Tolerance of foreign religions and cults was a stable of Roman politics from the beginnings of the Republic to the closure of the Empire in the Latin West, as expansion along its network of roads, trade routes, and sea lanes resulted in encountering foreign cults. Tolerance and respect, as well as a readiness to borrow and adapt foreign gods and goddesses, was Roman custom.

Evidence of this attitude emerges early on with the influence of the Etruscans and Greeks. Their deities were accepted as Rome's own. Apollo was adopted as a symbol of virtue and austerity, Zeus was assimilated to Juppiter, Hera to Juno, and Athena to Minerva. This trinity eventually became the focus of a new Roman state religion. As Rome marched east, Cybele, Mithras, Isis, Serapis, and countless other foreign cults gained entrance into its polity. This practice was called an *evocatio*, where deities were invited to Rome where they would be honored with monuments and games.[21]

Roman political attitudes toward Judaism are instructive, for they are emblematic of how Rome approached and defined foreign religions and cults.[22] During the reigns of Julius and Augustus Caesar, Jews were tolerated and given legal rights within the empire. During the reigns of Titus, Vespasian, Trajan, and Hadrian, they nearly lost such status. They slowly regained their religious privileges under the Antonines and Severii. With Diocletian, they regained the full status granted a *religio licita* and, according to the *Codex Theodosianus*, Jews lived under the *lex Judaeorum* until 398 CE.[23]

Initially, Judaism fulfilled Roman criteria for tolerance because of legal protections afforded Jews by Julius Caesar, who granted Jews exemptions from imperial taxes and military service.[24] Despite Jewish revolts against Rome, state tolerance of Judaism continued because of political and religious concessions made by Jews to Rome in the wake of the Trajanic and Hadrianic wars.[25] Pagan Rome could afford to be tolerant of Judaism in the second, third, and fourth centuries because the religion ceased to be a political danger. As a result, the Roman state permitted the Sanhedrin to be reconstituted, and the office of the Patriarch was again filled. Judaism regained its status as a legal religion (*religio licta*) after its rabbinic leadership agreed to give up active religious proselytism among gentiles. Although Jews did not participate in the state cults, this mattered little for it was legal for them not to do so. More significant to Rome was that Jews were no longer an active adversary of the tutelary gods and their emperors. In brief, Judaism could be tolerated as the religion of a small and comparative static minority without radical or subversive religious doctrines. That is to say, since it was no longer an enemy to the political order, Judaism was tolerated by the *imperium Romanum*.

Roman rulers confirmed the existing privileges of an ancient sanctuary when they conquered a region and welcomed numerous oriental cults into Rome. The principal motive for religious tolerance was political. Foreign cults were useful. As William Chase Green remarks, Rome did not want its polity to follow the Greek pattern of a land divided into a chessboard of petty states.[26] One way to avoid a land divided is to practice religious tolerance. Thus, whenever old gods descend because of their inadequate *numina*, new gods that protect the polity ascend. As Livy notes, when Rome faced Hannibal in crisis during the Second Punic War (218–201 BCE) foreign cults swept into Rome.[27] Dionysus of Halicarnassus states that Roman priests consulted the Greek Sibylline Books in times of unrest. This resulted in the importation of new gods and rituals into Rome.[28] Macrobius tells of inviting a protective deity from Carthage to desert the foreign state and come to Rome where the deity would be honored and celebrated with monuments and games.[29]

Not all foreign cults and deities were accepted. Selectivity was Roman political policy. If beneficial to the state and if its adherents were able to coexist with the mores of the Roman state religion, then a religion or cult was tolerated. Little tolerance was exhibited toward religious practices thought politically subversive such as human sacrifice or divination or those actions thought to promote insurrection and immorality. Livy reports that Rome rejected the cult of Bacchus-Dionysus because it promoted drunken orgies and allowed women to prostitute themselves by allowing them to be out in the evening.[30]

Augustus opposed the Isis cult, and, after the expulsion of Christians from the synagogues, Christianity no longer enjoyed the legal protection that was granted to Judaism as a *religio licita*. Starting with Nero in 64 CE, Roman emperors began to persecute devotees of this new cult. However, such intolerance was selective and short-lived. The cults of Mithras and Isis were well integrated into the Roman state by the time of the late Republic. Pliny the Younger notes that the Flavians embraced Isis, and Commodus incorporated Serapis into the official prayers of the new year.[31] Indeed, much to the distaste of Pliny, new "oriental" temples dotted the towns of Italy and continued to do so until the edicts of later Christian emperors. Before these edicts, Constantine had legitimized Christianity.[32]

Why was there Roman acceptance of foreign cults and deities? Principally, toleration of religions was important in maintaining the stability of the Roman state. Indeed, the benefits offered generally outweighed any losses. Moreover, the benefits offered by foreign gods and goddesses could be enjoyed by natives and foreigners, citizens and noncitizens, the elite and nonelite alike. Perhaps the most significant stabilizing factor of the presence of foreign cults was their familiarity to foreigners living within Roman territory. As the Republic and Empire expanded territorially and commercially, it encompassed more and more foreigners. For the state to maintain stability, the cults, creeds, and deities of Etruscans, Sabines, Faliscans, Latins, Greeks, Syrians, and Egyptians demanded toleration. These peoples needed to be appeased, unified, and given a sense of identity within the polity if Rome were to maintain domination. Roman toleration and adoption of foreign religions and cults did just that.

Religion in the pagan Roman world had a civic and consensual dimension. Participation in civic cults was mandatory to preserve the *pax deorum*. Thus, the Roman state saw it as beneficial that various deities and their followers coexisted. Tolerance of foreign religions and cults allowed followers to span social rank, geography, and local traditions. Moreover, religious toleration allowed for a sense of freedom from Roman domination. This formed a cohesive force among foreigners. As excavations from London to Dura Europos illustrate, followers of Mithras, Bal, Zeus, Isis, or Yahweh arriving from the same province, city, or town formed *collegia* on the basis of their common ethnic and religious traditions. From the time of the late Principate onwards, peoples from Rome to the frontiers celebrated many of the same rituals and festivals. Religion united the Roman state and allowed Rome to exercise political control. In the words of Polybius:

[T]he most distinctive excellence of the Roman state . . . [was] . . . its attitude to the gods . . . [and] [this] holds the Roman state together.[33]

This sense of belonging was furthered by Rome's role as an important religious center, where some emperors openly worshiped foreign deities.

5. Religious Intolerance

We have considered the political foundations of tolerance that carried Persian, Egyptian, Syrian, and Anatolian cults to regions outside their homes. We have also tried to explain the political and social origins of religious tolerance. Now the political origins of religious intolerance require attention. The development of a divine Roman imperial autocracy is central to this story.

By the middle of the third century, hastened by successful or unsuccessful usurpations and the violent deaths of emperors, it became clear that the Senate and military alone could no longer secure stability for the throne. A consensus emerged: to secure the state, another foundation alongside legalistic and militaristic ones was necessary. Thus, a new religious basis for the Roman state evolved, grounded in a single deity and the divinity of the emperor as its earthly regent. It is not merely the gods of Rome, the Roman Senate, and Roman legions that secure the state: god and emperor secure it as well.

This is the background against which emperors like Decius, Valerian, and Gallineus undertake their task of securing the Empire. Their efforts were to unite all the deities of the state and to harness them to the work of state restoration under divine imperial auspices. As Juppiter Optimus Maximus became dim, under Aurelian, "*Sol dominus imperii Romani*" embodied the idea of a unifying deity to correspond to the sole earthly ruler of the world. With this came the beginnings of a religious transformation of the person of the emperor and even more so, his direct deification. By the reign of Gallienus, Augustus is called *deus* instead of *divus*. The political meaning is that Augustus and his "heirs" are really divine, not merely dead men. Significantly, acceptance of this claim became the criterion for state toleration of foreign religions and cults. It also carried with it a heightened willingness of emperors to sacralize and tolerate or desacralize and not tolerate religious communities on the basis of political loyalty to the Roman state.

The idea that the felicity of heaven and earth depended on an imperial savior clashed with Christian faith and piety. But other events were brewing as well. When a disaster such as an earthquake or invasion occurred, it was assumed that the gods were angered with men. Here ruler and populace might demand a persecution—generally of the Christians—in order to placate the wrath of an outraged heaven. In such a case, the attitude of provincial governor and emperor determines the severity of the repression. It is to the governors that Tertullian addresses his apologia; it is to emperors that Origen does.

The grounds for Roman intolerance, repression, and persecution of the church were the unwillingness or inability of Christians to accept the divinization of the emperor and prostration before the gods of Rome and the emperor in acts of sacrifice. Thus, after his ascension, Decius took in hand a persecution of the Christians in several stages. First came measures against the leaders of the Church, beginning with the imprisonment of the bishop of Rome, who was put to death on January 20, 250 CE. Then, the persecution was pressed more fully in March. A third stage of more decisive action was undertaken in June when certificates of having made sacrifice to the pagan gods were required of all Romans, including Christians, from small children to the priests. The enforcement of this order was controlled by the Roman administration. The penalty for disobedience was death. What political factors led to an intolerance of Christianity? What political motives impelled Decius to turn executioner?

The answer lies in the change that had converted the Principate, based on republican juristic concepts, into an *imperium* that justified imperial religious absolutism. Decius was revolutionary. He demanded much more than an expiatory supplication of the gods to restore the *pax deorum*. He demanded loyalty to the emperor whose reign guaranteed divinely ordained order of the state. He did this because the primary purpose of the offering was the welfare of the emperor, sustainer of the state. Here notably, which god received the sacrifice was of secondary importance. Sacrifice was a test of imperial loyalty, but it was not a political motivation pure and simple. Questions of religious tolerance and intolerance were coming to the fore.

The precise legal basis for the persecution of Christians remains impossible to determine. Was it founded upon successive decisions of Roman magistrates acting under their wide discretionary powers (*coercitio*), with such decisions gradually hardening into law? Or was there a direct imperial pronouncement proscribing the sects? The latter appears likely, for, despite the tolerance of the Roman state, the church was resolute in its defiance of these new Roman laws.

The Christian community ever more strongly claimed to be an *imperium in imperio*. Immediately before the Decian persecution, Origen declared that Christ (and therefore his followers) was stronger than the emperor and all his officers, stronger than the Senate and the Roman people.[34] He looked for a day when the heathen cults should disappear and loyalty to the emperor no longer attested by pagan cult acts. Thus was removed the possibility of an understanding. Moreover, the claim of the church to dominion, illustrated by the illusion that some emperors were Christians, was too high to admit pagan reconciliation. But why was this so? It had not generally been the case in the past.

Here it is important to explore once again an unsettled question. It is not clear whether the order of Decius had as its motive persecution of Christians. With the Roman world on the brink of disaster, an act in which every member of the Roman world should do individual homage to the gods of Rome appears primarily a political measure. It seems that Decius did not demand from Christians an abjuration of faith but that they should join in a *supplicatio* such as Rome had traditionally employed in times of crisis.

Nonetheless, the very idea of the renewal of felicity on earth by the savior-ruler clashed with Christian doctrine. Thus, a return to the *status quo ante* seemed out of the question. Shortly, another persecution was launched under Valerian in August 257 CE, where a similar set of conditions were offered. Rome demanded no more than the minimum of obedience, not that Christians must abandon their faith, claiming that Christians should add to their faith a willingness to respect traditional religious formalities. This was necessary because it attested loyalty to the state and emperor.

Christians, such as Cyprian, answered that they would not cease to pray for the welfare of emperors but could only do so to the one true god.[35] Clearly, Christians like Cyprian wanted to separate state and emperor from the gods, let alone from their triune God. But it must have appeared to many Roman aristocrats and commoners that, if the Roman Juppiter, Juno, and Minerva were successfully challenged by the Christian Father, Son, and Holy Spirit, the *pax deorum* and *pax Romana* would dissolve. The gods angered would surely punish Rome, one god and emperor not withstanding.

The swift political dissolution of the *pax Romana* already signaled the religious disaffection of the *pax deorum*. Valerian's response was to break up the corporate life of the church. The persecution began with the arrest of leading churchmen but then took a novel course. Believers were not called to sacrifice. Rather, religious meetings and entry to cemeteries were forbidden under pain of death. The Roman state was severing-off the bureaucratic heart of the church. Around the cemeteries, particularly in the catacombs, workshops and rooms had been formed for the social life and administration of the church. It was here in Rome that the bishop Xystus, deacons, and clergy were arrested and put to death. In a year came a new rescript ordering the immediate execution of all clergy. Dionysius of Alexandria and Cyprian fell, and, like all highly placed Christians who clung to their faith, they suffered confiscation as well as death. Humbler folk, as long as they did not disobey the former edict or provoke the magistrates to action, were left alone. The persecution lasted three years, ending with Valerian's imprisonment on Persian soil. It did not overthrow the church. In the words of Cyprian, the *disciplina Romana* could not prevail over the *divinitus tradita disciplina*.[36]

When Valerian was taken prisoner and killed by the Persians, Gallienus broke with his father's policy against the Christians. Eusebius reports that Gallienus extended his concessions to that country after the fall of Macarianus (261 CE) and Aemilianus (262 CE).[37] This imperial decree gave tolerance and security to the church. When the emperor acted on petition from the bishops, he admitted that they possessed a legal status. When the emperor restored to the bishops churches and cemeteries, he confirmed the legality of the church's possessions. When the emperor pronounced Christianity neither outside the law nor against the law, he confirmed Rome's tolerance of another foreign religion. This was an important step. Christianity had been reclassified from a *superstitio* to a *religio*. It would take Constantine some forty years later to refine the status of Christianity to a *religio licita*.

Gallienus' murder was followed by a violent reaction. There were scattered martyrdoms, mostly in Italy, during the short reign of Claudius II, but it was not in his power to undo or counter the consequences of the edict of Gallienus. His decree of toleration (following Green's five questions): (1) affirms the legal status of Christianity; (2) acknowledges Christianity as constructive socially within the Roman state; (3) justifies the existence of Christianity as an erroneous, accidental but nonetheless constructive part of Roman political reality; (4) recognizes the doctrinal fault lines between the Roman imperial religion centered on a savior-emperor and Christianity centered on the Savior-Christ but justifies tolerance of the church on the basis that it is better for the state to cure Christianity by the treatment of tolerance than the knife of intolerance; and (5) affirms that there are political, historical, and legal factors that justify state tolerance for Christianity.

Tolerance of Christians furthered the Roman *pax deorum*, and quite a change this was. From the time of Trajan, it was established that Christianity carried as its consequence the penalty of death. Even Gallienus did not rescind this judgment. This awaited the verdict of Constantine and Licinius with the Edict of Milan in 313. Until that year, the church was never granted express recognition as a lawful corporation. It remained after Gallienus neither a *religio licita* nor a *religio inlicita*.

6. Between Religious Tolerance and Intolerance

There persisted an imperial anxiety over the possibility that the hard-won peace and security of the Mediterranean world should be threatened from within by foreign religions and cults. The establishment of the *pax Romana* depended upon a *pax deorum*. But the price was high—even a municipal fire-brigade or any other *collegia* in an Asian city was too perilous an association to receive imperial sanction. This concern deepened with the Christians. Here, the Caesars were faced by no municipal association but by a far-flung secret brotherhood.

The idea of an exclusive faith, which was not part of the henotheism, cultic polytheism, and inclusive monotheism of the Republic and Empire, was foreign to Roman political praxis. A common response was to interpret such a faith as merely a veil for a deep-rooted hostility to state and society since these sectaries were bent on turning the world upside down. When repression

of a religious cult occurred, it was politically motivated. Religious intolerance was practiced to avert social peril or to domesticate a foreign religion
that endangered the legitimacy of the state. However, Roman policy generally was not to repress local religions and cults but to affiliate them to its own
pantheon.

Between state and church, there stood no greater obstacle to reconciliation than the worship of the emperor. Pagans of the second century CE could
not understand the Christian objections to this tribute of respect to the ruler
of the Roman world. Marcus Aurelius thought it a perverse obstinacy. By the
third century, however, a subtle but important shift apparently occurred,
orchestrated by Diocletian and then Aurelian. What if the emperor were not
a god but a God's vice-regent on earth? Thus, Diocletian and Aurelian were
not Juppiter, but Jovius, Juppiter's representative, and their colleagues were
not Hercules, but Herculius.

Diocletian and his colleagues considered themselves *dis geniti* and *deorum
creatores* to whom *adoratio* should be offered. In pagan houses as well as in
temples of the imperial cult, the genius of the emperor was to be honored
for the *natalis caesaris* (birthday of the emperor), for the *natalis imperii* (anniversary of his ascension to power), and for the health of the imperial family,
at the *vox publica* each year, and at the *vota quinquinalia*. But to be God's representative rather than fully divine is a dramatic shift in religious ontology.
If this shift actually occurred, the way to an understanding between pagan
ruler and Christian subject opened up. Now even the *proskynêsis* (prostration)
before the emperor was not the worship of the god but an outward symbol of
homage to God's representative on earth. It appears to be the case because, in
the last persecution of Christians, the cult of emperors played a very subordinate part. The Christian Church of the third century was clearly prepared to
respond to these advances. The appeal with which Origen had concluded his
True Discourse seemed in a fair way answered.

After Gallienus, the Roman state no longer considered that Christians constituted a danger to the Empire. Experience proved that Christians might be
a peculiar brand of malefactors, but now Roman magistrates were not under
the legal obligation of proceeding against the church. This initiative could be
undertaken by any Christian. With a recantation of faith, the believer secured
state immunity from punishment. However, such actions appear to have been
rare. There are even signs to suggest the foundations of Christian tolerance
toward the Roman state. Throughout all the persecutions, no Christian had
raised the standard of revolt. There was not only a strong pacifist strain in
the church, as exemplified by Origen and Tertullian,[38] but, from the time of

the early apologists, Christians had affirmed their loyalty to the emperor. His power, however much abused, was God-given. Thus, prayers for the emperor formed a part of Christian worship. Melito had the vision that church and Empire were ordained in the Providence of God not for enmity but for cooperation. This explains why many Christians were prepared to give their loyalty to the Roman state, which guaranteed order and justice. Their claim was that it not demand apostasy from their faith. Lactantius was not only a Christian, but he was also a Roman who shrank in terror from the thought that one day, according to his scriptures, the Roman Empire would pass as had the empires of Babylon and Alexander.[39]

Keeping the results of Green's survey in mind, it appears that, by the late third century, the Roman state and the Christian Church: (1) accepted the role of other "religions"; (2) acknowledged, tolerated, and saw each "other" as constructive; (3) justified the existence and persistence of the state as constitutive of reality; and (4) recognized that the religious and theological fault lines that separate state and church centered on the divinity of the emperor. Once the emperor was defined as a divine-representative, but not divine, a justification of mutual tolerance emerged; therefore, (5) they accepted that political, historical, and theological factors are at play in expressions of tolerance and intolerance for each other. Thus, choices were beginning to be made by the Roman state and Christian Church to promote tolerance of the other.

7. Theological Tolerance and Intolerance

From our precipice of history, the timidity of the Caesars in the face of Christianity seems remarkable. This is the background against which Diocletian undertook his task of reorganization and reform. He wanted to unite all the peoples of the Empire, to harness them to the work of imperial regeneration. To accomplish this, he excluded no one who was prepared to do his part. He also thought that it should be made easy for Christians to do their part as well. Statesmanship could hardly come to any other conclusion. Here, Diocletian initiated new theological understandings of tolerance that would replace older religious ones. As God's representative on earth, Diocletian is the delegate of Juppiter as Jovius, while Maximian is the delegate of Hercules as Heraclius. Moreover, those who were willing to hold office were freed from the obligations of "pagan" sacrifice.

Despite rigorists in the church, these policies had positive results. Christians joined the army in large numbers, and no religious difficulties arose. Then, according to Lactantius, "some time" before the general persecution, a public sacrifice was offered, in the presence of Diocletian and Galerius, for purposes of learning the will of heaven.[40] The Christians crossed themselves to ward off evil from demons. No augury ensued, and the chief priest, Tagis, proclaimed this was so because of the presence at the rite of profane persons. Diocletian was furious. It was one thing to tolerate Christians, another to allow them to disturb a solemn religious rite. At Nicomedia in the winter of 302/3 CE, Galerius pressed upon his Augustus the necessity of a rigorous persecution. Diocletian resisted but agreed to refer the question to the oracle of the Milesian Apollo, who answered, "*ut divinae religionis inimicus.*"[41] Diocletian could no longer resist but demanded no blood be shed.

The oracle offered a justification for religious intolerance however high the political and social price might be. Christianity was an "unfriendly" religion. It was one thing to tolerate Christians, another not to be tolerated by them. Eusebius and Lactantius note that Christians were known by their mere presence, breath, or word to scatter the designs of demons; and, if they made the sign of the cross, no answer from the gods can be obtained.[42] In brief, what was perceived as Christian mixogony ignited imperial fury.

I shall not detail the persecutions against the Christians that would unfold. Others have done this admirably. In brief, desacralization and intolerance intensified. Christian churches were destroyed, houses used for worship were demolished, all assemblies for worship forbidden, scriptures and liturgical books were burned. Higher-class Christians were deprived of legal privileges, and all Christians were placed outside the law. They could not defend their rights in courts. Those who persisted in their Christianity were deprived of freedom.[43] In due time the clergy was imprisoned.[44] When Diocletian fell ill, Galerius issued the bloody edict commanding all men, women, and children to sacrifice and make libation on penalty of death. The western Augustus, Maximian, and later the eastern Augustus, Maximin Daia, complied. Diocletian's abdication is the sequel to the victory of Galerius.

Other horrors would follow, but focus falls on the years 308–309 CE. After July 308 CE, the persecution in Palestine was halted. Maximin Daia hoped to become Augustus. That hope was ignored by Diocletain and Galerius and then outright refused by Galerius. In response, Maximin unleashed a new edict in 309 CE. Temples were to be rebuilt, and everyone was to be present at the public sacrifices and eat the offerings to the deities. Every article sold in market was to be sprinkled with sacrificial blood. The popular response was swift. According to Eusebius, this edict was judged burdensome and excessive by non-Christians.[45] Thus, by March 310 CE, persecutions waned. The Roman East was sick of bloodshed. On April 30, 311, the unexpected happened. Galerius, the promoter of persecution, now suffering from a horrible illness, issued an edict of toleration. It is preserved by Lactantius and translated into Greek by Eusebius.[46] The persecution would end, and Christians were accorded legal recognition. The tolerance, which the church enjoyed in the early years of Diocletian's reign, was restored.

The edict is instructive for a study of sacralization and desacralization, tolerance and intolerance in the later pagan Roman period. It is issued "for the profit and advantage of the State." All things are to set right

according to ancient laws and public order [*disciplinam*] of the Romans and further to provide that the Christians . . . who had abandoned the way of life [*sectam*] of their own fathers should return to sound reason [*ad bonas mentes*]. . . . [T]he Christians had become possessed by obstinacy and folly . . . and instead of following those institutions of the ancients which perhaps their ancestors had first established . . . they were at their own will and pleasure making laws for themselves . . . acting upon them and were assembling in different places people of different nationalities. After we decreed that they should return to the institutions of the ancients, many were subjected to danger, many too were completely overthrown; and when most persisted in their determination and we saw that they neither gave worship and due reverence to the gods nor practiced the worship [*observare*] of the god of the Christians, considering our most gentle clemency and our immemorial custom by which we want to grant indulgence to all men, we have thought it correct in their case too to extend the speediest indulgence to the effect that they may be once more free to exist [*sint*] as Christians, and reform their churches [*conventicula componant*] always provided that they do nothing contrary to public order [*disciplinam*]. Further by another order we shall inform judges [*iudicibus*] what conditions the Christians must observe. Thus in accordance with this our indulgence they will be bound to entreat their god for our well-being and for that of the State and for their own so that on every side the State may be preserved unharmed and that they themselves might live in their homes in security.

At the opening of Galerius' edict, the language of earlier constitutions is recalled—the *mala voluntas* and *stultitia* of the Christians. In their breaking through the wall of partition that separates one religion from another, a Roman fear persists of Christian cosmopolitanism. Only the state is the foundation of cosmopolitanism. Hence, nothing must be done by Christians *contra disciplinam*. Finally, Galerius conditions religious toleration on Christian prayers for emperor and Empire. Coercion is implied: no Christian prayers results in Roman state intolerance of Christianity.

The edict suggests that religious toleration presupposes the existence of a state. The state deems it necessary to make a collective profession of a specific religion legal only if its members recognize the legitimacy of the state and its gods. Once the state tolerates a religion, it can disapprove of it, for toleration

presumes an authority that again may become coercive. The prayers availed
Galerius nothing. A few days after the issue of the edict he was dead. Lactantius rationalized that God permitted the great persecution in order to bring
pagans within the community of a Christian Church. Eusebius argued such
prayers were providential for a Christian Roman state, which would soon
have as its new emperor Constantine, a Christian emperor ruling a pagan
empire and bound to a pagan past. Here, out of political and religious necessity, Roman and Christian notions of tolerance and intolerance merge.

8. Tolerance Divine

The Roman world was divided between the two victors Constantine and
Licinius. They met in Milan and in June 313 CE, Licinius, with the agreement
of Constantine, published a letter in Nicomedia granting complete freedom
of belief.[47] What is striking is how different its tone is from the edict of Galerius published two years earlier. Religious toleration combined sacralization with individual choice, rights, liberty, benevolence, and devotion is its
theme:

Since we saw that freedom of worship ought not be denied, but that to each man's
judgment and will the right should be given to care for sacred things according to each
man's free choice, we have already some time ago bidden the Christians to maintain
the faith of their own sect and worship. But since in that edict, by which such right
was granted to the Christians, many and varied conditions clearly appeared to have
been added, it may well have come about that after a short time many were repelled
from practicing their religion.[48] Thus, when I, Constantine Augustus, and I, Licinius Augustus had met at Mediolanum [Milan] and were discussing all those matters which relate to the advantage and security of the state, among the other things
which we saw that would benefit the majority of men we thought first of all that those
conditions for which reverence for the Divinity is secured should be put in order by
us to the end that we might give to the Christians and all men the right to follow
freely whatever religion each had wished, so that thereby whatever supreme Divinity [Summa Divinitas] exists in the heavenly seat may be favorable and propitious
to us and to all those who are placed under our authority. Thus by a salutary and
most fitting line of reasoning we came to the conclusion that we should adopt this
policy—that our view should be that to no one whatsoever should we deny the liberty to follow either the religion of the Christians or any other cult which of his own
free choice he has thought to be best adapted for himself, in order that the supreme
Divinity, to whose service we render our free obedience, may bestow upon us in all in
all things his favor and benevolence. Wherefore we would that your Devotion should
know that it our will that all those conditions should be completely removed which
were contained in our earlier letters addressed to you concerning the Christians [and

which seemed to be entirely perverse and alien from our clemency][49] these should be removed and now in freedom and without restriction let all those who desire to follow the religion of the Christians quickly do so without any molestation or interference. We felt that the most complete information should be furnished on this matter to your Carefulness that you may be assured that we have given to the Christians complete and unrestricted liberty to follow their religion. Further, when you see that this indulgence has been granted by us to the Christians, your Devotion will understand that also to others a similar, free, and unhindered liberty and freedom of cult has been granted, for such a grant is befitting to the peace of our times, so that it may be open to every man to worship as he will. This has been done by us so that we should not seem to have dishonored any religion.

What are the motives behind the edict? On traditional grounds, the imperial aim is clear and simple. After a decade of internal strife and foreign invasion, the Roman state wants divine favor back. Thus, the Emperors returned all confiscated churches to the Christians with restoration provided either by the Imperial Treasury or by private persons—*sine pecunia et sine alla pretii petitione*. Even individual reparations were offered, as well as an indemnification to all who were deprived of land they wanted to purchase.

However important a return of divine favor may be for the Roman state and its rulers, there is more to this edict than that. It appears an exclusive religious tolerance has been replaced by an inclusive theological tolerance. Reasons for such a theological "shift" require some reflection. I would suggest that the Edict of Milan is based on the later Roman theological principles of inclusive monotheism and cultic polytheism, which accepts the existence of a great number of gods but holds that all gods are essentially one and the same. Thus, which name or rite according to which a god or goddesses is invoked makes little or no difference. There is one divinity worshiped throughout the world in diverse manners, customs, and many names.

The totality of the gods constitutes the divine world. However much a deity is intent on his honor, he never disputes the existence of other gods. They are all ever-lasting ones. What is fatal is if a deity is overlooked. Thus, as advocates of inclusive monotheism and cultic polytheism, Constantine and Licinius adopted inclusive religious tolerance as the political policy that best guaranteed the security of the Roman state and the *pax deorum*. Once religious tolerance becomes an accepted part of public life, framed as a kinship expression of Roman religious custom and the practice of age, old Roman civic virtues and neglected gods are appeased, and political and social harmony is restored.

In this edict, there is no breach with a wider "pagan" past. Once the god-kinship was abandoned, the rest of Hellenistic and Persian theories of sovereignty could be adopted with hardly any change in language. Precisely as the Hellenistic kings had for a guiding principle the divine *Logos*, and Persian monarchs held kingly power as a trust from their god, since the time of Diocletian and Aurelian, emperors assumed the place of representation with the ruling deity. Eusebius' theory of Christian sovereignty is a symbol of the way in which a Greco-Roman-Persian past was carried into a Christian present.

Eusebius celebrated the first Edict of Toleration by publishing his *History of the Church*. He formulated for the first time the theory of Imperial and Christian sovereignty, which remained the foundation of the East Roman world for over a millennia. In 324 CE, the transformation of Byzantium into Constantinople began. Pagan temples were not destroyed. Pagan statues were collected and housed in Constantinople as an adornment for the city. Just as Rome had her Fortuna—her fortune—Constantinople had her Tyche. The only limit of Constantine's toleration was that sacrifice was banished from the second Rome on the Bosporous. Constantinople stood as a Christian Rome.

The social reasons for such a political and theological "shift" require brief reflection, again from the pagan perspective. Among later Romans, the progressive decay of traditional religious and civic traditions undermined the needs of self-reliance, self-sufficiency, tranquility, and apathy and promoted the will for a new religious tolerance. The anonymity and loneliness of life in the great new cities, where one was a cipher, reinforced the need for a community of divine friends and helpers. What the individual did with the solitariness in this age was to form small private clubs devoted to the worship of individual gods, old and new, or to join philosophical schools dedicated to the common bond of mutual tolerance and friendship.

There were not only social reasons for these changes but "pagan" philosophical and religious ones as well. Significant is a revival of Pythagoreanism under Platonic auspices as a cult and way of life. Pythagoras is presented as the inspired sage, a counterpart of Zoroaster, Ostanes, and Manes. What is taught in his name is a detachable theurgic rather than rational self, which, once activated, allowed an escape from this world of darkness and penance to one of light and salvation. In such *katharsis*, the soul becomes one with the divine.

Here we enter the world of Neoplatonism with its novel notions of friendship.[50] Friendship took on the aura of a divine rather than human constellation of kinship, familial, and civic relationships. The thoughts of men and women became increasingly preoccupied with the techniques of individual salvation through holy books, prophetic inspiration, and revelation; or by oracles, dreams, and waking visions. Others found salvation in ritual by initiation in esoteric *musteria*.[51] In brief, we encounter the starting point for a new and entirely different kind of *religio*. Here the emperor becomes in the words of Marcus Aurelius, "a kind of priest and minister of the gods."[52] Here the agent does not determine what motivates ethical action, higher authorities do—a supreme divinity, divinities, emperors, and their interpreters.[53] Intentional action can have either beneficent, neutral, or negative consequences on the agent. This depends on the efficacy of an agent's divine knowledge of religious praxis. Thus, what accelerates at the close of antiquity is the practice of the theological virtues of charity and forgiveness. Significantly novel here is that theological virtue becomes the foundation of religious tolerance.

We are already within a late Roman rhythm. A new term, *grace*, also appears in later Platonists such as Porphyry, Iamblichus, and Proclus, a word that symbolizes a new shift in emphasis. Briefly, Iamblichus proposes that Soul is a separate self-subsistent hypostasis, dependent on and inferior to Intelligence.[54] Proclus goes on to argue that while Soul's essence is eternal, her activities take place in time.[55] This leads both to emphasize that human souls only contain the *logoi* operative within Universal Soul, but not within Intelligence. This is because no human soul can know the Forms as long as she remains a fallen soul.

Iamblichus and Proclus argue that both Soul and Intelligence exist under an appropriate mode on successive levels of reality.[56] However, union between the divine and human only occurs through appropriate ritual actions. The rituals that invoke the gods are a voluntary bestowal of divine power.[57] The human soul blessed by such power gains salvation. This claim resulted in the claims by Iamblichus and his heirs that theurgy, not philosophy, leads to divine union.[58] Hence, there is an emphasis in pagan Neoplatonism of the need for divine grace, combined with a new human receptiveness toward such grace. Without it the salvation of the soul is impossible.

Here a metaphysics of the will, rather than one of reason alone, emerges.[59] This is where divine grace (and providence) come into play. Plotinus describes the One as will, and as love, of itself.[60] Significantly, divine grace is seen as the product of divine will, or "undiminished giving," which is the nature of divine activity.[61] Within the intelligible world will, giving, and order imply one another. Thus, unaffected and unconcerned, the One wills reality as a spontaneous out-flowing (*prohodos*) of itself throughout the totality of Being. Then, at the levels of Intellect and Soul, there is a turning back (*epistrophe*), wherein Soul and Intellect contemplate the One and so receive form and order. Here, we encounter for the first time the notion of a divine, nonreflective, selfless tolerance.

9. Tolerance and Intolerance Divine

The later years of the reign of Constantine stand beyond the scope of this chapter. Nonetheless, the pagan contexts of Constantine's policy of religious tolerance and sacralization as well as desacralization and intolerance require brief comment. The approval of the gods was necessary for the maintenance of the Roman polity. Prescribed rituals were followed in giving the gods the offerings and prayers they were entitled to receive for their protection of the state. The emperor, as *pontifex maximus*, was designated to offer sacrifices for the sake of the empire. Some of these pagan practices changed when Constantine became Christian emperor. He shied away from performing sacrifices offered on the Capitoline in Rome. Elsewhere, according to the pagan historian Zosimus, Constantine agreed to participate in religious festivities to placate his soldiers but refused to perform sacrifices.[62] These practices were followed by all emperors after Constantine, with the exception of Julian the "Apostate."

A sense of the changes to come appears in 333 CE. In this year, Constantine authorized the inhabitants of a group of towns in Umbria to build a temple to the Gens Flavia, with the restriction that the temple should not be polluted by superstition, which meant that he agreed to an imperial cult only if sacrifices were not performed. Again as high priest, Constantine had the right to direct the construction and removal of temples. He used this power after the death of Licinius to confiscate precious objects from the temples in the east and the destruction of specific sanctuaries. Some temples were located on biblical sites. Others were destroyed because they were offensive to the new Christian standards of morality.

The temple of Aphrodite at Aphaca in Phoenicia was destroyed because of the practice of sacred prostitution. The temple of Aegeae in Cilicia was demolished because it was a locus of anti-Christian polemics.[63] Dedicated to Aesculapius, and publicized in the *Life of Apollonius of Tyana*, a second-century competitor to Christ, the temple's existence was not tolerated. There occurred as well the complete demolition of a Roman temple that stood on the supposed site of Christ's crucifixion and tomb in Jerusalem. Not only was the temple destroyed, but the stones and soil defiled by pagan sacrifices were removed until the holy place where the resurrection occurred appeared. Over this cave a church was built. All this activity supported new imperial notions of the holiness of places and objects touched by Christ.[64] It also was precise in its targets. Not all pagan temples were destroyed, but a precedent was set. Eventually, pagan cult activities persisted only in sacred caves, at sacred springs, and around sacred trees.

Such Christian political changes in standards of tolerance and intolerance have their origins in long-standing pagan traditions of sacralization and desacralization. Participation in pagan civic and religious cults was mandatory to preserve the *pax deorum* and to show political loyalty to the Roman rulers. This practice continued but now under new auspices. First, the Roman state had to be desacralized of its divine pagan patrons and, second, resacralized for its divine Christian ones. These activities were undertaken under the aegis of a novel theological criterion by Constantine—exclusive monotheism. As advocates of exclusive monotheism, Constantine and the Christian emperors who followed would increasingly come to practice religious intolerance. Thus commences a new Christian era that takes us beyond these later "pagan" horizons of religious and theological tolerance and intolerance.

Nonetheless, what accelerates at the close of pagan antiquity is the practice of the theological virtues. More specifically, religious maintenance of the *pax deorum* drove social and religious tolerance, while a political conception of imperial power, as a trust from God, established the conditions for the possibility of an inclusive theological tolerance. Once an identification of ruler with deity was replaced by the notion of the emperor deriving his power from God, such a wide-ranging tolerance became state policy. This was possible because now the emperor's aim was imitation, not identification with God. Fundamental to a political policy of inclusive tolerance was the adoption of two essential theological principles: inclusive monotheism and cultic polytheism. Inclusive monotheism accepts the existence of a great number of deities but holds that all gods and goddesses are essentially one and the same. Cultic polytheism allows for the practice of rites and rituals associated with all deities and holds it makes little or no difference under which name or according to which rite a deity is invoked.

This raises a fundamental question for our study. What are the necessary and sufficient conditions for a public policy of tolerance for nonbelievers in foreign religious communities? The Roman resources for tolerance seem to suggest that only a theological policy of inclusive monotheism, cultic polytheism, and ruler as regent of God met conditions that allowed for the political practice of inclusive religious tolerance. When these conditions were not met, we encounter a public policy of exclusive tolerance for nonbelievers in selected religious communities. When exclusive monotheism became the theological norm in the later Christian Empire, tolerance of cultic polytheism all but disappeared, save in domesticated form in the Christian cult of the saints. *In nuce*, inclusive tolerance was slowly replaced by exclusive tolerance in the case of Judaism and by inclusive intolerance in the case of paganism. But even here Christian emperors like pagan emperors before them viewed a public policy of tolerance and intolerance in largely political terms. In this sense, there is little difference between the policies of Marcus Aurelius, Diocletian, Constantine, and Justinian.

10. Tolerance Ancient and Modern

Greco-Roman notions of tolerance have little in common with modern theories of tolerance. The two traditions have different metaphysical assumptions, ontologies, views of the "Self," the "religious other," distinct assessments of the grounds for religious toleration, and even disparate notions about the good(s) of tolerance. The ancient option is guided by a divinely sanctioned, politically justified, and legally grounded rationality; the modern one is driven by a state-mandated, individually sanctioned volition coupled to a juridically limited notion of rationality. In brief, Greco-Roman concepts of tolerance had their origins in the rational political obligations and social commitments all share for maintaining the state and the gods who protect it, not in emotivist, sensationalist, duty, utilitarian, or behavioral foundations and factors.[65] That is to say, Greco-Roman notions of tolerance were not based on modern concepts such as rationality, duty, utility, social development, or behavioral factors. Tolerance is a religious and civic virtue that maintains a divinely sanctioned cosmopolitan state ruled by a divine king or Senate and Caesars. This suggests that tolerance was not designed to help maintain individual rights or to increase the welfare of a group. Indeed, tolerance does not involve high risk or sacrifice to agent or group. Tolerance is grounded in a reasoned political reciprocity and social justice that had as its rationale the maintenance of the state.

What of modern understandings of religious tolerance? How do they differ from ancient ones? Here difference matters. Ancient theories of tolerance have much to do with reason, state, and public policy. Modern definitions of tolerance have much to do with will and little to do with reason, state, and public policy. The crucial difference between ancient concerns and motivational states on the one hand and modern ones on the other is that moderns have taken upon themselves the tolerant and intolerant activities earlier grounded in the divine. This change has significant importance for our study of tolerance. It is a harbinger of what emerges in the modern period—rationalist, emotivist, sensationalist, duty, or utilitarian theories of tolerance.

The explanation for this shift or change is a complex one that cannot be addressed fully here. Inclusive tolerance had its ancient philosophical origins in Marcus Aurelius, Plotinus, Iamblichus, and Proclus with their emphasis on rational choice (*prohairesis*) and theological notions of divine grace (*charis*) and divine giving (*didonai*). Inclusive tolerance has its modern philosophical origins in David Hume, Immanuel Kant, Jeremy Bentham, and John Stuart Mill, who radically truncated the role of rational choice in moral affairs. Hume reduced ethics to sentiments. Kant limited ethics to a categorical imperative, based on willful duty, not rational choice. In the shadow of Hume and Kant, Bentham and Mill claimed we not only have a sentiment but also a duty on the basis of the greatest good for the greatest number to tolerate others. *In nuce*, modern theories of tolerance rest primarily on Kant's distinction between goodwill, the possession of which alone is both necessary and sufficient for moral worth, and what he took to be a distinct natural gift, that of knowing how to apply general rules to particular cases.

Thus, we find the great divide between Greco-Roman theories of tolerance and modern ones. With modernity, the triumph of goodwill over reason and charity over justice is almost complete. Those characters so essential to the dramatic scripts of modernity are in place: a tolerant will has triumphed over tolerant reason. As a consequence, we leave this study with what has become a problem. There are consequences of any "turn." In this case, we witness a turn from reason to will as the foundation for tolerance.

Here a final question requires reflection: is a modern public policy of inclusive tolerance possible? It appears so, but I would like to suggest inclusive tolerance may be possible at a cost. The Stoics claimed the existence of eternal laws built into the very structure of reality that direct the actions of all rational beings. Roman theorists developed a doctrine of a law all rational peoples would recognize. The aim was to show that the principles of morals could be known by reason alone so that the whole human race could know how to live properly. Natural law doctrine would develop in its Christian varieties, in a rational Thomistic and in a voluntarist Grotian version. Followers of Aquinas argued that God's intellect is the source of law. Grotius' followers claimed that God's will is the source of law. Significant for this study is that Grotius greatly influenced Thomas Hobbes, Samuel von Pufendorf, John Locke, and, through them, much of modern theories of tolerance.

In the shadow of the European Enlightenment, religious belief was willfully separated from politics and public policy. With the eclipse of religion, theology, and theories of natural law, state and individually sanctioned voluntarist grounds for religious tolerance (or intolerance) are left. Thus, by the early eighteenth century, discussions of whether there is an objective morality largely ceased to center on natural law altogether. Two other options replaced it. Legal positivism emerged with the view that the only binding laws are those imposed by human sovereigns. Legal realism also emerged with the claim that legal rights are of value only in the service of the project of legitimizing certain gender, class, or race interests as the prime salient property of law. These options leave the executive or legislature alone in judging the political and legal foundations of religious tolerance and intolerance—on largely voluntarist and utilitarian grounds. If there are limits or constraints on sovereign or legislator, it does not invoke or imply any of the religious and theological aspects of natural law positions. With this loss, consequences follow.

Natural-law theorists treat morality as a matter of compliance with law. Obligation and duty, obedience and disobedience, merit and guilt, reward and punishment are central notions where virtue is a matter of following laws rationally or willfully. However, this is not a self-imposed law. In following it, we are obeying God. Thus, if natural law dictates tolerance for the other or for the nonbeliever, we practice tolerance because it is an eternal divine law built into the very structure of nature and the state. Here, a legal norm such as tolerance grants the legal right to tolerance. Significantly, it is not possible in natural law, as it is possible in legal positivism and legal realism, that a morally iniquitous law could be a valid legal rule.[66]

Modern theories of tolerance are not based on natural law. John Rawls' theory of justice is a case in point.[67] It is liberal because Rawls accepts that society must be built around value pluralism and the notion of liberty. Because of this, the state should not impose specific conceptions of the good life, and humans should be free to follow their own values within limits prescribed by a theory of fairness. He also argues that the principles of social justice are those that would be agreed upon by a group of rational, self-interested persons placed behind a veil of ignorance. Behind this veil, persons would have no knowledge of their personal circumstances but would choose rationally to adopt certain principles whose implementation would constitute a fair and just society.

According to Rawls, two principles, which are discussed below, determine what is to count as a fair or just distribution of benefits and costs among members of a society. Justice is that there be no arbitrary distinctions between persons in the assigning of basic rights and duties. The two principles resolve what Rawls calls the problem of value pluralism. The just resolution of such conflicts is that no single set of values has priority over others. Here, the state must not impose a particular ideal of the good life and the just society is not the good life of the community as a whole. Instead, the state should allow—tolerate—that its individual members pursue their own conception of the good within limits. The two principles of justice do this by determining the just distribution of primary social goods, such as rights, liberties, powers, income, and wealth, that are needed for the pursuit of the good. It appears that Rawls' position rests primarily on Hume's notion of moral sentiments, which are his "veil of ignorance," and Kant's distinction between goodwill— possession of which alone is both necessary and sufficient for moral worth— and what Kant took to be a distinct natural gift: that of knowing how to apply general rules to particular cases.

Rawls assumes that humans want to advance their own ends and are not concerned with those of others. He also claims that it is rational to choose to live in a society based on two principles of justice because people's not having knowledge of their own particular circumstances would lead them to adopt principles that favor one group, set of values, or notions of the good life over any other. These two principles are: (1) each person is to have an equal right to the most extensive total system of equal basic liberties compatible with a similar system of liberty for all; and (2) social and economic inequalities are to be arranged so that they are both (a) to the greatest benefit of the least advantaged, consistent with the just savings principle, and (b) attached to offices and positions open to all under conditions of fair equality of opportunity with the difference principle.[68]

Thus, Rawls' theory of social justice is Kantian in dimensions. We are free, rational agents. It is also antiutilitarian in that, for utilitarians, the right action is the one that maximizes overall utility impartially considered, and utility is the only thing of noninstrumental value, which means that justice and rights have only instrumental value and that the liberty and value of one person can be sacrificed for the greater good. In contrast, Rawls' theory implies that social justice has primacy over utility because no individual can be sacrificed for society's greater good. Rawls also discusses how a liberal state might accommodate the values of different cultures within one nation through the idea of an overlapping consensus of public opinion. It is on the basis of public consensus that tolerance rests.

Three observations: First, Rawls' theory is one of social justice because it defines the principles that should regulate the institutions of a society. Second, his derivation of the rules for a just society, while contractual, is not based on a politically, religiously, or theologically grounded social contract. It is based on the notion that these rules agree with individual reflective moral judgment. Third, reflective equilibrium is the key idea here. Such equilibrium is found in subjective reflection when there is no longer any need to adopt or revise our ethical theory to fit our specific moral judgments and no need to adopt or revise our moral judgments to fit the theory. It is the balance between these two processes that yields justice and tolerance in a society.

Rawls' position follows Hume and Kant, rather than Aristotle, who claimed that one cannot be rational, just, tolerant, and act in a "veil of ignorance" simultaneously. In the broad sense according to Aristotle, we act justly when practicing the other excellences of character and when we act out of respect for all concerned with respect for the law.[69] Ignorance and public opinion preclude justice and tolerance. Thus, regardless of how rationally grounded Rawls' theory claims to be, justice and tolerance cannot be based on subjective reflection and opinion alone. Justice and toleration require a foundation based in character and law.

Thus, in Alasdair MacIntrye's words, "Those characters so essential to modernity, the expert who matches means to end in an evaluative neutral way and the moral agent who is anyone and everyone who is not mentally defective, have no genuine counterpart within the classical tradition at all."[70] Indeed, it is difficult to envisage the exaltation of bureaucratic expertise in any culture in which the connection between practical intelligence and moral values are firmly established. But these are a reflection of a present age in which tolerance is atomistically reasoned, willed, and opined rather than morally and legally grounded with consequences that remain—as with the case of altruism— problematic.[71]

Conclusion

The focus of this study has been that political concerns produced a public policy of tolerance and intolerance for nonbelievers in Greco-Roman paganism. In the Roman Republic and Empire, the political foundations for religious tolerance and intolerance rested on religious and theological grounds. Acts of sacralization and desacralization complemented edicts of tolerance or intolerance. Roman authorities attempted to control religious communities by tolerating them and sacralizing their religious buildings and writings or by not tolerating religions and cults by desacralizing their religious shrines and texts. By altering the spatial and temporal rhythms of a religious community, Roman rulers attempted to set the boundaries of licit and illicit behavior, of tolerance and intolerance toward others.[72] The sacralization of space during the centuries that saw the establishment of numerous pagan cults was followed by an intense sacralization of space by Christians. Consequently, more than once Roman authorities, pagan and Christian, ordered the confiscation or the destruction of religious buildings and artifacts. The goal of such activity was to maintain a polity divinely grounded.

We should address for the final time the five questions raised by William

Scott Green at the beginning of his study: the role of other religions; the acknowledgment of different religions; the justification of other religions; the fault lines that justify religious tolerance and intolerance; and the historical, political, and/or behavioral factors that correlate with the tolerance or intolerance of other religions. (Greco-)Roman Pagan sources make a variety of consistent claims that:

(1) The major category of the endurance of religious others is *tolerare*, tolerance. The role of "other" religions is to maintain the peace, stability, and order of the community of gods that guarantee the existence of the polity. This is done by tolerating "others" as an extension of one's own political, civic, and social self. Thus, religious tolerance for others was assessed in terms of reciprocal impact, action, intention, and motivation. Intention and motivation are known and assessed by political and social criteria established on the basis of rational choice (*prohairesis*). Hence, actor and recipient, as rational beings, make such a determination. Consequently, a superhuman agent justifies the efficacy of the impact, action, intention, or motivation of human tolerance.

(2) Different religions are acknowledged, endured, or rejected based on whether they are politically constructive. All (foreign) religions and cults are differentiated on the basis of a religion's fidelity to the *pax deorum* and the *imperium*.

(3) Since the totality of gods and goddesses constitute the divine world and no deity ever disputes the existence of other deities, the existence of all divine powers is justified. Other religions are seen as errors, accidents, or evil if they refuse to be a constructive part of reality by honoring the *pax deorum* and the legitimacy of the Roman state.

(4) The fault lines that support tolerance or intolerance of religious divergence are political and civic. The extent to which religious teachings and rituals support political and social cohesion justifies state tolerance or intolerance of a religion.

(5) The expression of state tolerance or intolerance of a religion is largely a function of historical, political, social, and moral factors. If a religion supports the Roman state, its *mos maiorum*, and the *pax deorum*, the political choice is made to tolerate a religion or recognize it as a *religio licita*. If a religion does not or cannot meet these criteria, the political choice is made not to tolerate a religion or judge it a *religio inlicita*.

In the end, a study of tolerance is not an idyll for weary men and women who would, like Hamlet's crab, go backward. Hence, a turn from forgetfulness to memory is sometimes a virtue in itself. Thus, I suggest that all of us cross over to that foreign shore, overcome inertia, and translate ourselves to the matter of a pagan-sanctioned, inclusive tolerance. If we can do this, we might be able to glance over our shoulders along the ancient path indicated in this study and endure nonbelievers on reasonable political, religious, and theological grounds, and not merely on voluntarist and utilitarian ones.

Thus, what is tolerance? What is the meaning of politically building and cultivating, of religiously and theologically dwelling and thinking tolerance? Only in asking these questions do we hear *tolerare*. It takes more than a minute to think of this word, or even what originally it talked about, and to think whether as a word we moderns have anything in common with it. To whom is tolerance most manifest? We need to talk this way or the history of tolerance and intolerance becomes a nightmare from which we, Dedalus-like, are trying to awaken. I hope that Greco-Roman, indeed pagan, notions of tolerance might again occupy contemporary man's contemporary reflection. We cannot hide ourselves from the "ancient" matter of tolerance since what the word says or does not say shapes our contemporary thoughts. These thoughts, in turn, determine the character of our world. The Latin word *tolerare* requires rescue from the Museum for Historic Oddities and restoration to its proper milieu: thinking.

Notes

1. Tolerance and its cognates are reducible to an act of enduring or the capacity for endurance. The etymology of the English word *tolerance*—and its cognates *tolerant, tolerate,* and *toleration*—have their origins in the Latin *tolerare*—to endure—and *tolerans, tolerantis,* ppr. of *tolerare*. These terms have their origin in the verb *tolero,* which has its origins in the Greek verb *tlao*—to bear. *Tolero* as a passive verb forms the root of the noun *toleratio, onis*—a bearing, enduring of pain—and the adjective *tolerabilis*—that which can be born, is bearable. As an active verb, *tolero* also forms the root of the present participle *tolerans, antis*—bearing, enduring, tolerant, patient, the past participle *toleratus, a, um*—endured, the comparative adverb *tolerabiliter*—enduring rather patiently, and the adverb *toleranter*—enduring patiently. Compare A. Walde und J. B. Hofmann, *Lateinisches Etymologisches Woerterbuch,* 2nd ed. (Heidelbert: Carl Winter Universitaetsverlag, 1972), 688.

2. J. Neusner, "Theological Foundations of Tolerance in Classical Judaism," [this volume], 193–217.

3. Inclusive monotheism involves the practice of cultic polytheism. In the Hellenistic and Roman periods, Stoics, Pythagoreans, and later Platonists were advocates of inclusive monotheism, while, for Hellenistic kings and later Roman emperors, it was part of the politico-religious praxis of imperial statecraft. As early as the idylls of Theocritus (third century BCE), we have evidence that, as divine kings, Ptolemy I (Soter) and his heirs practiced inclusive monotheism and cultic polytheism—a belief in one God worshiped in many forms. Compare *P. Oxy.* 1611, II.38ff. As descendants of Apollo, Seleucus I and Antiochus I did as well.

Compare *O.G.I.S.* 213, 214. The third and fourth century CE Emperors and Caesars Diocletian, Galerius, Licinius, and Constantine adopted inclusive monotheism. Compare Lactantius, *de mort. Pers.* XXXIV; IVXIII; Eusebius, *HE.* VII.17; X.5.

I have enclosed a bibliography for all ancient sources at the end of the footnotes. As for the abbreviations, see my comments on abbreviations at the beginning of the bibliography.

4. Josephus, *Contra Apionem* I, 189.

5. *Letter of Aristeas* 310.

6. Ibid.

7. Polybius, *Histories* XXXI, II.

8. Josephus, *Contra Apionem* II, 65ff.

9. Josephus, *Jewish Antiquities* XII, 125ff.; XVI, 27ff.

10. This case was tried before M. Agrippa, counselor to Augustus, and won with the aid of the Seleucid court historian Nicolaus of Damascus. Elsewhere, citizens of the Greek cities of Cyrenaica attacked Jews on the pretext of nonpayment of taxes. Again M. Agrippa abrogated these measures on behalf of the Jews. *Antiquities* XVI, 160, 169.

11. See R. Rebuffat, "*Divinites de l'oued Kebir [Tripolitaine]*" in *L'Africa romana: Atti del VII convegno di studio*, edited by A. Mastino (Sassari, Sardinia: Naples, 1999), 119–159.

12. I am indebted to B. Caseau for this insight. Compare "Sacred Landscapes" in *Late Antiquity: A Guide to the Postclassical World*, edited by G. W. Bowersock, P. Brown, and O. Grabar (Cambridge, MA: Harvard University Press, 1999), 21–59.

13. Ibid., 21–22.

14. Plotinus almost persuaded Gallienus to allow for the establishment of a state where men could dwell under Plato's laws. Eventually, as we shall see, a tension emerges between the Roman State and the Christian Church with both locative and utopian dimensions. The Platonapolis of the philosophers would have been in Campania, while the Jerusalem of the Christians was in Heaven. Cf. Porphyry, *Life of Plotinus* XII.

15. Diogenes Laertius, *Lives of the Eminent Philosophers* VII.88.

16. Marcus Aurelius, *Meditations* III.11.

17. Ibid., IV.4.

18. Ibid., VI.44.

19. For this introductory material, I am indebted to a fine undergraduate essay by S. Abegg. Compare "Rome City of the Gods."

20. Livy, *History of Rome* VIII.ix.

21. See P. Garnsey and R. Saller, *The Roman Empire: Economy, Society, and Culture* (Berkeley: University of California Press, 1984), 164–177.

22. For an overview, see R. M. Berchman, "Pagan Philosophical Views of Jews and Judaism," in *Approaches to Ancient Judaism*, edited by J. Neuser, 12:1–94, esp. 11–16, USF Studies in the History of Judaism 158 (Atlanta: Scholars Press, 1997).

23. *Codex Theodosionus* 2.1.10.

24. Josephus, *Jewish Aniquities* 16.160–265.

25. See E. M. Smallwood, *The Jews under Roman Rule from Pompey to Diocletian* (Leiden: E. J. Brill, 1981), 467–538.

26. W. C. Green, *The Achievement of Rome: A Chapter in Civilization* (Cambridge: Cambridge University Press, 1938), 327.

27. Livy, *History of Rome* XXV.1.

28. Dionysus of Halicarnassus, *Roman Antiquities* IV.

29. Macrobius, *Saturnalia* III.ix.6–8.

30. Livy, *History of Rome* XXXIX.viii–xix.

31. Pliny, *Epistula and Panygericus* 49.

32. Lactantius, *de mortibus perecutorum* XXXXVIII.2–12

33. Polybius, *Histories* VI.lvi.

34. Origen, *Contra Celsum* II.79.

35. Cyprian, *Acta Cyprianus* 1.2.

36. Cyprian, *de lapsis* 5.

37. Eusebius, *Historia Evangelica* VII.13.

38. Tertullian, *Apologia,* 35.

39. Lactantius, *Divines Insitutiones* VII.15, 11.

40. Lactantius, *de moribus persecutorum* II.

41. Following Lactantius, *de mortibus persecutorum* X.

42. See Eusebius, *Historia Evangelica* VII.10.4, and Lactantius, *Divines Institutiones* IV.27.3.

43. Ibid., VIII.2.4.

44. Ibid., VIII.6.9.

45. Eusebius, *de martyriam Palestinae* IX.3.

46. Lactantius, *de mortibus persecutorum* XXXIV; Eusebius, *Historia Evangelica* VII.17.

47. It is preserved by Lactantius, *de mortibus persecutorum* XXXXVIII. Eusebius offered a Greek translation. Compare *Historia Evangelica* X.5.

48. At this point, the Latin text of Lactantius begins.

49. These words are only in the Greek text.

50. See R. M. Berchman, "Altruism in Greco-Roman Philosophy," in *Altruism in World Religions*, edited by Jacob Neusner and Bruce D. Chilton, 26–30 (Washington, DC: Georgetown University Press, 2005).

51. See R. M. Berchman, "Rationality and Ritual in Neoplatonism," in *Neoplatonism and Indian Philosophy*, edited by P. M. Gregorios, 229–268 (Albany: State University of New York, 2002).

52. *Meditations* 3.4.3.

53. See P. Brown, "The Rise and Function of the Holy Man in Late Antiquity," *Journal of Roman Studies* 61 (1971): 80–101.

54. *De Animae ap.* Stobaeus 1.365.5–22ff.

55. *Elementatio Theologica* 191.

56. Proclus, in *Platonis Theologiam* 1.19, p. 91.16–21.

57. Iamblichus, *De Mysteriis* 1.12; 1.14; 3.16–18.

58. Ibid., 2.11.

59. Jean Trouillard, John Rist, and Arthur Lovejoy have traced the metaphysical trajectories of this metaphysics of the will through their notions of the "Doctrine of Divine Love" and the "Principle of Plenitude." They will later become normative in the metaphysical systems of medieval Judaism, Christianity, and Islam. Compare J. Trouillard, *La Procession Plotinienne* (Paris: Presses Universitaires de France, 1955); J. Rist, *Eros and Psyche Studies in Plato, Plotinus, and Origen* (Toronto: University of Toronto Press, 1964), 76ff; A. Lovejoy, *The Great Chain of Being: A Study of the History of an Idea* (New York: Harper & Row, 1960).

60. *Enneads* VI.8.13.5ff; 15.1.

61. The source of this doctrine is Plato's account in *Timaeus* 29e–30a, of the divine motive for creation.

62. Zosimus, *New History* II.29.5.

63. See R. L. Fox, *Pagans and Christians* (New York: Knopf, 1989), 671–672.

64. See R. L. Wilken, *The Land Called Holy: Palestine in Christian History and Thought* (New Haven, CT: Yale University Press, 1992).

65. A similar judgment holds for altruism in Greco-Roman antiquity. See Berchman, "Altruism in Greco-Roman Antiquity," 1–30.

66. There is no time to enter into case law, but minimal reflection on modern legal theory offers numerous examples where a morally iniquitous law is a valid legal rule. Examples could be culled from Greco-Roman sources of morally iniquitous laws taken as valid legal rules, but the fundamental difference is that such laws cannot be rationalized and justified under natural law theory. They can within legal positivist and realist theories of law.

67. Compare J. Rawls, *Theory of Justice* (Cambridge, MA: Belknap Press of Harvard University Press, 1971); and *Political Liberalism* (New York: Columbia University Press, 1996).

68. Compare J. Rawls, *Theory of Justice*, 5.

69. Aristotle's theory of justice is largely presented in *Nichomachean Ethics* V.

70. Compare A. MacIntyre, *After Virtue: A Study in Moral Theory* (Notre Dame, IN: University of Notre Dame Press, 1981), 155.

71. See Berchman, "Altruism in Greco-Roman Antiquity," 28–30.

72. See Caseau, "Sacred Landscape," 20–59.

Bibliography of Ancient Sources

Many editions from which I have made (or taken) translations are included below. Some of the other texts are also included. Normally, the Loeb Classical Library, Oxford Classical Texts, or Teubner editions were used for classical authors. The Corpus scriptorum ecclesiasticorum latinorum (CSEL), Corpus Christianorum series latina (CChr.SL), Sources chrétiennes (SC), Die griechischen christlichen Schriftsteller der ersten Jahrhunderte (GCS), and Migne Patrologia Graeca and Patrologia Latina (PG and PL) series were used for patristic sources.

Abbreviations are from S. Schwertner, *Internationales Abkürzungsverzeichnis für Theologie und Grenzgebiete* (Berlin/New York: W. de Gruyter, 1993), supplemented by the *Journal of Biblical Literature* guidelines, the *Oxford Classical Dictionary*, and Liddell Scott Jones (LSJ). Much other material on the pagan authors can be found in the bibliography of G. Rinaldi, *La Bibbia dei Pagani*, vols. I and II (Bologna, Italy: EDB, 1998); and in J. C. Cook, *The Interpretation of the New Testament in Greco-Roman Paganism* (Tübigen: Mohr Siebeck, 2000).

Adamantius. *De recta in Deum fide*. Edited by W. H. van de Sande Bakhuyzen. Leipzig, 1901. GCS.

Albinus. *Didaskalikos* [= *Alcinoos, Enseignement des Doctrines de Platon*]. Edited by John Whittaker and Pierre Louis. Paris, 1990. CUFr.

Ambrose. *De paradiso*. Edited by K. Schenkl. Vienna, 1897. CSEL 32.1.

Ambrosiaster. *Pseudo-Augustini quaestiones veteris et novi testamenti*. Vol. CXXVII. Edited by A. Souter. Vienna, 1908. CSEL 50.

Arethas. *Scripta minora*. Vol. I. Edited by L. G. Westerink. Leipzig, 1968. BiTeu.

Aristeas. *Lettre d'Aristée à Philocrate*. Edited by A. Pelletier. Paris, 1962. SC 89.

Aristides. *L'apologia de Aristide. Introduzione versione dal siriaco e commento, Lateranum.* Edited by C. Vona. Rome, 1950. N.S. 16.

Aristotle. *Aristotle.* 23 vols. Cambridge, MA/London, 1969. LCL.

———. *The Complete Works of Aristotle.* 2 vols. Edited by J. Barnes. Princeton, 1984.

Aristobulus. See C. R. Holladay in the section on modern scholarship.

Ps. Aristotle. *Aristotelis qui fertus libellus de mundo.* Edited by W. L. Lorimer. Paris, 1933. CUFr.

Arnobius. *Adversus nationes.* Edited by C. Marchesi. Corpus Paravianum. Turin, 1953.

Asclepius. *Asclepius: A Collection and Interpretation of the Testimonies.* Vol. 1–2. Edited and translated by E. J. Edelstein and L. Edelstein. New York, 1975. This is a reprint of the 1945 edition.

Athanasius. *Athanasius Werke: Urkunden zur Geschichte des arianischen Streites.* Vol. 3.1. Edited by H. G. Opitz, 318–328. Berlin, 1935.

Athenagoras. *Legatio and De resurrectione.* Edited by W. R. Schoedel. Oxford, 1972.

Atticus. *Atticus Fragments.* Edited by É. des Places. Paris, 1977. CUFr.

Augustine. *Sancti Aurelii Augustini de civitate Dei.* Edited by B. Dombart and A. Kalb. Turnholt, 1950–1955. CChr.SL 47–48.

Celsus. *Der ALHQHS LOGOS des Kelsos.* Edited by Robert Bader. Stuttgart/Berlin, 1940. TBAW 33.

———. *Celsus. On the True Doctrine. A Discourse against the Christians.* Edited and translated by R. J. Hoffman. New York/Oxford, 1987.

Chaeremon:
    van der Horse, P. W. *Chaeremon: Egyptian Priest and Stoic Philosopher.* Leiden, 1984.

Chaldean oracles:
    Lewy, H. *Chaldaean Oracles and Theurgy: Mysticism, Magic and Platonism in the Later Roman Empire.* Paris, 1978.
    Oracles chaldaïques. Avec un choix de commentaires anciens. Edited by É. des Places. Paris 1971. CUFr.

Cyril of Alexandria. *Contre Julien.* Edited by P. Burgière and P. Évieux. Paris, 1985. SC 322.

Diodore of Tarsus:
Deconinck, J. *Essai sur la châine de l'Octateuqe avec une édition des Commentaires de Diodore de Tarse qui s'y trouvent contenus.* Bibl. de l'École des Hautes Études 195. Paris, 1912.

Diogenes Laertius. *Vitae Philosophorum.* 2 vols. Edited by H. S. Long. Oxford, 1964.

Dionysius of Halicarnassus. *Roman Antiquities.* 7 vols. Translated by E. Cary. Cambridge MA/London, 1943.

Doxographi Graeci. 4th edition. Edited by H. Diels. Berlin, 1965.

Epicurus. *Epicurea.* Edited by H. Usener. Leipzig, 1887.

———. *Epicuro Opere, Biblioteca de cultura filosofica.* Vol. 41. Edited by G. Arrighetti. Torino, 1973.

Eunapius. *Vitae sophistarum, Philostratus and Eunapius, The Lives of the Sophists.* Edited and translated by W. C. Wright. London, 1922.

———. *Eunapii vitae sophistarum.* Edited by G. Giangrande. Rome, 1956.

Eusebius:
    Eusebius. *Eusèbe de Césarée Contre Hiéroclès.* Introduced and translated by M. Forrat. Edited by É. des Places. Paris. 1986. SC 333.
        ———. *Ecclesiastical History.* 2 vols. Edited and translated by K. Lake and J. E. L. Oulton. Cambridge, 1980.

————. *Eusèbe de Césarée Histoire Ecclésiastique*. In *Livres* V–VII. Edited by G. Bardy. Paris, 1955. SC 41.

————. *Praeparatio evangelica*. In *Eusebius* VIII/1–2. Edited by K. Mras. Berlin, 1954–1956. GCS.

————. *Eusèbe de Césarée. La Préparation Évangélique*. Edited by Jean Sirinelli, Édouard des Places et al. Paris, 1974–1991. SC 206, 228, 262, 266, 369.

————. *Preparation for the Gospel*, Part 1, Books 1–9; Part 2, Books 10–15. Translated by E. Hamilton Gifford. Oxford, 1903.

————. *Demonstratio Evangelica*. In *Eusebius*, vol. VI. Edited by Ivar Heikel. Leipzig, 1913. GCS.

————. *The Proof of the Gospel*. 2 vols. Translated by W. J. Ferrar. London/New York, 1920.

Genesis. In *Septuaginta*. Vetus Testamentum Graecum Auctoritate Academiae Scientiarum Gottingensis editum, vol. I. Edited by J. W. Wevers. Göttingen, 1974.

Heraclitus. *Allégories d'Homère*. Edited by Félix Buffière. Paris, 1989. CUFr.

Hellenistic Jewish Authors:

Holladay, C. R., comp. and trans. *Fragments from Hellenistic Jewish Authors*. Chico, CA, 1989.

Hermetica:

Scott, W., and A. S. Ferguson, eds. *Hermetica. The Ancient Greek and Latin Writings Which Contain Religious or Philosophic Teachings Ascribed to Hermes Trismegistus*, vol. IV. London, 1968.

Corpus Hermeticum. Vols. I–IV. Edited by A. D. Nock and A.-J. Festugière. Paris, 1945–1954. CUFr.

Hippolytus. *Kommentar zu Daniel*. Vols. I–IV. 2nd edition. Edited by G. N. Bonwetsch and M. Richard. Berlin, 2000. GCS.

Iamblichus. *Les Mystères d'Égypte*. Edited and translated by É. des Places. Paris, 1966. CUFr.

————. *On the Pythagorean Way of Life*. Edited and translated by J. M. Dillon and J. Hershbell. Atlanta, 1991.

Inscriptions: Packard Humanities Institute CD ROM #7, 1991–1996 (Cornell Epigraphy Project and the Duke Documentary Papyri).

Jerome. *Hieronymus, Comm. in Danielem*. Edited by F. Glorie, Turnholt, 1964. With ET by G. L. Archer, *Jerome's Commentary on Daniel*. Grand Rapids, 1958. CChr.SL 75a.

————. *Commentaire sur S. Matthieu*. Vol. 2. Edited by É. Bonnard. Paris, 1979. SC 259.

Josephus. *Jewish Antiquities*. Vols. 1–9. Edited by R. Marcus. Cambridge, MA/London, 1969. LCL.

Julian. *The Works of the Emperor Julian*. Vols. 1–3. Edited and translated by W. C. Wright. Cambridge, MA/London, 1923. LCL.

————. *L'Empereur Julien. Oeuvres complètes*. Vol. I/1, I/2, II/1, II/2. Edited by J. Bidez, G. Rochefort, and C. Lacombrade. Paris, 1932–1972. CUFr.

————. *Iuliani imperatoris epistulae leges poematia fragmenta*. Edited by J. Bidez, F. Cumont, and C. Lacombrade. Paris, 1922.

————. *Iuliani imperatoris librorum contra Christianos quae supersunt*. Edited by C. J. Neumann. Leipzig, 1880.

Giuliano imperator contra Galilaeos. Edited by E. Masaracchia. Testi e Commenti 9, Roma, 1990.

————. di Mopsuestia, Teodoro. *Replica a Giuliano Imperatore. Adversus criminationes in Christianos Iuliani Imperatoris*. In *appendice Testimonianze sulla polemica antigiulianea*

in altre opere di Teodoro, con nuovi frammenti del "Contro i Galilei" di Giuliano, ed.
A. Guida. Biblioteca Patristica. Florence, 1994.

―――. Guida, A. "Frammenti inediti del 'Contra i Galilei' di Giuliano e della replica di
Teodora di Mopsuestia. *Prometheus* 9 (1983): 136–163.

Justin. *Justini Martyris apologiae pro Christianis*. Edited by M. Marcovich. Berlin/New York,
1994. PTS 38.

―――. *Justini Martyris dialogus cum Tryphone*. Edited by M. Marcovich. Berlin/New York,
1997. PTS 47.

―――. *Iustini Philosophi et Martyris Opera*. In *Corpus Apologetarum Christianorum*, vol. V.
Edited by J. C. T. Otto. Wiesbaden, 1969. Ps. Justin, Quaest. et Resp. ad Orth.; rep. of
1881 ed.

―――. *Qeodwrhvtou ejpiskovpou povlew" Kuvrrou pro;" ta;" ejpenecqeivsa" aujtw/' ejperwthv-
sei" parav tino" tw'n ejx Aijguvptou ejpiskovpwn ajpokrivsei.* Edited by A. Papadopou-
los-Kerameus. Zapiski Istoriko-filologicheskago fakulteta Imperatorskago s.-peter-
burgskago universiteta 36. St. Petersburg, 1895 (the above text of Ps. Justin with fifteen
additional questions; ed. G. Hansen; rept. Leipzig 1975).

―――. *Pseudo-Iustinus Cohortatio ad Graecos, De Monarchia, Oratio ad Graecos*. Edited by M.
Marcovich. Berlin/New York, 1990. PTS 32. (Ps. Justin).

Lactantius. *Institutions divines*. 5 vols. Edited by Pierre Monat. Paris, 1973. Vols. 1–2, SC
204/205.

―――. *The Divine Institutes Books*. Vol. I–VII. Translated by M. F. McDonald, O.P., FC 49,
Washington 1964.

―――. *Lactantius de mortibus persecutorum*. Edited and translated by. J. L. Creed. Oxford,
1984. OECT.

Libanius. *Selected Works*. Vol. 1. Edited and translated by A. F. Norman. Cambridge/
London, 1987. LCL.

Livy. *History of Rome*. 14 vols. Cambridge MA/London, 1984. LCL.

Macrobius. *The Saturnalia*. Translated by P. V. Davies. New York/London, 1969.

Maximus of Tyre. *Dissertationes*. Edited by M. B. Trapp. Stuttgart/Leipzig, 1994. BiTeu.

―――. *The Philosophical Orations*. Translated with notes by M. B. Trapp. Oxford, 1997.

Numenius. *Fragments*. Edited by Édouard des Places. Paris, 1973. CUFr.

Ocellus. *Ocellus Lucanus — Text und Kommentar*. Edited by R. Harder. Berlin, 1926.

Origen. *Contra Celsum. Translated with an Introduction and Notes*. Edited and translated by
H. Chadwick. Cambridge, 1953.

―――. *Die Schrift vom Martyrium*. Buch I–IV gegen Celsus (I). Buch V–VIII gegen Celsus.
Die Schrift vom Gebet (II). GCS Origenes I–II. Edited by P. Koetschau. Leipzig, 1899.

―――. *Origenes Contra Celsum*. Libri VIII. Texts and Studies of Early Christian Life and
Language, Supp. VigChr 54. Edited by M. Marcovich. New York, 2001.

―――. *Origène Contre Celse. Introduction, Texte Critique, Traduction et Notes*. Vols. 1–5. Edited
by M. Borret, S.J. Paris, 1967–1976. SC 132, 136, 147, 150, 227.

―――. *Origenes Matthäuserklärung II*. Die lateinische Übersetzung der commentariorum
series, GCS Origenes XI. Edited by E. Klostermann, Berlin, 1976.

―――. *Origenis de principiis*. Libri IV. Texte zur Forschung 24. Edited and translated by
H. Görgemanns and H. Karpp. Darmstadt, 1976.

Papyri Graecae Magicae:

  Betz, H. D. *The Greek Magical Papyri in Translation, including the Demotic Spells*. Chi-
cago/London, 1986.

Preisendanz, K. *Papyri Graecae Magicae. Die Griechischen Zauberpapyri*. 2 vols. Edited by
E. Heitsch and A. Henrichs. Stuttgart, 1973/1974.

Philo Byblos. *The Phoenician History. Introduction, Critical Text, Translation, Notes*. Edited by
H. W. Attridge and R. A. Oden Jr. Washington, D.C., 1981. CBQMS 9.

Photius. *Bibliotheca*. Edited by R. Henry. Paris, 1959.

Plato. *Platonis opera*. Vols. 1-5. Edited by J. Burnet. Oxford, 1900–1907. OCT.

———. *The Collected Dialogues of Plato*. Edited by E. Hamilton and H. Cairnes. Bollingen
Series 71. Princeton, 1961.

Pliny. *Letters and Panegyricus*. Translated by Radice. Cambridge, MA/London, 1969. LCL.

Plotinus. *Plotini Opera*, Vols. 1–3. Oxford, 1954–1982. OCT.

Porphyry. *Porphyrii philosophi platonici opuscula selecta*. Edited by A. Nauck. Leipzig, 1886.
BiTeu.

———. *Porphyrii de philosophia ex oraculis haurienda librorum reliquiae*. Edited by G. Wolff.
Hildesheim, 1962. First edition 1856.

———. *La vie de Plotin*. Vols. 1–2. Edited by Luc Brisson, Marie-Odile Goulet-Cazé,
R. Goulet, D. O'Brien et al. Histoire des doctrines de l'antiquité classique 6. Paris,
1982–1992.

———. *De l'abstinence*. Vol. I–III. Edited and translated with notes by J. Bouffartigue,
M. Patillon, A. Segonds, and L. Brisson. Paris, 1977–1995. CUFr.

———. *The Homeric Questions*. Edited and translated by R. R. Schlunk. Lang Classical
Studies 2. New York, 1993.

———. *The Cave of the Nymphs in the Odyssey*. Seminar Classics 609. Buffalo, NY, 1969.

———. *Porphyrii philosophi fragmenta*. Edited by Andrew Smith. Stuttgart/Leipzig, 1993.
BiTeu.

———. *Vie de Pythagore. Lettre a Marcella*. Edited by Édouard des Places. Paris, 1982. CUFr.

———. *PROS MARKELLAN*. Edited and translated, with commentary, by W. Pötscher.
Philosophia Antiqua 15. Leiden, 1969.

———. Dörrie, H. *Porphyrios' Symmikta Zetemata. Ihre Stellung in System und Geschichte
des Neuplatonismus nebst einem Kommentar zu den Fragmenten*, Zetemata 20.
München, 1959.

———. Sodano, A. R. *Porfirio. Lettera ad Anebo*. Naples, 1958.

Posidonius. *The Fragments*. Edited by L. Edelstein and I. G. Kidd. Cambridge Classical
Texts and Commentaries 13. Cambridge, 1972.

Proclus. *The Elements of Theology, a revised text with Translation, Introduction and Commentary*.
Edited by E. R. Dodds. Oxford, 1963.

———. *Platonic Theology*. Edited by H. D. Saffrey and L. G. Westerink. Paris, 1968–1981.

Ps. Sallustius. *Concerning the Gods and the Universe*. Edited by A. D. Nock. Hildesheim, 1966.
Reprint of 1926 edition.

Stobaeus. *Anthologium*. 5 vols. Edited by C. Wachsmuth and O. Hense. Berlin, 1884–1923.

Stoic Fragments:
Stoicorum veterum fragmenta. Vols. I–IV. Edited by Johannes von Arnim. Leipzig, 1903.
SVF.

Symmachus. *Relatio*. In *Prudence*, ed. M. Lavarenne, 85–113. Paris, 1963. CUFr.

Tertullian. *Tertulliani Opera*. Edited by E. Dekkers et al. Turnholt, 1954. CChr.SL 1–2.

———. *Quinti Septimi Florentis Tertulliani de anima*. Edited by J. H. Waszink. Amsterdam,
1947.

Theodore of Mopsuestia. See Julian.

Theodoret. *Theodoreti Cyrensis quaestiones in Octateuchum*. Textos y Estudios "Cardenal Cisneros" 17. Edited by N. Fernández Marcos and A. Sáenz-Badillos. Madrid, 1979.

Thesaurus Linguae Graecae (TLG). Thesaurus Linguae Graecae CD ROM #E, U. Cal. Irvine, 1999. The authors on the disk are listed by: L. Berkowitz and K. A. Squitier. Thesaurus Linguae Graecae. Canon of Greek Authors and Works. New York/Oxford, 1990.

Tübingen Theosophy: Theosophorum Graecorum Fragmenta. Edited by H. Erbse. Stuttgart, 1995. BiTeu.

Zosimus. *New History*. Translated by R.T. Ridley. Sydney, 1982.

5

RITUAL RESOURCES OF TOLERANCE IN
GRECO-ROMAN RELIGION

KEVIN CORRIGAN

1. Tolerance

The word tolerance comes from the Latin *tolero-tolerare*, which means "to endure," "to observe," "to bear," but also "to nourish" or "to sustain." There is no ready Greek equivalent. "To let things be" (*ean*), especially when managing slaves, is not good practice.[1] So, the word-roots for any religious tolerance in the Greco-Roman world do not look too promising at first glance. Yet tolerance within certain recognized boundaries was part of both Greek religion and of Greco-Roman paganism, given the restrictions of religion to the domain of ethnic community and polis for the Greeks that permitted other religions and cults, and to obedience or pietas in the Roman world that tolerated foreign deities and cults so long as they remained reasonably subject to the Roman gods, *mos maiorum*, the Senate and the Roman people.[2]

2. Ritual and Religion

The word *ritual* is also difficult to pin down since there is no clear boundary in antiquity between our modern categories of the sacred and the profane.[3] Where are we to draw a boundary, for instance, between the Olympic gods, the various forms of worship and ritual in Greek religion, and the ritual form of hexameter (with the invocation of the muses) in the *Iliad*, *Odyssey*,

Theogony, or *Works and Days?* Or again, between temple worship and magical rituals? Or between the organized consultation of oracles (such as Eleusis or Dodona), incubation and healing rituals (such as the medical/healing rituals introduced in the worship of Asclepius), and Greek (and Roman) drama at the Festival of the Greater Dionysus? The boundaries do not line up in the same way for the ancient world as they do for ours since there is no simple split between religion, art, poetry, science, magic, and philosophy. Even law and politics have a fundamental religious dimension as in the reforms of Solon in 594 BCE, of Kleisthenes in 507 BCE, and of Lycurgus later still from 338 to 326 BCE.[4] The birth of "philosophy" in the early ancient world, the shamanistic chariot ride of the young man/Parmenides to the greeting and revelatory discourse of the goddess, is ritual drama in which a youthful representative of the human community actively receives a divine message.[5]

Here, as throughout the ancient world, ritual is regarded as something given—by god, goddess, and/or the weight of immemorial tradition (an important consideration in the Greco-Roman world)—within community context, a set of established practices with symbolic value, in compliance with custom, obligation, reverence, and submission, that links the active/recipient community to the divine, whether in supplication, celebration, memorialization, and/or humility before the incommensurabilities of lived experience. In this light, epic, drama, philosophy, and science may also be forms of religious ritual, i.e., forms of a ritual that either "reconnects" (*religare*) the individual/community to reality in the bonds of piety that connect to the divine—according to an etymology to be found in Lucretius, Lactantius, and Tertullian—or "rereads" (*relegere*) human life as a connection to the divine—according to an etymology preferred by Cicero.[6] Some magical practices may appear to stand outside this working definition of ritual since they are essentially solitary attempts to bind a divine or semidivine power for good or ill or to invoke a higher power for salvific purposes. Yet magical practices, too, stand within an implied community insofar as they employ prescribed rites, formulas, and words and suggest an eavesdropping community in the self-conscious actions of the individual practitioner.[7] So much then for definitions of *tolerance, ritual,* and *religion.* Let me now take up the bigger questions of where we might find resources for thinking about tolerance in the *ethnos, polis,* or *pax Romana* by looking at some of the gaps, strange appearances/interventions in the translations from the Greek world into the Hellenistic and Greco-Roman worlds.

3. Introduction and Overview

There is a tension in any culture between the centripetal forces that tend to confirm its own identity and the centrifugal forces that move it beyond its own limits and self-definitions. In the first case, the culture sees itself in an exclusive way: it is itself by excluding others, whether the "others" are foreigners or strangers in its own midst. In the second case, the culture wishes to conquer and appropriate but also to trade with and encounter others. Implicit in both spheres is the often unexamined ambiguity between toleration and intolerance that is provoked into explicit realization either by accident or by catastrophe or by art or simply by a kind of wild-card force that prompts, within established rituals, the problem of the acceptance or rejection of the other.

Here I shall, first, give an overview of the whole question concluding with preliminary answers to William Scott Green's questions; second, take several examples initially from the world of Greek religion broadly understood, examples that perhaps do not always get sufficient emphasis; third, situate them in uneasy proximity to examples of simple intolerance that also plainly characterize a supposedly tolerant world and examine how these examples translate into the Greco-Roman world; and, finally, chart out some of the strengths and failures of tolerance in the cults and religions of that much broader set of worldviews before concluding with a second attempt to answer the major questions before us.

Monotheisms, in the words of Jacob Neusner, can barely tolerate each other, much less other religions.[8] By contrast, polytheisms may on the surface look much more attractive. Greek religion had no strict body of revealed teachings and no fixed binding rituals for every worshiper of every shrine. Each locality could have its own myths and practices. So the Greeks worshiped a multitude of spiritual beings of different ranks who filled all of nature, both the sky gods above (*superi*) and the many gods below (*inferi*). These deities were not displaced but, in some measure, summed up by the Homeric pantheon of a clan of gods, headed by Zeus, and bound together in a social organization similar to that of the Homeric clan-state, as also by the Hesiodic picture of a horrific history from Chaos, Gē, Ouranos, Kronos, and Rhea to Zeus, out of which there emerged the steady-state, though much troubled, predominance of Zeus and Hera.

Greek religion is already an amalgam of divinities related to Egyptian and Near-Eastern models. Dogma or belief is not what is important so much as practice and ritual, and there is no modern separation between politics, religion, private life, or warfare. Generals and soldiers, not priests, often decide on religious policy. Prophetic diviners (e.g,. Chalchas or Teiresias) are often the major religious figures since it is crucial to come up with the right interpretations of events and actions; sacrifice, consequently, is a strategic device to sway the gods to one's side.[9] The *naos*, shrine or temple (or later in Rome, the *templum* or *aedes*), marks a sacred space where sanctuary is possible and from which invaders must be kept away, just as the herald marks the truce and sacred space in which suspension of hostilities is possible.[10]

At the root of this, there is the intersection of two perspectives that it is easy to lose sight of: the horizontal perspective that links the human participants and the vertical perspective that links human beings and gods (above and below). The casual observer from outside (such as the modern observer who may see the gods as purely symbolic or the ritual as theatrical or fictional) would not see anything of the vertical axis, yet as Fritz Graf points out, it is this axis that in an important way determines the significance of the ritual:

Humans address the gods through the intermediary of prayers and sacrifices, through the smoke that rises, and through the blood that flows, and we expect a certain number of reactions from the potential recipients of the rite. First, we expect immediate signs that the sacrifice has been accepted or rejected, perceived through the inspection of the entrails and the observation of the flame; then, we expect signs that the gods will grant the wishes for the future, will grant the help and benevolence prayed for. This vertical communication is played out differently from the horizontal one and is consciously and carefully staged by the human actors: it is communication that is spoken about by the indigenous people. The chance observer from outside, uninformed about theology and mythology, perceives only the interaction of the horizontal ritual message whose signifiers are determined by an ancestral cultural tradition.[11]

How we are to get at this vertical dimension and whether this intersection of horizontal/vertical perspectives is any place to search for tolerance are very difficult questions (which I shall take up below), especially since the attempt to propitiate, to bind, and to procure favors is implicitly at least a local one with a specific focus. Nonetheless, threats to stability often necessitate what peaceful existence cannot achieve. Under the threat of the Persians, for instance, a Panhellenic system is naturally consolidated as Greeks from all over the Greek world defend their common religious heritage, and oracular sites such as those at Delphi and Dodona function in the background as Panhellenic sanctuaries with indisputable authority even across ethnic/religious boundaries. So, the Greeks are aware of foreign peoples who have their own gods, and they are uncertain how to articulate common ground.[12]

At the same time, the Greeks appear to have had certain resources for thinking about tolerance in an intolerant world. I shall mention only the following here:

(1) The sacred place as a sanctuary (civic or rural), from which invasion and murder are outlawed.[13]

(2) The cognate function (among many others) of Zeus/Jupiter as "friend and protector of strangers," Zeus the "merciful," etc., summed up in the Baucis and Philemon or Orion myths in which the gods in disguise visit good religious people and reward them for their faithfulness and welcome to anonymous strangers.[14]

(3) The remarkable openness of some cults beyond the barriers of race, gender, or class, the Mysteries of Eleusis, for instance. Moreover, the lesser and greater rites were actually related to the welcome of the divine stranger, Demeter, sorrowing for her lost daughter, Persephone, as recounted in the *Homeric Hymn to Demeter*. Here we have a "vertical" axis whose significance we have lost. Nonetheless, the openness of the mysteries to *everyone* (except murderers and non-Greek-speaking initiates) down to late antiquity and their eclipse with Christianity is noteworthy.[15]

Further contrast between the Athenians/Hellenes and the Romans is useful. In the fifth century BCE, the Athenians simply sought to have colonies participate in the rites of their mother city or to impose the cult of Athena on fractious allies. So boundary stories of "Athena, ruler of Athenians" have been found in Samos, Kos, and Chalcis and probably mark Athens' wish to dominate their allies by confiscating land.[16] The Romans, by contrast, seem to be a mixture of different tendencies: they extended Roman citizenship from the outset to ex-slaves and allies. In one sense, this represented Rome's own enlightened best interests. Unlike Greece, where priesthoods ran in particular families and some annual priests were appointed by the city and where priests in different cults could be male or female, Roman priests with exceptions (e.g., female priests of Ceres and the Vestal Virgins) were men, appointed for life, and drawn from the senatorial order.[17] This concentrated power in the hands of the very few; religion is very much tied to political power, and the gods have everything to do with the preservation and expansion of Roman power, especially since successful competition for military conquest abroad was an ultimate means of guaranteeing political prestige at home. But power is not simply subordinated to religion, for, in the empire, senators often listed their priesthoods as first of the public offices they had held, even out of chronological order.[18]

So religious duty, a sense of *pietas*, and respect for the *mos maiorum* have their own dimension, and this situation, perhaps paradoxically, creates both a strong conservative centripetal tendency and yet an openness to other religions that is connected simultaneously to the *mos maiorum* and the centrifugal tendencies of tolerant expansionism. The Romans long believed, for instance, that the origins of Rome lay in the East. Roman magistrates sacrificed each year at Roma and at nearby Lavinium to the *penates* (or sacred objects/deities thought to have been brought from Troy by Aeneas).[19] There was, therefore, a living sense of Roman traditions passed on from outside Italy or even from the Greek midland. This deeply rooted belief is amply attested to by the numbers of Romans initiated into the mysteries of the Great Gods on Samothrace. Up to a third of the extant recorded names are Roman, so much so that the inscription regulating entry of noninitiates was actually bilingual (in Greek and Latin), something without parallel at any other Greek sanctuary.[20] Some sense, therefore, of a larger perspective, inclusive of foreign rituals, was part of the general stratigraphy of the Roman self-representation of origins, present status, and destiny.

Typically perhaps, therefore, one finds tensions in the Roman attitude to foreign deities and cults. Greek cults are not simply a matter of control. The Romans admired their antiquity and nobility. The Eleusinian Mysteries, for instance, were regarded by Cicero as having given not only the best hope for some continuous life after death, but the *vera principia* of civilized life itself.[21] Generally, therefore, Roman rule supported Greek religious practices and, except for Roman colonies (where inevitably in "expat" situations the colony mirrored the religious institutions of Rome),[22] did not impose Roman cults upon others. The antiquity and admirability of Greek cults were in tune with conservative Roman *auctoritas*. So, for instance, emperors visiting Greece participated in local sacrifices and festivals and were even initiated into the Eleusian Mysteries. And the emperor Hadrian restored many Greek temples in Athens and the Greek provinces as part of a larger project to promote Athens as the center of a revived Panhellenic movement.[23] On the other hand, in the second century BCE the cult of Bacchus that had become widespread in Italy and that was open to all ranks, men and women, was suppressed throughout Italy not only because it permitted the intermingling of the sexes but also apparently because it posed a pan-Italian network threat to traditional authority with its own strong internal leadership.[24] And in 181 BCE, books with Pythagorean doctrines discovered in a coffin supposedly containing the body of King Numa were burned on the advice of a Roman magistrate who decided that they were destructive of Roman religion.[25] Similar expulsions

occurred in the first century CE, and adherence to Roman ideology was oblig-
atory for everyone, emperors included. Although Stoicism was closely related
to traditional Roman practices, Marcus Aurelius, for instance, kept his *Meditations* or *To Himself* strictly to himself. And the divinity of the emperor was
not based upon earlier Greek cultic practices but framed in Roman practices
such as the apotheosis of Romulus.[26]

At the same time, the Greek pantheon was absorbed into the Roman pantheon with a specifically Roman focus in each case; and Jupiter, already associated with the Egyptian Ammon and the Etruscan highest sky-god Tinia,
absorbed the role of the Phrygian god Sabazios. But there was no equivalent of the associated Greek myths with immoral divine doings or a Hesiodic
Theogony. Jupiter Optimus Maximus was simply the ultimate protector of the
city, not the lover of Ganymede. As Dionysus of Halikarnassos emphasized
in his history of Rome in the first century BCE, Romulus "rejects all the traditional myths concerning the gods that contain blasphemies . . . [as] unworthy
of their blessed nature."[27] As Rome conquered the east, the cults of Cybele,
Mithras, Isis, Serapis, and many other deities were invited to Rome.[28] How
the Romans negotiated these introductions is interesting in itself: first, they
typically purged foreign cults of their foreign, Greek, or other unseemly practices. According to Dionysius again, the Romans allowed no secret Bacchic
mysteries and no male-female all-night vigils.[29] And although the worship of
Cybele (*Magna Mater*) kept its own Phrygian male and female priests, by senatorial decree no Roman could take part in the procession: "So careful are the
Romans to guard against religious practices that are not part of their own traditions."[30] Second, they threw a religious committee at the problem of interpretive divination. The sybilline books, a collection of prophecies/prophetic
writings purportedly coming in Greek from the sybil or seeress of Cumae in
south Italy (though in fact there were many sibyls—Delphi, Libya, Phrygia,
etc., according to Varro in Lactantius, *Div. Inst.* 50, 6), were the responsibility of the *quindecimviri* (a special college of "fifteen"), who were consulted in
times of crisis and sometimes advised the introduction of a foreign cult, presumably both to propitiate the powerful gods of foreign peoples and to augment the overall solidity of the *pax Romana* built upon the consensus of all
the gods (*pax deorum*) under the leadership of Jupiter and rooted in the traditional *penates*.[31] The *quindecimviri* were consulted, for example, before the
building of the temple to Ceres, Liber, and Libera in 493 BCE; before send-
ing an embassy to bring the god of Asclepius in snake-form from Epidauros
to Rome after a serious epidemic in 293 BCE, where Greek continued to be
used proudly by Romans in incubating/healing rites in Rome; and before the

importing of *Mater Magna* herself to Rome in 205–204 BCE.[32] So tolerance of foreign religions was mediated by crisis, prophecy, collegial divination, and ritual transformation or restriction. But the benefits for Rome were considerable. To embrace important foreign deities in their own way was to augment the *pax deorum* and the prestige of Rome by offering a focus for familiar identities to foreigners within the Roman world, just as to recognize the existing rights and privileges of ancient sanctuaries on foreign conquered territories was to sacralize the Roman world and avoid, as W. C. Green indicates,[33] the pitfall of fragmented city-states.

In the cases of Judaism and Christianity, the situation was more complicated and, ultimately, fatal. As Robert Berchman notes very well, at the end of the republic and the beginning of the empire (Julius Caesar and Augustus Caesar, respectively), Jews were given legal rights, as well as exemption from taxes and military service; and despite the revolts against Rome (especially 66–70 and the fall of Masada in 73) and Hadrian's banning of Jews from Jerusalem in 131, Rome could pursue a policy of tolerance because of concessions made by Jews to Rome after the Trajanic and Hadrianic wars and because Jews were no political threat after the first century to the whole picture of the inclusive polytheism of Rome.[34] In other words, the sense of identity of the whole *pax deorum* was not destroyed by the ethnic and religious identities of either Jews or other ethnic groups. As Berchman observes, inclusive monotheism and cultic polytheism were effectively parts of Roman political praxis in the republic and empire.[35]

However, with (a) the advent of more unified orthodoxies in the Jewish and Christian worlds in the third century on (i.e., distinct bodies of dogma and practice), (b) the enforcement of the divinity of the emperor, and (c) the requirement of pagan sacrifice under pain of death,[36] we witness the rise of Christianity as an exclusive monotheism that somehow manages to break the old Roman mold, a mold, first, of intolerance by persistent, brutal persecution to any major threat to its overall religious identity and, second, of the attempt to foster inclusive tolerance after the weariness of useless butchery through the major edicts of Gallienus (260), Galerius (311), and Constantine and Licinius (Milan, 313). In these edicts, we can already see the claims of a natural, rational law that—according to later terminology—participates in an eternal LOGOS and accords with the *mos maiorum* as binding upon all peoples.[37] Whether Stoic or not, there is an implicit rational claim upon the just reciprocity of all peoples. Already in the *Constituto Antoniana* by Caracalla in 212, in which Roman citizenship was given to all free inhabitants of the empire, the express purpose of such a move[38] was to fill the gods' sanctuaries or, in other words, to reinforce a dwindling Roman sense of community. Just over one hundred years later, this diminished sense of Roman religious identity was no longer able to withstand the force of an exclusive monotheism that brooked no rivals and addressed itself to all humanity. Earlier with figures like Philo, Clement of Alexandria, and some pagan polytheists, there was the sense that human beings could pursue truth in many different ways and yet be part of the same universe. Greeks had charged both Jews and Christians that their practices were "new"—Celsus, for instance, had argued in the 170s that Christians were little more than Jews, who were, in turn, derivative Egyptians.[39] Josephus had defended the antiquity of Judaism, and Origen had refuted Celsus. Some Christians had argued that Greek ideas prefigured their own or that, even in Greek rituals, Christian truths were embedded. Philo, in turn, had argued for the antiquity of Moses and for reading the Pentateuch intertextually as resonating with Plato (the *Timaeus*, for instance), an idea that is supported by both the Christian Justin and later by Numenius.[40] In this world, there are conflicts but still fertile intertextual resonances that bespeak a certain tolerance. Judaism had seemed at times to polytheists to be assimilable because, even as monotheistic, it did not impose itself on non-Jews by proselytism.[41] But the force of Christianity and the weakness of Roman religious community under the old *pax deorum* drove a fatal wedge into Greco-Roman religion from which its traditional sense of religious identity was not able to recover. Tolerance had its limits/limitations, and those limitations cut the blood off from the heart. Among the many ironies of this death knoll, one is that none of the formulations or grammar/syntax of any of the major Christian doctrines of the fourth or fifth centuries occurred in a world hermetically sealed off from Platonic, Aristotelian, and Stoic categories or from Plotinus, Porphyry, and Iamblichus—despite the protestations of people like Tertullian (earlier) to the contrary—even the complex phenomenon of monotheism and desert spirituality in Egypt, Syria, Palestine, etc., that is so distinctively Christian and that was a major driving force in the later Christianization of Europe. Indeed, this phenomenon has recently been traced back before Athanasius, Antony of Egypt, Pachomius to the school of Mani where we know both Jewish and Buddhist ascetics/monks played a significant role.[42]

3.1. Preliminary Conclusions

Here, then, in a preliminary way, we can address the five questions raised by William Scott Green: (1) the role of other religions; (2) the acknowledgment or rejection of different religions; (3) the justification of other religions; (4) the fault lines that justify religious tolerance or intolerance; and (5) the historical, political, and/or behavioral factors that correlate with the tolerance or intolerance of other religions. This study of Greco-Roman sources tends to favor the following preliminary answers:

(1) Tolerance is a somewhat checkered business that depends upon the manageability of other religions, that is, upon their capacity to maintain and augment either a sense of Panhellenic identity or, later, the Roman *pax deorum* and to avoid the fragmentation of that stability by the sacralization of a larger, more inclusive Roman world. Threats to stability, crises, and an openness to acknowledged necessity mediated by prophecy, collegial divination, and ritual transformation or restriction frequently provoked a tolerance that a political policy of tolerance could not achieve. Yet, arguably, there is an element in the Greco-Roman psyche that recognizes the implicit rights of the dispossessed as its own *penates* and, within the horizontal dimension of ritual and the centripetal/centrifugal forces of the Roman community, a vertical, religious dimension that recognizes an implicitly human dimension of relatedness to the divine that is unified under the worship of a single deity with a polytheistic family or families. In this sense, the Greco-Roman world functions as an inclusive monotheism and a cultic polytheism (as Berchman has argued in the previous chapter). But it remains unclear whether binary oppositions between "monotheism" and "polytheism" or "tolerance" and "intolerance" are really useful, in the first case, because they are later philosophico-theological categories and, in the second case, both because they are later categories and because they do not go far enough to catch the religious resonances between different traditions.

(2) and (3) Different religions are acknowledged, rejected, merely endured, or welcomed as religiously constructive on the basis (a) of threats to religious/political/medical stability, as well as upon their capacity (b) to augment the religious-political constitution, (c) to provide sets of familiar focus for a more cosmopolitan society, (d) to link Rome both to its foreign past and its imperial future, (e) to augment a more inclusive religious identity, and (f) to recognize the rational/religious claims and needs of all people according to a more universal law grounded in nature and *logos*. Justification follows the same criteria, but it is to be based also upon religious rituals such as divination, priestly collegiality, etc., and a sense of the *mos maiorum* that may include implicit kinship links with the foreigner.

(4) The fault lines that support intolerance are crisis, fear, paranoia, prejudice, racism, or the simple indigestibility of intractable political demands or exclusivist religious claims. What seems to support tolerance, by contrast,

are crisis, fear, paranoia, and weariness of butchery that seems to get one nowhere with apparent fanatics, but also a sense of what it means to be a religious Roman in a Greco-Roman world with universal claims based upon a law that binds or should bind all peoples and a natural sympathy for selective forms of what it means to be a stranger in a strange land.

(5) The expression of tolerance or intolerance of a religion immediately correlates with historical, political, and behavioral factors that are, in different ways at different times, shot through with other social, moral, and religious dimensions that make a simple cause-effect correlation always problematic. But, in general, legitimizing a religion involves drawing it within the circle of concerns that supports the *pax deorum* and *mos maiorum*, and delegitimizing it involves the opposite, unless it becomes too powerful and indigestible to swallow. It then either destroys the host organism or gets vomited out or remains a long-term lingering infection of the digestive tract—as we shall see below.

4. Tolerance and Ritual in an Expanded Sense

We have observed that the Greeks worshiped a multitude of spiritual beings of different ranks who filled all of nature, both the sky gods above (*superi*) and the many gods below (*inferi*) and that these deities were, in some measure, summed up by the Homeric pantheon of a clan of gods, headed by Zeus and bound together in a social organization similar to that of the Homeric clan-state, as also by the Hesiodic picture of a horrific history from Chaos, Gē, Ouranos, Kronos, and Rhea to Zeus, out of which there emerged the steady-state, though much troubled predominance of Zeus and Hera.

But herein there lie several puzzles (not least the question of the appropriate nature of divinity itself). If Greco-Roman polytheism is tolerant within the limits of tribe/clan and *dea Romana* (for Greece and Rome, respectively), nonetheless, there is a shared legacy of a most intolerant war at Troy and of a pantheon of competing gods who are anything but tolerant, together with human champions who strive to be equally intolerant. What meaning can tolerance have against this background? Is tolerance actually a feature of human weakness rather than divine self-sufficiency? Are failure and the incommensurabilities of experience embedded in religious rituals and ritualized through art, law, philosophy, at the root of tolerance rather than any active policies— at least, when taken together with the capacity of human beings to recognize something legitimate beyond their own claims and codes? Here I want to suggest several important resources for thinking about tolerance emerging out of early Greek religious rituals that proved to be crucial for the Greco-Roman world: epic, drama, philosophy, mystery religions, and cults.

4.1 Epic and Ritual

For a culture in exile that created the *Iliad* and *the Odyssey*, woven into complex hexameter forms that celebrated a glorious past and an unflinching heroic code of conduct, part of the real achievement was not so much the glorious deeds of war and ritualized intolerance but the capacity to recognize the face of another *ethnos* and to represent the conditions under which the hometown hero, Achilles, could actually break the mold of the heroic code itself. The very forms of the *Iliad* intensify this recognition of the other: (a) instead of the entire war and sack of Troy, fifty-five not-too-glorious days in which Patroclus and Hector (among others) are killed and Achilles' own death is presaged in his butchering of Hector; (b) by means of montage, parataxis, simile, instead of the absent Argive home-life, the women and city-life of Troy, especially Andromeda and Astyanax; and (c) instead of the pure exultation of the sack of Troy, the three threnodies—by Andromache, Hecuba, and Helen—which lead to the conclusion of book 24 over the grave-barrow of "Hector, breaker of horses." What is remarkable is that Homer—or a whole line of rhapsodes—could so clearly depict the face of the other *ethnos* as to inscribe in the death of Hector the fate of his/her own *ethnos*. This is not tolerance, of course, but a radical stretching of the artistic/religious imagination by a memorializing ritual so as to include the other both as other and yet simultaneously as oneself. And this stretching of the imagination also undergirds the remarkable scene (framed on a knife point between the potentially deadly angers of Achilles and Priam, justified by the heroic code)[43] in which Priam—to his horror—clutches the knees of the man who has killed his son and Achilles—to his own amazement— agrees to give up Hector. ". . . The two remembered," side by side, each his own loss. Then, Achilles, as it were, sees who Priam is for the first time: "How could you dare to come alone to the ships of the Achaians and before my eyes, when I am one who have killed in such numbers such brave sons of yours? The heart in you is iron. Come, then, and sit down upon this chair and you and I will even let our sorrows lie still in the heart for all our grieving."[44] And the conclusion of this meeting is an image of pure reflexivity: Priam and Achilles gaze at each other in wonder.[45] The roots of any genuine possibility for tolerance are implicit here in the fabric of this fundamental ritual: the recognition of the other and of the other's claim *despite* one's own anger and heroic status (and despite the eventual fall of Troy presaged in the death of Hector and the shared losses of Priam and Achilles).

By contrast, the final lines of the *Aeneid* do not suggest a better, more tolerant world, for they lie in uneasy proximity to the death of Hector in *Iliad*, 22, as, on this occasion, the outsider, Aeneas, kills the home champion, Turnus, to avenge the death of Pallas and simultaneously to bring about the destiny of Rome's conquest of the world. When Aeneas recognizes Pallas' belt worn by Turnus, "on fire with rage and terrible in his anger . . . in hot anger he sank the sword in Turnus' chest. His limbs collapsed in cold and his life fled with a groan complaining under the shades."[46] In these bleak final lines, Virgil seems to problematize both the heritage of Troy and the future destiny of Rome: is Aeneas to be driven by rage and bloodlust like the Homeric hero, without any deeper recognition of the other, or is he capable of becoming the Roman hero inspired by *pietas*, namely, by a sense of duty to the Roman gods, state, and family combined with *gravitas*, *dignitas*, and a sense of clemency even in victory? The gap between the two conceptions is what Virgil seems to call into question, especially since the memory of the dispossessed, the outcast, pervades the whole poem.[47]

4.2 Drama and Ritual

Broadly speaking, epic celebrates the clash not between different religions so much as between different tribes or clans. Even the *Iliad* suggests possibilities of more peaceful existence and the recognition of others' claims,[48] whereas the *Aeneid* problematizes the gap between passion and *pietas*. Whatever view one adopts about the meaning of myths (whether their origins are to be sought in relation to historical events or rituals or initiatory rites of passage),[49] the myths represented in Homer and Hesiod and in Greek drama are clearly spiritual ways of thinking about issues fundamental to society and of stretching the public imagination to recognize both its own limitations and the claims of the other in a broader context. This is true not only in relation to the gods in the plays of Aeschylus and Sophocles: human beings have to recognize that they are only human and as nothing before the gods' knowledge of things, as in the Delphic commandment "know thyself"[50] and Socrates' *Apology*[51]; but it is also true of the introduction of foreign deities and of the clan's tolerance of foreigners in its midst. The entry of Dionysus to the Greek world has profound repercussions for the emergence of drama itself, for many elective cults (the Orphic and the Eleusinian Mysteries), and for alternative theogonies from the Archaic period on,[52] but the fact that one had to lose one's mind, to be possessed in the service of God, was never easily accepted, as we can see not only in Herodotus and Demosthenes[53] (in classical times) but later in the repression of the cult of Bacchus by the senate in the 180s BCE,[54] in the criticisms of Livy (who says that the Bacchants had become "almost a second nation"[55]), and later still in those of Christians (such as Justin and Athenagoras).[56] And Euripides' *Bacchae* presents this profound unease in what is an almost indigestible form: the terrible death of Pentheus has led some interpreters to think of him as a martyr against irrational, religious fanaticism, yet this is not a plausible interpretation of the somewhat myopic, semidelusional character. We are instead presented with an irresolvable problem: either find a means of accepting the impulses to fury, ecstasy, and the sublime and acknowledge the hypocrisies that suppress these impulses or be destroyed by them. Again, *tolerance* is just the wrong term for such a dilemma, for tolerance suggests dispassionate detachment, whereas the *katharsis*, recognition, reversal, fear, and pity that Aristotle identifies as characteristics of drama in his *Poetics* involve some form of self-admission and transformation that has to be involved in dealing more adequately with forms of worship and viewpoints hitherto outside one's experience or excluded from recognition.

Nowhere is this perhaps clearer than in Euripides' *Medea*, a play that had a significant afterlife in Roman drama from Ennius to Ovid and Seneca. Medea, a devotee of Hecate and one of the great sorceresses of the ancient world, was the daughter of King Aeetes of Colchis who helped Jason obtain the golden fleece, fled with him afterwards, and cut her brother's body into pieces and threw them overboard to stop the pursuit behind Jason's ship. By magic she restored the youth of Jason's father, Aeson, and tricked the daughters of Pelias into killing their own father. Later, when Jason forsook Medea to marry the daughter of King Creon of Corinth, Medea kills both Creon and his daughter and then her own two children to take revenge on Jason before fleeing to Athens in a winged chariot. In other words, Medea is about as "barbarian" as it is possible to be, a barbarian witch who cannot be trusted or crossed.

In Euripides, Medea is presented for the most part as an ordinary young woman until the end when her magical powers are more prominent and Jason is presented—arguably—as a not very sympathetic character. The chorus generally sympathizes with Medea. In Seneca, by contrast, Medea's magical rituals are emphasized throughout, Jason is perhaps more sympathetic, and Medea kills the children on-stage (not off-stage, as in Euripides). In both plays, oaths feature prominently. Jason has sworn to keep faith with Medea but has broken his trust. For Greco-Roman religion, no one can support oath-breaking, and the gods will punish anyone who breaks an oath sworn by the gods.[57] At the same time, Medea's murder of the children is out of all proportion to Jason's crime, yet it possesses its own devastatingly "foreign" logic.

In Euripides' play, the audience is, therefore, faced with a terrible dilemma: sympathetic to Jason as they naturally are, they must nonetheless acknowledge his guilt and simultaneously recoil in horror before Medea's crime. The play provokes them into simultaneous acknowledgment and rejection and yet also poses a direct challenge: acknowledge the rights of the barbarian and the woman in your midst or your future hope for civilized life will be taken from you. This is not a plea for tolerance but a complex religious drama that turns the tolerance/intolerance disjunction inside out.

Again, Seneca's play sits in uneasy proximity to that of Euripides (however much Seneca might have borrowed from earlier Roman versions); despite the more sympathetic treatment of Jason, there is enough evidence to suggest that Medea could be seen by the audience to be an instrument of divine justice for Jason's having invaded the sea (Neptune) with the Argonauts and for having broken his oath with her.[58] But Jason has the final word in the play: "Travel up above through the high expanses of the heavens; bear witness that wherever you go there are no gods (*testare nullos esse, qua veheris, deos*)."[59] The verb *testare* in Jason's mouth bears a definite irony. But what does he mean? That there are no gods at all or that there are no gods wherever Medea goes or, again, that, when such trust is broken with apparent success, then we have no moral right to call the powers invoked in such a process "gods"?[60] Whatever the case, Seneca's play opens up the question of what can count as divinity in the case of competing claims and suggests that there is no divinity invoked in oath-breaking. In other words, there may well be a higher standard than the preferred viewpoints of rival deities. As in Plato's *Euthyphro*, so in this implicit (Stoic?) question, the claims of justice and ordinary morality are more basic to human life than different representations of divinity. As Socrates puts it: "Is the holy holy because the gods love it or do the gods love it because it is holy?"[61] As soon as this question gets asked, I suggest, a new standpoint for tolerance (and intolerance) emerges since there is now a chance at least that, while different divinities might be worshiped, no absolute privileging of a single viewpoint is to be guaranteed. It is true that this can be just another covert form of totalitarianism: I anathematize everybody except myself in the name of an empty absolute! But, in principle, it doesn't have to be this way since one may be able to respect the vulnerability and provisional quality of every viewpoint, including one's own, while leaving an open, undetermined space for a larger viewpoint beyond each. This is, of course, one of the great qualities of the dramatic novel, as Mikhail Bakhtin observed: namely, that it be multivoiced, genuinely heteroglossial, and involved with the here and now, rather than an infinitely removed epic distance. Drama provides an immensely important resource for thinking about tolerance or going beyond tolerance: an open space where the dance of life can return upon itself, that is, the orchestra.

4.3 From Drama to Philosophy

This leads us to one of the most important ritual resources for tolerance in the Greek and Greco-Roman worlds—the birth of philosophy. This birth is to be found not only in pre-Socratic philosophy, especially Heraclitus and Pythagoras who seem to epitomize an axial age of religious expression in the sixth century and who stand alongside Confucius and Lao Tzu in China, Siddharta Gautama in India, and Zoroaster in Persia; not only in the search for divinity and immortality in the cosmos in the theologies, theogonies, and cosmologies of the early thinkers and the practices of Orphic groups and Pythagorean brotherhoods/sisterhoods; and not only in the development of a new sense of inwardness and shared, common logos in Heraclitus and with the immortality of soul in Pythagoras and Empedocles;[62] it emerges also in step with Hesiod's and Solon's view that Zeus is concerned with justice[63] and especially with one of the primary concerns of Greek drama: the realization that the consequences of injustice (particularly, murder) are so unrelenting that a reorientation of the entire divine-human cosmos is required to effect a lasting resolution. Orestes' justifiable killing, on one set of principles, of Klytemnestra to avenge the murder of Agamemnon eventually requires in Aeschylus' Oresteia a superhuman feat of tolerance-creation, namely, the concerted attempt to persuade the Erinyes, the furies, in and beyond a court of law at Athens (the Areopagus)—before human jurors, Apollo, and Athena— to become the Eumenides, the benevolent ones, and to forgive their eternal pursuit of Orestes, a murderer. Whatever one is to make of one of the greatest trilogies in the history of drama, the Oresteia puts ritual persuasion and violence at the center of civic life as a matter of survival and suggests that forgiveness cannot come about without a transformation of the polis and cosmos as we know them.

Philosophy is born in the midst of all these fruitful streams (and more), at first as a search for what gives birth to and binds everything—water (Thales), ocean-infinite (Anaximander), earth-whole (Xenophanes), logos (Heraclitus), one-many (Pythagoras, Empedocles, Anaxagoras); then, as a logos given to a young man by the goddess (Parmenides), and later still as conversation between two or more that may start in jest, perplexity, and ordinary life but that has a deeper serious and, indeed, divine purpose. Such conversation has to be tolerant since the possibility of disagreement/refutation/lampoon is built into it from the start (the Sophists, Protagoras, Gorgias; comic drama: Aristophanes; and Socrates).

There is one other religious feature of the birth of philosophy with Socrates that is important for the question of tolerance: humility and the Delphic Oracle. Socrates may be ironic, hybristic, absurd—literally, "out of place," "unique"[64]—but he insists (a) that the Delphic pronouncement that he is the wisest in Greece was the beginning of his mission to prove the god right—despite his own initial skepticism, (b) that the Delphic commandment "know yourself" has to mean that human knowledge is as nothing beside divine knowledge, and (c) that he knows nothing beyond the one advantage he has over the rest of the population, that he alone knows that he knows nothing.[65] However problematic these claims may be, this is the birth of a very strange sort of tolerance, one that will not allow others to remain unthinkingly intolerant, and of a way of life that insists we cannot determine the world according to our own preferences. Where we do not have the ultimate mastery, where man is not the measure of all things,[66] the proper service of "the god" is to overthrow our prejudices, to subvert our notions of position, power, and morality, and to recall all human beings (apparently anyone who will participate in conversation) to what is really important, not external signs of rank but internal, moral worth and openness to a reality more important than themselves that saturates and sustains the whole of nature. This at least is the gist of Socrates' defense at his trial and it is also summed up in the beautiful prayer at the end of the *Phaedrus*:

Pan and all you other gods in this place, grant me to become inwardly fair, and as for everything I possess externally, may it be harmonious with my inner disposition. May I consider the wise man healthy, and may I have as much gold as only the moderate person can take away and carry.[67]

The spirit of Socratic philosophy embodied in this prayer and initiated by the Delphic Oracle gives us some sense of the civilizing, moderating force of such oracles in human life, a force for the civilizing combination of rationality, unbridled creativity, and yet menace represented in both the Apollo and Dionysus statues of the period (or later copies thereof).

From Tolerance to Intolerance. Polytheisms, like monotheisms, however, can only tolerate so much. Tolerance has a lot to do with size, with who has the significant majority, and with paranoia. Socrates did not manage to survive in the city, but he would never have gotten started in the village. This is the reason he needs the city to practice his own form of religious ritual—and yet, just as according to the Delphic Oracle, the one whom Apollo loves most is not the wealthiest donor with pretensions to grandeur but the unknown herdsman from Thessaly who regularly says his prayers and cares for his animals,[68] so Socrates is able to speak for the village, as it were, i.e., for the non-aristocratic peoples. But the limiting principle still stands: people tend to be intolerant and paranoid, and the more so the smaller the community.

In the telling example recounted by Caseau and Berchman[69] of Roman legionaries consecrating first the genius of Gholaia (in Libya) before the consecration of their own gods and, then later, upon the abandonment of the camp, the locals desecrating the temples of the Roman divinities, there are two fundamentally different perspectives: (1) the relative sizes of the threat and (2) the disproportionate size between the *pax Romana* and the occupied colony. The Romans could afford to be tolerant: their size and colonizing power permitted them to assimilate the divinities of others; the occupied people could not afford to relinquish what in fact defined them. And the Romans did need to propitiate foreign gods before occupying foreign lands and to sacralize the place with all appropriate deities. By analogy, one may plot the significance of state intolerance in classical Athens. Socrates' trial was no isolated incident but one in a series of trials against "free thinkers" (Anaxagoras, Diagoras, Protagoras, Euripides—and perhaps Aristotle, too).[70] The evidence may be sketchy, but it is still there. It was also linked to other shocking events—the mutilation of the herms and the profanation of the mysteries earlier in 415 BCE (the latter thought to be by Alcibiades, Socrates' pupil), a blatant case of desacralization by an individual outside the community. Impiety (*asebeia*), though not extensively defined at the time, was a real threat to the mutually enforcing relation between religion and politics. Profanation of the mysteries was so serious a charge that, when the case was brought to the assembly in 415, the assembly was cleared of noninitiates.[71] The charges against Socrates (listed in Plato's *Apology*) were also of compelling "size": (1) of refusing to recognize the gods recognized by the state (in Plato's *Apology*, Socrates argues that he does recognize the gods, though not in the same way as the prosecution—a surprising admission);[72] (2) of introducing new deities (in Plato's *Apology*, the most disturbing evidence is Socrates' daimonion—to have a direct hotline to divine will undermines the principles of communal religious and political life and bespeaks what we might call today potential "fascist terrorism");[73] and (3) of corrupting the youth (in the *Clouds*, Strepsiades adopts perjury on Socrates' advice—to break the oath that binds the foundation of state religion is to challenge the heart of piety. Alcibiades had done just this in profaning the mysteries).[74] Socrates was, therefore, a gadfly of serious proportions, and "democratic Athens" was not liberal and open-minded if faced with such deviant actions and opinions.

Philosophy as Ritual from Plato to Late Antiquity. Pierre Hadot has emphasized that much of ancient philosophical thought must be understood as a
form of ascetic practice and preparation, a spiritual exercise, and not academic philosophy with departmental status as we know it today.[75] I want to
suggest that philosophy of the whole period (but particularly that of Plato) is
a form of ritualized practice that casts the masks of drama into a more directly
participant dramatic dialogue no longer in honor of Dionysus (alone) but
now in pursuit of a much larger, inclusive world. If philosophy is a form of
lived community experience that reconnects one to the divine, then philosophy's rituals are conversations (dialogue/dialectic), walking together (*peripa-
tetos*)—a *methodos*, a way of being on the path ("two going together," as Plato
likes to quote from Homer)[76] that opens up an entirely new sacred space for
thinking about tolerance and yet, at the same time, clearly goes beyond such
categories as tolerance/intolerance (even polytheism/monotheism). Such a
methodos (a) casts into doubt familiar categories and representations of divinity; (b) provides a critique of stories about the immoral doings of the gods
and of human immorality masquerading as morality (as in the *Republic*) yet
remains connected to the myths of the past and rethinks the position of the
state's gods (as in the *Phaedrus*); (c) likens its ascending steps to the lesser
and greater Eleusian Mysteries (as in the *Symposium*), makes its dialectic resonate with a different kind of sacrifice that "assembles" and "cuts" the joints
of "reality" (as in "collection and division," e.g., Phaedrus, Sophist, etc.),
and "rubs" all its conceptions, images, words together, as it were, to create a
sacred light (as in the *Seventh Letter*); (d) builds into itself, as an integral part
of its being, the possibilities of subversive refutation ("with well-meaning
refutations," *Seventh Letter*) and of the presence, however uncomfortable, of
the nonpersuaded other (e.g., Thrasymachus in the *Republic*); and (e) allows
for a new indeterminacy of what is more ultimate than conventional representations of the gods (e.g., the "good" in the *Republic*, the "beautiful" in the
Symposium or "the what is" as opposed to the traditional Greek pantheon in
the *Phaedrus*), while (f) opening up a space, to supplant any privileged position for Socrates, for the "stranger"—female or male—who becomes a major
interlocutor in the *Symposium* and later dialogues.[77] One could hardly have a
more radical model for tolerance on a hitherto unimagined scale than this: an
open, relatively undetermined sacred space where the stranger assumes the
hierophantic role of linking the whole community to the divine. It has been
argued much in the latter half of the twentieth century that this is, in fact,
a totalitarian, tyrannical model, but, despite Bakhtin's assessment that the
later dialogues are monological and despite strong conservative tendencies in

the late *Laws*,[78] tyranny or intolerance is precisely what Plato repudiates most in the dialogues and letters.

In what follows, I briefly want to pick out certain key strands for framing this new resource for tolerance in Plato, Aristotle, and, later in the Greco-Roman world, with the Stoics, Plotinus, Porphyry, and Iamblichus. With this new model of conversation (upon which the intimate formulae of mystical union will later be built—the *monos pros monon* or "alone to alone" formula, in particular),[79] there come new models of understanding diversity, address, and ideal behaviors. In Plato's later dialogues, there are the following recognitions: (a) A new philosophical rhetoric of persuasion is required that will know how to speak intelligently to a multiplicity of addressees: even the violence of one word to all is not enough (this is in the *Phaedrus*);[80] and (b) the paradigm for understanding the cosmos as a whole is a model (the statue—*agalma*) of an "intelligible living creature," inclusive of all species:

It would be an unworthy thing to liken it to any nature that exists as a part only; for nothing can be beautiful which is like any imperfect thing; but let us suppose the world to be the very image of that whole of which all other animals both individually and in their tribes are portions. For the original of the universe contains in itself all intelligible beings, just as this world like the fairest and most perfect of intelligible beings, framed one visible animal comprehending within itself all other animals of a kindred nature.[81]

It is the first time we have such a vivid picture of a shared, potentially intelligible earth. The model for understanding creative divinity also changes radically: ungrudging, nonjealous divinity, capable of giving freely of itself, instead of jealous, territorial gods and goddesses.

Let me tell you then why the creator made this world of generation. He was good, and the good can never have any jealousy of anything. And being free from jealousy, he desired that all things should be as like himself as they could be. This is in the truest sense the origin of creation and of the world, as we shall do well in believing on the testimony of wise men: God desired that all things should be good and nothing bad, so far as this was attainable.[82]

Aristotle takes this a major step further, building significantly upon the Pythagorean-Platonic living-holistic model. For Aristotle, there has to be an aspect of life that goes beyond even enlightened human self-interest, and this aspect is religious in the deepest sense that it is concerned with "the best things," namely, divine things (see *Nicomachean Ethics* 6, 7) or the sphere of *Sophia*, contemplative wisdom. Partly, this is because human beings are not the summit of best organic development: "for there are other things much more divine in their nature" (such as heavenly bodies). Partly, it is because, if contemplative wisdom (*Sophia*) were restricted to practical/political wisdom (*phronēsis*), there will not be a perspective "concerned with the good of all animals." In other words, *Sophia* is ultimately a divine perspective that gives insight into and simply lets be the best interests of all animals without manipulating them for the perceived goals of the human race or of those other animals that possess practical wisdom (*phronesis*) and without doing anything with or to them (*praxis* and *poiēsis*). *Sophia*, therefore, appears to be that remarkable intersection where divine self-understanding and human understanding/ self-understanding meet in a tolerance of the highest kind that goes far beyond religious and ethnic divisions to cross the boundaries between species in order to gain insight into what is good "for men, fish . . . and all animals."[83] In sum, I suggest, we are here in the presence, not of RELIGION—with its ethnic, cultic, creedal divisions, however important these may be—but of what I shall refer to in the lower register (since it can slip by without one noticing it) of "religion," namely, a perspective that includes other interests but cannot be simply identified with or reduced to ethnic, political, or even perhaps imperial terms.

Something of this Aristotelian-scientific conception lies at the heart of the Hellenistic period, pervades the whole range of Stoic thought from Zeno of Citium, through Cicero and Epictetus to Marcus Aurelius in late antiquity, and perhaps empowers some of the major scientific inquiries of the age, especially Posidonius, whose interests in ocean currents have made him the mascot of contemporary oceanographers. But what I want to focus briefly on here is the Stoic conception of wholeness that lies behind the *pax Romana* and the *pax deorum* and that grounds religious tolerance as a matter of policy in the republic and empire. Here we find again that philosophical identity was not strictly demarcated from or opposed to religion or politics or the formulations of law directed to all rational peoples. Philosophical commitment was a religious commitment, as the wholesale use of the term *philosophia* to denote a complete way of committed religious life by the Christian fathers of the third and fourth centuries attests.[84] Adherence to a philosophical "school" was a question not only of mind but of heart (*mens/cor*; *nous/kardia*; *apatheia/puritas cordis*) and of relationship to/understanding of divinity.[85] So, in Marcus Aurelius, a committed Stoic, there is a strong sense of the intrinsic interrelatedness (a) of the common brotherhood of all humanity (see also in Cicero, Epictetus, etc.) within the larger living universe of all beings pervaded by divine *logos*, (b) of the functions of emperor, an individual human being representative of the whole species, and (c) of the vocation of divine-human community in everyday life.

So, *Meditations* 4:4:

If thought is something we share, then so is reason. . . .

And if so, we share a common law. And thus are fellow citizens. . . .

And in that case, our state must be the world.

Meditations 6:44:

My city and state are Rome—as Antoninus. But as a human being? The world.

So for me, "good" can only mean what's good for both communities.

And *Meditations* 5:27:

"Live with the gods." He is living with the gods who continually displays his soul to them, as content with what they have apportioned, and as doing what is willed by the spirit, the portion of himself which Zeus has given to each person to lead and guide them. . . .

And yet, at the same time, Marcus Aurelius persecuted the Christians. Shades of intolerance inhabit the most inclusive vision, just as for Plato the "good" casts the largest shadow (*corruptio optimi pessima*).

Later Antiquity. We do not have space to follow out this complex line of thought with full vigor but can only point out several major features in later antiquity:

(1) With Iamblichus and Proclus in late antiquity, the new emphasis upon theurgy—doing the work of God/god—as opposed to theology—talking about God/god—catches and develops something that was part of philosophy as ritual from the very beginning but that is lost sight of in the press of ordinary affairs.

(2) Similarly, the late antique focus on the theological virtues in both these thinkers is presumably to rival Christian and Jewish religious traditions, but it simultaneously catches up and develops something implicit in the earlier philosophical tradition, especially from Plato to Plotinus.

(3) The religious dimension of thought and practice can be found in invocation/philosophical rituals in Plotinus[86] and also in Gnostic texts (e.g., Nag Hammadi "Sethian" texts),[87] but it is also predicated upon two crucial features of such practice: (a) the notion that all peoples spontaneously, though mostly unconsciously, worship the same, one God and (b) that, while different appropriations or affirmative theologies are legitimate, we really know nothing of God's essence itself; and, therefore, negative theology in conjunction with kataphatic theology is the proper, humble, human way of opening up the indeterminate space where all human beings and all beings

can appropriately worship God in heart, mind, perception, life, or mere existence.

In relation to (a), Plotinus writes at the beginning of *Ennead*, VI, 5, 1ff. "A common opinion (*ennoia*) affirms that what is one and the same in number is everywhere present as a whole, when all human beings are naturally and spontaneously moved to speak of the god who is in each of us one and the same." This is a remarkable statement, but the word *ennoia* (almost "innate concept" by contrast to *epinoia*, "reflection") could be used in almost just this way by thinkers as different as Philo, Origen, Porphyry, Basil the Great, and Gregory of Nyssa.[88]

In relation to (b), Skeptics, Neoplatonists, Jews, Christians, and Gnostics, in different ways (as Jacques Derrida in an insightful article has implicitly pointed out: *Comment ne pas parler: denegations*[89]), might be able to maintain different versions of such a view, ranging from the One beyond being (in Plotinus, Porphyry, Proclus), to the One beyond the One beyond being (in the extreme negative theology of Iamblichus),[90] to Being beyond determinate beings (in Basil the Great, Gregory of Nyssa, Ps. Dionysius, Bonaventure, Aquinas). This, however, was a powerful resource for tolerance that did not properly survive the strains and tensions of other doctrinal and civilizational necessities.

(4) Finally, following Theophrastus' treatise *On Piety*, Porphyry in his *De Abstinentia*, after presenting a history of sacrifice, rejects animal sacrifice on the basis of other animals' kinship with us even in cognitive ability and in recognition of the demands of justice and then goes on to present one of the most compelling comparative case studies of the rejection of such killing in the earlier Greek golden age and among the Egyptians, Jews, Syrians, and Persians. The whole text is imbued with the vivid understanding (even if, elsewhere in Porphyry's writings, he takes a harsh view of Christians) that tolerance of other religions/nations or species is *not enough* for it implies a false superiority and an unwarranted management model. We have to allow ourselves to be *transformed* by the superior practices of other religions and other ages if we can only overcome the prejudices inculcated in us by social, political, moral, and religious thinking. Passive tolerance is plainly insufficient, but even active tolerance is not enough. Transformability is a real, if dangerous, path of openness to the other, and it is a primary quality of authentic religious experience—whether of Abraham, Moses, Jesus, Plato, the Stoics, Plotinus, Athanasius, Gregory of Nyssa, Proclus, or Damascius.

4.4 Community, Religious Identities, and Cults in the Late Greco-Roman World

Finally, we provide a brief note on community, cult proliferation, philosophy, and different sorts of "religion" in the late Greco-Roman world. If we assume, on the basis of the sources available to us from across the spectrum of the Greco-Roman world, (a) that there is something distinctive about the religious/vertical dimension—in however many combinations with other dimensions of social, political, individual life it may occur—and (b) that (no matter how difficult it may be to pinpoint precisely because it cannot be isolated) this dimension has the ability to transfix and mold other human interests either into a broader view of human and animal community (as Porphyry claims for the whole of antiquity) or to give purpose and meaning to individual lives (as in the case of stories such as Baucis and Philemon or temple inscriptions in gratitude and advertisement for healing), then we can see that this spirit, in different combinations and particularly when finely intermeshed with political and factional interests, may be *the* most powerful resource (i) for understanding both tolerance and intolerance, (ii) for thinking about the complex nature of communities that helps to drive or destroy civilizations, and (iii) for shedding significant light upon the complex relation of the *pax deorum/pax Romana* and the proliferation of cultic identities in the late empire. If religion is not just one of a bundle of characteristics defining ethnic, civic, or imperial identity, but the principal defining characteristic[91] (and one that does not always need material or expansionist success to justify itself[92]), then against the background of dwindling Roman religious community we have noted in the times of Caracalla above, we can see in the proliferation of cultic identities in this period the unleashing of a powerful, multiedged, and dangerous force that the Romans had long realized possessed the capacity to cut right across and to subvert other dimensions of the political spectrum but that they were increasingly powerless to control. The many cults of this period offered, in short, *religious* identities to their members.[93]

Instead of a typical view that "conversion" before the rise of Christianity was a philosophical and not a religious phenomenon,[94] people were clearly capable of being converted not simply to philosophical ideas but to new religious ways of life (as Lucius to the worship of the goddess Isis at the end of Apuleius' *Golden Ass*). Philosophy and the many different cults were not necessarily hostile to Greek or Indian or Syrian or Persian religion and were not inherently more meaningful than official Greco-Roman religious practices. But they were different ways of living out a relation to the gods, to others, and to oneself that could leap across political, ethnic, or even religious divides, and they were, therefore, dangerous to any weakened religious-political community of the whole empire.

The ability of the religious spirit to leap across the divide between hitherto different or irreconcilable dimensions is one of the most important resources for religious tolerance; it may well lead to what seems to modern eyes a dangerous or uncritical syncretism, e.g., late Christian, "Naassene" attempts to find Christian rituals prefigured in pagan rituals,[95] or again, the apparent contradiction of the Christian bishop of Troy celebrating ancient pagan rituals one day of the year on the plain of Hisarlik in the second and third centuries.[96] But, I suggest, it is also the reason Philo can see something crucial for Jewish life *immediately* in Plato and can link it instinctively and persuasively to Moses or the reason Numenius can recognize Plato to be "an atticizing Moses."[97] On the other hand, "religion" also exists within the divisions and is a major force, thereby, for cultic separation and intolerance, often with equally powerful rationality as the development of doctrine/creeds (an inherently reasonable and even open-minded process in itself, if one is trying to make the best sense of a mystery on the basis of *all* the evidence) in Judaism and Christianity attests or, not quite so reasonable perhaps, the forbidding of intermarriage from both sides between Jews and Christians in late antiquity. In other words, the greatest resource for tolerance, one could argue, is that there is a "religious" dimension of life; and the greatest resource for intolerance is that there is a RELIGIOUS category. But nothing is quite so simple since "religious" and RELIGIOUS are two conditions that cannot easily be told apart precisely because they can pervade each other in myriad combinations. Is Antigone in Sophocles' play of the same name, for instance, a fanatical, terrorist saboteur or an intelligent young girl with a different, religious vision? The quality that permits me to recognize something akin in the other, no matter how foreign, can also be the quality that empowers me to exclude the other entirely.

There are two further complicating factors of the ambiguities of tolerance and religion in late antiquity. The British historian Christopher Dawson argued in the last century that civilizations decay when they lose touch with the religious roots that first inspired their emergence and nurtured their full development.[98] For Greco-Roman religion, the sense of religious purpose and shared community built upon the *mos maiorum* was a driving force in the expansion of Roman *imperium*. By contrast, the dwindling sense of religious community and the proliferation of alternative identities in the cults of the later empire promoted a more open-handed tolerance (in the Edict of Milan, particularly) that proved to be dangerous and, worse still, based upon little else than the crumbling foundations of an exhausted system. In order to be tolerant, one has to have a real foundation from which one can be tolerant. Otherwise, the checks are blank.

On the other side of the issue, basic tolerance is only the minimal threshold for any kind of self-understanding, much less spiritual or human understanding of the other. Artistic/mythical rituals stretch the human imagination to confront the unimaginable, the incommensurable, or to open an indeterminate space in which otherness can be imagined differently. Philosophical ritual, in a similar but even more far-reaching way, extends that open space of possibility to the brotherhood of humanity based upon the shared law and sympathy of nature, reason, and spirit as well as the intrinsic values of a cosmic and hypercosmic order that empowers but resists our capacity to know or determine.

5. Conclusion

To reply to William Scott Green's five questions a second time: in answer generally to (1)–(5), we have suggested that the categories of tolerance/intolerance do not quite address the principal issues suggested by the whole history of Greco-Roman religion, namely, that while tolerance is crucial in an intolerant world, the really dangerous issue is the need inherent in religious rituals themselves for self-transformability—the capacity to go beyond oneself to the divine and to the other—or, in other words, the problem (a) that there are "religious"/ RELIGIOUS dimensions that pervade religions and cut across the political/civic/ social fields that accompany and interpenetrate them and (b) that only from the viewpoint of the "religious" dimensions or something like them can otherwise insuperable doctrinal or existential divides be viewed for what they are, namely, real, living issues that somehow or other have to be respected yet transcended in ordinary life.

Re (1), other religions both threaten and yet augment the *pax Romana–pax deorum*. All gods need to be propitiated and included to the degree that this does not weaken the stability of the whole. Yet even threats to stability, crises, imperfections, incommensurabilities, and absences of due proportion— mediated by prophecy, divination, and ritual transformation (or restriction) in state religion or artistic and philosophical ritual—provoked a tolerance and a potential self-transformability that mere tolerance on its own could not achieve. This tolerance of other religions and, generally, a refusal by Rome to impose its own forms of worship upon others, together with a respect for the antiquity/venerability of other traditions, produced a new sense of the community of all human beings rooted in the perceived kinship of everything in the divine. Inclusive monotheism and cultic polytheism can, therefore, dwell uneasily but amicably side by side, but they cannot withstand the ultimate force of the abused children, namely, the related, exclusive monotheisms of the Jews and Christians. The Romans cleaned up the myths of the Greeks and sanitized the narrative out of their own stories only to be overwhelmed by the power of a simple story from elsewhere that they were never able to assimilate.

Re (2) and (3), different religions are acknowledged, rejected, merely endured, or welcomed as religiously constructive on the basis of all the features noted above: (a) threats to stability; (b) capacity to augment the constitution of the whole; (c) ability to provide familiar focus for different groups in an increasingly cosmopolitan society; (d) resonances between Rome's foreign religio-political past and its imperial future; and (e) the increasing need to recognize the claims of others and of other religions on the explicit grounds of a shared, common law grounded in nature, *logos,* and the divine and an implicit link of common "religious" inheritance despite the difference of RELIGION. Justification, therefore, also ranges from sheer political/social/medical expediency to "religious" kinship and must simultaneously—given the Roman's extraordinary attachment to religion—have included multiple motives.

Re (4) and (5), the fault lines that support intolerance are always with us: crisis, fear, paranoia, prejudice, racism, RELIGION, and intractable political-religious demands. The fault lines that support tolerance are the inclusive and expansionist religious sensibilities that went into the forging of a civilization always imperiled by external failures and internal factional intolerances, as well as those ritual forms that question, reflect upon customary ritualistic practices and open up indeterminate spaces for rethinking justice and religious claims/responsibilities. Shared universal law, negative theology—or a *balance* between negative and affirmative theologies—and an instinctive recognition in all traditions (Greco-Roman, Jewish, and Christian) that, despite differences all human beings worship "one and the same" God are, perhaps, the most important fault lines of all. Fault lines destroy older configurations and lead to the birth of new ones. Finally, the historical, political, and behavioral factors that correlate with the tolerance or intolerance of other religions are complex indeed, but they should not be isolated, I have suggested, from "religious"/RELIGIOUS (including artistic, philosophical, cultic) considerations that always, in some measure, accompany and pervade them. To isolate them is, I suggest, the typical modern mistake of dividing history or contemporary life up into all its lowest common denominators—

social, political, intellectual, legal, philosophical, scientific, etc.—and then being forced to relegate religion to what is none of the above: pure madness or fantasy. Yet, without fantasy, there would never even be a human world, much less a divine-human horizon of possibility. And without certain forms of madness, the sheets would never get crumpled in the first place.

Bibliography

Adkins, L., and Roy A. Adkins. *Dictionary of Roman Religion*. Oxford: Oxford University Press, 1996.

Armstrong, A. H., ed. *Classical Mediterranean Spirituality: Egyptian, Greek, Roman*. World Spirituality 15. New York: Crossroads, 1986.

Beard, M., J. North, S. Price. *Religions of Rome*. 2 vols. Cambridge: Cambridge University Press, 1998.

Berchman, R. M. "Altruism in Greco-Roman Philosophy." In *Altruism in World Religions*, edited by Neusner and Chilton, 1–30.

———. "Pagan Philosophical Views of Jews and Judaism." In *Approaches to Ancient Judaism*, edited by Jacob Neusner, 1–94. Atlanta: Scholars Press, 1997.

Bowersock, W., P. Brown, and O. Grabar, eds. *Late Antiquity: A Guide to the Postclassical World*. Cambridge, MA: Harvard University Press, 1999.

Bremmer, J. N. *Greek Religion*. New York: Oxford University Press, 1994.

Burkert, W. *Greek Religion: Archaic and Classical*. Translated by John Raffan. Cambridge, MA: Harvard University Press, 1985. German original: 1977.

Caseau, B. "Sacred Landscapes." In *Late Antiquity*, edited by Bowersock et al., 21–59.

Cole, S. G. "The Mysteries of Samothrace during the Roman Period." *Aufstieg und Niedergang der römischen Welt* 2.18.2: 1564–1598.

Corrigan, K. "Body and Soul in Ancient Religious Experience." *In Classical Mediterranean Spirituality*, edited by A. H. Armstrong, 360–83.

Dubourdieu, A. *Les origins et le développement du culte des Pénates à Rome*. Rome and Paris: École française de Rome, 1989.

Ferguson, J. *Greek and Roman Religion: A Source Book*. Park Ridge, NJ: Noyes Publications, 1980.

Fowden, G. "Religious Communities." In *Late Antiquity*, edited by Bowersock et al., 82–106.

Graf, Fritz. *Magic in the Ancient World*. Translated by F. Philip. Cambridge, MA: Harvard University Press, 1997. French original: 1994.

Hine, H. M., trans. Medea/Seneca. Warminster, UK: Aris & Phillips, 2001.

Kraemer, R. S., ed. *Maenads, Martyrs, Matrons, Monastics: A Sourcebook on Women's Religions in the Greco-Roman World*. Philadelphia: Fortress Press, 1988.

Martin, L. H. *Hellenistic Religions: An Introduction*. New York and Oxford: Oxford University Press, 1987.

Mikalson, J. D. *Religion in Hellenistic Athens*. Berkeley: University of California Press, 1998.

Mylonas, G. E. *Eleusis and the Eleusinian Mysteries*. Princeton, NJ, and London: Princeton University Press, 1961.

Neusner, J. *Approaches to Ancient Judaism*. USF Studies in the History of Judaism 12. Atlanta: Scholars Press, 1997.

Neusner, J., and B. Chilton, eds. *Altruism in World Religions*. Washington, DC: Georgetown University Press, 2005.

Price, Simon. *Religions of the Ancient Greeks*. Cambridge: Cambridge University Press, 1999.

Scheid, J. *An Introduction to Roman Religion*. Translated by Janet Lloyd. Bloomington: Indiana University Press, 2003. French original: 1988.

Notes

1. Further on *tolero*, see R. M. Berchman in this volume. For *ean*, see Plato's ironic usage in relation to Agathon in *The Symposium* 175 b.

2. See J. Scheid, *Introduction to Roman Religion*, 28: "Civic rationality that guaranteed the liberty and dignity of its members both human and divine . . . and guaranteed the established order and ruled out any power founded upon fear." If this describes the effect of traditional religious practice at Rome, then even Lucretius' debunking of the place of the gods in order to dispel fear (in the *De Rerum Natura*) was in accordance with traditional Roman practice.

3. Latin: *ritus*. Again, no exact Greek equivalent, though *telestika* (initiatory rites), *orgia* (secret rites), *leitourgia* (public service/worship of the gods)—in the mysteries or Bacchic cult-worship—or *hiera* (sacred things) or *ergon* (work) or *praxis* (business) or *threskeia* (religious worship/observance) are approximates. See Bowersock et al, *Late Antiquity*, under ritual, and Scheid, 30–38; and for the modern sacred/profane distinction in relation to Roman thought, Scheid, 23–25.

4. Compare Price, *Religions of the Ancient Greeks*, 78–81.

5. See the proem to Parmenides' ritualistic journey and reception of a *logos* that he must not change in any detail.

6. On *religio*, see Scheid, *Introduction to Roman Religion*, 22. For Greek religion generally, see Burkert, *Greek Religion*, and Bremmer, *Greek Religion*; on the Hellenistic period, Martin, *Hellenistic Religions*, and Mikalson, *Religion in Hellenistic Athens*; and for the Roman period, Beard et al. *Religions of Rome*, vol. I, and Scheid, passim.

7. Compare, generally, Graf, *Magic in the Ancient World*.

8. Jacob Neusner, "Theological Foundations of Tolerance in Classical Judaism" [this volume].

9. Compare Price, 1–3, and Xenophon, *Anabasis* 5.3.4–13; for sacrifice, see Scheid, 79–110.

10. ". . . in a holy circle," *Iliad* 18, 504. For differences between Greek and Roman practices, see Beard et al., vol. II, no. 4.1; 4.4; Price, 150.

11. Graf, 214.

12. Compare Price, 1–10.

13. See Caseau, *Late Antiquity*, edited by Bowersock et al., 21–59; Price, 47–66.

14. Compare Price, 2 and 11–46. See also Lucretius, *De Rerum Natura* 5.1023: "It is just for all of us to feel compassion for those who are weak."

15. See especially Mylonas, *Eleusis and the Eleusinian Mysteries*.

16. Compare Price, 65, 151.

17. Scheid, 129–46; Beard et al., vol. II, chap. 8.

18. Price, 151.

19. Dionysius of Halicarnassus, I.64; 67.4. For the *penates* and *di manes*, see Scheid, 166–79.

20. Compare Cole, "The Mysteries of Samothrace," 1564–1598; Dubourdieu, *Les origines et le développement . . .* , 125–50; Price, 147–48.

21. Cicero, *De legibus* 2.14.36.

22. Beard et al., vol. I, 313–63.

23. Pausanias I.18, 6–9.

24. See generally Kraemer, *Maenads, Martyrs . . .* ; Price, 153–54; Beard et al., vol. I, 91–96; vol. II, 12.1.

25. Pliny, *Natural History* 13, 84–87.

26. Compare Price's account, 155–56.

27. Dionysius of Halicarnassus 2.18.3; Compare Price, 153.

28. Scheid, 143–44; Berchman (in this volume); Price, 108–25.

29. Dionysius of Halicarnassus 2.19.2.

30. Ibid., 19.5; trans. Beard et al., 153.

31. Scheid, 121–23.

32. Very helpful are the chronology-tables in Scheid, 193–212.

33. W. C. Green, *The Achievement of Rome: A Chapter in Civilization* (Cambridge: Cambridge University Press, 1938), 327 (cited in R. M. Berchman in this volume).

34. For an accessible account of the broader—and harrowing—history of Judaism from Babylon to Rome, see R. J. Hoffmann, trans., *Porphyry's Against the Christians: The Literary Remains* (Amherst, MA: Prometheus Books, 1994), 95ff.

35. See R. M. Berchman in this volume, "Greco-Roman Paganism," n. 3.

36. The Edict of Decius in 250 CE for sacrifice; deification of Julius Caesar (*Lex Rufrena*), 42 BCE; Augustus, 14 BCE; Claudius, 54 CE; Vespasian and Titus, 79–81, etc. See Scheid, chronology.

37. Compare Berchman's surely correct claim, ". . . the Edict of Milan is based on the later Roman theological principles of inclusive monotheism and cultic polytheism, which accepts the existence of a great number of gods but holds that all gods are essentially one and the same" (Compare the edict: ". . . so that . . . whatever supreme Divinity exists in the heavenly seat may be favorable and propitious to us and to all those who are placed under our authority") (Berchman in this volume). See further subsection, "Philosophy as Ritual from Plato to Late Antiquity," below.

38. Preserved in a papyrus at Giessen, see G. Fowden, *Late Antiquity*, edited by Bowersock et al., 85.

39. Preserved in Origen, *Contra Celsum*, trans. H. Chadwick (Cambridge: Cambridge University Press, 1953); compare Price, 159.

40. Fragment 8, 13 *Des Places*.

41. Fowden, *Late Antiquity*, 84.

42. See Gedaliahu G. Strousma, "The Manichaean Challenge to Egyptian Christianity," in *The Roots of the Egyptian Christianity*, eds. Birger A. Pearson and James E. Goehring, 307–19 (Philadelphia: Fortress Press, 1986); and W. Harmless, *Desert Christians: An Introduction to the Literature of Early Monasticism* (Oxford: Oxford University Press, 2004), 436–39. The claim is interesting and worth considering on its own merits, even if the search for origins may tend to be unduly territorial at times.

43. *Iliad* 24, 558–60; 583–85.

44. *Iliad* 24, 519–23, trans. R. Lattimore (Chicago: University of Chicago Press, 1951). All quotations from the *Iliad* are taken from this translation.

45. *Iliad* 24, 629–33.

46. *Aeneid* 12, 938–52.

47. See the assessment of W. R. Johnson (in *The Aeneid*, trans. S. Lombardo [Indianapolis, IN: Hackett, 2005]): "Whether by his own design or as a reflection of Rome's collective consciousness, countervailing its celebration of the warrior in triumph is the persistent memory of the outcast, the exile, who speaks with the voice of the dispossessed, of Trojan, not Roman, Aeneas" (lxx).

48. See also, for example, the series of contrasts between the cities at peace under justice and at war under terror wrought by the lame god, Hephaestus, on the shield of Achilles (*Iliad* 18), dominated finally by the dancing/threshing floor and the fearful, heroic purpose of the shield itself.

49. For different views of myth, see Price, 15–19; K. Corrigan/E. Glazov-Corrigan, *Plato's Dialectic at Play: Argument, Structure and Myth in the Symposium* (University Park: Pennsylvania State University Press, 2004), 220–24.

50. For comment on the commandment as a counsel of humility, see U. von Wilamowitz, *Der Glaube der Hellenen* (Berlin: Weidmannsche buchhandlung, 1932), 123.

51. *Apology* 21a ff.

52. See, e.g., Price, 117ff.

53. Ibid., 115–16.

54. Ibid., 153–54.

55. Livy, *History of Rome* 39, 9.4, 10.5–7, 13.8–14.

56. Price, 160.

57. See Hine, *Medea/Seneca*, 19–20.

58. Ibid., line 4—*profundi saeve dominator maris*—and page 112.

59. Ibid., l. 1027.

60. Ibid., 31–33.

61. Plato, *Euthyphro* 10c–11b.

62. See Werner Jaeger, *The Theology of the Early Greek Philosophers*, trans. from the German manuscript by Edward S. Robinson (Oxford: Oxford University Press, 1960 [1947]); and K. Corrigan, "Body and Soul in Ancient Religious Experience," 360–83. The notion of a kinship of soul across species boundaries is evidently of importance for a consideration of tolerance (e.g., in Xenophanes, fragment 7a West, Pythagoras upon seeing someone beating a puppy is reported to have said: "Stop. That is the soul of a friend of mine; I recognize the voice") as is also the notion of the World Soul of which we and all other things are parts.

63. Compare Hesiod, *Works and Days* 220–62; Solon 1, 1–32 (and discussed in H. Lloyd-Jones, *The Justice of Zeus* [Berkeley: University of California Press, 1971], 43–45); Aeschylus, *Agamemnon* 750–81; Sophocles, *Antigone* 449–70.

64. *Atopos*; see *Symposium* 221c.

65. *Apology* 29b.

66. Compare Protagoras, *Die Fragmente der Vorsokratiker*, 6th ed., 3 vols., Berlin, 1951–1952, eds., H. Diels and W. Kranz, 80 b1.

67. *Phaedrus* 279 b–c.

68. For Porphyry's version *De Abstinentia* 2.16, as Price observes (140, n. 38), from Theopompus, *Die Fragmente der griechischen Historiker*, eds. F. Jacoby, J. Engels, E. Theys (Leiden and Boston: Brill, 1998), 115F 344.

69. Berchman in this volume; Caseau in *Late Antiquity*, edited by Bowersock et al., 21ff.

70. Price, 82–88.

71. Ibid., 84; Andocides 1.12, 29, 31.

72. *Apology* 35d.

73. *Apology* 31c–d.

74. For the charges, see *Apology* 24b and ff.

75. P. Hadot, *Philosophy as a Way of Life: Spiritual Exercises from Socrates to Foucault* (*Exercices spirituelles*), trans. M. Chase (Oxford and Cambridge, MA: Blackwell, 1995).

76. *Iliad* 10, 224; Plato, *Protagoras*, 348d; *Symposium*, 174 d3.

77. For example, Diotima, the Mantinean stranger, in the *Symposium*, and the Eleatic and Athenian strangers in some of the later dialogues—*Sophist, Statesman, Laws*.

78. See especially Karl Popper, *The Open Society and Its Enemies,* Vol. 1: *The Spell of Plato* (Princeton, NJ: Princeton University Press, 1971)

79. See K. Corrigan, "'Solitary' Mysticism in Plotinus, Gregory of Nyssa, Proclus and Pseudo-Dionysius," *Journal of Religion* 76 (1996): 28–42.

80. *Phaedrus* 271 cff.

81. *Timaeus* 30 c.

82. *Timaeus* 29 e–30 a.

83. *Nichomachean Ethics* 6, chap. 7.

84. So, in Gregory of Nyssa's life of his sister Macrina, everyone sits down to eat at the *trapeza tes philosophias* (table of philosophia); see *Patrologia Graeca* 46.

85. Even for monastic usage in the fourth century CE, see now R. Sinkewicz, trans., *Evagrius of Pontus: The Greek Ascetic Corpus* (Oxford: Oxford University Press, 2003).

86. For a striking instance, see *Ennead* V 8, 7, 1–10.

87. See John D. Turner, "Ritual in Gnosticism," in *Gnosticism and Later Platonism*, ed. John D. Turner and Ruth Majercik (Atlanta: Society of Biblical Literature, 2000), 83–140.

88. For usage, see L. Ayres, *Nicea and Its Legacy* (Oxford: Oxford University Press, 2004).

89. In H. Coward and T. Foshay, eds., *Derrida and Negative Theology* (Albany: State University of New York Press, 1992).

90. Compare R. T. Wallis, *Neoplatonism*, 2nd ed. (London: Duckworth), 1995.

91. Price, 141.

92. After all, one of the characteristic features of a religious view is that it not be solely dependent upon external criteria of success or approval—that something should be worth doing either for God's approval or simply for itself—because it is the right or holy thing to do or more generally for the sake of another set of values or another life than the usual dictates of historical existence.

93. Compare Price.

94. Ibid., 140–41.

95. Ibid., 161–66.

96. A. H. Armstrong, "The Way and the Ways: Religious Tolerance and Intolerance in the Fourth Century A.D.," *Vigiliae Christianae* 38 (1984): 1–17.

97. Fragment 8, 13, *Des Places*.

98. For example, Christopher Dawson, *Progress and Religion* (Washington, DC: Catholic University of America Press, 2001); *The Gods of Revolution* (London: Sidgwick and Jackson, 1972); *The Formation of Christendom* (New York: Sheed and Ward1967), etc.; the dangers of such a view are, of course, that it may provide only a dominant or one-sided view of history, and it, therefore, can only be applied cautiously.

PART 4

CHRISTIANITY

6

TOLERANCE AND CONTROVERSY IN CLASSICAL CHRISTIANITY

The Gospel according to Matthew and Justin Martyr

BRUCE CHILTON

Christianity's classical sources emerged during a period of several hundred years after the writing of the New Testament. The early centuries of the Common Era saw the birth of a new religion separate from Judaism, with distinctive sacraments, creeds, and scriptures. Christians believed their theology made them globally different from others; Jewish observers and Roman magistrates agreed only too vociferously. By the second century, Christians called themselves a new or third race that transcended conventional differences between Jews and Greeks.[1]

Two common misunderstandings need to be avoided before we can map the resources of tolerance that Christianity developed during this crucial period.

First, the distinctive features characteristic of the new religion were not all in place at the end of the first century. The New Testament represents a transitional moment between the teachings of Jesus, who was firmly grounded in the Judaism of his time, and the faith in Jesus that produced a new religion. Once that transition was achieved, writings of the second century articulated characteristically Christian practices, institutions, and documents. Even the New Testament was only codified as a "standard" of scripture (a canon, from the Greek term *kanon*) during the second century. Before then, only the scriptures of Israel were canonical for those who believed in Jesus. So it stands to reason that we will not be able to consider Christian resources of tolerance unless we consider patristic literature, the writings of Christianity's theologians, called the "fathers (*patres* in Latin) of the Church," in addition to the New Testament.

The second misunderstanding directly impinges on the topic of tolerance. Throughout its classical period, Christianity was a minority movement, whether within the Roman Empire or within the Jewish population (in territorial Israel as well as in the Diaspora). Working with historical references, as well as with estimates from scholars and archaeologists, a sociologist has recently woven a plausible picture (complete with maps and graphs) of the demographic rise of Christianity through the fourth century.[2] He estimates the Christian population at some 15 percent of the Roman Empire by the time of Constantine (although I personally would make that number nearer to 10 percent at the beginning of the fourth century). Christianity's thought regarding tolerance was, therefore, in no sense mainline, and Christians had to deal with many different relationships with people more powerful than they, groups that did not share their faith. In order to address the topic, we need to be guided by representative New Testament and patristic sources that reflect these relationships.

Two such sources immediately suggest themselves.

The Gospel according to Matthew is by far the most frequently quoted of the Gospels within the classical period (and down to our day). Its first position in the New Testament is no coincidence but reflects Matthew's wide acceptance within the Catholic Church—that is, the Church taken as a whole (*katholikos*), throughout the Mediterranean world—during the second century and later. Of all the Gospels, Matthew is also the most concerned with social relations. The only Gospel that has Jesus use the word "church" (*ekklelsia),* Matthew deals in detail with issues of community discipline (including excommunication) and relations with those outside the community. The decision to consult Matthew in particular, therefore, comes as a matter of course.

During the second century, a philosopher from Samaria named Justin, who converted to Christianity, addressed an *Apology* to the reigning Roman emperor and engaged in a *Dialogue* with a Jewish interlocutor.[3] Justin's attempt to assure the acceptance, or at least the toleration, of Christianity did not succeed, in that he himself died a martyr. But his thought and approach became paradigmatic within patristic theology and at the same time addresses a range of groups that Christianity engaged over the issue of tolerance.

Matthew and Justin both show that Christians did not think of everyone not like them as representing the same kind of "other." The notion of the "other" (frequently capitalized) that has become fashionable in postmodernist theory presumes a dichotomy between self and other that is not applicable to most people in most times, and certainly not to Christians in the first centuries of their movement. As the work of Edward W. Said illustrates, the roots of the postmodernist usage *other* lie in existentialist and postcolonialist theory, both of which have their uses in particular contexts.[4] But in communities that do not think of themselves as collections of individuals and within societies that have no hegemonic share in power, *self* and *other* are by no means uniform concepts. Classical Christianity prior to its acceptance within the Roman Empire corresponds to this exception to postmodern theory: its view of itself was communal (specifically including possessions, for example), and its predicament was one of powerlessness until Constantine's Edict of Milan.

Fortunately, Matthew and Justin present comparable views of how Christians should relate to those who do not share their faith. Without deploying a dichotomist model of self and other, these documents set out three different types of relationship, each of which demands a particular kind of tolerance and discipline from believers. The adjustment given a community or individual toward those outside will differ dramatically, according to whether these outsiders are (1) persecutors, (2) disputants who use a common religious language to impugn the claims of the Church, or (3) people from another religious world altogether. The purpose of this paper is to set out the three types of relationship addressed by Matthew and Justin, to explain how these attitudes developed, and then to suggest ways in which an appreciation of all three—especially in their interactions among one another—*helps to explain the emergence of intolerance within Christianity.*

Persecutors and the Response of Witness

According to Matthew 5:38–48, Jesus commanded his followers to love their enemies (compare Luke 6:27–36):[5]

You heard that it was said, Eye for eye and tooth for tooth. Yet I say to you, Not to resist the evil one, but whoever cuffs you on your right cheek, turn to him the other as well. And to the one who wishes to litigate with you, even to take your tunic, leave him the cloak as well! And whoever requisitions you to journey one mile, depart with him two! Give to the one who asks you, and do not withhold from the one who wishes to borrow from you. You have heard that it was said, You shall love your neighbor and you shall hate your enemy. Yet I say to you, Love your enemies, and pray for those who persecute you, so you might become descendants of your father in heavens. Because he makes his sun dawn upon evil people and good people, and makes rain upon just and unjust. For if you love those who love you, what reward have you? Do not even the customs-agents do the same? And if you greet only your fellows, what do you do that goes beyond? Do not even the Gentiles do the same? You, then, shall be perfect, as your heavenly father is perfect.

Jesus calls for love of enemies without expectation of reward. But the pragmatic character of the demand makes his teaching all the more paradoxical. What is the source of his demand that enemies should be loved?

Jesus' teaching in this regard came into full focus during his last months in Jerusalem, although it has deep roots in his experience before that time. By uncovering those circumstances, we can appreciate the distinctiveness of his ethics. Despite his naiveté concerning the politics of Rome, and therefore the growing threat of execution at the hands of Pontius Pilate, Jesus knew that he courted danger during this period. The constant threat took a toll on his followers, as Jesus well knew. They actually had to be ready to give up wealth and family, to ruin their lives if necessary. The message that God's kingdom was to be all consuming, dissolving even Caesar's power, made it tolerable to bear the Romans' cross if necessary. Jesus speaks of doing that when he refers to his followers as a whole (Matthew 16:24–27), not only his own fate.

Both Jesus (who taught publicly between the death of John the Baptist in 21 CE and his own death in 32 CE) and Matthew (written in Damascus c. 80 CE) understood the threat of Roman soldiers, who were authorized to take what they needed from pilgrims and force them into labor. The teaching represented in Matthew 5:38–48 is not, as commonly supposed, a timeless adage against resistance to any and all injustice but a strategy of coping with soldiers who took what they needed, by violence if necessary. In the face of the Roman Empire's evil, retaliate with the good that provides by example the prospect that justice might prevail, as well as a chance of avoiding harm. Popular theology has persistently taken this teaching out of its original social context and made Jesus into a philosopher of blanket nonresistance. But his powerful wisdom speaks from the conditions he and the Matthean community faced. Mahatma Gandhi and Martin Luther King rightly saw that Jesus did not teach acquiescence to evil but an exemplary retaliation that shows evil up for what it truly is.

This teaching directly fed into Justin's conception of martyrdom. The term derives from the Greek term *martus*, which means a "witness," with *marturia* standing for the abstract noun (as in such English phrases as "giving witness" or "producing evidence"). But becoming a "witness" took on new significance as Roman law authorized the persecution of Christians simply for being Christians. In a correspondence during 111 CE with Pliny, governor of Bithynia and Pontus in Asia Minor, the Roman emperor Trajan confirms this policy.[6] Recognition of the gods of Rome (specifically by means of divine honors of incense and wine offered to the emperor's image) is all that should be required of those denounced as Christians. The ultimate question was not their faith or their religious practice as such, but whether they were loyal to the Roman Empire and emperor. They were given every incentive—including by the use of torture, if necessary—to renounce their former "atheism," the perceived danger in the Christian refusal to worship idols. They were killed for their stubbornness if they repeatedly refused to accede to the offer of clemency in exchange for their repentance.

Justin's *Apology* is, among other things, a brilliant assault on the legal logic involved in this sort of prosecution. Ordinarily, legal proceedings are designed to get criminals to confess their crimes, for which they are punished. In this case, however, no wrongdoing is admitted. Instead, one admits to being a Christian and then—by sacrificing to the emperor's image—abjures Christianity. Then, to compound the impression of some kind stage play, the magistrate buys this alleged repentance, showing just how vain a belief in idols is (*Apology* 3–14). Excoriating Rome for its equivalent of a "don't-ask-don't-tell" policy became the stock and trade of Christianity's apologists, especially Tertullian later in the second century. But Justin is the first prominent apologist (that is, defender of Christianity within the legal and philosophical setting of the Roman Empire), and he shows explicitly that the aim of martyrdom, as in Matthew's teaching of turning the other cheek, is the conversion of one's persecutor.

Dispute and the Response of Argument

In the nature of the case, Christianity developed from within Second Temple Judaism, and its emergence as an autonomous religion is marked by a series of disputes that take their terms of reference from Judaism. Over the course of time, these controversies framed a fresh system of belief, emotion, and practice. Argument, therefore, became a systemic concern, and Jesus' teaching in regard to resurrection provides a case in point.

Matthew, like Mark and Luke, presents Jesus' perspective as part and parcel of sharp controversy. Sadducees are portrayed as asking a mocking question of Jesus, designed to disprove the possibility of resurrection.[7] Because Moses commanded that, were a man to die childless, his brother should impregnate his widow for him, suppose there were seven brothers, the first of whom was married. If they all died childless in sequence, whose wife would the woman be in the resurrection (Matthew 22:23–28; compare Mark 12:18–23; Luke 20:27–33)?

Jesus' response is categorical and contentious (Matthew 22:29–32):

Jesus replied and said to them, You are deceived, knowing neither the Writings nor the power of God! Because in the resurrection they neither marry nor give in marriage, but are like angels in the heaven. But concerning the resurrection of the dead, have you not read what was said to you—by God—saying, I am the God of Abraham and the God of Isaac and the God of Jacob? He is not God of the dead, but of the living. The crowds heard and were overwhelmed by his teaching.

Of the two arguments Jesus uses, the one from scripture is the more immediately fitting in context, an appeal both to the nature of God and to the evaluation of the patriarchs in early Judaism. If God identifies himself with Abraham, Isaac, and Jacob, it must be that, in his sight, they live. And those three patriarchs—once we join in this analogical reflection—are indeed living principles of Judaism itself: they are Israel as chosen in the case of Abraham (see Genesis 15), as redeemed in the case of Isaac (see Genesis 22), and as struggling to identity in the case of Jacob (see Genesis 32). That evocation of patriarchal identity is implied, rather than demonstrated,[8] but the assumption is that the hearer is able to make such connections between the text of scripture and the fulfillment of that scripture within present experience.

Yet, that implicit logic of the argument from scripture only makes the other argument seem all the bolder by contrast. The direct comparison between people in the resurrection and angels is consonant with the thought that the patriarchs must live in the sight of God, since angels are normally associated with God's throne (so, for example, Daniel 7:9–14). So, once the patriarchs are held to be alive before God, the comparison with angels is feasible. But Jesus' statement is not only a theoretical assertion of the majesty of God, a majesty that includes the patriarchs (and, by extension, the patriarchs' comparability to the angels); it is also an emphatic claim of what we might call divine anthropology. Jesus asserts that human relations, the usual basis of human society and divisions among people (namely, sexual identity), are radically altered in the resurrection.[9] That claim of substantial regeneration and transcendence became a major theme among the more theological thinkers who followed Jesus, beginning with Paul.

But, especially as presented by Matthew, the victory of Jesus' logic implies the collapse of the Sadducees'. They are "deceived" as well as ignorant. Justin raised that attribution of ignorance to a new level. He argues systematically that the prophets, beginning with Moses and including David, attested Christ. The central meaning of the scriptures of Israel, according to this reading, was how God became man, not particular requirements or commandments. Justin sets his *Dialogue with Trypho, A Jew* in the period after the revolt under Simon called Bar Kokhba (*Dialogue* 1.3), which lasted between 132 and 135. Thematically, Justin disputes Trypho's conception of the permanent obligation of the law (chapters 1–47) and sees the purpose of scriptures in their witness to Christ's divinity (chapters 48–108), which Justin says justifies and indeed requires the extension of the divine covenant to gentiles (chapters 109–136). Trypho, therefore, is portrayed as arguing in agreement with the axiom of the Mishnah that the systemic meaning of the scriptures is the law, while Justin argues that their systemic meaning is Christ.

Justin spells out the structure of the prophetic tradition beginning with Moses more precisely in his *Apology* (32.1), insisting that "all we affirm to have learned from Christ and the prophets who preceded him is only truth" (23.1). He invokes Moses as the "first prophet," citing Genesis 49:10–11, Jacob's prophecy that the scepter of rule would not depart from Judah (*Apology* 32.1). By treating Moses in this way, as the author who gave voice to *Jacob's* (that is, Israel's) blessing and the agent of the prophetic Spirit (compare *Apology* 44), Justin can proceed through the prophets (Isaiah, above all) to speak of their reference to Christ and then focus on David's testimony—as both prophet and king—within the Psalms (*Apology* 40.1).

These extensive citations over a long run of chapters systematize the claim of the risen Jesus among the disciples in Luke 24:44 (compare v. 27) that "it was necessary for all the Scriptures to be fulfilled in the Law of Moses and the Prophets and the Psalms concerning me." A setting of communal instruction and worship, akin to the meetings of Christian worship as Justin briefly describes them (*Apology* 67.3), at which the apostles' memoirs or the writings of the prophets were read and studied, is the likely point of origin of Justin's christological tradition of reading the scriptures of Israel.

In concluding her penetrating reading of the *Dialogue*, Tessa Rajak suggests that ". . . it is perhaps not wholly far-fetched to suggest that the *Dialogue with Trypho*, though presented as an apologetic dialogue, is less a discussion than a Christian *pesher* on Isaiah and the other prophets."[10] Rajak is appropriately tentative in making this suggestion because the *Dialogue* does not comport with the genre of *pesher* ("interpretation") in providing a continuous commentary on Isaiah or any other prophet. But a similar technique is instanced in episodic exegeses of scripture also discovered at Qumran.

In a recent study of the usage of scripture attributed to James, the brother of Jesus, in Acts 15, namely, Amos 9:11, it has been pointed out that an analogy to the episodic usage of that passage by James is offered by the texts of Qumran designated *florilegia* by the editors. In one citation (in 4Q174 3:10–13), the image of the restoration of the encampment of David is associated with the promise to David in 2 Samuel 7:13–14 and with the Davidic "branch" (compare Isaiah 11:1–10), all taken in a messianic sense.

Given the expectation of a son of David as messianic king within early Judaism (see *Psalms of Solomon* 17:21–43), the messianic application of the passage in Amos, whether in (in 4Q174 3:10–13) or by James in Acts 15, is hardly strange. On the other hand, it is striking that the passage in Amos—particularly, "the fallen hut of David"—is applied in the *Damascus Document* (CD 7:15-17), not to a messianic figure but to the law that is restored. Clearly, neither Trypho nor the rabbis innovated the insistence that the prophets attested the Mosaic Law.

Indeed, the book of Amos itself makes Judah's contempt for the Torah into a pivotal issue (Amos 2:4) and calls for a program of seeking the LORD and his ways (Amos 5:6–15), so it is perhaps not surprising that "the seeker of the law" is predicted to restore it in the *Damascus Document*. Still, CD 7:15–20 directly refers to the "books of the Torah" as "the huts of the king," interpreted by means of the "fallen hut of David." Evidently, there is a precise correspondence between the strength of the Messiah and the establishment of the Torah, as is further suggested by the association with the seeker of the law *not only* in the *Damascus Document* but also in the *florilegium*. This kind of interpretation, although pursued to different ends, by means of briefer citations, and without a framing argument such as Justin's, offers a useful analogy to the treatment of scripture in the *Dialogue* as well as in the *Apology*.

The Essene interpretation and Justin evidently go their separate ways when it concerns the Torah. By insisting upon Moses' role as a prophet, indeed the first prophet, Justin contends with the portrait of Moses that animated rabbinic literature from the second century onward, where Moses appears preeminently as the giver of the Torah, both in writing and in the oral tradition of the sages. Justin does not engage rabbinic literature in any detail (even as interpreted in the *Mekilta*, the only second-century Midrash according to many critical estimates) and sometimes makes apparent errors in what he takes to be the practice of Judaism in his time. Yet he does know that he is confronting a Jewish *paradosis* ("tradition") unlike his own, and he warns Trypho away from it (*Dialogue* 38.2, 120.5), while maintaining his own ground within a setting of traditional learning (*Second Apology* 10.1–2).[11] The particular passage that Justin uses to make his case is quite striking because rabbinic interpretation in its most popular form during the second century—as represented in the Targumim, designed for usage within synagogues—also understood Genesis 49:10–11 as a messianic prophecy.[12] In that choice, as in his argument as a whole, Justin insists that the Christians and the Jews cannot both be correct in their interpretations.

People from Another Religious World and the Response of Inclusion

As contrasted with the modern assumption that Christianity is a religion for non-Jews, Jesus' encounter northwest of Galilee with a gentile woman highlights the ingrained prejudice and xenophobia that he shared with most rural Jews (Matthew 15:21–28). While Jesus was staying in a house in that area, trying to escape Herod Antipas' attempt to kill him, a woman described as Syro-Phoenician in Mark 7:24–30 (that is, an Aramaic-speaking non-Jew who came from the ancient coastal region of Phoenicia in present-day Lebanon) found him. Matthew underscores the woman's foreign pedigree by calling her a "Canaanite" (Matthew 15:22), referring to a group that, according to the Torah, was to be removed from the land of Israel, and by having Jesus insist he was sent only to "the lost sheep of the house of Israel" (15:24). She asked Jesus to exorcise her daughter from an unclean spirit. He refused, "It is not good to take the bread of the children and throw it to the dogs" (Matthew 15:26).

He had rebuffed her with the brutal comparison of female gentiles to dogs. Expressing that sentiment in gentile territory was asking for trouble. And the woman gave it to him, and very much to the point; the verbal victory went to her, at the expense of Jesus (Matthew 15:27): "But she said, Indeed, Lord: even the dogs eat from the scraps which fall from the table of their lords."

The contrast with the story of the centurion in Capernaum (Matthew 8:5–13) is eloquent. The woman's location, her designation as a non-Jew with no evident interest in Judaism, as well as her sex and that of her daughter, all show that she was impure in ways the centurion was not. Yet her instinct to accept any help Jesus might give was stronger even than his reactive refusal of her; he relented and agreed to deal with her daughter's unclean spirit.

Although the Gospels present Jesus as a rabbi whose teachings developed over time, early Christians from the second century onward believed their faith was based on eternal truths concerning the Son of God, truths that went beyond issues of the Jesus of history. For that reason, Christianity can only be understood when the eternity of Christ and Christ's capacity to make himself

known from the beginning of creation to people who could not have known
Jesus in his historical circumstances are fully taken into account. The fathers
of the Church could even adopt Plato as one of their own.

Justin argued insistently that the prophets inspired the best of Greek philosophy. In taking Moses as a prophetic figure, of course, Justin had aligned
himself with the portrait of Philo, and that alignment bears fruit. Like Philo
(*De aeternitate mundi* 17–19), Justin believes that Plato imitated Genesis in
the *Timaeus* (*Apology* 59–60).[13] His statement of the analysis is actually more
aggressive than Philo's (44.9):

Whatever both the philosophers and poets said concerning the immortality of the
soul or punishments after death or about perception of things heavenly or similar
doctrines they were able to understand and explain because they borrowed the essential features from the Prophets.

This perspective is by no means limited to cosmological issues, but specifically includes ethics (44:8): "So when Plato said, 'The responsibility of choice
is for him who makes it, God is not responsible,' he took it from the prophet
Moses."

The paucity of explicit reference to Philo in Justin has troubled some commentators,[14] but it should be kept in mind that Justin is sometimes least
explicit when he is most influenced by other literary sources. He paraphrases
the satire against those who make idols (*Apology* 9), for example, without citing its source in Isaiah 44 or its repetition in Acts 17. Justin explicitly writes as
a philosopher[15] and, for that reason, absorbs literary influences more than he
cites them. Citation is not routine; scripture is specified when there is a matter of doubt or Justin believes the scriptural meaning is deeper than a literary
motif.

Justin famously portrays Socrates as executed for his opposition to idols
(*Apology* 5.3–4), so close is the fit between the prophets and Greek sages. To
Justin's mind, a rejection of *eidolothuta* (food sacrificed to idols) remains a
constitutive feature of faith in Jesus (*Dialogue* 24), as was the case of James'
teaching, according to Acts 15:19–21. That agreement with the apostolic decree
is striking because Justin goes very much his own way as compared to James
when it comes to circumcision.

The comparison between Philo and Justin shows the extent to which Judaism in the first century and Christianity in the second century relied upon the
revival of Platonism to provide them with a way of expressing how their respective religions were philosophically the most appropriate. The Platonic picture
of perfect intellectual models was their common axiom, invoked in Philo's
rhythmic, elegant Greek and in Justin's controversial, rhetorical Greek. One

can easily imagine a debate between Philo and Justin. Had it occurred, that would have been an encounter between Judaism and Christianity in antiquity on philosophical terrain that they both claimed and with which both were comfortable. Had they met and disputed, Judaism and Christianity would have been represented as approximate equals on a level playing field.

But that meeting never happened. Not only one hundred years divided what were by then two different religions,[16] but watershed events did as well. The Temple in Jerusalem had been burned under Titus in 70 CE and dismantled at Hadrian's order in 135. Judaism was still tolerated in a way Christianity was not, but it was now under suspicion, the remnant of a destroyed nation that had rebelled, and it needed to reconstitute itself as a postnational and postcultic religion in the wake of the failed revolts against Rome that resulted in the double destruction of the Temple.

The rabbis who invented a new form of Judaism during the second century did so not on the basis of Platonism but on grounds of a fresh intellectual contention. They held that the categories of purity established in their oral teaching, as well as in scripture, were the very structures according to which God created and conducted the world. The Mishnah, the principal work of the rabbis, is less a book of law (which it is commonly mistaken for) than a science of the purity that God's humanity—that is, Israel—is to observe.[17]

So complete was the rabbinic commitment to systematic purity at the expense of Platonism, Philo's own work was not preserved within Judaism but only became known as a result of the work of Christian copyists. And the very philosophical idiom that the rabbis turned from as a matter of survival—apologetic argument—was what Justin turned to, also as a matter of survival.

Dangerous Hybrids: Making Tolerance Intolerant

Perhaps it was inevitable that, within the New Testament and patristic literature, the target of one kind of tolerance should be confused with another. Matthew instances this phenomenon when, in the context of discussing excommunicating a person from the Church, Jesus advises his followers that "he will be to you as a Gentile and a customs-agent!" (Matthew 18:17). In this case, however, because the disputant has put himself into the position of someone from another religious world (the third case above) by refusing the discipline of the Church, the principle of tolerance established in the story of the Canaanite woman does not apply. By making a hybrid of two principles of tolerance, intolerance is produced.

A cognate but more dramatic hybrid, that of disputant and rank outsider, is evident in the treatment of Jews in Matthew. This Gospel proves inventive in attributing to Jews blame for Jesus' death, although crucifixion was a uniquely Roman punishment in the time of Jesus. Nonetheless, Jews willingly call down responsibility for shedding Jesus' blood on themselves *and their children*, and this after Pilate—the only person with authority to order the execution—has washed his hands of guilt (Matthew 27:24–25). Matthew also passes on the legend of Pilate's wife (27:19), although prefects of Pilate's rank were not authorized to bring their wives on posting. In any case, Pilate and his entourage resided in Caesarea, not Jerusalem. Matthew is sensitive to the latter fact and has the wife "send" a message to Pilate.

Justin pursues the removal of Jews from the field of tolerance by insisting that the prophets forecast the transfer of the prophetic Spirit from Israel to Christians. In his recent study of the Binding of Isaac (interpretations of Genesis 22), Edward Kessler has characterized Justin as illustrating "a pervasive patristic supersessionist teaching, which is known as the doctrine of replacement theology."[18] The basis of this teaching, however, as Kessler clearly indicates, is not a claim about the standing of one community in relation to another but an analysis of prophecy. As Justin says (*Dialogue* 29.2, see also 32.2):

For these words have neither been prepared by me, nor ornamented by human art; but David sang them, Isaiah evangelized them, Zechariah proclaimed them, and Moses wrote them. Are you acquainted with them, Trypho? They are contained in your Scriptures, or rather not yours, but ours. For we are persuaded by them; but you, though you read them, do not recognize the mind that is in them.

At its theological foundation, Justin's "supersessionism" is no greater than Paul's, who offered an analysis of the obscured reading of scripture among Jews (2 Corinthians 3:12–18)[19] that has clearly influenced Justin here as much as Paul's teaching of the "mind" of Christ (1 Corinthians 2:16).

In his *Dialogue*, Justin portrays Trypho as being limited to the immediate reference of scripture, enslaved by its specification of laws. Justin is committed to a typological reading of scripture, the Christian norm during the second century. The prophets were understood to represent "types" of Christ, impressions on their minds of the heavenly reality, God's own son. Trypho, by contrast, is portrayed as becoming lost in the immediate minutiae of the prophetic text. So prevalent was this understanding of Judaism by the end of the century that Christians such as Clement of Alexandria and Tertullian called any limitation to the immediate reference of scripture (its "literal meaning") the "Jewish sense."

Justin presents the shift in the possession of the Spirit that animates the scripture, moreover, in a way Paul does not. While Paul famously still hopes that "all Israel will be saved" (Romans 11:26), Justin is categorical—by means of Isaiah 51:4 and Jeremiah 31:31—that "there is to be an ultimate Law and Covenant superior to all, which now must be kept by all people who claim God's inheritance" (*Dialogue* 11.2–3). This eternal covenant (Isaiah 55:3–4) establishes who is a true, spiritual Israelite and Judaite and who is not (*Dialogue* 11.5), taking the place of all other aspirants to those names. As Philippe Bobichon has said, "*nous ne sommes plus dans une logique d'accomplissement (comme dans le Nouveau Testament), mais de substitution.*"[20] (We are no longer within the logic of fulfillment [as in the New Testament], but of substitution.) Bobichon makes plain that supersession and replacement are not one and the same. The way in which Justin makes the transition from one to the other is instructive and prepares the way for yet another move.

The periodization of prophecy is the key to Justin's position in this regard. In taking this position, I take a different view from those who attempt to explain Justin on the basis of a periodization of scripture. Philippe Bobichon attempts such a reading, arguing that "*[p]our l'Apologiste, precepts <<éternels>> (destiné à toute l'humanité) et preceptes de la Loi (reservés à Israël) entretiennent un rapport d'inclusion: ils eminent du même Dieu et s'inscrivent dans une même économie salvatrice.*"[21] (For the Apologist, "eternal" precepts [intended for all humanity] and precepts of the Law [reserved for Israel] together foster a relationship of inclusion: they derive from a single God and are inscribed in a single economy of salvation.) That "inclusive" reading is accurate, it seems to me, but its generative term of reference is "the prophetic Spirit" in Justin, rather than being determined by the nature of particular texts or a specific view of salvation history.

Bobichon's reading represents a simplification of the argument of Theodore Stylianopoulos, who argues that Justin divides scripture into "(1) ethics, (2) prophecy, and (3) historical dispensation."[22] Treating scripture as conditional indeed permits Justin to get out of the force of Trypho's observation that Jesus kept the law (*Dialogue* 67.5–6), but that is because the whole of scripture is prophetic, so that any part of it might prove to be binding or to be conditional in the light of what attests to Christ. For that reason, a "ritual" requirement—such as avoiding *eidolothuta*—might remain crucial, while an "ethical" requirement—such as leaving part of a field unharvested for the benefit of the poor (which receives treatment in an entire tractate of the Mishnah)—might receive no emphasis.

Basic to Justin's view of prophecy are the Gospels' portrayal of John the

Baptist as the successor of the prophets and Justin's claim that prophecy came to an end after Jesus' death (*Dialogue* 51.1–52.1–4). The former theme, of course, is taken directly from the Gospels (Luke 16:16; Matthew 11:13), but the latter idea is also attested—and in surprising sources. From the time of 1 Maccabees (4:46), Jewish teachers had held that the era of prophecy had come to an end, so that the time had come to await a prophet; and this notion is specifically endorsed by rabbinic literature during the second century and later as part of the explanation for the destruction of the Temple.[23] Although no connection is made to Jesus, the Talmud also dates portents of the Temple's demise to the period "forty years years before the destruction of the Temple" (Bavli, Yoma 39b; compare Yerushalmi, Sota 6:13). As in the case of his messianic exegesis and his recourse to arguments reminiscent of Philo's, Justin appears to adapt motifs of Judaism available to him.

His purpose, however, goes beyond the supersession or even the replacement of Judaism. Justin appears clearly to believe that, with the defeat of Bar Kokhba, Judaism is coming to an end. Referring again to Genesis 49 (this time, v. 8), Justin declares that there will be two comings of Christ, "that in the first he would be suffering, and that after his coming there would be neither prophet nor king in your race, and—I added—that the Gentiles who believe in the suffering Christ will expect his coming again" (*Dialogue* 52.1). Once these sufferings of Christ had been accomplished,[24] Israel no longer had a place, which is the reason Isaiah predicts the devastation of Judea (*Apology* 47) as well as the conversion of the gentiles (49) and the reason— finally—even the seal of the covenant in Genesis 17 itself, as Rodney Werline has explained, is completely reinterpreted (citing *Dialogue* 16): "For Justin, then, circumcision is the sign for the recent historical national disaster for the Jews."[25] To this extent, Justin stands not simply for supersession or replacement but for the elimination of Israel as commonly understood on the basis of the prophetic Spirit. Now "[t]hose who justify themselves and say they are children of Abraham will desire to inherit along with us even a little place, as the Holy Spirit cries aloud by Isaiah [a citation of 63:15 follows]" (*Dialogue* 25.1; compare 55.3).

The "Spirit of prophecy" is precisely what Targum Jonathan to the prophets, largely extant during the second century, said would return to Israel in the mouths of the prophets at the end of time.[26] Justin's reply—echoing targumic language—is that "the prophetic Spirit" has already made its move. He produces a hermeneutic of Christian experience out of Jesus' prophecy in Matthew, that "the kingdom of God shall be taken from you and given to a nation producing its fruit" (Matthew 21:43), as well as the declaration of Paul and Barnabas that, having attempted to speak to the Jews in Pisidian Antioch, "we turn to the Gentiles" (13:36). The speech of Paul in Pisidian Antioch bears comparison with Justin's approach to scripture and the range of texts cited. At the same time, when Paul and Barnabas make their claim, they do so as envoys of the Holy Spirit (13:2).

Prophecy as a contemporary phenomenon is an emphatic theme of Luke–Acts, and it is a major aspect of Justin's argument (*Dialogue* 88). Indeed, Justin becomes so enthusiastic in his argument that he makes false prophecy among Christians into an argument that the Spirit is among them (*Dialogue* 82). Christian failings, on this reading, become stronger than Jewish virtues. In an attempt to save Justin from his own trenchancy, Sylvain Sanchez has argued that there were, after all, other forms of Judaism in the second century that Justin does not mention.[27] Given what he says about any form of Judaism he can think of, that was their good fortune.

Christianity after Constantine was, therefore, not innovative in becoming anti-Judaic. Intolerance, understood here as a distortion of principles of tolerance, simply armed itself during that period. Prominent Christian leaders not only embraced a model of state-sanctioned religion but also pressed to extend its reach to permit orthodox Christians to attack their competitors.

In addressing the Emperor Theodosius, Bishop Ambrose of Milan most clearly expresses the emergent attitude toward Judaism and Jews, whom he wants treated as if they were heretics (that is, disputants). Far to the east of Ambrose, in Callinicum on the Euphrates, the local bishop had encouraged the plunder and arson of a synagogue. Concerned by such behavior as a breach of public order, Theodosius directed that the bishop rebuild the synagogue at his own expense. Ambrose's response, in a letter of December 388 CE, is infamous, but its argument is worth more than the general characterization it usually receives (Epistle 40.8):

This, I ask, Emperor: that you turn your vengeance upon me, and, if you consider this act a crime, that you impute it to me. Why order the absent to be punished? I am present here before you, and confess my guilt. I proclaim that I set the synagogue on fire, or at least ordered others to do so, that there might not be left a building in which Christ is denied. If you ask me why I have not burned the synagogue in my neighborhood, I answer that its destruction has already been begun by the judgment of God, and my work was at an end.

F. Homes Dudden, a sympathetic biographer, goes on to describe the "really astounding perversity" of Ambrose's argument, where he says that, since similar actions had been taken against churches under the emperor Julian, the burning of a synagogue could also be overlooked. To Dudden's mind, the whole incident is an example of "how religious prejudice could so warp the judgment of a good and wise man as to cause him to condone the crimes of robbery and arson, and actually plead the unpunished outrages of brutal mobs and heathen persecutors as precedents for pardoning fanatical Christian criminals."[28]

Dudden wrote during a time that brought all too salient examples of the atrocities that Ambrose's argument and attitude warranted. He explains that "unbalanced zeal" on the part of Ambrose "induced him to step outside his proper province, and inflict an undeserved humiliation on a monarch who was doing his best." To Dudden's mind, the whole business was "surprising."[29] Undue enthusiasm has been the diagnosis of many religious ills since the eighteenth century, but "zeal" as such has been considered a virtue during most of the history of Christianity. It only becomes a problem when its purpose turns destructive, and religious arson is without question a good example of that. The real culprit in this argument is not Ambrose's zeal or some defect of his temperament, a momentary loss of self-control, or a lapse in his sense of propriety or law. Ambrose clearly believes that setting fire to synagogues is not a bad thing to do.

What shapes Ambrose's attitude is his sense of history, his conviction that the judgment of God—unfolding historically since the conversion of Constantine, as Eusebius taught—was against all those who heard the scriptures of Israel read every week and yet did not turn to Christ. Behavior such as the mob's at Callinicum, from his point of view, simply helps God's will along. By his own testimony, he would have done the same thing in Milan, except the synagogue there was already on the way out.[30]

For Ambrose, Theodosius is emperor for the service of true religion to which the maintenance of civil law is secondary (Epistle 40.11). That general point of view permitted him to make an argument on behalf of the Christian arson when he preached in Theodosius' presence on this subject. "In plain words, honor the least of Christ's disciples and pardon their faults, that the angels may rejoice, that the apostles may exult, that the prophets may be glad."[31] The means chosen for removing the synagogue were imperfect, but that did not make it any less divine will in history. Finally, Ambrose argues for the tolerance of intolerance when it is in a good cause.

In Ambrose's case, as in Eusebius', the union of the Roman Empire and the Catholic Church signals a fundamental change in the order of social experience and conduct. Judaism is now treated as a peculiar, passing problem, which history is in the process of resolving on behalf of the Church. That shows how powerful and how political the Christian conception of history could be. Within this context, we can understand Lee McDonald's observation that "[s]ome of the most intense Christian writers against the Jews (Aphrahat, Ephraem, Chrysostom, Cyril of Alexandria, and even Augustine of Hippo) are from the fourth and fifth centuries, when the Jews were still active in proselytizing Gentiles and having significant successes among the Christian population."[32] The issue, however, is not merely competition with a perceived "heresy" in itself, which had been the perennial environment of the primitive Church and the early Church. For the Orthodox and Catholic Church, the very existence of Judaism, whether conceived of as offering heretical options within Christianity or as a social entity outside the Church, was at best to be tolerated only until the work of history was done.

In order to frame the issue of Judaism and of heresy in this way, teachers of the Church practiced selective tolerance. They made all Jews the equivalent of Sadducees and then tolerated unruly mobs who attacked Jews, so that the religion that found its voice during a period of sustained martyrdom condoned persecution. What permitted that distortion was not just a matter of violent temperament or deep prejudice or the abuse of power (all of which were plentiful). At a systemic level, what was more important was the theological mistake that promoted a willingness (a) to trade one kind of tolerance against another and (b) to take three distinctive kinds of teaching in regard to tolerance, designed for differing groups of people, and reduce them to a social policy regarding a single "other" that was more the construct of the persecutors than the expressed identity of those they persecuted. If Christianity were guided by canonical and patristic sources, it would have insisted then and would insist now upon all three principles of tolerance as irreducible and on the enduring requirement to come to terms with the reality of official resistance, of religious disputes, and of encounter with people whose experience seems foreign to our own, as intrinsic aspects of living in a disunited world.

Notes

1. See *The Epistle to Diognetus* 1. Of course, this claim to transcend racial boundaries did not prevent ethnic and racial constructions of the religion; see Denise Kimber Buell, *Why This New Race? Ethnic Reasoning in Early Christianity* (New York: Columbia University Press, 2005).

2. Rodney Stark, *Cities of God: The Real Story of How Christianity Became an Urban Movement and Conquered Rome* (San Francisco: HarperCollins, 2006). Although evocative, I have criticized Stark's findings for their generality; see Bruce Chilton, *Abraham's Curse: Legacies of Child Sacrifice* (New York: Doubleday, 2008).

3. See the chronology of Miroslav Marcovich, *Iustini Martyris Dialogus Cum Tryphone:*

Patrische Texte und Studien (Berlin: de Gruyter, 1997), 1. He places the *Dialogue* during the period 155–160, after the *Apology*, c. 150–155. I follow his Greek text of the *Dialogue*; as well as the two volumes of Philippe Bobichon, *Justin Martyr. Dialogue avec Tryphon. Édition critique:* Paradosis 47.1, 2 (Fribourg: Academic Press, 2003). For the *Apology*, I follow André Wartelle, *Saint Justin. Apologies. Introduction, Texte Critique, Traduction, Commentaire et Index* (Paris: Études Augustiniennes, 1987), who places the *First Apology* in 153–154 (p. 35) and the *Second Apology* shortly thereafter.

4. See Edward W. Said, *Orientalism* (New York: Pantheon, 1978).

5. For a consideration of the social conditions and historical circumstances in Jesus' experience that this teaching reflects, see Bruce Chilton, *Rabbi Jesus: An Intimate Biography* (New York: Doubleday, 2000), 46, 197–289.

6. This Pliny is called "the Younger," to distinguish him from his uncle and adoptive father, a famed historian and naturalist. See Pliny, *Letters*, The Loeb Classical Library, trans. William Melmoth and W. M. L. Hutchinson (London: Heinemann, 1923); Betty Radici, *The Letters of Pliny the Younger* (London: Penguin, 1969).

7. Acts 23:8 makes out that the Sadducees deny resurrection altogether, and that is also the judgment of Josephus. I have argued that, despite these unequivocal statements (or, rather, precisely because they are so unequivocal), we should be cautious about what the Sadducees denied; see Bruce Chilton, *The Temple of Jesus: His Sacrificial Program within a Cultural History of Sacrifice* (University Park: Pennsylvania State University Press, 1992), 82. The Sadducees' position is attributed to them only by unsympathetic observers, such as Josephus (*The Jewish War* 2 §165–166) and various Christians (Mark 12:18–27; Matthew 22:23–33; Luke 20:27–38; Acts 23:6–8).

8. For Jesus' characteristic attitude toward scripture, see Bruce Chilton, *A Galilean Rabbi and His Bible: Jesus' Use of the Interpreted Scripture of His Time* (Wilmington, DE: Glazier, 1984); also published with the subtitle, *Jesus' Own Interpretation of Isaiah* (London: SPCK, 1984).

9. It is commonly asserted that Jesus accorded with accepted understandings of resurrection within Judaism; see Pheme Perkins, *Resurrection: New Testament Witness and Contemporary Reflection* (London: Chapman, 1984), 75.

10. Tessa Rajak, "Talking at Trypho: Christian Apologetic as Anti-Judaism in Justin's *Dialogue with Trypho the Jew*," in *The Jewish Dialogue with Greece and Rome: Studies in Cultural and Social Interaction*, 511–533, Arbeiten zur Geschichte des antiken Judentums und des Urchristentums XLVIII (Leiden: Brill, 2001), 531.

11. See Theodore Stylianopoulos, *Justin Martyr and the Mosaic Law*, Society of Biblical Literature Dissertation Series 20 (Missoula, MT: Scholars Press, 1975), 50, who thinks that, because Justine was a Samaritan, he believed tassels were scarlet rather than blue (*Dialogue* 46.5) and that hot water should not be drunk on the Sabbath (19.3 [sic! this is 29.3]). It seems risky, however, to base an argument about Justin's thought on his Samaritan background, both because second-century Samaritanism is not a known quantity (see Reinhard Pummer, *The Samaritans*, Iconography of Religions 23.5 [Leiden: Brill, 1987]) and because it is not even clear that Justin had been a Samaritan by anything but race. Tessa Rajak reads *Dialogue* 29 to mean that Justin had been a pagan, so that the term *genos* should only be understood of his people (120), not his thought; Rajak, "Talking at Trypho," 512. In a brief but helpful treatment, Peter Philhofer, "Von Jakobus zu Justin. Lernen in den spätschriften des Neues Testaments und bei den Apologeten," in *Religiöse Lernen in der biblischen, fruuhjüdischen und frühchristlichen Überlieferung*, Wissenschaftliche Untersuchungen zum Neuen Testament 180,

eds. Beate Ego and Helmut Merkel, 253–269 (Tübingen: Mohr Siebeck, 2005), 265, states: "*Justin sieht sich in einter Schultradition: Er hat eine Lehre empfagen, die er seinerseits nun weitergibt.*" ("Justin sees himself in the tradition of a school: he has received teaching, which he in turn hands on.")

12. See Bernard Grossfeld and Moses Aberbach, *Targum Onqelos on Genesis 49: Translation and Analytic Commentary*: SBL Aramaic Studies 1 (Missoula, MT: Scholars Press, 1976). Grosffeld was an early advocate of what has since become a consensus, that the earliest Targumim represent Judaism during the second century, not only within rabbinic discussion but as that discussion was intended to influence popular practice and belief; see Bruce Chilton, "The Targumim and Judaism of the First Century," *Judaism in Late Antiquity. Part Three, Where We Stand: Issues and Debates in Ancient Judaism* (volume two), Handbuch der Orientalistik 41, ed. J. Neusner and A. J. Avery-Peck, 15–150 (Leiden: Brill, 1999).

13. Justin also uses this argument as a weapon in his dispute with Marcion. The theme as a whole is explored in J. C. M. Van Winden, *An Early Christian Philosopher: Justin Martyr's Dialogue with Trypho chapters one to nine. Introduction, Text and Commentary:* Philosophia patrum (Leiden: Brill, 1971).

14. Bobichon, *Justin Martyr*, I.81–82.

15. Wartelle, *Saint Justin*, 246, cites the same theme among other apologists, as well as writers in the classical tradition.

16. See Bruce Chilton and Jacob Neusner, *Judaism in the New Testament: Practices and Beliefs* (London and New York: Routledge, 1995).

17. To this extent, the rabbinic project is more Aristotelian than Platonic; see Jacob Neusner, *The Theology of the Oral Torah: Revealing the Justice of God* (Montreal: McGill-Queen's University Press, 1999).

18. Edward Kessler, *Bound by the Bible: Jews, Christians and the Sacrifice of Isaac* (Cambridge: Cambridge University Press, 2004), 19.

19. On the necessary element of supersessionism in Paul, see Bruce Chilton. *Rabbi Paul: An Intellectual Biography* (New York: Doubleday, 2004).

20. Philippe Bobichon, *Justin Martyr*, Paradosis 47.1, 2. On the phrase, "*la race israélite (israèlitikon genos) véritable, spirituelle*," see Bernard Meunier, "Le clivage entre Juifs et chrétiens vu part Justin (vers 150)," in *Le Judaïsme à l'aube de l'ère chrétienne. XVIIIe congres de l'ACFEB (Lyon, September, 1999)*, Lectio Divina 186, eds. Philippe Abadie and Jean-Pierre Lémonon, 333–344 (Paris: du Cerf, 2004), 336. This leads to his conclusion (344): "*le judaisme est à la rigueur hébergé par le chrétiens, ce n'est en aucun case l'inverse.*" (Judaism is ultimately hosted by the Christians, and in no case the reverse.)

21. See Philippe Bobichon, "Préceptes éternels de la Loi mosaïque et le *Dialogue avec Tryphon* de Justin Martyr," *Revue Biblique* 111.2 (2004): 238.

22. Stylianopoulos, *Justin Martyr and the Mosaic Law*, 55.

23. Peter Schäfer, *Die Vorstellung vom heiligen Geist in der rabbinischen Literatur*, Studien zum Alten und Neuen Testament 28 (München: Kösel, 1972).

24. A probable awareness of the Birkhat ha-Minim causes Justin to reinterpret Galatians 3:10 in *Dialogue* 95–6. As Judith Lieu, "Accusations of Jewish Persecution in Early Christian Sources, with Particular Reference to Justin Martyr and the *Martyrdom of Polycarp*," *Tolerance and Intolerance in Early Judaism and Christianity*, eds. Graham N. Stanton and Guy G. Stroumsa, 279–295 (Cambridge: Cambridge University Press, 1998), 291, says: "On the one hand, the scriptural 'cursed be everyone who hangs on a tree' anticipates how the Jews would

treat both Christ and Christians, yet, on the other, it also sets into sharp relief the Christian response of steadfastness and forgiveness. . . ."

25. Rodney Werline, "The Transformation of Pauline Arguments in Justin Martyr's *Dialogue with Trypho*," *Harvard Theological Review* 92, no. 1 (1999): 90.

26. See Bruce Chilton, "Prophecy in the Targumim," in *Mediators of the Divine: Horizons of Prophecy, Divination, Dreams and Theurgy in Mediterranean Antiquity*, South Florida Studies in the History of Judaism 163, ed. R. M. Berchman (Atlanta: Scholars Press, 1998), 185–201.

27. Sylvain Jean Gabriel Sanchez, *Justin Apologiste Chrétien*, Cahiers de la Revue Biblique 50 (Lyon, France: Edition Gabalda, 2000), 253.

28. F. Homes Dudden, *The Life and Times of St. Ambrose*, vol. II (Oxford: Clarendon, 1935) 371–379, 378.

29. Ibid., 379.

30. Commentators frequently surmise that the synagogue had been struck by lightning, but it was more the victim of history, with or without natural collaboration.

31. Ambrose recounts this sermon in a letter to his sister Marcellina (*Epistle* 41.26), which was also written in December of 388 CE.

32. See Lee Martin McDonald, "Anti-Judaism in the Early Church Fathers," in *Anti-Semitism and Early Christianity: Issues of Polemic and Faith*, ed. C. A. Evans and D. A. Hagner (Minneapolis: Fortress, 1993), 217; and Leonard Rutgers, *The Hidden Heritage of Diaspora Judaism* (Leuven, Belgium: Peters, 1998).

7

ROMAN CATHOLIC UNDERSTANDING OF RELIGIOUS TOLERANCE IN MODERN TIMES

The Second Vatican Council (Vatican II)

WILLIAM REISER, S.J.

The major questions that Catholic theologians will be reflecting on during the twenty-first century will most likely come as a result of Christianity's interface with the other major world religious traditions. The twentieth century brought Catholic theology, uneasily but irreversibly—and eventually with some intellectual relief—into modern historical consciousness.[1] Nearly every aspect of the Catholic Church's life and teaching has been rethought in terms of extensive archaeological, cultural, linguistic, and historical research. In light of the forces for globalization that have been increasingly at work in human societies, questions relating to Christian belief and practice are being raised in a mental environment quite different from anything we have seen since, perhaps, the ancient church moved from a Palestinian to a Hellenistic cultural context and religious thought-world.[2] The issues of religious tolerance, dialogue, and cooperation are not merely inescapable; they belong to what Pope John XXIII referred to, in positive terms, as "the signs of the times."[3] In order to understand Catholic thinking about religious tolerance at the present time, one needs to turn to the Second Vatican Council, often referred to as "Vatican II."

Sources

Because of their high level of teaching authority, anyone who wants to know what the Roman Catholic community thinks and believes about a particular issue must take into account the church councils.[4] Scripture is considered to be the starting point for theological reflection; the councils belong to the church's tradition and mark stages in the unfolding of the biblical revelation. Yet although conciliar teaching is authoritative, it would be misleading to think of it as incapable of further development. The way the Catholic Church understands and then presents its message, its mission, and even its identity is necessarily affected by the historical and cultural settings in which it finds itself. Theological understanding, like every other exercise of the human mind, cannot circumvent historical process or escape the limitations of perspective that time and space impose.

Throughout the history of the Catholic Church there have been numerous provincial or regional councils or "synods," but the Western church also recognizes twenty-one universal or "ecumenical" councils—assemblies with representation from all the local churches or dioceses. The Second Vatican Council (1962–65) was an ecumenical council; its character and importance for Catholic life and thought, for theology and pastoral practice, cannot be overestimated.[5] The sixteen conciliar documents of Vatican II constitute the most authoritative voice to date with respect to many aspects of Catholic teaching; and yet, even though the council clarified and updated church teaching, the work of theology has continued. In the matter of the Catholic Church's thinking about the world religions, viewed as mediators of divine presence, we might do well to think of a theological trajectory. The council could not have settled once and for all the relationship between Christian faith and the other religions because, among other things, all the relevant questions have not yet surfaced. Nevertheless, the council acknowledged the existence of the religions and saw them in a positive light. The fact of their existence thus forces theologians to ask whether (and if so, how) they fit into a scheme of providential design. The creation of a mature theology of world religions is going to take some time.

The principal Vatican II documents for our topic are the Declaration on the Church's Relation to Non-Christian Religions (*Nostra aetate*) and the Declaration on Religious Freedom (*Dignitatis humanae*). Two further documents, the Decree on Ecumenism (*Unitatis redintegratio*) and the Decree on the Missionary Activity of the Church (*Ad gentes*), as well as a section (nos. 13–16) from the Dogmatic Constitution on the Church (*Lumen gentium*), should also be taken into account. These documents proceed from a faith-conviction, a spiritual vision about human origins, that guides the Catholic Church's assessment of the other world religions. Let me explain what this faith-conviction is.

How the Different Religions Are Understood

For the Catholic community, God created the human race as one and not as a countless multitude of individuals. The Decree on Missionary Activity (*Ad gentes*) states: "For it has pleased God to call human beings to share in his own life not merely as individuals, without any unifying bond between them, but rather to make them into a people in which his children, who had been widely scattered, might be gathered together in unity."[6] Corresponding to this unity, there would be, ideally, a single faith centered on the one God who revealed himself to Abraham, formed and guided the people of Israel, and unsurpassably manifested himself in Jesus of Nazareth. The oneness of God thus underlies the call to unity among all nations and races, and that oneness appropriately comes to fullest expression in a oneness of belief and practice. Thus, the Catholic Church envisions itself as a symbolic expression of the unity that God intends for the human race.[7]

Yet, what are we to make of the fact that there is more than one religion? Did God "will" that, in the matter of religious belief and practice, pluralism should reign as much as it does in other aspects of human social existence?[8] For Catholic theology, religion is "naturally" present within the human con-stitution, a sign of humanity's orientation toward the divine. The fact that there is a variety of religions should occasion no more surprise than the fact that there is a variety of languages, cultures, or philosophical worldviews. According to Catholic theology, however, the Christian faith, with its deep roots in the traditions of the Hebrew Bible, is privileged since, within this par-ticular history, the one God chose to reveal himself by speaking "directly" to (or from within) the religious receptors of a particular people. The term used to describe this revelation is *supernatural*. Accompanying this supernatural revelation is the call to mission, that is, to preaching, proclaiming, and bear-ing witness to the truth that God wishes to make known to the world through the body of believers.

The Catholic Church, therefore, sees itself related to the other religions as if in a series of concentric unities. The Dogmatic Constitution on the Church puts it this way:

All human beings are called to the new people of God. . . . For all the nations of the earth, therefore, there is one people of God since it draws its citizens from all nations, but the kingdom is not earthly in character, but heavenly. For all the faithful scattered throughout the world are in communion with the rest in the holy Spirit. . . . [T]o this catholic unity of the people of God, which prefigures and promotes universal peace, all are called, and they belong to it or are ordered to it in various ways, whether they be catholic faithful or others who believe in Christ or finally all people everywhere who by the grace of God are called to salvation.[9]

After delineating how the Catholic Church is related to those awaiting or seeking baptism, and in various degrees, to other Christian ecclesial bodies, the decree turns its attention to the non-Christian religions:

In the first place, there is the people to whom the testaments and promises were given and from whom Christ was born according to the flesh. . . . But the plan of salvation also embraces those . . . who hold the faith of Abraham and along with us they worship the one merciful God. . . . There are others who search for the unknown God in shadows and images; God is not far from people of this kind since he gives to all life and breath and everything. . . . There are those who without any fault do not know anything about Christ or his church, yet who search for God with a sincere heart and, under the influence of grace, try to put into effect the will of God as known to them through the dictate of conscience: these too can obtain eternal salvation. Nor does divine Providence deny the helps that are necessary for salvation to those who, through no fault of their own, have not yet attained to the express recognition of God yet who strive, not without divine grace, to lead an upright life.[10]

Salvation, understood here as entrance into the afterlife in union with God and all the righteous, is possible for people of other religious traditions—and even for those unaffiliated with any religion, provided they follow the divine law as imprinted within their conscience.

Turning to the Declaration on the Church's Relation to Non-Christian Religions, we find the council speaking more specifically. The decree first sets out the relevant church teaching:

All nations are one community and have one origin, because God caused the whole human race to dwell on the whole face of the earth. They also have one final end, God, whose providence, manifestation of goodness and plans for salvation are extended to all. . . .[11]

After listing seven fundamental questions about the meaning of human life—"What is a human being? What is the meaning and purpose of our life? What is good and what is sin? What origin and purpose do sufferings have? What is the way to attaining true happiness? What are death, judgment and retribution after death? Lastly, what is that final unutterable mystery which takes in our lives and from which we take our origin and towards which we tend?"[12]—the decree considers four world religions: Hinduism, Buddhism,

Islam, and Judaism—the religions "associated with the development of civili-
sation."[13] By specifying these fundamental questions, the decree is furnish-
ing criteria in terms of which to assess the adequacy of the religions. In other
words, religions can be evaluated in terms of how effectively they address
those existential concerns that constitute the core of religious belief and
thereby shape ethical and religious practice. The positive aspects of Hinduism
are noted first: "in Hinduism the divine mystery is explored and propounded
with an inexhaustible wealth of myths and penetrating philosophical investigations, and liberation is sought from the distresses of our state either through
various forms of ascetical life or deep meditation or taking refuge in God with
loving confidence." Next comes Buddhism, where "the radical inadequacy of
this changeable world is acknowledged and a way is taught whereby those with
a devout and trustful spirit may be able to reach either a state of perfect freedom or, relying on their own efforts or on help from a higher source, the highest illumination." The positive intent of other religions is also recognized:
"other religions which are to be found throughout the entire world strive in
various ways to relieve the anxiety of the human heart by suggesting 'ways,'
that is teachings and rules of life as well as sacred rites."[14]

   With Muslims, the religious ties are much closer since the Catholic Church
shares with the Muslim community Abrahamic faith. Muslims "venerate
Jesus as a prophet," they esteem Mary as his virgin mother, they await the resurrection of the dead, and they "have regard for the moral life and worship
God especially in prayer, almsgiving and fasting."[15] But no. 4 of *Nostra aetate*
makes it clear that the Catholic Church's deepest ties will always lay with Judaism because of the spiritual heritage that Jews and Christians share. Thus, we
read:

For the church of Christ recognises that the beginnings of its faith and election are to
be found already among the patriarchs, Moses and the prophets in accordance with
God's saving mystery. It states its belief that all believers in Christ, children of Abraham according to faith, are included in the same patriarch's calling and that the salvation of the church is mystically prefigured in the exodus of the chosen people from
the land of slavery. Hence the church cannot forget that through that people with
whom God out of his ineffable mercy deigned to enter into an ancient covenant, it
received the revelation of the old Testament and is nourished from the root of the
good olive tree, onto which the branches of the wild olive tree of the gentiles have
been grafted.[16]

Jesus, Mary, the apostles, Paul—and practically the whole first generation of
Christians—were daughters and sons of Abraham.[17]

   We may conclude from this look at the declaration *Nostra aetate* that the

Catholic Church does not view the other religions primarily as more or less adequate ways to God (although clearly members of these religions can reach eternal salvation). Vatican II does not image the world religions as many equal spokes on a wheel. The church seems to view them, rather, in terms of degrees of unity with itself as the visible expression of that communion God desires the human race to have with himself and with one another. The major question to ask for evaluating the legitimacy of other religions, therefore, appears to be this: does a given religion, through its moral teaching and particular way of relating to God, promote the unity of the human race? A religion is constructive in the measure that it teaches and cultivates the unity of peoples—a unity that is not advocated for the pragmatic reason of ensuring our survival but as the expression of our common origin and destiny in the mystery of God.

The general attitude of the Catholic Church in the documents of Vatican II toward the other world religions is one of respect and appreciation for the role each plays in securing unity and peace for the human race.

The "Constructive" Elements in Other Religions

According to no. 2 of *Nostra aetate*, the world religions—in particular, those "associated with the development of civilization"—help human beings find answers to the most profound questions about meaning and life and "strive in various ways to relieve the anxiety of the human heart."[18] Indeed, there is to be found in them "a ray of that truth which enlightens everyone."[19] This truth is located primarily in the social and moral teaching of the religions, although the Catholic Church acknowledges in Hinduism the elements of asceticism, meditation, and "taking refuge in God with loving confidence."[20] In addition, no. 3 notes, as we have seen, that Muslims worship the God of Abraham, esteem the moral life, and engage in the ascetical practices of almsgiving and fasting. Then, no. 5 observes:

We cannot, however, call upon God the Father of all if we refuse to behave like sisters and brothers towards certain people created to the image of God. The relation of man and woman to God the Father, and their relation to their fellow human beings, are linked to such a degree that scripture says: "Whoever does not love, does not know God" (1 Jn 4, 8).[21]

The "we" here refers to the Christian faithful, but the statement contains a striking religious universal: every man and every woman, because of her or his relation to the Creator, is by that very fact brother and sister to one another. Thus, wherever human beings truly love one another, present there is the mystery of God, transcending all religious boundaries. Insofar as religions lead their adherents to live out the human being's fundamental relationship with the Creator, they contribute—in the words of the author of the book of Revelation—to the construction of "a new heaven and a new earth" (Rev 21:1).

The positive or constructive elements within cultures (and, thus, within their religions) cannot be dismissed as hostile to the Christian experience since Christian faith, while rooted in a particular history and set of narratives, is—in the council's view—transcultural. These positive elements may be drawn from sacred writings, rituals and devotions, moral insight, popular wisdom or proverbs, music, art, social organization, philosophy, forms of meditation and contemplative practices, both popular and monastic spiritualities, and lessons learned from a history of suffering. Elements are not to be imported into the Christian faith without theological discernment, but the sheer existence of such elements contributes to a climate of mutual understanding and tolerance. The most constructive element of all would be the desire, born from the depths of religious experience, for unity and peace.

Which Teachings Justify Tolerance or Invite Intolerance?

From a Catholic perspective, the word *tolerance* might not be all that serviceable because, to some ears, it skirts the notion of truth. Joseph Ratzinger (now Pope Benedict XVI) explained the difficulty this way:

Are tolerance and belief in revealed truth opposites? Putting it another way: Are Christian faith and modernity compatible? If tolerance is one of the foundations of the modern age, then is not the claim to have recognized the essential truth an obsolete piece of presumption that has to be rejected if the spiral of violence that runs through the history of religions is to be broken? Today, in the encounter of Christianity with the world, this question arises ever more dramatically, and ever more widespread becomes the persuasion that renouncing the claim to truth in the Christian faith is the fundamental condition for a new universal peace, the fundamental condition for any reconciliation of Christianity with modernity.[22]

In attempting to answer this question, then-Cardinal Ratzinger argued, citing an important New Testament text: "Truth and love are identical. This sentence—if the whole of its demand is understood—is the surest guarantee of tolerance; of an association with truth, whose only weapon is itself and, thereby, love."[23] Tolerance by itself would prove to be an unsteady platform on which to build the unity of the human race precisely because the human mind searches for truth; and truth is, following Plato, inseparable from the good—and from the mystery of God (here the cardinal cites Mark 10:18).[24] Moreover, one cannot talk about truth without considering the notion of freedom and, as the council does, the dignity of the human person. As a consequence, we might say that the notion of religious tolerance does not stand apart from the notions of truth and freedom.[25] Of course, the very idea of religious tolerance has evolved. Writing shortly before the final text of the Declaration on Religious Freedom (*Dignitatis humanae*) was voted on and promulgated, the North American theologian John Courtney Murray explained some forty years ago the outdated reasoning that was blocking the decree's passage:

> The theory of religious tolerance takes its start from the statement, considered to be axiomatic, that error has no rights, that only the truth has rights—and exclusive rights. From this axiom a juridical theory is deduced, which distinguishes between "thesis" and "hypothesis." The thesis asserts that Catholicism, *per se* and in principle, should be established as the one "religion of the state," since it is the one true religion. Given the institution of establishment, it follows by logical and juridical consequence that no other religion, *per se* and in principle, can be allowed public existence or action within the state (which, normally, in this theory, is considered to be identical and co-extensive with society). Error has no rights. Therefore error is to be suppressed whenever and wherever possible; intolerance is the rule. Error, however, may be tolerated when tolerance is necessary by reason of circumstances, that is, when intolerance is impossible; tolerance remains the exception. Tolerance therefore is "hypothesis," a concession to a factual situation, a lesser evil.[26]

In the minds of some of those attending the council, Murray seems to be implying, the other religions had to be "tolerated" because the alternative would be not only doctrinal wars over who possesses the truth but political instability as well.

The Declaration on Religious Freedom represents a major advance in church teaching on the matter of conscience and religion. The declaration argues that, because human beings have been endowed with reason, they are morally obliged to seek the truth about the origin and destiny of their lives (nos. 1 and 3). This proposition is hardly new to Catholic theology, of course; Paul was thinking along these lines in the opening chapter of his letter to the Romans.[27] The Catholic Church also insists that such searching ultimately orients human beings toward the mystery of God revealed in Jesus Christ. Again, this proposition reflects a conviction whose genesis takes us back to the early church and to the celebrated phrase of the second-century Christian apologist, Justin Martyr, "seed of the Word."[28] But the council also insists that any response to God can only be a response in faith and such faith can never be coerced; it must come from freedom (no. 2). Religious freedom is understood to be a basic human right. However certain we may be of the existence of God and the obedience that is due him, religion cannot trump conscience. The declaration states:

People grasp and acknowledge the precepts of the divine law by means of their own consciences, which they are bound to follow faithfully in all their activity, so as to come to God, their end. They must not be forced to act against their conscience. . . . The practice of religion of its very nature consists principally in internal acts that are voluntary and free, in which one relates oneself to God directly; and these can neither be commanded nor prevented by any merely human power.[29]

While religious groups have the right to share their message with others, they may not do so in ways that compromise another person's freedom: "But in propagating their religious belief they must always abstain from any kind of action that savours of undue pressure or improper enticement, particularly in regard to the poor or uneducated."[30] Scripture—divine revelation—does not explicitly affirm a person's right to be free from coercion and pressure when it comes to making religious assent, but this certainly was the example of Christ (nos. 9 and 11). The declaration makes what is implicit in Scripture explicit:

One of the chief catholic teachings, found in the word of God and repeatedly preached by the fathers of the church, is that the response of people to God in faith should be voluntary; so no one must be forced to embrace the faith against her or his will. . . . It is, therefore, entirely in accord with the nature of faith that every kind of human coercion should be excluded from religion.[31]

Yet, it has taken the Catholic Church centuries to appreciate the existence and importance of this right. The declaration concedes as much when it says:

Thus the *leaven of the gospel has long been at work* in the minds of people and has played a part *in the course of time* in the *growing recognition* of the dignity of the human person, and in *the maturing* of the conviction that in religious matters this dignity must be preserved intact in society from any kind of human coercion.[32]

One reason for the Catholic community's slowness in coming to this insight might have been the uncritical way in which it often interpreted the text of Matthew 28:19–20 with respect to teaching all nations. The text reads: "Go therefore and make disciples of all nations, baptizing them in the name of the Father and of the Son and of the Holy Spirit, and teaching them to obey everything I have commanded you." These final words of Jesus to his followers are understood to be a "divine command" (no. 14). The Catholic Church's mission to teach and baptize is invested, therefore, with the highest religious warrant. Whoever refuses to listen and pay heed would be resisting God, and the person who resists God becomes guilty of sin. A narrow reading of Matthew 28:19–20 leaves only the following option: either open oneself to the Christian message or alienate oneself from God.[33]

Nevertheless, sacrosanct as conscience is, the human person, together with his or her conscience, never stands outside the human circle in the sorry kind of independence that comes with isolation. Giuseppe Alberigo comments:

> The text avoids an individualistic interpretation of freedom of conscience; it does not allow for public life a purely private conception of religion that is rooted in an agnostic theory of tolerance and puts all religions on the same level; it does not grant the state tutelage over religion, but neither can the religions or the Churches use state-sponsored coercion to preserve their public status.[34]

The last point of this text should probably be underlined. When the Catholic Church —or any religion—is by treaty or by tradition aligned with the state, intolerance is enabled, and repression frequently follows. No matter how compelling the claims of revealed truth may be, therefore, religion is never entitled to violate individual freedom. Furthermore, genuinely religious truth is "humble"; it neither seeks nor needs power and privilege in order to authenticate and protect itself.

Social and Cultural Mechanisms That Enable or Disable Religious Tolerance

One of the hottest theological topics in recent years has been "inculturation." Given its presence in so many different societies and cultures, the Catholic Church has been keen to allow and to welcome those elements of indigenous cultures that have helped people profess and practice Christian faith within their own cultural idiom.[35] While inculturation is hardly new to the church's experience, the fact that Christian belief was, for centuries, so deeply impregnated by Western culture tended to blind theologians to what happens when the Christian narrative inserts itself and takes root in different cultural settings. For the scholastic theology that dominated Catholic intellectual life prior to the Second Vatican Council, the difference between the truth of doctrinal propositions and the language or thought forms in which these truths were expressed was so negligible as to be virtually nonexistent. The diversity and pluralism within the Catholic community's theological, spiritual, and liturgical traditions went largely unnoticed.[36]

Vatican II recognized the importance of inculturation in its Decree on Missionary Activity (*Ad gentes*) in two places. Connecting inculturation with Jesus' Incarnation, the council wrote:

The church, so that it may be able to offer to all the mystery of salvation and the life brought by God, ought to insert itself into all these groups [who have never been exposed to the gospel] with the same thrust with which Christ himself, by his incarnation, bound himself to the particular social and cultural conditions of the people among whom he lived.[37]

The idea here is that by "accommodating" itself to a specific context, the divine mystery set the pattern for the subsequent missionary practice of Christian apostles.

A second passage goes into greater detail:

The seed which is the word of God, germinating from good soil, watered by the divine dew, absorbs moisture and transforms and assimilates it into itself, so that finally it bears much fruit. Indeed, as with the economy of the incarnation, the young churches . . . take over, in a marvelous exchange, all the riches of the nations. . . . From the customs and traditions of their own peoples, from their wisdom and learning, from their arts and sciences, these churches borrow everything which can contribute to praising the glory of the creator. . . . As a result, avenues will open up for a more profound adaptation in the entire area of Christian life. [Aided by sound theological reflection] the Christian life will be adapted to the character and disposition of each culture; particular traditions together with the special endowments of each national family, illumined by the light of the gospel, will be made part of a catholic unity.[38]

Exposure to new cultural and social contexts encourages toleration whenever such contact has enabled the Catholic Church to accommodate itself to diversity. The same can be said with respect to pluralism within a society. The experience of pluralism can trigger defensive responses within any group that fears losing its historical and cultural identity. But the alternative—the building of conceptual walls, the flight into stereotyping, the construction of ghettos—is neither socially healthy nor a guarantee of the group's survival. Pluralism encourages religious tolerance to the degree that pluralism is accepted and not lamented as a fact of life—another of the positive conceptual forces that Vatican II set in motion. This openness merits some attention.

In his opening address to the council, Pope John XXIII said:

In the daily exercise of our pastoral office, we sometimes have to listen, much to our regret, to voices of people who, though burning with zeal, are not endowed with too much sense of discretion or measure. In these modern times they can see nothing but prevarication and ruin. They say that our era, in comparison with past eras, is getting worse, and they behave as though they had learned nothing from history, which is, none the less, the teacher of life. They behave as though at the time of former Councils everything was a full triumph for the Christian idea and life and for proper religious liberty.

We feel we must disagree with these prophets of gloom, who are always forecasting disaster, as though the end of the world were at hand.

In the present order of things, Divine Providence is leading us to a new order of human relations. . . .[39]

The Second Vatican Council approached the modern world from the confident perspective that the Spirit of God is at work in human history. The council's purpose was not to identify error and condemn it but to notice what is good and positive and to affirm it. Later in his address, John XXIII told the council:

At the outset of Second Vatican Council, it is evident, as always, that the truth of the Lord will remain forever. We see, in fact, as one age succeeds another, that the opinions of men follow one another and exclude each other. And often errors vanish as quickly as they arise, like fog before the sun.

The Church has always opposed these errors. Frequently she has condemned them with the greatest severity. Nowadays, however, the Spouse of Christ prefers to make use of the medicine of mercy rather than that of severity. She considers that she meets the needs of the present day more by demonstrating the validity of her teaching rather than by condemnations. . . . [People today] are ever more deeply convinced of the paramount dignity of the human person and his perfections, as well as of the duties which that implies. Even more important, experience has taught men that violence inflicted on others, the might of arms, and political domination, are of no help at all in finding a happy solution to the grave problems which afflict them.[40]

The extent to which Vatican II was continuous or discontinuous with the past remains a very alive question. The Catholic Church had been slow to acknowledge the historical fact of doctrinal development and equally slow in appropriating the fact that every human institution (and its statements) is profoundly conditioned by time and culture. Indeed, taking into account "the methods of research" and "the literary forms of modern thought," John XXIII had called attention to the difference between the substance of dogmatic propositions and the form in which they are expressed.[41]

But doctrinal development involves more than the reformulation of ancient teachings; it is also about newness and, at times, correction.[42] Over the centuries, the Catholic Church presented its doctrines as "truths," and it understood "truth" to be essentially timeless and unchanging—a philosophical posture that initially rendered the notion of doctrinal development theologically dangerous. While I do not wish to take up the questions surrounding doctrinal development in this paper, I believe it would be worth quoting the observation of the cultural historian Charles Freeman:

Reason is a means of finding truths through deductive and inductive logic. These truths may be valuable in themselves in helping us understand who we are (the theory of evolution), but they have also, through medicine, for instance, transformed human life. We are free to apply the fruits of reasoned thought to some of our greatest needs, in many areas with enormous success. Yet built into a tradition of rational thought is the necessity for tolerance. It is the only way in which it can progress. Reason also provides external standards of truth, often, for instance, from empirical evidence. This helps take personal animosity out of debates in that disputes over the interpretation of external evidence are normally less abrasive than those between human beings struggling to assert or maintain their personal authority. History suggests that conflicts between religions tend to be more destructive than those between scientists! In this sense, the price to pay for the assumption that there can be doctrinal certainty has been a heavy one.

Philosophically, therefore, it becomes crucial to define the areas where certainty is possible and those where it is not. This was another of the intellectual achievements of the Greeks. *Pace* Plato, they understood that the nature of the divine, if such spiritual force exists, cannot be grasped when there is no external evidence for it. The troubles described in this book come not from the teachings of Jesus or from the nature of Christians themselves (though arguably one can trace them to Paul), but from the determination to make "certain" statements about God. Tragically, the pressures to do so, many of them political and economic, were intensified by the introduction of the concept of an afterlife, in which most would be punished eternally for failure to adhere to what was eventually decided to be orthodox.[43]

The problem for religion seems to become rather obvious, once we start speaking of truths. If one religion is true, then the other religions are logically reckoned to be false. And on a lesser scale, if one church lays claim to the fullness of truth, then the other faith communities are to one degree or another deficient—an awkward position to maintain when one is trying at the same time to encourage ecumenical dialogue. Vatican II attempted to move beyond this impasse, at least in terms of our living alongside one another, by proposing that there exists a "hierarchy of truths."[44] Instead of thinking about degrees of separation, Vatican II chose to think in terms of degrees of union, that is, levels or circles of shared conviction about the relation between human beings and God and the moral life. Tolerance does not seem to be possible whenever we start to measure another religion in terms of truth and error because the only response to error is to correct it or to put it down.

A properly theological understanding of truth requires that we distinguish the notion of truth from the notion of correctness. Doctrinal propositions, like propositions in general, are determined to be correct or incorrect with respect to an underlying conceptual framework. As human understanding advances, those frameworks often change. When they do, what was considered to be correct or coherent at one time may turn out to be incorrect by a later norm or standard. The notion of truth, however, involves more than making correct statements. Truth cannot be discovered apart from "doing" or living what one professes to be "true." Religious truth is, thus, often viewed as a "path" or "way" that leads to freedom, life, enlightenment, wholeness, communion, and peace. As a way, "truth" must be walked. To evaluate a religion or a church, therefore, one has to start by examining the day-to-day practice of its members and how, through that practice, those members are becoming whole and more fully human. However counterintuitive it sounds, truth is ultimately linked to faith. Orthodoxy, on the other hand, is a matter of doctrinal correctness. In crafting its beliefs in terms of a creed, the ancient church was spelling out and making coherent what was contained in narrative form in the Gospels. It is important to remember, however, that a scriptural notion of truth has more to do with eschatology than with metaphysics. The intellectual and religious horizon of the Gospels remains eschatological. Truth, like the Gospel concept of the kingdom of God, bears an already/ not-yet character.

Vatican II presented an understanding of divine revelation that was personal and relational. Revelation consists not so much of propositions but of God communicating or sharing God's own self with human beings.[45] Yet, a personal, relational approach to revelation implies a personal and relational understanding of truth, and only a personal and relational understanding of truth can serve as the theological basis of genuine religious tolerance. Vatican II may not be the Catholic Church's final word about the relation of the church to the other religions, but the council showed itself remarkably sensitive to the presence and action of the Spirit beyond the church's spiritual and doctrinal boundaries.

The most effective and reliable means of promoting religious toleration offered by Vatican II, I suggest, is ecumenical contact and dialogue. The council opened the door to common worship on the part of Catholics and other Christians under "certain special circumstances." It encouraged Catholics to "get to know the outlook" of their "separated fellow Christians": "their history, their spiritual and liturgical life, their religious psychology and culture."[46] It urged meetings among Christian groups for the discussion of theological problems. It called for ecumenical sensitivity in the way theology courses are taught in Catholic seminaries and divinity schools. Catholics and others can collaborate in the work of social justice and peacemaking.[47] And the council reminded Catholics of how deeply they are united with many other Christian groups through a common baptism.[48]

Summary and Conclusion

In addition to ecumenism, culture itself can be an agent of toleration, as when the church finds itself in a new cultural setting and is thereby forced to let the seed of faith take root in different soil. One recognizes and then surrenders any subtle ambition for uniformity; we are not all cut from the same mold and, thus, cannot be forced into one. The experience of cultural difference can be both challenging and liberating, provided one has the freedom to step out of familiar thought patterns and learn how to listen. Toleration is promoted further by the religious pluralism and social diversity that characterize so much of modern life. No one is helped if communities come to blows over differences of religious belief. Finally, toleration becomes easier as one pinpoints the heart of religion in terms of people's experience of the divine, especially as that experience leads them to want unity and, at the same time, to abandon every effort to co-opt someone else's freedom. Although redefining truth along theological lines sounds more like a theoretical than a practical means for promoting religious toleration, reconceiving truth in the way I have sketched can protect us from letting differences of belief become the source of suspicion, distrust, avoidance, and violence. Vatican II moves in that direction through one of the major strands in its understanding of divine revelation.

Pulling together the lines of thought to be found in the conciliar texts, we return to the five key questions posed by William Scott Green and answer each of them briefly. First, *what is the role of other religions in the documents of Vatican II?* Religious pluralism is viewed in the documents as an obvious aspect of contemporary experience. The council does not celebrate religious diversity; it accepts it. As expressions of the striving of the human spirit for wholeness and community, the religions testify—each in its own way—to the fact that human beings come from God and by nature are oriented toward the transcendent.

Second, *does Vatican II acknowledge the other religions, reject them, endure them, or find them to be religiously constructive? Does the council treat them generically or are they differentiated?* The other religions are certainly acknowledged, although the council does not suggest that God "willed" there should be many religions. The religions are constructive insofar as they encourage their adherents to pursue peace and unity. The council appreciates that each religion is distinctive, but its descriptions of the major religions is brief and reveal a lack of sustained, in-depth engagement with them—a deficiency that the council wanted the church to overcome.

Third, *how does Vatican II account for the existence and persistence of other religions? Are they viewed as errors, accidents, the consequence of evil, a constructive part of the social world, or some combination of these options?* Religions arise in response to the human being's searching for answers to the most basic questions about existence. Since the questions about where we come from, why we are here, and what our ultimate destiny might be are not going to disappear, religion is not going to disappear, either. Religion also speaks to humanity's need for moral order and its need to understand and live with suffering. In addition, through ritual and meditative practice, each religion furnishes a "path" by which human beings enact their relationship with the divine mystery. To the degree that they contribute to wholeness and peace, religions are constructive. Vatican II does not speak of the other religions in terms of ignorance and falsehood, but neither does it find in them "the fullness of grace and truth."[49]

Fourth, *since there are divergent, sometimes opposed views of other religions, what are the doctrinal fault lines within Catholic theology that have produced this divergence? Where do the documents of Vatican II justify tolerance? Where might they yield ground to intolerance?* The fault line within Catholic theology perhaps resulted from interpreting biblical texts such as Acts 4:12 so literally that the Catholic Church fell into an exclusivist view of salvation.[50] The positive desire that human beings should be saved, coupled with a strong rejection of pagan religion, led the Catholic Church to view itself as the sole ark of salvation. Some early Christian thinkers, however, recognized that there was moral and even spiritual goodness outside the Christian horizon. They accounted for this by appealing to the mind's orientation toward truth and to their religious conviction that truth was one and that it came from God. Thus, there emerged a tension between the faith conviction about the unique role played by Jesus in God's providential plan and the experience of knowing people who were God-fearing but not automatically drawn to seek baptism. Vatican II recognized in no. 16 of the Dogmatic Constitution on the Church that salvation is possible outside the church. The council went out of its way to avoid leaving any grounds for intolerance when it encouraged Catholics to engage in dialogue and cooperate with members of other religions, even to "preserve and promote those spiritual and moral good things as well as the socio-cultural values which are to be found among them."[51]

Fifth, *are there historical, political, and/or behavioral factors that correlate with the expression of tolerance in modern Catholic thinking? With intolerance? And what determines whether tolerance or intolerance will prevail?* On a practical level, tolerance seems to be enhanced whenever the church finds itself in a multicultural, religiously pluralist society and when, at the same time, Catholics are sufficiently secure about their own religious identity that they can enter into a dialogue and collaborate with followers of other religions. Conversely, religious intolerance is likely to be fueled when people sense that their cultural identities are being threatened. On a theological level, tolerance is encouraged in the measure that believers perceive rays of truth in the other religions since all those rays originate in God, who is truth itself. One invites intolerance whenever communities behave as if they own the truth, conflating truth with orthodoxy. If salvation is possible to followers of other religions, then God must be sharing himself with them in and through those religions—an implication that Vatican II did not develop.

In his address at the University of Regensberg, titled "Faith, Reason and the University: Memories and Reflections," Benedict XVI sketched what he considers an important contribution that Catholic theology can make to interreligious dialogue, namely, its insistence upon the connection between faith and reason.[52] Vatican II was presupposing this connection when it spoke of "a ray of that truth which enlightens everyone."[53] According to the Pope, no religion should espouse a belief or a behavior that is essentially irrational—which violence is by its very nature—in the name of God. Whatever is genuinely of God will not violate the canons of intelligibility, and both violence and the intolerance that gives rise to it are intrinsically unreasonable. The Pope's unfortunate quotation about Muhammed and the sword required explanation and apology, but the overall point of his address remains timely. Tolerance alone may not be enough to enable religions to exist alongside each other. They should also be talking with one another and, at times, challenging each other, so that the truth that is God and the truth that the mind seeks do not diverge, tearing apart the human family.

Notes

1. The Canadian theologian Bernard J. F. Lonergan, S.J., explained that Catholic theology prior to the Second Vatican Council was deeply rooted in a classicist culture that sheltered the church from "the chill winds of modernity." See Lonergan, *A Second Collection*, ed. William Ryan and Bernard Tyrell (Philadelphia: The Westminster Press, 1974), 93ff. He also wrote: "[C]lassicism is no more than the mistaken view of conceiving culture normatively and of concluding that there is just one human culture. The modern fact is that culture has to be conceived empirically, that there are many cultures. . . ." See Lonergan, *Method in Theology* (London: Darton, Longman & Todd, 1972), 124.

2. The significance and challenge of the church's finding itself in a brand-new cultural context was developed by the German Jesuit theologian Karl Rahner in "Toward a Fundamental Theological Interpretation of Vatican II," *Theological Studies* 40 (1979): 716–727.

3. John used the expression (which comes from Matthew 16:3) in his 1963 encyclical letter *Pacem in Terris* (no. 126). The Second Vatican Council employed the phrase in its Pastoral Constitution on the Church in the Modern World (*Gaudium et spes*), no. 4; and in its Decree on Ecumenism (*Unitatis redintegratio*), no. 4. The official Latin title of the Vatican II decrees is taken from the opening two or three words of the Latin text.

4. Conciliar teaching is more authoritative than Canon Law. In his Apostolic Constitution officially publishing the 1983 Code of Canon Law, John Paul II wrote: "Therefore the new Code which is promulgated today necessarily required the previous work of the council" (*Code of Canon Law: Latin-English Edition* [Washington, DC: Canon Law Society of America, 1983], xii). And again: "The instrument which the Code is fully corresponds to the nature of the Church, especially as it is proposed by the teaching of the Second Vatican Council in general and in a particular way by its ecclesiological teaching. Indeed, in a certain sense this new Code could be understood as a great effort to translate this same conciliar doctrine and ecclesiology into *canonical* language. If, however, it is impossible to translate perfectly into *canonical* language the conciliar image of the Church, nevertheless the Code must always be referred to this image as the primary pattern whose outline the Code ought to express insofar as it can by its very nature" (xiv). For a discussion of the status of conciliar teaching, see Francis A. Sullivan, S.J., *Magisterium: Teaching Authority in the Catholic Church* (Mahwah, NJ: Paulist Press, 1983); see also Sullivan's book *Creative Fidelity: Weighing and Interpreting Documents of the Magisterium* (Mahwah, NJ: Paulist Press, 1996), esp. 162–174.

5. For more background, see Norman P. Tanner, *The Councils of the Church: A Short History* (New York: The Crossroad Publishing Co., 2001).

6. Paragraph no. 2. Quotations from the conciliar documents are taken from volume 2 of Norman P. Tanner, English ed., *Decrees of the Ecumenical Councils*, 2 vols. (London and Washington, DC: Sheed & Ward and Georgetown University Press, 1990); see 1011. All scriptural quotations in this paper are from the New Revised Standard Version.

7. The divine plan, then, is "that the entire human race may form one people of God, come together as the one body of Christ, and be built into the one temple of the holy Spirit." Such unity corresponds to "the profound wish of all humankind." See *Ad gentes*, no. 7 (Tanner, 1017).

8. The August 6, 2000, Declaration from the Congregation for the Doctrine of the Faith (CDF) titled "*Dominus Iesus*" (On the Unicity and Salvific Universality of Jesus Christ and the Church) distinguished *de facto* from *de iure* religious pluralism. Those who propose that *de facto* pluralism is positively willed by God, the declaration argues, have succumbed to the relativistic mind-set that has infected modern Western thinking. The declaration was signed by Joseph Ratzinger (now Pope Benedict XVI), who was then prefect of the CDF. It can be found in *Origins* 30 (September 14, 2000), 209–219, as well as on the Vatican website. *Dominus Iesus* occasioned considerable response from theologians concerned about the effect the declaration would have on ecumenism. For instance, see Francis A. Sullivan, "The Impact of *Dominus Iesus* on Ecumenism," *America* 183, no. 13 (October 28, 2000): 8–11; also, *Sic et Non: Encountering Dominus Iesus*, ed. Stephen Pope and Charles Hefling (Maryknoll, NY: Orbis Books, 2002).

9. No. 13 (Tanner, 859–60).

10. No. 16 (Tanner, 861).

11. No. 1 (Tanner, 968). This comparatively brief decree has a very interesting history. Initially, those who drafted the document wanted the council to make a statement on the church's relationship with Judaism. The council, they believed, simply could not ignore the Holocaust and whatever complicity Christian theology had unwittingly provided by its failure to understand and contextualize various New Testament texts. Resistance came from two directions: from those who insisted upon taking those biblical texts literally and from church leaders living in the Arab world who feared that a statement on Judaism would be interpreted as the church's siding with the state of Israel politically in the conflict between Jews and Muslims. See Giuseppe Alberigo and Joseph Komonchak, eds., *History of Vatican II* (Maryknoll, NY, and Leuven, Belgium: Orbis Books and Peeters, 2003), 4:135–193 and 546–559. See also Section II of Edward Idris Cardinal Cassidy, *Ecumenism and Interreligious Dialogue: Unitatis Redintegratio, Nostra Aetate* (Mahwah, NJ: Paulist Press, 2005)

12. No. 1 (Tanner, 968).

13. No. 2 (Tanner, 969).

14. No. 2 (Tanner, 969).

15. No. 3 (Tanner, 969).

16. No. 4 (Tanner, 970).

17. For an assessment of what has happened since *Nostra aetate*, see Elena Procario-Foley, "Heir or Orphan? Theological Evolution and Devolution before and after *Nostra Aetate*," in *Vatican II Forty Years Later*, ed. William Madges, 308–339, College Theology Society Annual 51 (Maryknoll, NY: Orbis Books, 2006).

18. Tanner, 969.

19. Ibid.

20. Ibid.

21. Ibid., 971.

22. Joseph Cardinal Ratzinger, *Truth and Tolerance: Christian Belief and World Religions* (San Francisco: Ignatius Press, 2004), 210.

23. Ibid., 231. The text is: "Whoever does not love does not know God, for God is love" (1 John 4:8).

24. Ibid., 230. The gospel text is: "Jesus said to him, 'Why do you call me good? No one is good but God alone.'" Pages 231–258 of *Truth and Tolerance* examine the connection between truth and freedom, although without ever drawing on the council's Declaration on Religious Freedom (*Dignitatis humanae*).

25. David Hollenbach, a Catholic ethicist, has suggested that tolerance can actually deepen alienation in society because it tends to "neutralize potential conflicts." He writes: "The standard response to the diversity of groups and value systems in Western political culture has long been an appeal to the virtue of tolerance. Tolerance is a live-and-let-live attitude that avoids introducing conceptions of the full human good into political discourse. . . . [W]hen the pluralism of diverse groups veers toward a state of group conflict with racial or class or religious dimensions, pure tolerance can become a strategy like that of the ostrich with its head in the sand." See Hollenbach's essay "Is Tolerance Enough? The Catholic University and the Common Good," *Conversations on Jesuit Higher Education* 13 (1998): 8.

26. John Courtney Murray, S.J., played a major role in the development of the conciliar decree on religious freedom. His report entitled "Religious Freedom" can be found at http://www.georgetown.edu/users/j1h3/Murray/1965ib.htm.

27. See Rom 1:18–23.

28. The phrase "seeds of the Word" appears in no. 11 of the Decree on Missionary Activity (*Ad gentes*). This expression seems to be equivalent to the phrase "a ray of that truth which enlightens everyone" in no. 2 of *Nostra aetate* (see Tanner 1020 and 969). In chapter 13 of his *Second Apology*, Justin remarked how philosophers, poets, and historians had participated in "the seminal Divine Word." From his own experience he knew the similarities and differences between the teachings of Plato and those of Christ. Justin tells us: "Indeed, all writers, by means of the engrafted seed of the Word which was implanted in them, had a dim glimpse of the truth." See Justin Martyr, *The Second Apology* in *Writings of Saint Justin Martyr*, The Fathers of the Church (New York: Christian Heritage, Inc., 1948), 133.

29. No. 3 (Tanner, 1003).

30. No. 4 (Tanner, 1004).

31. No. 10 (Tanner, 1006-07).

32. No. 12 (Tanner, 1009). Emphasis added.

33. Mark 16:15–16 contains a similar message. The next step, which I shall not take here, would be to examine Vatican II's Decree on the Missionary Activity of the Church (*Ad gentes*) alongside John Paul II's encyclical letter of December 7, 1990, "On the Permanent Validity of the Church's Missionary Mandate" (*Redemptoris missio*), which he wrote for the twenty-fifth anniversary of *Ad gentes*. The encyclical can be found on the Vatican website.

34. Giuseppe Alberigo and Joseph Komonchak, eds., *History of Vatican II* (Maryknoll, NY, and Leuven, Belgium: Orbis Books and Peeters, 2003), 5:453.

35. See, for example, Michael Paul Gallagher, *Clashing Symbols: An Introduction to Faith and Culture* (Mahwah, NJ: Paulist Press, 1998); Aylward Shorter, *Toward a Theology of Inculturation* (Maryknoll, NY: Orbis Books, 1989).

36. No. 4 of the Decree on Ecumenism (*Unitatis redintegratio*) contains this remarkable affirmation of diversity and pluralism: "All in the church must preserve unity in essentials. But let all, according to the gifts they have received, maintain a proper freedom in their various forms of spiritual life and discipline, in their different liturgical rites, and even in their theological elaborations of revealed truth" (Tanner, 912). And later in no. 17: "What has just been said about legitimate variety must also be taken to apply to the differences in theological expression of doctrine. In the study of revelation east and west have followed different methods, and taken different steps, towards their understanding and confession of God's truth. It is hardly surprising, then, if from time to time one tradition has come nearer to a full appreciation of some aspects of a mystery of revelation than the other, or has expressed it to better advantage" (Tanner, 917).

37. No. 10 (Tanner, 1019-20).

38. No. 22 (Tanner, 1030-31). No. 40 of the Constitution on the Sacred Liturgy (*Sacrosanctum concilium*) addresses the delicate yet vital issue of how to incorporate "the elements from the traditions and particular talents of individual peoples" into worship (Tanner, 829).

39. *The Documents of Vatican II*, ed. Walter M. Abbot (New York: Herder & Herder and Association Press, 1966), 712. On the history of the council, see Giuseppe Alberigo, *A Brief History of Vatican II* (Maryknoll, NY: Orbis Books, 2006).

40. Abbot, *Documents*, 715–16.

41. Ibid., 715.

42. See, for example, John T. Noonan, *A Church That Can and Cannot Change: The Development of Catholic Moral Teaching* (Notre Dame, IN: University of Notre Dame Press, 2005).

43. Charles Freeman, *The Closing of the Western Mind: The Rise of Faith and the Fall of Reason* (New York: Alfred A. Knopf, 2003), 337–38.

44. This celebrated phrase appears in no. 11 of Vatican II's Decree on Ecumenism (*Unitatis redintegratio*): "When comparing doctrines with one another, they [Catholic theologians joined with other Christians in common study of the divine mysteries] should remember that in catholic doctrine there exists an order or 'hierarchy' of truths, since they vary in their connection with the foundation of the christian faith" (Tanner, 915).

45. To cite No. 2 of the council's Dogmatic Constitution on Divine Revelation (*Dei verbum*): "It has pleased God, in his goodness and wisdom, to reveal *himself.* . . . By thus revealing *himself* God . . . in his great love speaks to humankind as friends . . . so as to invite and receive them into relationship with *himself*" (Tanner 972; emphasis added). In other words, revelation means that the divine mystery shares itself with human beings; doctrinal propositions and biblical texts are finite, linguistic expressions of God's self-communication.

46. Decree on Ecumenism (*Unitatis redintegratio*), nos. 8 and 9 (Tanner, 914).

47. Ibid., nos. 9–12 (Tanner, 914–15).

48. Ibid., no. 22 (Tanner, 919). To see how seriously the church has taken Vatican II's call for dialogue, see Francesco Gioia, ed., *Interreligious Dialogue: The Official Teaching of the Catholic Church (1963–1995)* (Boston: Pauline Books and Media, 1997).

49. Decree on Ecumenism, no. 3 (Tanner, 910). See also John 1:17.

50. The text reads: "There is salvation in no one else, for there is no other name under heaven given among mortals by which we must be saved."

51. Declaration on the Church's Relation to Non-Christian Religions (*Nostra aetate*), no. 2 (Tanner, 969).

52. The address, which drew considerable attention because it quoted an unflattering view of Islam that appears in a fourteenth-century manuscript, was given on September 12, 2006. It can be found on the Vatican website.

53. Declaration on the Church's Relation to Non-Christian Religions, no. 2 (Tanner, 969).

8

THE LATTER-DAY SAINT DOCTRINE

OF SALVATION

Religious Exclusivity, Tolerance, and Accommodation

DANNY L. JORGENSEN

Introduction

The Latter-day Saint (LDS or Mormon) religion was established in 1830 as the only restoration of the original Church of Jesus Christ.[1] It, like Christianity generally, intends to provide universal salvation for humanity exclusive of all other religions. Latter-day Saints of the nineteen century, like most other Americans, took the Christian Bible mostly literally as gospel and history. Religions other than those deriving from biblical traditions were considered illegitimate. All biblical religions except for Mormonism, furthermore, were thought to be at least partly incorrect. This included Judaism and all other forms of Christianity—Orthodox, Catholic, Protestant, or anything else— that were regarded as apostate versions of the most primitive doctrine and organization of the Church of Christ.[2]

The Church of Jesus Christ of Latter-day Saints today counts more than twelve million members worldwide, a little more than half of them outside of North America.[3] There are about a half a million members in Europe; nearly a half million in the Pacific; about three million Latter-day Saints reside in Mexico, South America, or the Caribbean; and almost a million live in Asia. The LDS African membership of around two hundred thousand is relatively small but growing. Sociologist Rodney Stark projects that there will be at least sixty million and perhaps as many as two hundred and sixty-five million Mormons worldwide by 2080.[4] There currently is considerable scholarly debate over the actual number of active Latter-day Saints, with some arguing that nearly half of the official membership is inactive.[5] Mormonism, nevertheless, is a substantial minority religion in North America and the world today.

Viewed from the standpoint of the sociology of culture, knowledge, and religion, absolutist or exclusivistic claims to truth, such as those found in the Latter-day Saint religion, can be expected to result in exceptional intolerance, hostility, and even aggression toward other cultural forms and nonbelievers.[6] The conviction that a religion is absolutely, exclusively, and universally true readily results in highly cohesive social organizations (characteristically, sects) with powerful leaders—especially when they are sustained by charismatic authority, extraordinarily committed followers, singular values and norms, and self-justifying ideologies of intolerance and sometimes violence toward outsiders. Opposition to such a religious group tends to reinforce and intensify its absolutist convictions and the related social dynamics. Access to social and political power may enable such a religious group to exert dominance over other religions and nonbelievers, while a lack of access to power tends to produce a sense of persecution within the religious group and sometimes withdrawal from the larger society.

The central task of this essay is to explain why such intolerance and even hostility toward other religions and peoples *is not* the case for the Latter-day Saint religion in the world today. The Mormon doctrine of salvation—involving rather complex imagery of the Godhead, the cosmos, history, and the location of humanity within this immense context—provides the key to understanding this religion's exclusivistic worldview as well as its toleration of other religions and nonbelievers.[7] The Latter-day Saint religion—like many other religions in the world today—acknowledges the social realities of globalization and religious pluralism, yet it remains fully committed to having exclusive authority for the universal salvation of humanity.

The Latter-day Saint Scriptures

The Church of Jesus Christ of Latter-day Saints formally was organized by the American prophet Joseph Smith Jr., on April 6, 1830, in the state of New York.[8] It took the Christian Bible, King James Version, as the foundational scripture and literal word of God insofar as it was translated correctly.[9] The uniquely Latter-day Saint Book of Mormon, understood as a second testament to Christ, provided another scripture.[10] It, as translated by Joseph Smith from ancient records, tells of the migration of biblical, old-world peoples to the New World; their subsequent conversion by Jesus Christ; and their pre-Columbian deviation from Christianity. The revelations of Joseph Smith and his prophetic successors up to the present day are recorded in a third scripture, titled the Doctrine and Covenants.[11] The Mormon canon is completed by the Pearl of Great Price, a volume containing Smith's partial retranslation of the King James Bible, his rendition of other sacred documents, and additional revelations of Latter-day Saint prophets.[12]

Scriptural Images of Human History

The early Latter-day Saints, like many Americans, believed that the Christian Bible provided a substantially literal history of humanity. All humanity was understood as descended from Adam and Eve, Noah, and especially Abraham as chronicled by the Bible and, according to Old Testament history, divided by race, ethnicity, tribe, or lineage into three main categories: (1) Jews—God's chosen people; (2) the descendents of Cain who because of their disobedience to God had been marked—commonly understood as dark skin color resulting in African peoples; and (3) Gentiles—everyone else.[13] The Jews were distinguished further by patriarchal tribes and lineage, especially from Abraham onward, perhaps implicitly accounting for the existence of Asian peoples.[14]

For the Latter-day Saints, the Book of Mormon resolved the biblical mystery of Native Americans by identifying them as descendants of ancient Israelites. Native Americans, according to the Book of Mormon account, mostly were the descendants of Lehi through his sons, Nephi and Laman, all of whom were Israelite immigrants to the New World. Following their conversion to Christianity at the Resurrection, the descendants of Nephi and Laman divided into warring factions, ultimately culminating in the destruction of the Christian Nephites by the apostate Lamanites. It was this Lamanite remnant that was present in the New World and named "Indians" by Columbus.

Early Mormons of European descent envisioned themselves as members of the tribes of Israel—specifically of the House of Joseph through Ephraim—having been transformed by some mystical means into Jews, a belief that was common enough among Euro-American peoples of the period.[15] Humanity thereby was understood as divided by God into racial or ethnic groups constituting Jews, dark-skinned Africans (and African Americans) as well as implicitly Asian people of color, gentiles, and Lamanites. God's plan for humanity was conceptualized in terms of these divisions of humanity by biblical lineage into discrete racial or ethnic groups.

God's Plan for the Salvation of Humanity

The Latter-day Saint religion, like Christianity generally, holds that faith in Jesus Christ is necessary for human redemption from the biblical Fall and eternal salvation. The Mormons—taking common Christian thinking as their basic point of departure—regarded the Jews as the people chosen by God to prepare the way for his plan, that being the eventual advent of the Savior.[16] Ultimately, they believed, the Jews would convert to Christianity and, consequently, there was no urgency in proselytizing them.[17] They understood the basic Christian mission to be the conversion of the gentiles. For the Mormons, this necessarily included the conversion of other Christians to the restored Church of Christ since all other forms of Christianity had fallen into apostasy following the death of the original apostles. Guided by the Book of Mormon, the Latter-day Saints assumed a special mission to the Lamanites (or Native Americans), expressly the reclaiming of these people to Christianity.[18]

In short, then, the Latter-day Saint religion, as sociologist Armand Mauss observes, embraced the Pauline commitment to the universal salvation of the Children of Abraham (or all God's people) from the beginning to the present. Early Mormonism, however, envisioned universal salvation in terms of priorities based on biblical imagery of lineage and its unique understanding of scripture. Mauss succinctly summarizes the sequence for gathering the descendants of Abraham as: "Ephraim and Manasseh first; Judah whenever it was ready; the other or 'lost' tribes of Israel whenever they were brought out of obscurity by the divine schedule; then the Gentiles; and finally the descendants of Cain."[19]

Latter-day Saint images of human history and these divisions of humanity into racial and ethnic categories gradually were transformed in the twentieth century with the scientific rejection of race as a meaningful distinction among human groups, globalization, and the success of this religion worldwide.[20] The LDS Church no longer encourages the previous distinction between themselves (as Israelites) and gentiles (outsiders). Greater sensitivity to Native Americans has resulted in formally dropping most references, outside of the language of scripture, to Lamanites. Joseph Smith authorized the baptism of a few African Americans and the ordination of select African American men to the priesthood, but Brigham Young (his immediate successor) prohibited African Americans from using their priesthood or being

ordained to the Mormon priesthood.[21] The church's success in South American, particularly Brazil where such ethnic heritage often is ambiguous, reinforced by American protests against this policy, contributed to considerable
internal pressure to overturn the semiofficial ban on black priesthood membership.[22] In 1978 this matter was rectified by prophetic revelation confirming
that people of color were as eligible for priesthood as any other worthy male
member.[23]

The early Latter-day Saint religion was directed primarily to the conversion of Native Americans, generally without a great deal of success (except
among Pacific Islanders as well as much later Central and South Americans),
and other Christians.[24] It, like many other Christian missionary efforts, discovered that attempts to convert non-Christians, particularly in the East and
Africa, required a different message from the previously successful appeals
to those already converted to Christianity. Over the past twenty or so years,
the Latter-day Saint conversion strategy increasingly has been reoriented to
teaching basic principles of Christianity before the more distinctive or unique
elements of this religion. In short, then, the contemporary Latter-day Saint
religion is oriented to converting all of humanity to its form of Christianity
with little specific regard for the older racial and ethnic categories or their
underlying scriptural rationale.

The Latter-day Saint Plan of Salvation

The Latter-day Saint understanding of God's plan for human salvation
involves unique concepts of the nature of Godhead, connections among premortal life, mortal life, and the spirit world as well as complex imagery of
multiple realms (kingdoms) of heaven and a realm of outer darkness (or the
approximate LDS version of Christian hell). Mormon salvation, much like
that of Christianity in general, requires belief in God, faith in Jesus Christ,
baptism by immersion for the remission of sin, laying on of hands for receipt
of the confirming gifts of the Holy Ghost (speaking in tongues, prophecy,
revelation, visions, healings, interpretation of tongues, miracles, and so on),
proper prayer, as well as obedience to God's laws and ordinances. Depending on the choices an individual makes, she or he may progress toward godhood and attain an exalted, god-like state and eternal life as a member of
God's family in the celestial world. Ultimately, then, Latter-day Saint salvation promises the conforming believer the possibility of attaining godhood
and reigning with God and Christ as a priest and king or priestess and queen,
along with other saved family members, in the celestial world eternally.

The Nature of God

Joseph Smith, the founding LDS prophet, taught that the supreme biblical God attained Godhood by a process like what is experienced by human beings. Smith preached in a funeral sermon that "God himself was once as we are now, and is an exalted man, and sits enthroned in yonder heavens!"[25] Having progressed in meeting all of the tests faced by humanity, God achieved the knowledge and power to gain supremacy over all gods and worlds. "In the beginning," Smith preached, the head of the Gods called a council of the Gods; and they came together and . . . [prepared] a plan to create the world and people it."[26] Openly acknowledging that he was teaching a doctrine of the plurality of gods and clearly turning trinitarianism on its head, Smith remarked in another sermon that "I have always declared God to be a distinctive personage, Jesus Christ is a separate personage from God the Father, and that the Holy Ghost was a distinctive personage and a Spirit: and these three constitute three distinctive personages and three Gods. If this is in accordance with the New Testament, lo and behold! We have three Gods anyhow, and they are plural: and who can contradict it!"[27] The founding Mormon prophet also taught his followers that there is a female deity, a Mother in Heaven, who is the wife (or consort) of God the Father.[28] Little is known about this female deity, and the LDS Church today does not emphasize her, but the Mother in Heaven is acknowledged in a popular Mormon hymn.[29]

Another important feature of Smith's revelations about the nature of God is a materialist metaphysics. God, he revealed, is a material (or embodied) being, explaining that the eternal elements—principally, spirit in the form of intelligence (mind or soul)—are nothing more or less than a higher form of matter. This spirit-matter forms the essence of everything, including God, Christ, premortal humanity, and embodied human beings. Or, in other words, spirit beings also have form—one that differs in essence only from mortal embodiment.[30]

The Cosmos and Multiple Worlds of Human Existence

Joseph Smith further taught that all human beings—as composed of the prime element of spirit-matter—are eternal; they existed in the beginning with God, and they are the premortal creation (literally, the off-spring) of God. In other words, the Latter-day Saint religion holds that human beings are the spirit children of God the Father who exist in a premortal world before they are born and embodied in mortal life. Following death, human beings become disembodied (resume a spirit-matter form) and go to the world of spirits to await judgment and resurrection. The Mormon spirit world is sub-divided into paradise and prison. Those who accepted the Latter-day Saint gospel await resurrection in paradise, while everyone else waits in prison. Fol-lowing the resurrection, based on their judgment, human beings go to the celestial world, terrestrial world, telestial world, or outer darkness.[31]

The *celestial world* represents the highest level of glory, and it is reserved for those who are in the process of becoming exalted, having accepted the Latter-day Saint gospel and fulfilled other requirements for salvation. The *terrestrial world*, the second level of glory, is for people who basically were good but did not accept the fullness of the gospel and who were worldly. The *teles-tial world*, the third level of glory, is for people who did not accept the gospel and/or have no testimony of Jesus Christ, as well as those who were sinners. Liars, sorcerers, adulterers, and whoremongers are among the sinful specifi-cally mentioned in scripture.[32] The telestial world, however, is not unpleas-ant, being part of heaven, even if it is a lesser level of celestial glory. *Outer darkness*, the Latter-day Saint equivalent of hell, is for the sons of perdition: those who have committed the unpardonable sin— the sin of having known but rejected the fullness of the Latter-day Saint gospel and having joined Lucifer (the devil).

Eternal Salvation

The Latter-day Saint religion holds that human beings—as premortal spirit children of God—received instructions from the Heavenly Father on his plan of salvation. Mortal life (or earthly human existence) is a time when these spirits, having been embodied, are tested and make decisions. Reject-ing Christian doctrines of original sin and predestination, the prophet Joseph Smith revealed that people by way of God-given agency and the decisions they make may progress to and attain exaltation and, ultimately, godhood. Or, in other words, they may achieve a god-like state and eternal life with God and Christ in the celestial world.

God's plan for salvation as taught by the Latter-day Saint religion requires people to abide by the commandments of God, as revealed in scripture, for righteous living. Critical to those commandments are the performance of cer-tain actions and ordinances. To be valid, these actions and ordinances must be performed in specific ways with the person by authorized members of the priesthood of the Church of Jesus Christ of Latter-day Saints. They include repentance from sin, prayer, Christian baptism by immersion, the confirm-ing laying on of hands for the gifts of the Holy Ghost, and certain unique rit-uals that only are performed in God's temple. Prayer, for instance, must take a specific form, and baptisms as well as the other ordinances require particular form and language as provided by scripture.

The basic temple rite is an endowment whereby a member enters into a covenant with God. By way of temple ritual, marriage may be extended beyond mortality to eternity, and other temple rituals involve sealing parents and children as well as other family members together eternally. In the ultimate salvation rite performed exclusively in a Latter-day Saint temple, a priesthood member and his spouse enter into a covenant with God whereby they receive a promise of eternal life in the celestial world. Finally, a ritual baptism by proxy may be performed in the temple for the living or the dead. This rite provides those who lived before the Latter-day Saint restoration and/or those who did not receive the gospel message with the opportunity to embrace Latter-day Saint Christianity and attain eternal salvation.

God's plan of salvation as understood by the Latter-day Saint religion is historically specific. People who lived from Adam to Jesus were resurrected with Christ, judged, and moved on to the realms of glory or outer darkness. Everyone born since the beginning of Christianity will be resurrected and judged in two stages at the time of Christ's Second Coming. All of those in paradise will be judged at the first of these resurrections. On the morning of the first resurrection, everyone worthy of the fullness of the gospel—namely, obedient Mormon priesthood members, their wives, and their families—will be resurrected to reign with Christ as kings and priests or queens and priestesses during the millennium. Everyone else with a testimony of Christ but without the fullness of the Mormon gospel will be resurrected in the afternoon, ushering in the millennium. The second resurrection, at the end of the millennium, is for those people who are awaiting judgment in spirit prison. Those judged worthy of some level of celestial glory will be first, followed by the sons of perdition who will be sent to outer darkness.

The Latter-day Saint Religion in a Pluralistic World

In response to the specific questions posed by William Scott Green, it should be clear from the foregoing that the Latter-day Saint religion, in its classic sources as they have developed to the present, envisions other religions, particularly the biblical traditions, as a part of God's plan for humanity and salvation.[33] Mormonism takes little notice of religions other than those derived from the Bible. The Latter-day Saint religion holds that it exclusively is the route to humanity's eternal salvation. Yet, almost everyone eventually will earn eternal salvation and some degree of glory in heaven.

Mormonism treats Judaism, much like Christianity in general, as a part of God's plan to prepare a select people for the advent of Christ. The Latter-day Saint religion, unlike some other forms of Christianity, takes the Old Testament of the Christian Bible seriously, drawing on it specifically in the development of organizational forms, temple rituals, and the fundamental values and norms of daily life. The Old and New Testaments in Latter-day Saint theology (as well as all of its other scriptures) are fully indexical, mutually elaborating, and incomplete without one another, comprising mere parts of a larger whole. Other forms of Christianity, in spite of their apostasy, also are all a part of God's plan from a Latter-day Saint perspective. The most salient feature of other forms of Christianity from a Mormon standpoint is not that they are wrong but rather that they—much like other forms of biblical religion—are incomplete revelations. Other Christianities more specifically are seen as constructive in providing believers with a testimony of the Christ and enabling them to achieve some degree of glory and eternal salvation.

Islam, for the early Latter-day Saints and most other Americans, was an exotic religion about which they knew little. Islam, nevertheless, implicitly was recognized as an Abrahamic religion and part of the biblical tradition. This Abrahamic kinship with the descendants of Ishmael was acknowledged more explicitly in the 1970s when the Latter-day Saints began developing specific missions to Muslims worldwide. Hence, the Latter-day Saint religion regards Islam in much the same way as Judaism and Christianity, namely, as one of the biblical religions but an incomplete revelation.[34]

Mormonism, much like most other new religions, initially experienced a lack of acceptance, leading to considerable tension with the people, culture, and society of the United States. From the formal organization of the church in 1830, the Mormons moved from New York to Ohio, then to Missouri and Illinois, until reaching the valley of the Great Salt Lake in 1847, in what became the Utah Territory of the United States. These moves were provoked in part because of conflict with other Americans and the socially dominant institutions, some of it resulting in violence.[35] The Mormons consequently developed and sustained a collective sense of being persecuted for their religion as God's chosen people through these experiences.[36]

The collective Mormon identity as a peculiar and persecuted people was reinforced by their relative isolation in the intermountain American West from headquarters in Salt Lake City, Utah, as well as their social, cultural, economic, and political dominance within this region of the United States. This collective identity lasted into the middle of the twentieth century.[37] Following the end of World War ii, the Latter-day Saint religion rapidly accommodated to American culture and society.[38] Mormons have assimilated into the larger sociocultural fabric to such an extent that literary critic Harold Bloom concluded that this religion and its people now are quintessentially American.[39] While the Latter-day Saint religion and its people largely have accommodated to the pluralism of a global society, some observers detect signs of retrenchment today.[40] Even so, there is little indication that Latter-day Saint exclusivity will result in any substantial rejection of religious pluralism or the coexistence it has accommodated with other cultures or religions.

In responding further to the important issues raised by William Scott Green, it is useful to review briefly what is known specifically about Latter-day Saint relations with other people and religions. Mormonism generally is highly respectful of other culture and religions, and it encourages the retention of cultural identities so long as they contain no religious elements in competition with the Latter-day Saint religion. It, in other words, unlike many religions, does not permit much of any retention of distinctive cultural heritages by converts that include features of potentially rival religions. The structure and organization of the Latter-day Saint religion and its normative expectations for the membership are extraordinarily uniform in whatever culture it is found. It, for instance, permits the use of languages other than English but little cultural variation from the largely American structure of worship, ritual, and recommended lifestyle.[41]

Summarizing the Mormons' treatment of Native Americans in the intermountain West of the United States historically, sociologists Bruce Chadwick and Stan Albrecht observe that "[u]ndoubtedly, both kindness and cruelty existed, but the overall evidence suggests that Latter-day Saints, because of their beliefs about Indian Americans' belonging to the House of Israel and the church's responsibility to help them flourish as a people, treated Indian Americans much more humanely than most others did on the American frontier."[42] Sociologist Armand Mauss is much less certain, however, that the Mormon view of Native Americans was all that different from other Americans once the Latter-day Saints were located in the West and encountered conflict with some of the tribes.[43]

Until recently the LDS Church sponsored special services and programs for Native Americans, including opportunities to attend Brigham Young University. In reviewing studies of the consequences of church membership and participation in these programs for Native Americans, Armand Mauss concludes that those who did not fully assimilate to American Mormonism exhibited conflicted identities. In more recent years, the Saints' lack of success in converting North American native peoples combined with the considerable receptivity to Mormonism in Central and South America (among peoples commonly of mixed Native and European backgrounds) has resulted in redefinition of the Book of Mormon message and its understanding by the American membership as well as Mesoamerican converts.

Early Mormonism inherited much of the existing history of the tensions and conflict between Judaism and Christianity.[44] Joseph Smith, however, reconceptualized Mormon Christianity with powerfully significant Hebraic overtones. The Latter-day Saints envisioned themselves literally as the new Israelites, linked by lineage, scripture, and ritual to the Jews, past and present. Ultimately, Smith taught, there would be two zionic gatherings, one of Jews in Israel and another of Saints in America, in preparation for the coming of the Messiah and his millennial reign on earth. It, therefore, is hardly surprising that sociologists find Mormons historically to be much lower than other Americans on measures of anti-Semitism.[45] Those studies, furthermore, are supported by several accounts by Jews of favorable relationships with Mormons in the American West.[46]

From 1852 to 1978, the Church of Jesus Christ of Latter-day Saints prohibited people of black ancestry from holding the priesthood, and it did little proselytizing among Africans or African Americans. Sociologist Armand Mauss carefully examined Mormon views of African Americans before 1978.[47] He found little difference between Latter-day Saints and other white Americans, both of whom exhibited religious hostility toward blacks resulting in prejudice and discrimination. Mauss endeavored to sort out the connections among religious orthodoxy, provincialism, and hostility, as well as their relationship to prejudice and discrimination for non-Mormon and Mormon Americans. He concluded that religious provincialism (rather than orthodoxy) is associated most strongly with religious hostility toward outsiders (blacks, Jews, and so on) and that it, in turn, is what produces prejudice and discrimination. Hence, Mormons have tended in most sociological studies to express highly favorable views toward Jews and Native Americans while reflecting negatively prejudicial views and discriminatory actions toward blacks, much like other white Americans.[48]

Since 1978, the LDS Church has engaged in various public relations efforts to change its racist public image, and it has sought actively to convert black Americans and Africans.[49] For many Mormons, the 1978 revelation resolved the "race issue." Armand Mauss, based on survey data of the American population, concludes that prejudice and discrimination toward blacks has declined among Latter-day Saints at rates equal to or greater than those for other white Americans. Since the LDS Church does not collect data on ethnicity, it is difficult to know how successful it has been in converting African Americans. Even so, a few African Americans now are prominently presented and promoted by the church and its programs. One study by social scientists Cardell Jacobson, Tim Heaton, Dale LeBaron, and Trina Hope found that black Americans "felt reasonably accepted in the LDS Church."[50] All of the available data on African Americans who convert to and remain active in the Latter-day Saint religion seems to support this general conclusion.[51]

Mormonism, like many American sects, has found Africa (as well as portions of Eastern Europe and Russia) to be hostile to its missions. Even so, when not legally prohibited, the Latter-day Saints have actively pursued African converts since 1978 with some success. Cardell Jacobson, Tim Heaton, Dale LeBaron, and Trina Hope, in reviewing what little is known about Mormonism in Africa, conclude that "[t]he overall impression from [interviews with African members] . . . is that racial tension is not a major problem of the LDS Church in Africa."[52] Armand Mauss concludes that "[a]ll believers of all lineages thus finally became the children of Abraham, as the apostle Paul had promised," in the Latter-day Saint religion.[53]

Summary and Conclusion

The Latter-day Saint restoration of the Gospel and Church of Christ exclusively provide for the universal and eternal salvation of humanity according to God's plan. Only those who embrace the exclusive fullness of the Latter-day Saint gospel and are otherwise obedient to God's commandments will become exalted, god-like beings and attain eternal life in the celestial world as a part of the family of God and Christ. The Latter-day Saint religion, notwithstanding this exclusivity, recognizes that not everyone will convert to Mormonism; and those who do not implicitly will have additional opportunities to do so in the worlds beyond mortal earthly existence. Although the highest degree of glory in heaven is reserved for obedient Latter-day Saints, all other godly people will receive some degree of heavenly glory and eternal life. This presumably will include at least most all good people of other religions besides Mormonism. Only the very few individuals, the sons of perdition, who reject God and Christ as well as follow Lucifer, will be relegated to outer darkness (or hell).

In spite of Latter-day Saint exclusivity, this theodicy directly acknowledges nonbelievers and other religions, as well as encourages Mormon toleration of them and these differences. Put somewhat differently, Latter-day Saint theodicy recognizes pluralism, accepts it, and requires toleration of cultural and religious differences. Obedience to God's commandments as found in the

Latter-day Saint scriptures, especially the Christian Bible as reinforced by the Book of Mormon, prohibits actions harmful to the welfare of other human beings—except only in self-defense or other similarly justifiable ways. Mormonism thereby avoids the potentially negative sociological consequences of religious exclusivity and absolutism.

Twenty-first-century Mormonism is thoroughly committed to the Pauline promise of Christian universalism inclusive of all of God's children. The Latter-day Saint religion and its people, notwithstanding a history of tension and conflict with outsiders, has accommodated to worldwide cultural and religious pluralism. The Latter-day Saints, because of their sense of special affinity with Jews and Judaism, as well as their distinctive mission to the indigenous peoples of the Americas and the Pacific, exhibit little hostility, prejudice, or discrimination toward these groups. With the 1978 revelation specifically directing the Latter-day Saint religion to include people of black African descent in God's plan with all human rights and privileges, the previous hostility, prejudice, and discrimination toward these peoples has decreased significantly among the Latter-day Saints.

Since the 2003 global religion poll discussed by Professor Green apparently did not gather information specifically on Latter-day Saints, it is difficult to know with certainty how they might have responded to the survey questions.[54] Even so, it is possible to suggest how the Latter-day Saint religion, in its classic sources and what is known about its practice (as discussed here), most likely would respond to those questions. Mormonism clearly holds that it exclusively is the path to human salvation, yet its view of salvation acknowledges that most all of the adherents of other religions also will go to heaven and achieve some degree of glory, as well as eternal salvation. Contemporary Latter-day Saint theology recognizes all of God's children as equal and none of them as superior to the others. While Mormons generally have favored intra-faith marriages, they also see interfaith unions as outstanding opportunities for conversion; and, as with other minority religions in the United States and elsewhere, interfaith marriage is a common practice and accepted reality. The Latter-day Saint religion would find it difficult to respond to questions about punishments for disobedience to God. The Heavenly Father envisioned by this religion is more a God of love and compassion, although Mormons clearly anticipate facing judgment based on obedience to his commandments.

The Latter-day Saint religion ultimately is extraordinarily optimistic about humanity and its prospects for redemption and eternal salvation. There is no doubt about what God expects of humanity. These matters are clearly defined by scripture. Yet, the Latter-day Saint religion recognizes precious few unpardonable sins. In this respect, it sees God the Father as exceptionally tolerant of human disobedience and mistakes. The only specifically unpardonable sin is the rejection of God's plan, the redemptive power of Christ, combined with deliberate opposition to God in league with Lucifer. Yet, even the sons of perdition may have future opportunities in other worlds to redeem themselves and obtain eternal salvation. For the Latter-day Saint religion, human beings are embryonic gods, capable of progressing to godhood by way of God's plan for them. Such a theology leaves little room for intolerance of others or hostility, aggression, and violence toward them—except in self-defense—no matter their culture or religion.

Notes

1. Although there are more than one hundred varieties of the Latter-day Saint religion, all references here specifically are to the Church of Jesus Christ of Latter-day Saints headquartered in Salt Lake City, Utah, the largest single group, unless noted otherwise.

2. Insofar as Islam was recognized by the Latter-day Saints as a biblical or Abrahamic religion, it too was believed to be partly incorrect.

3. See *Church Almanac* (Salt Lake City, UT: Deseret News, 2006). Also see Jeffery L. Sheler, "The Mormon Moment: The Church of Latter-day Saints Grows by Leaps and Bounds," *US News and World Report*, November 13, 2000.

4. Rodney Stark, "The Rise of a New World Faith," *Review of Religious Research* 26 (1984): 18–27; also see Stark, "Modernization and Mormon Growth: The Secularization Thesis Revisited," *Contemporary Mormonism: Social Science Perspectives*, ed. Marie Cornwall, Tim B. Heaton, and Lawrence A. Young, 13–23 (Urbana: University of Illinois Press, 1994); Stark, "So Far, So Good: A Brief Assessment of Mormon Membership Projections," *Review of Religious Research* 38 (1996): 174–178; and Stark, "A Theoretical Assessment of LDS Growth," *Latter-day Saint Social Life: Social Research on the LDS Church and Its Members*, ed. James T. Duke, 29–70 (Provo, UT: Religious Studies Center, Brigham Young University, Bookcraft, 1998).

5. See Peggy Fletcher Stack, "Keeping Members a Challenge for LDS Church: Mormon Myth: The Belief That the Church Is the Fastest-Growing Faith in the World Doesn't Hold Up," *Salt Lake Tribune*, June 22, 2006.

6. An excellent contemporary overview of the sociologies of knowledge and religion is provided by Steve Bruce, *Religion in the Modern World: From Cathedrals to Cults* (New York: Oxford University Press, 1996). Also see Peter L. Berger, *The Sacred Canopy: Elements of a Sociological Theory of Religion* (Garden City, NY: Doubleday, 1967); Bryan R. Wilson, *Religious Sects: A Sociological Study* (London: Weidenfeld and Nicolson, 1970); Max Weber, *From Max Weber: Essays in Sociology*, trans. and ed. H. H. Gerth and C. Wright Mills (New York: Oxford University Press, 1946); Max Weber, *Max Weber on Charisma and Institution Building: Selected Papers*, ed. S. N. Eisenstadt (Chicago: University of Chicago Press, 1968); and Max Weber, *The Sociology of Religion*, trans. Ephraim Fischoff (Boston: Beacon Press, 1963).

7. For a more comprehensive interpretation of this matter, see Douglas J. Davies, *The Mormon Culture of Salvation: Force, Grace, and Glory* (Burlington, VT: Ashgate, 2000).

8. A sound overview of the Saints is provided by Leonard J. Arrington and Davis Bitton, *The Mormon Experience: A History of the Latter-day Saints*, 2nd ed. (Urbana: University of Illinois Press, 1992). Also see James B. Allen and Glen M. Leonard, *The Story of the Latter-day Saints*, 2nd ed. (Salt Lake City, UT: Deseret Book Company, 1992).

9. See "Articles of Faith of the Church of Jesus Christ of Latter-day Saints," accessed at www.lds.org/library, on November 5, 2006 (also reprinted in Joseph Smith, *History of the Church of Jesus Christ of Latter-day Saints*, 7 vols., ed. B. H. Roberts [Salt Lake City, UT: Church of Jesus Christ of Latter-day Saints, 1902–1932], 4:535–41), hereafter cited as *History of the Church*.

10. Joseph Smith, trans., *The Book of Mormon* (New York: Doubleday, 2004).

11. *The Doctrine and Covenants of the Church of Jesus Christ of Latter-day Saints* (Salt Lake City, UT: Church of Jesus Christ of Later-day Saints, 1982); hereafter cited as DC.

12. *The Pearl of Great Price* (Salt Lake City, UT: Church of Jesus Christ of Later-day Saints, 1982).

13. For an extended discussion of these themes, see Armand L. Mauss, *All Abraham's Children: Changing Mormon Conceptions of Race and Lineage* (Urbana: University of Illinois Press, 2003).

14. The logical possibility of extending Mormon arguments about biblical lineage to Asian peoples is purely speculative on my part. To the best of my knowledge the people of the East were a biblical anomaly for the early Mormons, and there were no explicit efforts to include them in world history according to the Bible.

15. See Mauss, *All Abraham's Children*, 17–40, for a detailed discussion of this belief among the Latter-day Saints, other Americans, and Europeans.

16. For discussions of Latter-day Saint views of Jews and Judaism, see Rudolf Glanz, *Jew and Mormon: Historic Group Relations and Religious Outlook* (New York: Waldron, 1963); Steve Epperson, *Mormons and Jews: Early Mormon Theologies of Israel* (Salt Lake City, UT: Signature Books, 1992); and Arnold Green, "Gathering and Election: Israelite Descent and Universalism in Mormon Discourse," *Journal of Mormon History* 25, no. 1 (1999): 195–228. For a summary of the scholarly literature on Mormon/Jewish relations, see Mauss, *All Abraham's Children*, 158–190.

17. See Arnold Green, "A Survey of LDS Proselyting Efforts to the Jewish People," *Brigham Young University Studies* 8, no. 4 (1968): 427–443.

18. See Mauss, *All Abraham's Children*, 41–157.

19. Ibid., 276.

20. Ibid.

21. Ibid., 212–30; Newell G. Bringhurst, *Saints, Slaves, and Blacks: The Changing Place of Black People within Mormonism* (Westport, CT: Greenwood, 1981); as well as Lester E. Bush and Armand L. Mauss, eds., *Neither White nor Black: Mormon Scholars Confront the Race Issue in a Universal Church* (Salt Lake City, UT: Signature Books, 1984) for sound discussions of this matter. Also see Roger D. Launius, *Invisible Saints: A History of Black Americans in the Reorganized Church* (Independence, MO: Herald Publishing House, 1988).

22. See Mary Lou McNamara, "Secularization or Sacralization: The Change in LDS Church Policy on Blacks," in *Contemporary Mormonism*, 310–325.

23. DC, Official Declaration 2. The Latter-day Saint religion maintains a lay priesthood consisting of all worthy male members.

24. Mauss, *All Abraham's Children*, notes that Mormons interpreted an obscure Book of

Mormon reference, Alma 63:5–8, as having extended Nephite—and, therefore, Israelite—identity to Polynesian peoples. Hence, the tremendous success of Mormonism in Polynesia was seen as fulfilling the special Latter-day Saint mission to the Lamanites. Likewise, the immensely successful Latin American missions were understood to involve the conversion of people of Lamanite descent.

25. Joseph Smith, "King Follet Sermon," April 7, 1844, 11 pages, accessed at www.utlm.org, on November 1, 2006, p. 3 (also reprinted in Smith, *History of the Church* 6:473–79).

26. Ibid., 5.

27. Joseph Smith, "Sermon on Plurality of Gods," June 16, 1844, 5 pages, accessed at www .utlm.org, on November 1, 2006 (also reprinted in Smith, *History of the Church*, 6:473-79).

28. See Linda P. Wilcox, "The Mormon Concept of a Mother in Heaven," in *Sisters in Spirit: Mormon Women in Historical and Cultural Perspective*, ed. Maureen Ursenback Beecher and Lavina Fielding Anderson, 64–77 (Urbana: University of Illinois Press, 1987); and Danny L. Jorgensen, "The Mormon Gender-Inclusive Image of God," *Journal of Mormon History* 27, no. 1 (Spring 2001): 95–126.

29. See Eliza R. Snow, "O My Father," in *Hymns of The Church of Jesus Christ of Latter-day Saints* (Salt Lake City, UT: The Church of Jesus Christ of Latter-day Saints, 1985), 292.

30. See Jacob Neusner, "Conversations in Nauvoo on the Corporeality of God," *Brigham Young University Studies* 36, no. 1 (1996–97): 7–30, for an invaluable comparative assessment of the Mormon God concept.

31. See DC, section 76.

32. Ibid., 76:82, 103.

33. William Scott Green, "The 'What' and 'Why' of Religious Toleration: Some Questions to Consider," this volume.

34. See Mauss, *All Abraham's Children*, 184–88.

35. See, for example, Marvin S. Hill, *Quest for Refuge: The Mormon Flight from American Pluralism* (Salt Lake City, UT: Signature Books, 1989).

36. R. Laurence Moore, *Religious Outsiders and the Making of Americans* (New York: Oxford University Press, 1986), astutely observes that this sense of persecution—no matter its externally observable conditions—is sociologically functional for producing a powerful sense of solidarity and identity among members of a religious sect.

37. See Thomas F. O'Dea, *The Mormons* (Chicago: University of Chicago Press, 1957); and Lawrence A. Young, "Confronting Turbulent Environments: Issues in the Organizational Growth and Globalization of Mormonism," in *Contemporary Mormonism*, 43–63.

38. See Klaus J. Hansen, *Mormonism and the American Experience* (Chicago: University of Chicago Press, 1981).

39. Harold Bloom, *The American Religion: The Emergence of a Post-Christian Nation* (New York: Simon and Schuster, 1992). Even so, it is not clear whether other Americans are willing to elect a Mormon as president of the United States. See Hannah Elliott, "A Mormon for President? Poll Says Probably Not; Pundits Not So Sure," *Associated Baptist Press*, July 25, 2006.

40. See Armand L. Mauss, "Refuge and Retrenchment: The Mormon Quest for Identity," in *Contemporary Mormonism*, 24–42.

41. The LDS Church, for instance, owns and operates the Polynesian Cultural Center on Oahu in Hawaii. Natives from throughout Polynesia who are Mormons attend Brigham Young University–Hawaii without paying tuition, and many of them are employed in a

work-study type program at the Polynesian Cultural Center. The center provides a glimpse of the external cultural characteristics (dwellings, tools, foods, and the like) of various Polynesian cultures, and a huge evening pageant displays Polynesian song and dance. Perhaps surprisingly, it is the most popular tourist attraction on the Hawaiian Islands. In observing all of this in 1990, I was struck by how almost all evidence of earlier Polynesian religion had been purged from the depictions and performances of these cultures. A large mural in the BYU student center portrays a traditional sacrifice ritual at a volcano, yet the natives are not depicted in the nude (as they surely would have been) but in what resembles Mormon temple dress, and there is no indication of actual human sacrifice.

42. Bruce A. Chadwick and Stan L. Albrecht, "Mormons and Indians: Beliefs, Policies, Programs, and Practices," in *Contemporary Mormonism*, 287–309.

43. Mauss, *All Abraham's Children*, 121–51.

44. Ibid., 158–211.

45. See ibid., 191–211, for an excellent summary of the sociological literature.

46. See Jack Goodman, "Jews in Zion," in *The People of Utah*, ed. Helen Z. Papanikolas, 187–220 (Salt Lake City: Utah State Historical Society, 1976); Louis C. Zucker, "A Jew in Zion," *Sunstone* (September–October 1981): 35–44; and Juanita Brooks, *The History of Jews in Utah and Idaho* (Salt Lake City, UT: Western Epics, 1973).

47. Mauss, *All Abraham's Children*, 218–230.

48. Ibid., 121–57.

49. Ibid., 231–66.

50. Cardell K. Jacobson, Tim B. Heaton, E. Dale LeBaron, and Trina Louise Hope, "Black Mormon Converts in the United States and Africa: Social Characteristics and Perceived Acceptance," in *Contemporary Mormonism*, 342.

51. See, for example, Jessie L. Embry, *Black Saints in a White Church: Contemporary African American Mormons* (Salt Lake City, UT: Signature Books, 1994); and Cardell Jacobson, ed., *All God's Children: Racial and Ethnic Voices in the LDS Church* (Springville, UT: Bonneville Books, 2004).

52. Jacobson et al., in *Contemporary Mormonism*, 344.

53. Mauss, *All Abraham's Children,* 276.

54. Baylor University, *The Baylor Religion Survey* (Waco, TX: Baylor Institute for Studies in Religion, 2005), did collect information from a small subsample of Latter-day Saints. The results for Mormons have not been published; although when they are available, these data may permit further analysis and interpretation of Mormons specifically.

PART 5

JUDAISM

9

THEOLOGICAL FOUNDATIONS OF
TOLERANCE IN CLASSICAL JUDAISM

JACOB NEUSNER

The three monotheist religions—Judaism, Christianity, and Islam—find it difficult to tolerate one another but impossible to tolerate any religion besides themselves. The logic of monotheism—there is only one God, who governs all things—yields little basis for tolerating other religions. So, while religious toleration forms a natural attitude for secular people who believe nothing or for polytheists who believe everything, religious resources of tolerance do not flow abundantly out of the theology of monotheism.

There are no theological foundations of tolerance in classical Judaism, only eschatological intimations that, at the end of days, all humanity will know the one true God. But that is not the same thing as a theological basis for tolerating error or those that commit error. In the here and now, no doctrines accord recognition to religions other than Judaism. And classical Judaism contains no doubt as to the outcome of history in the end-time: God will see to it that all of humanity accords recognition to him as the one true God, and, on that basis, now as part of the Israel that knows God, the exgentiles will inherit the world to come.

Let me begin with one detail and then turn to the comprehensive issues that require attention. Judaism, like Christianity and Islam, resolves the problem of evil that is endemic to monotheism by appeal to a last judgment and the promise of eternal life for those who are justified. In the eternal life, the anomalies of this world, where the wicked prosper and the righteous suffer, are resolved. Now the issue is this: do gentiles (not Israelites) enter into eternal life upon resurrection from the dead, as do Israelites? The entire issue of toleration is captured by a dispute that concerns eschatological tolerance of gentiles, defined as idolaters, as against Israelites, defined as those who know God: does the gentile at the end of days rise from the grave, stand in judgment, and gain a portion in the world to come, as do nearly all Israelites? The matter is subject to debate:

A.   R. Eleazar says, "None of the gentiles has a portion in the world to come, as it is said, 'The wicked shall return to Sheol, all the gentiles who forget God' (Ps. 9:17). 'The wicked shall return to Sheol'—these are the wicked Israelites. 'And all the gentiles who forget God'—these are the nations."

B.   Said to him R. Joshua, "If it had been written, 'The wicked shall return to Sheol—all the gentiles,' and then nothing further, I should have maintained as you do. Now that it is in fact written, 'All the gentiles who forget God,' it indicates that there are righteous people among the nations of the world who do have a portion in the world to come."

Tosefta Sanhedrin 13:2

What makes a gentile righteous is that he does not forget God. But remembering God entails acknowledging him and that makes the gentile into an Israelite. That is in line with the prophetic vision, recapitulated in the *Alenu* prayer, that, in the end of days, the whole of humanity will know God as Israel does now. All Israel has a portion in the world to come (M. San. 11:1) yields, "All who have a portion in the world to come are Israel." So, eschatological tolerance raises a prospect that, on second glance, does not yield toleration at all: gentiles enjoy eternal life but only as Israelites—and that is Joshua's view. Eliezer, for his part, does not dissimulate. But even if we treat Joshua's opinion as normative, we have no category, idolatry, or a religion devoted to a god other than the God who made himself known to Abraham, to which toleration is accorded. The category formation, tolerable religion other than that of the Lord, does not present itself in the classic rabbinic law and theology. That is because the systemic category formation that defines the social order that Judaism constitutes, called "Israel," precipitates the formation of its opposite, "non-Israel," outsider; and the "non-Israel" is defined as God's enemy: the idolater. The entire system aims at demonstrating God's justice and mercy, and, in that context, the outsider is justly excluded. There are nuances to the exposition of the matter that we shall consider, but the basic point registers: there are no theological foundations for toleration of idolatry or the idolater in classical Judaism.

Neither the philosophical nor the exegetical nor the mythic formulation sets forth a doctrine that validates difference from the monotheist norm. Monotheism by its nature begins with the intolerant position that there is only one God; so all other gods are false, and those that worship other gods than the God who made himself known in revelation—in the Instruction, or Torah, of Sinai—are enemies of God. To uncover the foundations for a policy of toleration, we must enter into the complexity of the law, theology, and narrative of classical Judaism.

For scripture, the starting point of Judaism, the community at large forms the focus of the law, and idolatry is not to be negotiated with by the collectivity of holy Israel. In its land, Israel is to wipe out idolatry, even as a memory. Scripture is clear that Israel is to obliterate all mention of idols (Ex. 23:13), not bow down to gentiles' gods or serve them but overthrow them and break them into pieces (Ex. 23:24): "You shall break down their altars and dash in pieces their pillars and hew down their Asherim and burn their graven images with fire" (Dt. 7:5). Israelites are commanded along these same lines:

"The graven images of their gods you shall burn with fire; you shall not covet the silver or the gold that is on them or take it for yourselves, lest you be ensnared by it; for it is an abomination to the Lord your God. And you shall not bring an abominable thing into your house and become accused like it."

(Dt. 7:25–26)

"You shall surely destroy all the places where the nations whom you shall dispossess served their gods, upon the high mountains and upon the hills and under every green tree; you shall tear down their altars and dash in pieces their pillars and burn their Asherim with fire; you shall hew down the graven images of their gods and destroy their name out of that place."

(Dt. 12:2–3)

Accordingly, so far as the written Torah supplies the foundations for the treatment of the matter by the rabbinic canon of the formative age, the focus of discourse concerning the gentiles is idolatry. Scripture's Halakhah does not contemplate Israel's coexisting, in the land, with gentiles and their idolatry.

The Religious System of Judaism in Its Normative Statement

The characterization of the Judaic theology of the gentiles requires attention to the entire corpus of canonical writings that all together define the norm. The canon of classical Judaism comprising scripture and the rabbinic legal and exegetical complements to scripture came to closure by the seventh century

CE. The rabbinic law, contained in the Mishnah, ca. 200 CE, a philosophical law code; the Tosefta, ca. 300 CE, complements the Mishnah; the Yerushalmi or Talmud of the land of Israel, ca. 400 CE, a commentary to thirty-nine tractates of the sixty-one topical expositions of the Mishnah and the Tosefta; and the Bavli or Talmud of Babylonia, ca. 600 CE, a commentary to thirty-seven tractates of the Mishnah and the Tosefta. The whole is constructed in dialogue with the law, narrative, and prophecy of scripture, with a privileged standing accorded to the Pentateuch or Torah of Moses.

The rabbinic sages of late antiquity set forth a religious system of the culture and social order of the community of which they speak, which they call "Israel," those concerning whom scripture tells its stories and to whom scripture addresses its law and prophecy. That religious system defines the way of life and the worldview of the Israel that embodies the one and explains itself in accord with the other. The world—all humanity—is divided, in accord with the Judaic system, into two classifications of persons, the gentiles and Israel. So our question becomes: what are the theological resources for tolerance of gentiles that classical Judaism nurtures? Why should gentiles enjoy the toleration of Israelites, meaning, why does God accommodate in the world that he made and now governs the presence of gentiles as well as Israelites?

The Halakhic system of the Mishnah, Tosefta, Yerushalmi, and Bavli speaks to a world that is not so simple. The land belongs to Israel, but gentiles live there too—and run things. And Israel no longer forms a coherent collectivity but a realm made up of individuals, with their distinctive and particular interests. The Halakhah of the rabbinic canon of the formative age commences its treatment of the same subject with the opposite premise: gentiles live side by side (whether or not in the land of Israel) with Israelites, and Israelites have to sort out the complex problems of coexistence with idolatry. And that coexistence involves not whole communities, the People (Israel) and the peoples, whoever they may be, but individuals, this Israelite living side by side with that gentile.

Moreover, the rabbinic documents use the occasion of idolatry to contemplate a condition entirely beyond the imagination of scripture, which is the hegemony of idolatrous nations and the subjugation of holy Israel. The topic of idolatry forms the occasion for the discussion of Israel's place among the nations of the world and of Israel's relationships with gentiles. Furthermore, the rabbinic system's theory of who Israel is finds its context in the contrast with the gentiles. The meeting point with the written Torah is defined by the indicative trait of the gentiles, which is their idolatry; that is all that matters about them.

Why Is Humanity Divided between Israel, the Unique Community of Humanity That Knows God, and the Gentiles, No Community at All, Who Do Not Know God?

We turn to the mythic explanation of why there are gentiles in the world and how they are to be assessed by Judaism. It is a narrative of the story of humanity in relationship to the one and only God of creation. The story recapitulates the history of Adam and Eve and their successors, ten generations from Adam to Noah that God found rebellious:

A. The generation of the flood has no share in the world to come,

B. and they shall not stand in the judgment,

C. since it is written, "My spirit shall not judge with man forever" (Gen. 6:3)

D. neither judgment nor spirit.

E. The generation of the dispersion has no share in the world to come,

F. since it is said, "So the Lord scattered them abroad from there upon the face of the whole earth" (Gen. 11:8).

G. "So the Lord scattered them abroad"—in this world,

H. "and the Lord scattered them from there"—in the world to come.

I. The men of Sodom have no portion in the world to come,

J. since it is said, "Now the men of Sodom were wicked and sinners against the Lord exceedingly" (Gen. 13:13)

K. "Wicked"—in this world,

L. "And sinners"—in the world to come.

Mishnah-tractate Sanhedrin 10:3

God wiped out the children of Adam, leaving only Noah—"righteous in his generation"—to regenerate the human race. The children of Noah, all humanity, are subject to seven religious obligations or commandments, for which violations are punished. Israel, whom we meet in a later chapter of the same narrative, is obligated to hundreds (the conventional number is 613, the combination of the days of the solar year and the bones of the body).

God tolerates the children of Noah so long as they keep the commandments assigned to them. God does not neglect the gentiles or fail to exercise dominion over them. For even now, gentiles are subject to a number of commandments or religious obligations. God cares for gentiles as for Israel, he wants gentiles as much as Israel to enter the kingdom of heaven, and he assigns to gentiles opportunities to evince their acceptance of his rule. One of these commandments is not to curse God's name:

A. "Any man who curses his God shall bear his sin" (Lev. 24:15).

B. It would have been clear had the text simply said, "A man."

C. Why does it specify, "Any"?

D. It serves to encompass idolaters, who are admonished not to curse the Name, just as Israelites are so admonished. ·

Bavli Sanhedrin 7:5 I.2/56a

Not cursing God, even while worshiping idols, seems a minimal expectation.

But, in fact, there are seven such religious obligations that apply to the children of Noah. If they observe these commandments, they are in good standing with God. It is not surprising—indeed, it is predictable—that the definition of the matter should find its place in the Halakhah of Abodah Zarah, Tosefta-tractate Abodah Zarah 8:4–6:

T. 8:4 A. Concerning seven religious requirements were the children of Noah admonished:

B. setting up courts of justice, idolatry, blasphemy [cursing the name of God], not practicing cruelty to animals, fornication, bloodshed, and thievery.

We now proceed to show how each of these religious obligations is represented as applying to gentiles as much as to Israelites:

C. Concerning setting up courts of justice—how so [how does scripture or reason validate the claim that gentiles are to set up courts of justice]?

D. Just as Israelites are commanded to call into session in their towns courts of justice.

E. Concerning idolatry and blasphemy—how so? . . .

F. Concerning fornication—how so?

G. "On account of any form of prohibited sexual relationship on account of which an Israelite court inflicts the death-penalty, the children of Noah are subject to warning," the words of R. Meir.

H. And sages say, "There are many prohibited relationships, on account of which an Israelite court does not inflict the death-penalty and the children of Noah are [not] warned. In regard to these forbidden relationships the nations are judged in accord with the laws governing the nations.

1. "And you have only the prohibitions of sexual relations with a betrothed maiden alone."

The systemization of scripture's evidence for the stated proposition continues:

T. 8:5 A. For bloodshed—how so?

B. A gentile [who kills] a gentile and a gentile who kills an Israelite are liable. An Israelite [who kills] a gentile is exempt.

C. Concerning thievery?

D. [If] one has stolen, or robbed, and so too in the case of finding a beautiful captive [woman], and in similar cases:

E. a gentile in regard to a gentile, or a gentile in regard to an Israelite—it is prohibited. And an Israelite in regard to a gentile—it is permitted.

T. 8:6 A. Concerning a limb cut from a living beast—how so?

B. A dangling limb on a beast, [which] is not [so connected] as to bring about healing,

C. is forbidden for use by the children of Noah, and, it goes without saying, for Israelites.

D. But if there is [in the connecting flesh] sufficient [blood supply] to bring about healing,

E. it is permitted to Israelites, and, it goes without saying, to the children of Noah.

As in the case of Israelites, so the death penalty applies to a Noahide, so b. San. 7:5 I.4–5/57a: "On account of violating three religious duties are children of Noah put to death: on account of adultery, murder, and blasphemy." R. Huna, R. Judah, and all the disciples of Rab say, "On account of seven commandments a son of Noah is put to death. The All-Merciful revealed that fact of one of them, and the same rule applies to all of them." But just as Israelites, educated in the Torah, are assumed to exhibit certain uniform virtues, e.g., forbearance, so gentiles, lacking that same education, are assumed to conform to a different model.

Gentiles, by reason of their condition outside of the Torah, are characterized by certain traits natural to their situation, and these are worldly. In addition, the sages' theology of gentiles shapes the normative law in how to relate to them. If an Israelite is by nature forbearing and forgiving, the gentile by nature is ferocious. That explains why, in the Halakhah as much as in the Aggadah, gentiles are always suspect of the cardinal sins, bestiality, fornication, and bloodshed, as well as constant idolatry. The Judaic theology of the gentiles, which sees them as an undifferentiated phalanx of enemies of God, who worship idols deliberately ignoring the truth, leaves little basis for affirming altruistic conduct toward "others." On the contrary, even ordinary transactions that express simple compassion are subjected to doubt:

A   They do not leave cattle in gentiles' inns,

B   because they are suspect in regard to bestiality.

C   And a woman should not be alone with them,

D   because they are suspect in regard to fornication.

E   And a man should not be alone with them,

F   because they are suspect in regard to bloodshed.

G   An Israelite girl should not serve as a midwife to a gentile woman,

H   because she serves to bring forth a child for the service of idolatry.

I   But a gentile woman may serve as a midwife to an Israelite girl.

J   An Israelite girl should not give suck to the child of a gentile woman.

K   But a gentile woman may give suck to the child of an Israelite girl,

L   when it is by permission.

                              Mishnah-tractate Abodah Zarah 2:1

A   They accept from them healing for property,

B   but not healing for a person.

C   "And they do not allow them to cut hair under any circumstances," the words of R. Meir.

D   And sages say, "In the public domain it is permitted,

E   "but not if they are alone."

                              Mishnah Abodah Zarah 2:1–2

The prevailing attitude of suspicion of gentiles derives from the definition of gentiles: idolaters, enemies of God. One should not anticipate a rich repertoire of rulings on how one must sacrifice for the welfare of the gentile-other. I cannot point to narratives that suggest one must, let alone laws that obligate it.

That view of matters is embodied in normative law, as we have seen. The law of the Mishnah corresponds to the lore of scriptural exegesis; the theory of the gentiles governs in both. Beyond the Torah, there not only is no salvation from death, but there is not even the possibility of a common decency. The Torah makes all the difference. The upshot may be stated very simply. Israel and the gentiles form the two divisions of humanity. The one will die but rise from the grave to eternal life with God. When the other dies, it perishes; that is the end. Moses said it very well: choose life. The gentiles sustain comparison and contrast with Israel, the point of ultimate division being death for the one, eternal life for the other.

If Israel and the gentiles are deemed comparable, the gentiles do not acknowledge or know God; therefore, while they are like Israelites in sharing a common humanity by reason of mythic genealogy—deriving from Noah—the gentiles do not receive in a meritorious manner the blessings that God bestows upon them. So much for the points of stress of the Aggadah. When it comes to the Halakhah, as we have seen, the religious problematics focus not upon the gentiles but upon Israel: what, given the world as it is, can Israel do in the dominion subject to Israel's own will and intention? That is the question that, as we now see, the Halakhah fully answers. For the Halakhah constructs, indeed defines, the interiority of an Israel sustaining God's service in a world of idolatry: life against death in the two concrete and tangible dimensions by which life is sustained: trade and the production of food, the foci of the Halakhah. No wonder Israel must refrain from engaging with idolatry on days of the festivals for idols that the great fairs embody—then especially. The presentation of the Halakhah commences with the single most important, comprehensive point—as usual.

The gentiles deprived themselves of the Torah because they rejected it, and, showing the precision of justice, they rejected the Torah because the Torah deprived them of the very practices or traits that they deemed characteristic, essential to their being. That circularity marks the tale of how things were to begin with in fact describes how things always are; it is not historical but philosophical. The gentiles' own character, the shape of their conscience, then, now, and always, accounts for their condition—which, by an act of will, as we have noted, they can change. What they did not want, that of which they were by their own word unworthy, is denied them. And what they do want condemns them. So, when each nation comes under judgment for rejecting the Torah, the indictment of each is spoken out of its own mouth, and its own self-indictment then forms the core of the matter. Given what we know about the definition of Israel as those destined to live and the gentile as those not, we cannot find surprising that the entire account is set in that age to come to which the gentiles are denied entry.

When the gentiles protest the injustice of the decision that takes effect just then, they are shown the workings of the moral order, as the following quite systematic account of the governing pattern explains (from the Bavli tractate Abodah Zarah 1:1 I.2/2a–b:

A. R. Hanina bar Pappa, and some say, R. Simlai, gave the following exposition [of the verse, "They that fashion a graven image are all of them vanity, and their delectable things shall not profit, and their own witnesses see not nor know" (Isa. 44:9)]: "In the age to come the Holy One, blessed be He, will bring a scroll of the Torah and hold it in his bosom and say, 'Let him who has kept himself busy with it come and take his reward.' Then all the gentiles will crowd together: 'All of the nations are gathered together' (Isa. 43:9). The Holy One, blessed be He, will say to them, 'Do not crowd together before me in a mob. But let each nation enter together with [2B] its scribes, 'and let the peoples be gathered together' (Isa. 43:9), and the word 'people' means 'kingdom': 'and one kingdom shall be stronger than the other' (Gen. 25:23)."

We note that the players are the principal participants in world history: the Romans first and foremost, then the Persians, the other world-rulers of the age:

C. "The kingdom of Rome comes in first."

H. "The Holy One, blessed be He, will say to them, 'How have you defined your chief occupation?'

I. "They will say before him, 'Lord of the world, a vast number of marketplaces have we set up, a vast number of bathhouses we have made, a vast amount of silver and gold have we accumulated. And all of these things we have done only in behalf of Israel, so that they may define as their chief occupation the study of the Torah.'

J. "The Holy One, blessed be He, will say to them, 'You complete idiots! Whatever you have done has been for your own convenience. You have set up a vast number of marketplaces to be sure, but that was so as to set up whorehouses in them. The bathhouses were for your own pleasure. Silver and gold belong to me any how: "Mine is the silver and mine is the gold, says the Lord of hosts" (Hag. 2:8). Are there any among you who have been telling of "this," and "this" is only the Torah: "And this is the Torah that Moses set before the children of Israel (Dt. 4:44)." So they will make their exit, humiliated.

The claim of Rome—to support Israel in Torah-study—is rejected on grounds that the Romans did not exhibit the right attitude, always a dynamic force in the theology. Then the other world rule enters in with its claim:

K. "When the kingdom of Rome has made its exit, the kingdom of Persia enters afterward."

M. "The Holy One, blessed be He, will say to them, 'How have you defined your chief occupation?'

N. "They will say before him, 'Lord of the world, We have thrown up a vast number of bridges, we have conquered a vast number of towns, we have made a vast

number of wars, and all of them we did only for Israel, so that they may define
as their chief occupation the study of the Torah.'

O.   "The Holy One, blessed be He, will say to them, 'Whatever you have done has
     been for your own convenience. You have thrown up a vast number of bridges, to
     collect tolls, you have conquered a vast number of towns, to collect the corvée,
     and, as to making a vast number of wars, I am the one who makes wars: "The
     Lord is a man of war" (Ex. 19:17). Are there any among you who have been telling
     of "this," and "this" is only the Torah: "And this is the Torah that Moses set be-
     fore the children of Israel' (Dt. 4:44)." So they will make their exit, humiliated.

R.   "And so it will go with each and every nation."

As native categories, Rome and Persia are singled out; "all the other nations"
play no role, for reasons with which we are already familiar. Once more, the
theology reaches into its deepest thought on the power of intentionality, showing that what people want is what they get.

But matters cannot be limited to the two world empires of the present age,
Rome and Iran, standing in judgment at the end of time. The theology values balance and proportion, seeks complementary relationships, and therefore treats beginnings along with endings, the one going over the ground of
the other. Accordingly, a recapitulation of the same event—the gentiles' rejection of the Torah—chooses as its setting not the last judgment but the first
encounter, that is, the giving of the Torah itself. In the timeless world constructed by the rabbinic canon of the formative age, what happens at the outset
exemplifies how things always happen, and what happens at the end embodies
what has always taken place. The basic thesis is identical—the gentiles cannot
accept the Torah because, to do so, they would have to deny their very character. But the exposition retains its interest because it takes its own course.

Now, the gentiles are not just Rome and Persia but others; and of special
interest, the Torah is embodied in some of the Ten Commandments—not to
murder, not to commit adultery, not to steal; then the gentiles are rejected for
not keeping the seven commandments assigned to the children of Noah. The
upshot is that the reason that the gentiles rejected the Torah is that the Torah
prohibits deeds that the gentiles do by their very nature. The subtext here is
already familiar: Israel ultimately is changed by the Torah, so that Israel exhibits traits imparted by their encounter with the Torah. So too with the gentiles,
by their nature they are what they are; the Torah has not changed their nature.

Once more a single standard applies to both components of humanity, but
with opposite effect, as seen in the Sifré to Deuteronomy CCCXLIII:IV.1ff.:

1. A.   Another teaching concerning the phrase, "He said, 'The Lord came from
        Sinai'":

B. When the Omnipresent appeared to give the Torah to Israel, it was not to Israel alone that he revealed himself but to every nation.

C. First of all he came to the children of Esau. He said to them, "Will you accept the Torah?"

D. They said to him, "What is written in it?"

E. He said to them, "'You shall not murder' (Ex. 20:13)."

F. They said to him, "The very being of 'those men' [namely, us] and of their father is to murder, for it is said, 'But the hands are the hands of Esau'" (Gen. 27:22). 'By your sword you shall live' (Gen. 27:40)."

At this point, we cover new ground: other classes of gentiles that reject the Torah; now the Torah's own narrative takes over, replacing the known facts of world politics, such as the earlier account sets forth, and instead supplying evidence out of scripture as to the character of the gentile group under discussion:

G. So he went to the children of Ammon and Moab and said to them, "Will you accept the Torah?"

H. They said to him, "What is written in it?"

I. He said to them, "'You shall not commit adultery' (Ex. 20:13)."

J. They said to him, "The very essence of fornication belongs to them [us], for it is said, 'Thus were both the daughters of Lot with child by their fathers' (Gen. 19:36)."

K. So he went to the children of Ishmael and said to them, "Will you accept the Torah?"

L. They said to him, "What is written in it?"

M. He said to them, "'You shall not steal' (Ex. 20:13)."

N. They said to him, "The very essence of their [our] father is thievery, as it is said, 'And he shall be a wild ass of a man' (Gen. 16:12)."

O. And so it went. He went to every nation, asking them, "Will you accept the Torah?"

P. For so it is said, "All the kings of the earth shall give you thanks, O Lord, for they have heard the words of your mouth" (Ps. 138:4).

Q. Might one suppose that they listened and accepted the Torah?

R. Scripture says, "And I will execute vengeance in anger and fury upon the nations, because they did not listen" (Mic. 5:14).

At this point, we turn back to the obligations that God has imposed upon the gentiles; these obligations have no bearing upon the acceptance of the Torah; they form part of the ground of being, the condition of existence, of the gentiles. Yet even here, the gentiles do not accept God's authority in matters of natural law:

S.   And it is not enough for them that they did not listen, but even the seven religious duties that the children of Noah indeed accepted upon themselves they could not uphold before breaking them.

T.   When the Holy One, blessed be He, saw that that is how things were, he gave them to Israel.

Now comes another parable, involving not a king but a common person:

2. A.   The matter may be compared to the case of a person who sent his ass and dog to the threshing floor and loaded up a *letekh* of grain on his ass and three *seahs* of grain on his dog. The ass went along, while the dog panted.

B.   He took a *seah* of grain off the dog and put it on the ass, so with the second, so with the third.

C.   Thus was Israel: they accepted the Torah, complete with all its secondary amplifications and minor details, even the seven religious duties that the children of Noah could not uphold without breaking them did the Israelites come along and accept.

D.   That is why it is said, "The Lord came from Sinai; he shone upon them from Seir."

Along these same lines, the gentiles would like to make a common pact with Israel but cannot have a share in God, as explained in the Sifré to Deuteronomy CCCXLIII:IX.2:

A.   Thus the nations of the world would ask Israel, saying to them, "'What is your beloved more than another beloved' (Song 5:9)? For you are willing to accept death on his account."

B.   For so Scripture says, "Therefore they love you to death" (Song 1:3).

C.   And further: "No, but for your sake are we killed all day long" (Ps. 44:23).

Now comes the envy of the gentiles, their desire to amalgamate with Israel, and Israel's insistence upon remaining a holy people, a people apart:

D.   [The nations continue,] "All of you are handsome, all of you are strong. Come and let us form a group in common."

E.   And the Israelites answer, "We shall report to you part of the praise that is coming to him, and in that way you will discern him:

F.   "'My beloved is white and ruddy . . . his head is as the most fine gold . . . his eyes are like doves beside the water-brooks . . . his cheeks are as a bed of spices . . . his hands are as rods of gold. . . . His legs are as pillars of marble. . . . His mouth is most sweet, yes, he is altogether sweet' (Song 5:10-16)."

G.   When the nations of the world hear about the beauty and praiseworthy quality of the Holy One, blessed be He, they say to them, "Let us come with you."

H.   For it is said, "Where has your beloved gone, O you fairest among women? Where has your beloved turned, that we may seek him with you" (Song 5:1).

Israel's is not the task of winning over the gentiles. That is God's task, and it will be done in God's own good time:

I.   What do the Israelites answer them? "You have no share in him: "I am my beloved's and my beloved is mine, who feeds among the lilies'" (Song 6:3).

The various gentile nations rejected the Torah for specific and reasonable considerations, concretely, because the Torah prohibited deeds essential to their being. This point is made in so many words, then amplified through a parable. Israel, by contrast, is prepared to give up life itself for the Torah. But that is because Israel is transformed by the Torah into a kingdom of priests and a holy people.

In the Classical Sources of Judaism, What Is the Role of Other Religions?

The Halakhah finds difficult the differentiation of pagans into distinct nations, treating all gentiles as equivalent in connection with idolatry, on the one side, and cultic uncleanness, on the other. All gentiles constitute sources of uncleanness analogous to corpses, all with uniform consequences. And, along these same lines, rabbinic Judaism affords through differentiation no recognition to other religions. All form media of idolatry, and while the rabbinic sages know that diverse idols are served through diverse liturgies, all other religions fall into the same category. None is worse than any other. The Aggadic narratives differentiate Babylonia, Persia, Greece, and Rome, in constructing a theology of history that places Israel at the fifth and final phase of human history, once more, the eschatological resolution of all matters in favor of one God, who made himself known at Sinai to the children of Abraham, Isaac, and Israel. But when those narratives do differentiate one nation and its gods from another, it is only to impute to all of them the same wicked qualities, as at Leviticus Rabbah 13:5.

Are Different Religions Acknowledged, Rejected, Merely Endured, or Religiously Constructive? Are Other Religions Treated Generically or Differentiated?

Since other religions are treated generically and not differentiated from one another, classical Judaism faces the task of explaining the presence in the world of idolatry that defined the everyday context of Israel's existence. First, they maintained, gentiles act as though they do not really mean to honor idols. By the standard of respect shown by Israel to God, gentiles fail. Second, gentiles cannot transform the natural world into an object prohibited for Israelite use by reason of its forming an idol. Thus, we find in the Mishnah-tractate Abodah Zarah 3:4–5:

A. Peroqlos b. Pelosepos "Pericles the Philosopher" asked Rabban Gamaliel in Akko when he was washing in Aphrodite's bathhouse, saying to him, "It is written in your Torah, 'And there shall cleave nothing of the devoted thing to your hand' (Deut. 13:18). How come you're taking a bath in Aphrodite's bathhouse?"

B. He said to him, "They do not give answers in a bathhouse."

C. When he went out, he said to him, "I never came into her domain. She came into mine. They don't say, 'Let's make a bathhouse as an ornament for Aphrodite.' But they say, 'Let's make Aphrodite as an ornament for the bathhouse.'

D. "Another matter: If someone gave you a lot of money, you would never walk into your temple of idolatry naked or suffering a flux, nor would you urinate in its presence.

E. "Yet this thing is standing right at the head of the gutter and everybody urinates right in front of her.

F. "It is said only, '. . . their gods' (Deut. 12:3)—that which one treats as a god is prohibited, but that which one treats not as a god is permitted."

M. A.Z. 3:4

A. Gentiles who worship hills and valleys—

B. these hills or valleys are permitted, but what is on them is forbidden for Israelite use,

C. as it is said, "You shall not covet the silver or gold that is upon them nor take it."

D. R. Yosé says, "Their gods are on the mountains, and the mountains are not their gods. Their gods are in the valleys, and the valleys are not their gods."

E. On what account is an *asherah* prohibited? Because it has been subject to manual labor, and whatever has been subject to manual labor is prohibited.

F.   Said R. Aqiba, "I shall explain and interpret the matter before you:

G.   "In any place in which you find a high mountain, a lofty hill, or a green tree, you
      may take for granted that there is an idol there."

M. A.Z. 3:5

Idolatry is rejected, not acknowledged, but the action of the idolater
imparts the status of idolatry to what is, in fact, neutral. It is all a matter of
intentionality. That is, the pagan imparts power to the idol by reason of his
own will, which is, therefore, corrupt and corrupting. Here are the norms set
forth by Mishnah-tractate Abodah Zarah 4:4–6, joined with Tosefta's com-
plement as indicated. The Mishnah text is given in boldfaced type, so to differentiate it from the Tosefta's amplification.

**M. 4:4 An idol belonging to a gentile is prohibited forthwith [when it is made].
And one belonging to an Israelite is prohibited only after it will have been worshiped. A gentile has the power to nullify an idol belonging either to himself or
his fellow gentile. But an Israelite has not got the power to nullify an idol belonging to a gentile.**

T. 5:6 The pedestals which gentiles set up during the persecution [by Hadrian]—
even though the time of persecution is over—Lo, these are forbidden. Is it possible
that an idol which a gentile nullified—is it possible that it should be deemed prohibited? Scripture says, "The graven images of their gods you shall burn with fire" (Deut.
7:25). That which he treats as a god is prohibited. And that which he does not treat as
a god is permitted. Is it then possible that an idol which a gentile nullified should be
deemed permitted? Scripture says, The graven images of their gods . . .—Whether he
treats it as a god or does not treat it as a god, it is forbidden.

T. 5:7 How does one nullify [an idol]? A gentile nullifies an idol belonging to himself
or to an Israelite. But an Israelite does not nullify an idol belonging to a gentile [cf.
M. A.Z. 4:4C–D].

T. 5:9 At what point is it called "set aside [for idolatrous purposes]"? Once some concrete deed has been done to it [for that purpose].

T. 5:10 What is one which has been worshiped? Any one which people worship—
whether inadvertently or deliberately. What is one which has been set aside? Any
which has been set aside for idolatry. But if one has said, "This ox is for idolatry,"
"This house is for idolatry," he has said nothing whatsoever. For there is no such
thing as an act of consecration for idolatry.

**M. 4:5 How does one nullify it? [If] he has cut off the tip of its ear, the tip of its
nose, the tip of its finger, [if] he battered it, even though he did not break off [any
part of] it, he has nullified it. [If] he spit in its face, urinated in front of it, scraped
it, threw shit at it, lo, this does not constitute an act of nullification.**

T. 5:8 A pedestal, the greater part of which was damaged—lo, this is permitted. One the whole of which was damaged is prohibited until one will restore it. That belonging to him is permitted, and that belonging to his fellow is prohibited. Before it has been sanctified, it is prohibited. After it has been sanctified, it is permitted.

M. 4:6 An idol, the worshipers of which have abandoned it in time of peace, is permitted. [If they abandoned it] in time of war, it is forbidden. Idol pedestals set up for kings—lo, these are permitted, since they set [images up on them only] at the time kings go by.

What emerges is the distinction between the Israelite's and the idolater's relationship to the idol. The gentile is assumed to be an idolater, and, once the idol is manufactured, it automatically is prohibited. But if it is made for an Israelite, it is assumed to be a piece of wood until the Israelite commits an act of worship. Then he, like the pagan, exercises his power of will to impart to the piece of wood the status of a false god. The gentile's idol lies outside of the Israelite's power of intentionality. To nullify it, the Israelite must acquire possession of it and then treat it as his own property. The gentile's power of intentionality governs, for example, when we assess whether an idol has been abandoned willingly or under duress. If the latter is the case, it is not nullified. The laws suffice to demonstrate that paganism and idolatry are not acknowledged but rejected, and it goes without saying are assigned no constructive task.

How Do the Classical Judaic Sources Justify, or Account for, the Existence and Persistence of Other Religions? Are the Other Religions Seen as Errors, Accidents, the Consequence of Evil, a Constructive Part of Reality, or Some Combination of Variation of These Options?

The normative sources do not justify idolatry. They account for its persistence only by appeal to God's plan for nature. God condemns the idolater, the gentile, for the blasphemous intentionality exhibited by the idol that he makes, as is shown in the Bavli tractate Abodah Zarah 4:6 I.2ff./54b–55a:

I.2 A. A philosopher asked Rabban Gamaliel, "It is written in your Torah, 'For the Lord your God is a devouring fire, a jealous God' (Dt. 4:24). How come he is more jealous against the worshipers of the idol than against the idol itself?"

B. He said to him, "I shall give you a parable. To what is the matter to be compared? To a mortal king who had a single son, and this son raised a dog for himself, which he called by his father's name, so that, whenever he took an oath, he exclaimed, 'By the life of this dog, my father!' When the king heard, with whom

was he angry? Was he angry with the son, or was he angry with the dog? One
has to say it was with the son that he was angry."

At this point, the question of the substantiality of the idol emerges; the
debate to this point is framed to presuppose the sages' position. Now we ask
how one can dismiss the power of idols in their own right:

C. [The philosopher] said to him, "Are you going to call the idol a dog? But there is
some substance to it."

D. He said to him, "What makes you say so?"

E. He said to him, "One time a fire broke out in our town and the entire town
burned up, but that temple was not burned up."

F. He said to him, "I shall give you a parable. To what is the matter to be compared? To a mortal king against whom one of the provinces rebelled. When he
makes war, with whom does he do it? With the living or with the dead? You must
say it is with the living he makes war."

G. He said to him, "So you're just calling it names—a dog, a corpse. In that case,
then let him just destroy it out of the world."

If God exercises so much power, then why not simply wipe out idolatry? Here we
once more ask a fundamental question, which receives a reasonable response:

H. He said to him, "If people worshiped something of which the world had no
need, he certainly would wipe it away. But lo, people worship the sun, moon,
stars, and planets, brooks and valleys. Now do you think he is going to wipe out
his world because of idiots?

I. "And so Scripture says, [55A] 'Am I utterly to consume all things from off the face
of the ground, says the Lord, am I to consume man and beast, am I to consume
the bird of the heaven and the fish of the sea, even the stumbling blocks of the
wicked' (Zeph. 1:2).

J. "Now simply because the wicked stumble on account of these things, is he going
to destroy them from the world? Don't they also worship the human being, 'so am
I to cut off man from off the face of the ground'?"

Nonetheless, Scripture itself attests to God's own recognition of the substantiality of idolatry. He is jealous of idolatry, and that shows he himself concedes
that idols compete. In the same line of questions figures, also, the possibility
that idols do some good. As before, the argument is framed through parables:

I.3 A.   General Agrippa asked Rabban Gamaliel, "It is written in your Torah, 'For
the Lord your God is a devouring fire, a jealous God' (Dt. 4:24). Is there jealousy,
except on the part of a sage for another sage, on the part of a great athlete for
another great athlete, on the part of a wealthy man for another wealthy man?"

B. He said to him, "I shall give you a parable. To what is the matter to be compared? To a man who married a second wife. If she is more important than she, she will not be jealous of her. If she is less than she, she will be jealous of her."

So much for the matter of gentile idolatry: to be a gentile means to be an idolater.

But cannot idolaters point to the great deeds of their gods in their temples? We turn now to concrete cases in which both parties concede something happens in a temple of an idol, whether healing, whether some other sort of supernatural event. The first of the two cases involves a rather complex parable. In the second, since sages form the conversation, texts of scripture are introduced and accepted as self-evident proof.

I.4 A. Zeno asked R. Aqiba, "In my heart and in your heart we both know that there is no substance whatsoever in idolatry. But lo, we see people go into a shrine crippled and come out cured. How come?"

B. He said to him, "I shall give you a parable. To what is the matter to be compared? To a reliable person who was in a town, and all the townsfolk would deposit their money into his care without witnesses. One man came and left a deposit in his charge with witnesses, but once he forgot and left his deposit without witnesses. The wife of the reliable man said to him, 'Come, let us deny it.' He said to her, 'Because this idiot acted improperly, shall we destroy our good name for reliability?' So it is with troubles. When they send them upon a person, they are made to take the oath, 'You shall come upon him only on such-and-such a day, and you shall depart from him only on such-and-such a day, and at such-and-such an hour, through the medium of so-and-so, with such-and-such a remedy.' When it is time for them to take their leave, it just happened that the man went to a temple of an idol. So the afflictions plea, 'It is right and proper that we not leave him and go our way, but because this fool acts as he does, are we going to break our oath?'"

From the parable, we turn to concrete cases in the everyday world:

I.5 A. Raba b. R. Isaac said to R. Judah, "There is a temple to an idol in our locale. When there is need for rain, the idol appears in a dream and says to them, 'Kill someone for me and I shall bring rain.' So they kill someone for her, and she brings rain."

B. He said to him, "If I were dead, no one could tell you this statement which Rab said, 'What is the meaning of the verse of Scripture, ". . . which the Lord your God has divided to all the peoples under the whole heaven" (Dt. 4:19)? [Since the letters of the word *divided* may be read as *smooth*, the verse means this:] this teaches that he made them smooth talkers, so as to banish them from the world."

C. That is in line with what R. Simeon b. Laqish said, "What is the meaning of the verse of Scripture, 'Surely he scorns the scorners, but he gives grace to the

lowly' (Prov. 3:34)? If someone comes along to make himself unclean, they open
the gate for him. If he comes along to purify himself, they also help him do so."

To summarize, the rationality of God's attitudes requires explanation.
He despises idolaters more than the idol because the idolaters act as though
there were substance to the idol. He does not concede any substance to the
idol and, therefore, bears the object no special malice. God does not destroy
things gentiles worship, since that would prove disproportionate.

The world order is defined by rationality, which finds its substance in the
rule of justice. Then the moral order of justice enters at just this point. Having established that idolaters subject themselves to God's hatred by reason of
their attitudes and consequent actions, we ask about the matter of fairness.
To explain matters, we turn to an account of how things came about—a reason we should call historical but sages would classify as paradigmatic. That is,
the sages' explanation, framed in terms of a narrative of something that happened, turns out to be a picture of how things now are—a characterization of
the established facts as these are realized under all circumstances and at any
time, the tenses, past, present, or future, making no difference. So when we
ask, "Why begin with the question of gentiles having entered the category of
death?" we take up a tale that casts in mythic-narrative form what constitutes
an analysis of characteristic traits. Not only so, but the narrative explicitly
points to the enduring traits, not a given action, to explain the enduring condition of the gentiles: that is how they are because that is how they wish to be.

So now the question becomes urgent: how has this catastrophic differentiation imposed itself between Israel and the gentiles, such that the gentiles,
for all their glory in the here-and-now, have won for themselves the grave,
while Israel, for all its humiliation in the present age, will inherit the world
to come? And the answer is self-evident from all that has been said: the gentiles reject God, whom they could and should have known in the Torah. They
rejected the Torah, and all else followed. The proposition then moves in these
simple steps:

(1) Israel differs from the gentiles because Israel possesses the Torah and
the gentiles do not;

(2) because they do not possess the Torah, the gentiles also worship idols
instead of God; and

(3) therefore, God rejects the gentiles and identifies with Israel.

Since We Know That, Within Religions, There Are Divergent, Sometimes Opposed, Views of Other Religions, What Are the Doctrinal Fault Lines Within the Religion That Produce This Divergence? Which Teachings Within the Sources of Judaism Justify Tolerance of Other Religions, and Which Justify Intolerance?

One teaching of the classical rabbinic canon justifies tolerance of gentiles, if none validates tolerance of idolatry. It is captured at our starting point: the eschatological resolution of the matter—that gentiles too may enjoy the resurrection and eternal life that represent Israel's destiny—requires attention. It is the one point in the system at which systemic thought about the other or the outsider comes into play. We engage with that thought when we ask, "What about gentiles in general?" All depends upon their own actions. Since the point of differentiation is idolatry as against worship of the one God, gentiles may enter into the category of Israel, which is to say, they recognize the one God and come to serve him. That means, whether now or later, some, perhaps many, gentiles will enter Israel, being defined as other Israelites are defined: those who worship the one and only God. The gentiles include many righteous persons. But by the end of days these God will bring to Israel. We find the following in Yerushalmi Berakhot 2:8 I:2:

A. When R. Hiyya bar Adda, the nephew of Bar Qappara, died Resh Laqish accepted [condolences] on his account because he [Resh Laqish] had been his teacher. We may say that [this action is justified because] a person's student is as beloved to him as his son.

B. And he [Resh Laqish] expounded concerning him [Hiyya] this verse: "My beloved has gone down to his garden, to the bed of spices, to pasture his flock in the gardens, and to gather lilies" [Song 6:2]. It is not necessary [for the verse to mention, 'To the bed of spices']. [It is redundant if you interpret the verse literally, for most gardens have spice beds.]

C. Rather [interpret the verse as follows:] My beloved—this is God; has gone down to his garden—this is the world; to the beds of spices—this is Israel; to pasture his flock in the gardens—these are the nations of the world; and to gather lilies—these are the righteous whom he takes from their midst.

Now, a parable restates the proposition in narrative terms; having chosen a different mode of discourse from the narrative one that dominates in the authorized history, Genesis through Kings, sages reintroduce narrative for an other-than-historical purpose, as here:

D. They offer a parable [relevant to this subject]. To what may we compare this matter [of the tragic death of his student]? A king had a son who was very beloved to him. What did the king do? He planted an orchard for him.

E. As long as the son acted according to his father's will, he would search throughout the world to seek the beautiful saplings of the world, and to plant them in his orchard. And when his son angered him he went and cut down all his saplings.

F. Accordingly, so long as Israel acts according to God's will he searches throughout the world to seek the righteous persons of the nations of the world and bring them and join them to Israel, as he did with Jethro and Rahab. And when they [the Israelites] anger him he removes the righteous from their midst.

It follows that Israel bears a heavy burden of responsibility even for the gentiles. When Israel pleases God, the righteous among the gentiles are joined to them, and when not, not. So while gentiles as such cannot inherit the world to come, they too can enter the status of Israel, in which case they join Israel in the world to come. And that is precisely what sages expect will happen.

This the gentiles will do in exactly the way that Israel attained that status to begin with, which is by knowing God through his self-manifestation in the Torah, therefore by accepting God's rule as set forth therein. In this way, the theology of rabbinic Judaism maintains its perfect consistency and inner logic: the Torah determines all things. That point is made explicit: if a gentile keeps the Torah, he is saved. But by keeping the Torah, the gentile has ceased to be a gentile and has become an Israelite, worthy even of the high priesthood. First comes the definition of how Israel becomes Israel, which is by accepting God's dominion in the Torah:

1.A. "The Lord spoke to Moses saying, Speak to the Israelite people and say to them, I am the Lord your God":

B. R. Simeon b. Yohai says, "That is in line with what is said elsewhere: 'I am the Lord your God [who brought you out of the land of Egypt, out of the house of bondage]' (Ex. 20:2).

C. "'Am I the Lord, whose sovereignty you took upon yourself in Egypt?'

D. "They said to him, 'Indeed.'

E. "'Indeed you have accepted my dominion.'

F. "'They accepted my decrees: "You will have no other gods before me."'

G. "That is what is said here: 'I am the Lord your God,' meaning, 'Am I the one whose dominion you accepted at Sinai?'

H. "They said to him, 'Indeed.'

I. "'Indeed you have accepted my dominion.'

J.   "'They accepted my decrees: "You shall not copy the practices of the land of
     Egypt where you dwelt, or of the land of Canaan to which I am taking you; nor
     shall you follow their laws.""'

Sifra CXCIV:ii.1

I cite the passage to underscore how matters are defined, which is by appeal
to the Torah. Then, the true state of affairs emerges when the same definition
explicitly is brought to bear upon the gentiles. That yields the clear inference
that gentiles have the power to join themselves to Israel as fully naturalized
Israelites, so the Torah that defines their status also constitutes the ticket of
admission to the world to come that Israel will enter in due course. Sages could
not be more explicit than they are when they insist that the gentile ceases to be
in the status of the gentile when he accepts God's rule in the Torah:

A.   ". . . by the pursuit of which man shall live":

B.   R. Jeremiah says, "How do I know that even a gentile who keeps the Torah, lo, he
     is like the high priest?

C.   "Scripture says, 'by the pursuit of which man shall live.'"

D.   And so he says, "'And this is the Torah of the priests, Levites, and Israelites,' is
     not what is said here, but rather, 'This is the Torah of the man, O Lord God'
     (2 Sam. 7:19)."

E.   And so he says, "'Open the gates and let priests, Levites, and Israelites will enter
     it' is not what is said, but rather, 'Open the gates and let the righteous nation,
     who keeps faith, enter it' (Is. 26:2)."

F.   And so he says, "'This is the gate of the Lord. Priests, Levites, and Israelites . . .'
     is not what is said, but rather, 'the righteous shall enter into it' (Ps. 118:20)."

G.   And so he says, "'What is said is not, 'Rejoice, priests, Levites, and Israelites,'
     but rather, 'Rejoice, O righteous, in the Lord' (Ps. 33:1)."

H.   And so he says, "It is not, 'Do good, O Lord, to the priests, Levites, and Israel-
     ites,' but rather, 'Do good, O Lord, to the good, to the upright in heart' (Ps.
     125:4)."

I.   "Thus, even a gentile who keeps the Torah, lo, he is like the high priest."

Sifra CXCIV:ii.15

What is at issue is no genealogy ("high priest") but keeping the Torah. To
be "Israel" represents not an ethnic but a theological classification. That is not
to suggest God does not rule the gentiles. He does—whether they like it or
not, acknowledge him or not. God responds, also, to the acts of merit taken by
gentiles, as much as to those of Israel. The upshot is that "gentile" and "Israel"

classify through the presence or absence of the same traits; they form taxo-
nomic categories that can in the case of the gentile change when that which is
classified requires reclassification by criteria of a supernatural character.

Are There Historical, Political, and/or Behavioral Factors That Correlate With the Expression of Tolerance in Judaism? With Intolerance? How Do You Explain the Choices Made Within the Religion for Tolerance and Intolerance?

Normative Judaism in its formative canon did not have the last word on the
matter at hand or any other. A long and complex history of exegesis and
amplification yielded other Aggadic-theological perspectives, other Halakhic
rulings. A massive complication intervened in the form of Christianity and
Islam. These represented challenges to not only the Judaic account of self-
manifestation in the Torah but also the Judaic classification of humanity into
those that know God and those that do not, monotheists and idolaters. As to
God's instruction, Christianity both affirmed scripture and added to the Torah
the New Testament and produced the Bible. For its part, Islam acknowledged
the revelation of the Bible and deemed the Qur'an to be the last, best word that
God set forth. So, neither conformed to the paradigm of classical Judaism: in
or out. And both monotheist religions explicitly rejected idolatry just as did
Judaism. Indeed, Christians accepted martyrdom for the sake of sanctifying
God's name (in the categories of Judaism) by rejecting pagan sacrifices. So, in
medieval and modern times, the classical version of matters confronted facts it
could not with facility dismiss or explain away.

At issue is whether Christianity and Islam are to be differentiated from
other religious traditions and accorded recognition as authentic monotheisms
in line with the revelation of the Torah at Sinai. Self-segregationist Judaism,
in closed communities, maintains the integrity of the classical traditions, but
other communities of Judaism take up diverse positions on that issue. Conservative, Modern/integrationist Orthodox, Reform, Reconstructionist, New
Age, Jewish Renewal, and other Judaisms do take up a more tolerant position
vis-à-vis Christianity and Islam than does the normative canon. Some find
authoritative foundations for differentiating Christianity and Islam from the
idolatry so rigorously rejected by God in the Torah.

But the classical position challenges theological toleration within Judaisms. The Torah is God's word, by the criterion of which all other claims to
speak for God are to be assessed—and by which, in one aspect or another, all

are found wanting. Accordingly, while, in part for political reasons, in part out of genuine conviction, Jews (whether practicing Judaism or not) express attitudes of tolerance and tolerate other religions, the classical response to the modern and contemporary challenge of religious toleration endures. That is, Judaism finds it difficult to validate those attitudes when its normative sources are interrogated. One would face formidable obstacles in attempting to compose out of the sources of the Halakhah and of the Aggadah a Judaic theology of Christianity and of Islam. A single narrative articulates the theological foundation of intolerance: the criterion of God's honest truth:

A. The books of the Evangelists and the books of the minim they do not save from a fire. But they are allowed to burn where they are,

B. they and the references to the Divine Name which are in them.

C. R. Yosé the Galilean says, "On ordinary days, one cuts out the references to the Divine Name which are in them and stores them away, and the rest burns."

D. Said R. Tarfon, "May I bury my sons, if such things come into my hands and I do not burn them, and even the references to the Divine Name which are in them.

E. "And if someone was running after me, I should go into a temple of idolatry, but I should not go into their houses [of worship].

F. "For idolaters do not recognize the Divinity in denying him, but these recognize the Divinity and deny him.

G. "And about them Scripture states, 'Behind the door and the doorpost you have set up your symbol for deserting me, you have uncovered your bed' (Is. 57:8)."

H. Said R. Ishmael, "Now if to bring peace between a man and his wife, the Omnipresent declared that a scroll written in a state of sanctification should be blotted out by water, the books of the minim, which bring enmity between Israel and their Father who is in heaven, all the more so should be blotted out,

1. "they and the references to the Divine Name in them.

J. "And concerning them has Scripture stated, 'Do I not hate them that hate thee, O Lord? And do I not loathe them that rise up against thee? I hate them with perfect hatred, I count them my enemies' (Ps. 139:21–22)."

Tosefta Shabbat 13:5

There are ways of nurturing attitudes of respect and toleration for religious difference—including the right of the other to err—out of the resources of Judaism. But compromise and dissimulation and negotiation of matters of truth do not form one of them.

10

TOLERANCE OF IDOLS AND IDOL WORSHIPERS IN EARLY RABBINIC LAW

The Case of Mishnah Tractate Avodah Zarah

ALAN J. AVERY-PECK

Jacob Neusner's study [in this collection] of the rabbinic sources that concern worship of gods other than the God of Israel reaches a single and incontrovertible conclusion regarding tolerance in classical Judaism. Professor Neusner phrases the matter clearly in his first paragraph:

There are no theological foundations of tolerance in classical Judaism, only eschatological intimations that, at the end of days, all humanity will know the one true God. But that is not the same thing as a theological basis for tolerating error or those that commit error. In the here and now, no doctrines accord recognition to religions other than Judaism. And classical Judaism contains no doubt as to the outcome of history in the end-time: God will see to it that all of humanity accords recognition to him as the one true God, and, on that basis, now as part of the Israel that knows God, the ex-gentiles will inherit the world to come.

That point emerges from and is abundantly supported by a profusion of biblical sources and rabbinic texts that elaborate those sources. No religion other than the religion of Israel can be justified or in any regard abided because the God of Israel is the only true God and the Israelite mode of worship is the only divinely sanctioned method of worship. All other worship is in error and subject to God's punishment. As Deut. 12:2–3, cited by Professor Neusner, and as a host of other passages make clear (Exod. 23:13; 23:24; Deut. 7:5; Deut.

7:25–26), Israelites are commanded to obliterate all mention of idols and physically to destroy all accoutrements of idol worship, the idols themselves as well as their altars and anything associated with them.

The written Torah accordingly does not contemplate Israel's coexisting with idol worshipers, and, within the context of such biblical thinking, the rabbis could develop no theological framework within which idols or those who worship them could be tolerated. They depict gentiles, rather, as enemies of God, enemies who deliberately ignore God's status as creator and ruler. As Neusner explains, while the rabbis imagine that gentiles will, at the end of time, arrive at the correct worship of the one God and, therefore, be saved, they could not, in rabbinic theology, be tolerated as gentiles. The rabbinic idea that, when gentiles worship and believe like Israelites, they will be subject to God's salvation like Israelites is not an indication of rabbinic tolerance of the other. It is, rather, an expression of the rabbis' certainty about the ultimate correctness of their own beliefs and about the error of the other. Within this framework, as Neusner shows, rabbinic Judaism offers no theology of tolerance: no theological structure within which gentiles' worship can be accommodated, let alone seen as an appropriate or efficacious manner of worshiping God.

As we shall see in the following, however, rabbinic theological intolerance captures only one aspect of the rabbis' handling of the problem of the relationship between Jews and gentiles. Indeed, the rabbis grant no legitimacy whatsoever to gentile religious practices. And yet, as we shall see, in the rabbinic legislation that controls day-to-day interactions between Jews and non-Jews, a very different and unexpected picture emerges.[1] For, in legislating for the concrete environment of the land of Israel in the first centuries, the rabbis are clear that social, cultural, and economic interactions between Jews and non-Jews are, with few limitations, both acceptable and appropriate. From the standpoint of theology, non-Jews might be murderers, fornicators, and engage in bestiality; but in the real-life world of the community and marketplace, they are perfectly appropriate customers, business associates, and neighbors. This point is clear even in the continuation of the Mishnah passage cited by Neusner that accuses non-Jews of bestiality, fornication, and murder (Mishnah Avodah Zarah 2:1):[2]

2:1 G.   An Israelite girl should not serve as a midwife to a gentile woman,

H.   because she serves to bring forth a child for the service of idolatry.

I.   But a gentile woman may serve as a midwife to an Israelite girl.

J.   An Israelite girl should not give suck to the child of a gentile woman.

K.   But a gentile woman may give suck to the child of an Israelite girl,

L.   when it is by permission.

Israelites may not directly support idol worship—I discuss indirect support below—and this includes serving as midwives for gentile women or suckling gentile babies. These actions undeniably give life to idol worshipers and, hence, to idolatry. But Israelites may accept such support from gentiles, even to the extent of having an Israelite child suckled by a gentile woman. Such interaction is seen in no way to harm the child, let alone to compromise the integrity of the Israelite religious community. This suggests that, beyond the rabbinic theology that refuses to tolerate non-Israelite religion, rabbinic social law in very concrete ways tolerates and, indeed, legitimates quite personal interactions between Israelites and gentiles. Without regard for their theology, in an environment in which Jews can realize significant benefits from living cooperatively with non-Jews, the Mishnah's rabbis seek every possible avenue to allow such interactions, even including, as we shall see in some detail, accommodating gentiles' idolatrous worship.

This means that there is a significant dichotomy within the rabbinic treatment of gentiles and their religion, and this has some impact on the answers we must provide to the questions posed by William Scott Green [in this collection]. On the one hand, the rabbinic tolerance for social and economic interactions between Jews and non-Jews does not change the answers Neusner provides for Green's first three questions. To summarize Neusner: (1) Non-Israelite religions represent the error of those who refuse to recognize God. (2) In the rabbinic literature, these religions are treated generically and as an undifferentiated mass. Any slight differentiation between the worshipers of one idolatrous system and another does nothing more than to impute to all systems the same theological error and wicked human qualities. (3) Non-Israelite religions persist not because they have any humanly conceivable value but because of God's larger plan for history, which will reach its eschatological fulfillment when all people recognize God's power and sovereignty. Thus, the only theological justification for the tolerance of idolatry is the Israelites' knowledge that God's plan is ultimately to bring idolatry to an end and bring all gentiles to the true worship of the God of Israel.

But this depiction of rabbinic theology does not fully respond to Green's fourth and fifth questions, which ask:

(4)   Since we know that, within religions, there are divergent, sometimes opposed, views of other religions, what are the doctrinal fault lines within the religion that produce this divergence? Which teachings within the sources you study justify tolerance of other religions, and which justify intolerance?

(5)   Are there historical, political, and/or behavioral factors that correlate with the expression of tolerance in the religion you study? With intolerance? How do you explain the choices made within the religion for tolerance and intolerance?

The answer to these questions is that, within the early rabbinic system, the theological justification for not tolerating gentiles is balanced by an apparent desire, perhaps even a need, to facilitate interactions that allow Israelites to participate in and benefit from the social, cultural, and economic world in which they live. We speak of a historical and political setting in which Israelites' cultural as much as economic life reflected the reality of a world shaped by exactly those people whom the Israelites' theological system insisted had no right even to exist upon the land of Israel. In the conflict between theological truths and economic and social reality, economic and social realities appear to have won. While theology took up a position of intolerance, the actual life of the Jew in the first centuries was guided by a legal system that permitted the broadest possible range of tolerance of the other, tolerance reflected in the law's facilitating close economic and social interactions.

Thus, even as the Mishnah associates gentiles with all manner of evil, it legislates for continuing and largely unimpeded economic interaction with them. In a very real and concrete way, in the actuality of the day-to-day life of the Israelite community, gentiles were to be tolerated. Scripture might have seemed clear when it stated (Deut. 12:3), "[Y]ou shall tear down their altars and dash in pieces their pillars and burn their Asherim with fire; you shall hew down the graven images of their gods and destroy their name out of that place." However this might have been, the rabbis acquiesced to the presence of idols and idol worship as a continuing fact of life, and so they were completely willing to establish a normative law within which Israelites would not only live alongside but would engage in mutually beneficial interactions with idolaters and, most strikingly, with many aspects of their worship.

The point emerges clearly and consistently in Mishnah Tractate Avodah Zarah (the title signifies "idolatry," meaning literally "foreign worship"), which presents laws controlling Israelites' business and other interactions with gentiles. The goal of the law is twofold. On the one side, the law regulates Israelite conduct so as to prevent Israelites from providing immediate financial or material support to gentiles' worship of idols. To support idolatry, e.g., by providing the idol worshiper with the paraphernalia needed in his ritual practice, would be to engage in the same theological error as taints the non-Jew; this an Israelite may not—with notable exceptions detailed below—do. At the same time, the law of Avodah Zarah explicitly permits all Israelite interactions with non-Jews that do not blatantly support idol worship. Before turning to the specific laws that illustrate these points, let me make clear what is noteworthy here:

1. Contrary to scripture's explicit demand that all places of idol worship be torn down and destroyed, according to the Mishnah, Israelites must simply avoid immediate contact with or direct support of idols and idolatry. Explicit in this is that the idol itself may continue to stand. Indeed, according to the Mishnah, under certain circumstances, Israelites may even participate in the manufacture of accoutrements of idol worship and they may frequent places in which idols are found.

2. While the Mishnah, as we already have seen, asserts that gentiles are suspect as regards bestiality, fornication, and bloodshed (M. A.Z. 2:1), the Mishnah's laws authorize ordinary business interactions with them. So the characterization of non-Jews that emerges from the rabbis' intolerant theology has little or no impact when the Mishnah considers the sorts of interactions Israelites may, in fact, have with these same people. They are tolerated as business partners, as neighbors, and as residents of one's same city.

3. The Mishnah's laws permit a wide range of interactions with gentiles, even ones that provide material or financial support for idolatry. This is permitted so long as the Israelite does not *intend* to support idolatry or so long as he can *imagine* that his actions do not directly support idol worship. The Mishnah thus places the economic life and well-being of Israelites in front of the biblical commandment to uproot idolatry from the land. Almost any action that can be interpreted as not supporting idolatry is permitted, no matter what its actual impact on the conduct of the non-Israelite cult.

With these general principles in hand, we turn to specific examples in the law of Mishnah Avodah Zarah that express these points. The general principle of the tractate, that Israelites may do business with gentiles so long as the dealings will not directly support idolatry, appears at Mishnah Avodah Zarah 1:1–1:2:

1:1 A.   Before the festivals of gentiles for three days it is forbidden to do business with them,

B.   (1) to lend anything to them or to borrow anything from them,

C.   (2) to lend money to them or to borrow money from them,

D.   (3) to repay them or to be repaid by them.

E.   R. Judah says, "They accept repayment from them, because it is distressing to him [that is, to the Israelite]."

F. They said to him, "Even though it is distressing to him now, he will be happy about it later."

1:2 A. R. Ishmael says, "Three days before them and three days after them it is prohibited."

B. But sages say, "Before their festivals it is prohibited, but after their festivals it is permitted."

Outside of a rather limited period immediately preceding a gentile festival, business interactions between Israelites and idol worshipers are normative and largely unrestricted. The anonymous law of M. A.Z. 1:1A–D wishes only to cut off such business relationships for three days prior to gentiles' festivals. The supposition is that anything given by the Israelite to the gentile in this period will directly support the upcoming pagan worship and that even money a gentile gives to an Israelite somehow would be in preparation for the gentile's worship and so should be forbidden. Notably, some authorities wish to reduce even this minor impediment to Israelite-gentile interaction. Judah, 1:1E, would allow Israelites to accept repayment of loans; the Israelite is, after all, only getting back what was his in the first place. While Ishmael, 1:2A, wishes also to prohibit Israelite-gentile interactions briefly following the gentile festival, sages at 1:2B, like the anonymous law of 1:1A, disagree. According to the majority view, Israelites may ignore the fact that what the gentile loans them may have just been used in idol worship or that the money with which he repays a loan or completes a business deal may have just been earned through commerce associated with idolatry.

Just as business interactions with gentiles are not significantly limited, so the Israelite's ability to go where he needs to go in order to engage in business with gentiles is largely unimpeded by the law. In the following, for instance, the general prohibition against going to a place in which there is an idol, M. A.Z. 1:4A–C, is tempered by a further rule (G, illustrated by H) that permits the Israelite to go to and do business in such places:

1:4 A. A city in which there is an idol—

B. [in the area] outside of it, it is permitted [to do business].

C. [If] an idol was outside of it, [in the area] inside it is permitted.

D. What is the rule as to going to that place?

E. When the road is set aside for going to that place only, it is prohibited.

F. But if one is able to take that same road to some other place, it is permitted.

G. A town in which there is an idol, and there were in it shops that were adorned and shops that were not adorned—

H. this was a case in Beth Shean, and sages ruled, "Those that are adorned are prohibited, but those that are not adorned are permitted."

An Israelite is to avoid doing business in an area in which there is an idol, though he may do business among idolaters, A–C. But even this prohibition is quickly tempered. First, the Israelite is not restricted from going to a place of idolatry, so long as the road he uses to get there has other destinations as well, D–F. At issue is not where he in fact is going but what it looks like he is doing. Idolatrous towns are not off limits, so long as the Israelite can avoid making a show of the fact that he is going to such a place. This is required so that other Israelites will neither get the wrong idea about this individual's intentions nor, encouraged by seeing another Israelite heading to a town in which idol worship takes place, come themselves to lessen their contempt for idolatry. The ruling at G–H is even more striking than that of A–C, for it permits exactly what A–C restricts: the Israelite may, in fact, enter and do business in a town in which there is an idol, so long as he does not do business in shops that are themselves adorned for idolatry. Even if it is clear that the Israelite is doing business with an idol worshiper, so long as there is no blatant and immediate evidence of that fact, the interaction is permitted.

The passages so far reviewed emerge from the idea that an Israelite may not openly and materially support idolatry. At Mishnah Avodah Zarah 1:8, this prohibition is relaxed:

1:8 A.   And they do not make ornaments for an idol:

B.   (1) necklaces, (2) earrings, or (3) finger rings.

C.   R. Eliezer says, "For a wage it is permitted."

An Israelite, it should go without saying, A–B, may not participate directly in idol worship by creating ornaments for an idol. What is striking is Eliezer's qualification of this rule, C. If the Israelite is paid a wage by a non-Jew, his creating of such ornaments is not viewed as his own participation in idol worship. He is, in Eliezer's view, just doing his job.

The fact that Eliezer's statement permits an Israelite materially to participate in gentiles' worship may account for its omission from a number of manuscripts of the Mishnah, including the one known to Rashi. Many medieval commentaries, indeed, suggest that Eliezer's statement should be excised from the text since it is, to them, incomprehensible that any rabbi would permit Israelites to create objects for use in a pagan cult. But the text as we have it is well supported by early manuscripts and makes a point that, in fact, is in line with the general tendency of the law of Avodah Zarah. So long as the Israelite may imagine that his actions do not directly support idol worship, they are permitted. Indeed, we shall see below at Mishnah Avodah Zarah 4:4 that an Israelite even may own an idol, so long as it has not previously been worshiped. This concept may be reflected in Eliezer's statement here. The object created by the Israelite for a wage is not in the status of an article of idolatry until it has actually been used in the pagan cult. Eliezer, therefore, permits creating it. The net result of this, of course, is that Israelites may work for gentiles and participate in business operations that support idolatry. Economic considerations lead to a level of tolerance that trumps theological concerns.

The passages we so far have discussed permit a range of behaviors that bring Israelites into close contact with idols and idolatry. In permitting these behaviors, these passages leave open what is perhaps the central issue for such discussions, the question of what constitutes a prohibited image or idol in the first place. This is an important question insofar as, while a strict definition that prohibits all images will preclude much Israelite contact with non-Jews, a laxer definition that does not deem images or icons invariably to be idolatrous will open up a range of possibilities for Israelite interaction with gentiles. As we might expect on the basis of the Mishnah's tendency to identify ways to permit Israelite interaction with gentiles, the Mishnah's authorities reject scripture's blanket prohibition on images and assert that one even can disregard a gentiles' own sense of whether or not an image or icon is an idol. According to the Mishnah, rather, Israelites are constrained to view as representing an object of idolatry only objects that seem to the Israelite himself to be idolatrous. Other objects, even ones that gentiles consider idols, are permitted. Several passages support this point. The first, at M. A.Z. 3:1, reads as follows:

3:1 A.   "All images [even those used only for ornamentation] are prohibited [such that an Israelite may not benefit from them],

B.   "because they are worshiped once a year," the words of R. Meir.

C.   And sages say, "Prohibited is only one that has in its hand a staff, bird, or sphere."

D.   Rabban Simeon b. Gamaliel says, "Any that has anything at all in its hand."

This passage develops the Mishnah's tendency to allow Israelites considerable contact with the accoutrements of idol worship. Meir, A–B, wishes to prohibit even ornamental images since they are worshiped. They must, he says, therefore be considered artifacts of idolatry. But sages and Simeon b.

Gamaliel, C+D, significantly limit the prohibition, saying it applies only in the case of images that clearly are meant to represent deities that have authority over the world. This is evidenced by the image's holding in its hand a sign of dominion, for instance, a staff, representing dominance; a bird, representing all humankind; or a sphere, representing the entire world (Babylonian Talmud Avodah Zarah 41a). While Simeon b. Gamaliel is more expansive in prohibiting any image that holds something in its hand, he equally moves away from scripture, which bans all images whatsoever. Simeon b. Gamaliel and sages, in contrast to scripture, seem intent on giving Israelites access to a cultural world in which images of all sorts were commonplace.

A second story advances this sort of thinking, showing that, for the rabbis, determination of the permissibility of an Israelite's contact with an icon depends on whether or not that object must necessarily be defined as a pagan divinity. The answer to this question, of course, will be crucial to Israelites' ability to participate in specific aspects of the economy and culture of the land of Israel in the first centuries. The following story is remarkable in its portrayal of a theological debate between Gamaliel and a pagan, Peroqlos, the son of Pelosepos, perhaps a corruption of the designation "the philosopher." Peroqlos claims to know the laws of Torah, and these, in his view, render impermissible Gamaliel's use of the bathhouse, in which stands a statue of Aphrodite, a statue Peroqlos considers a "devoted" thing—an object of idolatry. Gamaliel, by contrast, responds with a series of syllogisms through which he concludes that the statue cannot be an idol at all:

3:4 A.   Peroqlos b. Pelosepos asked Rabban Gamaliel in Akko, when he was washing in Aphrodite's bathhouse, saying to him, "It is written in your Torah, 'And there shall cleave nothing of a devoted thing to your hand' (Deut. 13:18). How is it that you're taking a bath in Aphrodite's bathhouse?"

B.   He said to him, "They do not give answers in a bathhouse."

C.   When he went out, he said to him, "I never came into her domain. She came into mine. They don't say, 'Let's make a bathhouse as an ornament for Aphrodite.' But they say, 'Let's make Aphrodite as an ornament for the bathhouse.'"

D.   "Another matter: Even if someone gave you a lot of money, you would never walk into your temple of idolatry naked or suffering a flux, nor would you urinate in its presence.

E.   "Yet this thing is standing there at the head of the gutter and everybody urinates right in front of her."

F.   "It is said only, '[Cut down the idols of] their gods' (Deut. 12:3)[3]—that which one treats as a god is prohibited, but that which one treats not as a god is permitted."

The substance of Gamaliel's argument should be clear: whatever pagans might think, the way the statue of Aphrodite is treated proves it is only an ornament, not an idol. As such, it is not subject to any prohibition. Gamaliel supports his view from scripture. Deuteronomy 12:3 demands that Israelites destroy gentiles' "gods." This means, he says, that images that are not *treated* as gods, even a statue of a known goddess, are permitted.

If the meaning of the passage is clear, its underlying assumptions deserve note: Peroqlos, a gentile, is depicted as knowing and showing respect for the laws of Torah, even if his understanding of the oral law is incomplete; and Gamaliel, a Jew, is represented as knowledgeable about idols, having an authoritative viewpoint on which, in fact, are objects of worship and which are nothing more than ornaments. The Mishnah's editors, thus, conceive there to be a remarkable level of interaction and discussion between Jews and non-Jews, interactions in which rabbis take seriously and respond carefully to non-Jews' inquiries. This represents a level of tolerance that is in line with what we have seen in Mishnaic law but which, we should recall, goes far beyond what either scripture or the rabbis' own *theology* would lead us to expect.

The significance of this passage for our understanding of tolerance in rabbinic law deserves further note. On the one hand, Gamaliel—and so the authorities behind the other passages we have reviewed—would claim not to "tolerate" idolatry at all; they simply are allowing Israelites contact with objects that, in their view, really are not associated with idolatry, or they are permitting Israelites to engage in acts that, in their view, do not directly support pagan worship. But the consequence of Gamaliel's position, and so the effect of the other laws we have discussed, in fact, is to accommodate Israelite contact with what gentiles themselves would have seen as aspects of their religious worship, and it is to permit Israelites to benefit economically and socially from the presence of idols and idol worship in the land of Israel. The extent to which this represents a significant level of tolerance of non-Jews must be made explicit.

Gamaliel engages a gentile in a philosophical debate, using syllogistic rhetoric common in his Greco-Roman setting. Along with this, Gamaliel is fully comfortable using a bathhouse built and presumably frequented by gentiles. Through his argument and his behavior, he facilitates Jewish life within a cultural and economic setting significantly shaped by the presence of gentiles and their worship. The theological intolerance of idolatry that emerges from the rabbinic exegetical literature and that is analyzed by Neusner thus is balanced by the rabbis' depiction of what is allowable and appropriate in actual

social and economic interactions with non-Jews. These interactions tolerate the other and the other's religious culture at a level and to an extent that
neither scripture nor the Midrashic texts cited by Neusner would lead us to
anticipate.

Gamaliel's attitude towards the statue of Aphrodite, it bears noting, is not
unique within the Mishnaic materials before us. The notion that an object is
or is not deemed an idol depending on how gentiles' treat it further is developed by Mishnah Avodah Zarah 4:4. This passage makes two points: first, an
Israelite may own an "idol" so long as it has never been worshiped; an object
is classified as an idol, that is, in light of its use rather than based on any characteristics intrinsic to its shape or manufacture. Second, following this same
theory, a gentile may "nullify" an idol, so as to render it permitted to an Israelite (he does this by cutting off the tip of one of its limbs or by otherwise
mistreating it; M. A.Z. 4:5):

4:4 A.   An idol belonging to a gentile is prohibited forthwith [when it is made].

B.   And one belonging to an Israelite is prohibited only after it will have been
worshiped.

C.   A gentile has the power to nullify an idol belonging [either] to himself or his
fellow.

D.   But an Israelite has not got the power to nullify an idol belonging to a gentile.

E.   He who nullifies an idol has nullified its appurtenances.

F.   [If] he nullified [only] its appurtenances, its appurtenances are permitted, but
the idol itself [remains] prohibited.

4:5 A.   How does one nullify it?

I B.   [If] he has cut off the tip of its ear, the tip of its nose, the tip of its finger,

C.   [if] he battered it, even though he did not break off [any part of] it,

D.   he has nullified it.

II E.   [If] he spit in its face, urinated in front of it, scraped it, threw excrement at it,
lo, this does not constitute an act of nullification.

III F.   [If] he sold it or gave it as a pledge on a loan—

G.   Rabbi says, "He has nullified it."

H.   And sages say, "He has not nullified it."

An object has no intrinsic status as an idol. That is a status that comes with,
and reflects, the gentile's attitude toward and use of the particular object.

Within this definition, if gentiles treat an object in ways Israelites find incommensurate with how one should treat a deity, the object need not be deemed an idol at all and so is permitted. An Israelite may be in its presence or otherwise benefit from it. The net result of this rule is that Israelites are permitted to be present in many places that scripture's much stricter definition of an idol would not allow.[4]

Let us review what we have seen in the passages of Mishnah Avodah Zarah that reflect on permissible and impermissible interactions of Israelites and gentiles. Mot notably, it appears that at stake in these materials is not a theological premise regarding the validity or invalidity of idol worship but, rather, the concrete reality of how Israelites will live in a world dominated by gentiles and their worship. Thus, even as the rabbis in the materials cited by Neusner are clear regarding the immutable differences between Jews and non-Jews, differences that leave no room for a theological tolerance of the other, they work very hard to allow Israelites to live in a world marked by the presence of idolatry. This is a world in which, in the day-to-day conduct of the Israelite's economic and social life, he will need to be in contact both with people who worship idols and with the idols and ornaments they create as aspects of their worship.

This means that the answer the sources before us yield for Green's fifth question—regarding reasons for the multiple and divergent views of other religions that emerge within a single tradition—must be carefully considered. If Gamaliel can use the bathhouse in which a statue of Aphrodite stands, if Israelites can work for gentiles and produce ornaments to be placed on idols, if businesspeople can interact and do business with idol worshipers, even in cities and in shops in which idols are prominent, then the rabbis of the Mishnah have deemed it both possible and appropriate—despite a theological stance that denies non-Israelite religion any legitimacy—to tolerate, if not that religion, then at least its practitioners and its paraphernalia.

It bears noting that the reason for this unexpected attitude is almost certainly sociological. What choice did the Mishnah's authorities have? The failed Jewish revolt against Rome of 70 CE, which led to the destruction of the Jerusalem Temple, and the failed Bar Kokhba revolt of 133–135 CE already had proved that scripture's approach, which demanded that idol worshipers and their idols be uprooted from the land, was not a viable option. The Mishnah's authors, through their laws if not their theology, thus found a way to accommodate to a reality they could not change, to the actuality of the world in which they would have to live. This was a world in which Jews would do business with pagans, travel through and live in their cities, enjoy their pub-

lic buildings and baths. We need not establish whether Rabban Gamaliel or
the anonymous authorities cited at Mishnah Avodah Zarah 4:7 (cited below)
in fact engaged gentiles in philosophical discussions. Either way, the framers of the Mishnah clearly believed that such interactions were conceivable
and depicted them as important contexts in which gentiles, even if they challenged Judaism, would do so with respect, and Israelites would respond by
explaining and justifying their own religious behaviors. Given the reality of
their world, did the Mishnah's framers have much of a choice in how to deal
with the other?

For their part, of course, the Mishnah's authors did not explain their
approach as necessitated by the reality of Israel's social and political powerlessness or as developed in order to benefit Israelites in their social and economic life. They presented it, rather, as, at base, commensurate with God's
own character and demands upon humanity. The Mishnah, thus, explains
that Israelites are obligated by God to display a fundamental level of civil
behavior toward pagans in order to assure peaceful relationships. Mishnah
Shebiit 5:9H–I (see also Mishnah Shebiit 4:3) accordingly permits Israelites,
during the sabbatical year, to assist gentiles in the performance of agricultural work that is forbidden to Israelites themselves, and it adds that Israelites
should greet gentiles "in the interests of peace." As the passage makes clear,
these are the same principles that apply in the relationship between Israelites who follow all aspects of the rabbinic purity laws and those who do not
(Mishnah Shebiit 5:9):

5:9 A.   [During the sabbatical year] a woman may lend to a neighbor who is sus-
         pected [of not observing the law] of the Sabbatical year: (1) a sifter, (2) a sieve,
         (3) a millstone, (4) or an oven.

B.   But she may not sift or grind [flour] with her [since the grain was gathered in
     violation of the law].

C.   The wife of a *haber* [one who observes rules of purity in everyday affairs] may
     lend to the wife of an ordinary Israelite [who does not observe those strin-
     gencies]: (1) a sifter, (2) or a sieve,

D.   and she may sift or grind or shake [dry flour] with her [since these actions can-
     not render either the utensils or the individuals who are involved ritually
     unclean].

E.   But from the time that [the ordinary Israelite woman] pours water over the flour
     [and thereby renders the flour susceptible to uncleanness, cf. Lev. 11:34, the wife
     of a *haber*] may not touch it [the flour],

F.   because one does not assist those who commit a transgression.

G. And all [of the allowances noted at A and C–D] were only made in the interest of peace.

H. And during the Sabbatical year one may assist gentiles [to do work that is forbidden to Israelites], but one may not assist Israelites [to do such work during the sabbatical year].

I. And one greets them [gentiles], in the interest of peace.

Gentiles and Jews are treated the same. So long as gentiles or nonobservant Jews are not violating the law as they conceive it, the pious Jew may participate in their activities, even if this involves an action the pious Jew would not be permitted to perform for his or her own benefit. On the one hand, we might not be entirely surprised by this approach, which takes into account the need to maintain peaceful community relationships. At the same time, to help those who ignore God's law and to greet them "in the interests of peace" is surely to settle for less than scripture, and even the rabbis themselves, imagines is God's ultimate plan for the world. Again, given no good options for how Israelites will face the world in which they live, the Mishnah's framers assert that accommodating idol worshipers and idolatry comports with God's will for the current age. Clearly expressing this point, Mishnah Avodah Zarah 4:7 argues that for good and logical reasons, God himself does not wipe out idolatry:

4:7 A. They asked sages in Rome, "If [God] is not in favor of idolatry, why does he not wipe it away?"

B. They said to them, "If people worshiped something of which the world had no need, he certainly would wipe it away.

C. "But, lo, people worship the sun, moon, stars, and planets.

D. "Now do you think he is going to wipe out his world because of idiots?"

E. They said to them, "If so, let him destroy something [that idolaters worship] of which the world has no need, and leave something that the world needs!"

F. They said to them, "Then we should strengthen the hands of those who worship these [things that would not be destroyed], for then they would say, 'Now you know full well that they are gods, for, lo, they were not wiped out!'"

God cannot destroy all objects of idol worship without destroying the entire world, and if he destroys only some idols, gentiles will believe that the objects that survive are truly gods. For this reason, God is compelled to allow idol worship to continue. The implication of this passage is important as regards Israelites' treatment of idols and idolaters. If God cannot and does not wipe out idolatry, what are his people, the Israelite nation, to do? Just as God does, Israelites must tolerate the existence of idols and those who worship them.

The point is made clear at Tosefta Berakhot 6:2, which reflects on God's tolerance of gentiles:

6:2 A.   One who beholds idolatry says, "Praised [be Thou, O LORD, King of the universe] who is slow to anger."

B.   One who beholds a place from which idolatry was uprooted says, "Praised [be Thou, O LORD . . . who uprooted idolatry from our land [= M. Ber. 9:1].

C.   "May it be thy will, LORD our God, that idolatry be uprooted from every place in Israel, and turn the hearts of thy servants to serve thee."

[ed. princ. adds: And outside the Land one need not recite this, for the majority of the inhabitants are gentile.]

D.   R. Simeon [says], "Even outside the Land one must recite this, for they are destined to convert,

E.   "as it says, 'At that time I will change the speech of the people to a pure speech, that all of them may call on the name of the LORD and serve him with one accord' (Zeph. 3:9)."

It is hardly surprising, B+C, that one who sees a place from which idolatry has been uprooted praises God for carrying out the divine will of bringing an end to idol worship, or that, D+E, one should in all places express the desire for an end to idolatry. What is surprising is at A. An Israelite who witnesses idolatry, rather than cursing the idolater, similarly should extol God because, in the continued existence of idolatry, we see evidence of a divine trait important to Israelites as much as to gentiles: God is slow to anger, and this means that God patiently waits for all sinners—whether gentiles or Israelites—to find the correct path. Israelites themselves have a clear reason to be thankful for this divine trait of forbearance.

Idolatry exists because God himself tolerates it. And this means that Israelites, in their objective of imitating God, have both reason and right also to be tolerant. Social, political, and economic reality remain in the background as the rabbis argue that tolerance of gentiles is justified because, in an ultimate sense, Israelites share with gentiles a reliance on God's patience and God's willingness to wait for people to come to the true faith. In the Mishnah's view, what distinguishes the two groups is only that Israelites already have made the first step, accepting the lordship of the one God, which gentiles will do only in some future age. In the meantime, God—and so the people of Israel—accepts their continued existence. The law of Avodah Zarah—contrary to the rabbis' theological system that cannot tolerate idol worship—legislates for the very real world that will exist until the age when God's plan for all humanity will be fully realized. Until that time, in the context of the workaday world, even if not in their deepest theological reflections, Israelites can accommodate the existence and false practices of people whom God himself has deigned to tolerate.

Tolerance, for the rabbis, means to tolerate the presence of—indeed, to coexist with and benefit from the presence of—non-Israelites in the Israelites' social and economic sphere. To the extent that this requires accommodating the other's religious practices, those practices are accommodated. This clearly falls short of what we in the modern world consider religious tolerance, signified today by a religious community's acceptance that members of other faith communities, no matter what their manner of worship or conception of God, not only have a right to their practices and beliefs but are, in an ultimate sense, correct in their religious perceptions and in their theology. As Neusner has shown, this is a definition of tolerance that classical Judaism does not meet and that, in line with the inner logic of Judaism's perception of God's covenant and law, it cannot support.

At the same time, we should not take lightly the extent to which the rabbinic approach does accommodate the other and the other's religious practices—even if it deems those practices ultimately wrong and destined for eradication. Jews, as an aspect of their monotheism and in line with the twin concepts of covenant and Torah, believe that they possess the only truth, and the power of that assertion sustained them throughout antiquity and into modern times. Even so, within the framework of this certainty that Judaism alone comprises the truth of God's revelation and the accurate statement of God's demands, Jews also developed a record of working to live in peace with others who do not share their faith or religious practices. The question of whether or not Judaism is a tolerant religion thus yields two answers, depending upon what we mean when we speak of tolerance.

Within classical Judaism, there can be no theological tolerance since that would mean giving credence to religious ideas known from the perspective of Torah to be incorrect. Even so, the law of classical Judaism demands a striking level of social tolerance and acceptance of the other. Surely, as we have seen in detail, this is a result of the concrete political, economic, and social circumstance in which the creators of rabbinic Judaism found themselves: there is no doubt that a stance that demanded other than accommodation of gentile neighbors would have hurt the Israelite community more than it would have damaged the other. And yet, in their own justification of this toleration, in the idea that God himself waits for non-Israelites to find their way to the true God and to true worship, we find the rabbinic judgment that all people, Israelites and non-Israelites alike, stand in a roughly comparable relationship to God: none of us stands in a perfect relationship to God, and all of us, therefore, are dependent upon God's willingness to wait for our return to the correct path. This rabbinic accommodation of the other does not meet contemporary notions of what it means to be tolerant. Still, in striking contrast to Judaism's Pentateuchal heritage, which allowed no accommodation of other religions, which it demanded that Israelites completely obliterate, the rabbinic developments and their justification for peaceful relationships with non-Jews are significant statements of the centrality of at least one aspect of tolerance within classical Judaism.

Notes

1. As background to the following discussion, compare the views of Sacha Stern, *Jewish Identity in Early Rabbinic Writings* (Leiden: Brill, 1994), with those of Gary G. Porton, *Goyim: Gentiles and Israelites in Mishnah-Tosefta* (Atlanta: Scholars Press, 1988). Stern focuses on the negative depictions of non-Jews and the restrictions governing Israelite–gentile interactions introduced in the Mishnah and significantly expanded in the Tosefta and, especially, the Talmudic literature. He thus describes a firm social and economic barrier between the two groups. While clear on the economic and social limitations imposed by rabbinic law, Porton, by contrast, notes the permeability of these laws and the wide range of social and economic contexts in which Jews and non-Jews are understood to interact. Citing Porton's view that the restrictions are comparatively few, Stern succinctly phrases the issue between them by responding, "few does not necessarily mean 'innocuous.' From the perspective of our sources, it was these restrictions which essentially characterized their interaction with non-Jews" (145). The disagreement between these scholars has its source in part in Stern's reliance on later Talmudic and Midrashic texts, which Porton excludes and which contain the bulk of the negative assessments of non-Jews. But an equal foundation of their disagreement is the failure, particularly prominent in Stern's study, to distinguish the rabbis' theological (and I would argue theoretical, utopian) system, in which non-Jews and their pagan worship can in no way be tolerated, from their laws controlling day-to-day life. As Porton argues and as we shall see in the following, these laws rather consistently, even if within certain limits, sanction interactions between Jews and gentiles. As William Scott Green's foundational questions lead us to do, we must, therefore, be conscious of the multiple and divergent views of other religions contained within a single tradition. It is this aspect of the question of tolerance with which the following discussion grapples.

2. Translations are taken from Jacob Neusner, *The Mishnah: A New Translation* (New Haven, CT: Yale University Press, 1988).

3. The complete verse is: "Break down their altars, smash their sacred stones and burn their Asherah poles in the fire; cut down the idols of their gods and wipe out their names from those places."

4. Notably, according to M. A.Z. 4:5E, urinating in front of an idol does not nullify its status as an idolatrous god. This is contrary to the position of Gamaliel, above, M. A.Z. 3:4D, that the fact that people urinate in front of the statue of Aphrodite in the bathhouse proves that it is not an idol but only an ornament. While rabbinic authorities clearly disagree on the details, the larger point is uncontested: not all statues or other images are idols, and even what gentiles might themselves consider gods do not necessarily have that status so as to be prohibited for Israelite contact.

PART 6

---◆---

ISLAM

11

SOURCES OF TOLERANCE AND
INTOLERANCE IN ISLAM

The Case of the People of the Book

IBRAHIM KALIN

Islam's encounter with other religions is as old as Islam itself. The two sources of Islam, i.e., the Qur'an and Hadith, contain extensive discussions, narrations, and injunctions on the various religious traditions before Islam and especially Judaism and Christianity. The Muslim awareness of the multiplicity of faith traditions is evident not only in the Qur'an but also in the sayings of the prophet Muhammad as well as in the later Islamic scholarship. Historically, the first Muslim community came into being within a fairly diverse society where Jews, Christians, pagans, polytheists, monotheists, fire-worshipers (Magians or Majus), and others lived together across the Arabian Peninsula. The major and minor religions that the Islamic world encountered from its earliest inception to the modern period make up a long list: the religious traditions of the pre-Islamic (*jahiliyyah*) Arabs, Mazdeans in Mesopotamia, Iran, and Transoxania, Christians (of different communions like Nestorians in Mesopotamia and Iran, Monophysites in Syria, Egypt and Armenia, Orthodox Melkites in Syria, Orthodox Latins in North Africa), Jews in various places, Samaritans in Palestine, Mandaeans in south Mesopotamia, Harranians in north Mesopotamia, Manichaeans in Mesopotamia and Egypt, Buddhists and Hindus in Sind, tribal religions in Africa, pre-Islamic Turkic tribes, Buddhists in Sind and the Panjab, and Hindus in the Panjab.[1] In short, Islam is no stranger to the challenge of other religions.

The fact that Islam is the last of the three Abrahamic faiths puts it in a special relationship with Judaism and Christianity. On the one hand, the Qur'an defines Jews and Christians as the People of the Book (*ahl al-kitab*) and gives them the status of protected religious communities (*ahl al-dhim-mah*) under the provision of paying a religious tax called *jizya* (compare the Qur'an, al-Tawbah 9:29). Within this legal framework, the People of the Book are accorded certain rights, the most important of which is the right of religious belief, i.e., no forced conversion. On the other hand, the Qur'an engages the People of the Book head-on as the primary counterparts of a serious dialogue on the unity of God, the Abrahamic tradition, some biblical stories, salvation, the hereafter, and the nature of Jesus Christ. The Qur'an is explicit and occasionally harsh in its criticism of certain Jewish and Christian themes because no serious dialogue is possible without raising the most fundamental issues.

In relation to the treatment of non-Muslims, we thus see a tension between what we might loosely call the requirements of law and theological doctrine. Islamic law grants certain rights to non-Muslims, including freedom of religion, property, travel, education, and government employment. These rights extend not only to Jews and Christians but also to other faith traditions such as the Manicheans, Hindus, and Buddhists. Muslims encountered these latter communities as the borders of the Islamic world expanded beyond the Arabian Peninsula. One of the major legal adjustments in this process was the enlargement of the concept of the People of the Book to include those other than Jews and Christians. This, however, was complemented by an economic system that allowed non-Muslims to move freely across the social strata of Muslim societies in which they lived. Following the vocation of Prophet Muhammad, Muslims always encouraged free trade and, therefore, unlike Christianity, did not have to discriminate against Jews as international merchants or money-lending usurers.

Socially, there was nothing in the Islamic tradition similar to the Hindu caste system that would have led to the treatment of Hindus in discriminatory manners. Instead, Muslims treated Hindus as members of a different socioreligious community whose internal affairs were regulated by Hindu, not Islamic, laws. Politically, Muslim rulers were more or less pragmatic and used relatively lenient legal provisions to ensure the loyalty of their non-Muslim subjects. Forced conversion or economic discrimination was not in the interest of the state or the Muslim communities. This socioeconomic and legal framework, thus, played a key role in the rapid spread of Islam and facilitated the development of a "culture of coexistence" in Muslim societies that had considerable non-Muslim populations from the Balkans and Anatolia to the subcontinent of India.

Legal protection, however, is not a license to theological laxity. The Qur'an sharply criticizes the Meccan polytheists and accuses them of failing to understand the true nature of God. Jews and Christians are not spared from criticism, some of which are general and some specific. The primary reason for the Qur'an's constant dialogue with them is its unflinching effort to hold them up to higher moral and religious standards than the Meccan pagans. As the two heirs or claimants to the legacy of Abraham, Jewish and Christian communities are expected to uphold the principles of monotheism and accept the new revelation sent through the prophet Muhammad. The Qur'an calls upon them to recognize Islam as part of the Abrahamic tradition:[2]

"Say: O People of the Book. Come to a word [kalimah] common between us and you: that we shall worship none but God, and that we shall ascribe no partners unto Him, and that none of us shall take others for lords beside God. And if they turn away, then say: Bear witness that we are they who have surrendered (unto Him)."[3]

Al-i Imran 3:64

The tension between theological certitude and legal protection is further complicated by another tension between the unity of the essential message of religions and the multiplicity of socioreligious communities. The tension is real with theological and political consequences. The problem is how to explain and then reconcile the discrepancy between the unity of the divine message and the diversity of faith communities to which the divine message has been sent. As I shall discuss below, the Qur'an seeks to overcome this problem by defining the plurality of socioreligious communities as part of God's plan to test different communities in their struggle for virtue and the common good (al-khayrat).

The universality of divine revelation is a constant theme in the Qur'an and forms the basis of what we might call the Abrahamic ecumenism of monotheistic religions. As the father of monotheism, Abraham is assigned a central role to represent the universalist nature of the divine revelation: he is the most important figure to unite Jews, Christians, and Muslims, despite the fact that Moses, Jesus, and Muhammad are also accorded special places in the Islamic tradition. While Abraham represents the pinnacle of this ecumenism, other prophets are seen as bearers of the same message, i.e., believing in the unity of God, worshiping him alone, and leading a virtuous life. "And before thy time We never sent any apostle without having revealed to

him that there is no deity save Me,—[and that,] therefore, you shall worship
Me [alone]!" (al-Anbiya 21:25).

The Qur'an presents this claim to universality as a trait of not only Islam
but also other Abrahamic faiths and calls upon Jews and Christians specifically to renew their bond with the father of monotheism. The true religion is
"islam" (with a small "i") in the sense of "surrendering oneself to God" fully
and unconditionally. Once this common denominator is secured, ritual differences and even some theological disparities can be overcome. The Qur'an
calls all to *islam* without making a distinction: "Do they seek a faith other
than in God [*din Allah*], although it is unto Him that whatever is in the heavens and on earth surrenders itself [*aslama*], willingly or unwillingly, since
unto Him all must return?" (Al-i 'Imran 3:83; compare also al-Ra'd 13:15). The
reference to the cosmological order of things, which we see in some Qur'anic
verses (compare al-Rahman 55:1–18; Isra 17:44), is of particular significance
since it establishes "surrendering to God" (*islam*) as both a cosmological
and human-religious principle. The universality of divine message extends
beyond revealed books all the way to the natural world.

This universalism, however, is always qualified by a reference to true faith
in God and His decision to send messengers to warn those who are mistaken.

"Say: 'We believe in God, and in that which has been revealed unto us, and that which
has been revealed unto upon Abraham and Ishmael and Isaac and Jacob and their
descendants, and that which has been vouchsafed by their Sustainer unto Moses and
Jesus and all the [other] prophets: we make no distinction between any of them. And
unto Him do we surrender ourselves [literally 'we're *muslims* to Him']."

Al-i 'Imran 3:84

These specific references to the prophets of Abrahamic monotheism
shows Islam's specific interest to have a constant dialogue with the People of
the Book and form a kind of religious alliance with them against the Meccan
polytheists. If the prophet Abraham is understood correctly as the father of
monotheism, then the theological differences between Jews, Christians, and
Muslims can be negotiated. The Qur'an is, thus, absolutely uncompromis-
ing on the fundamental Abrahamic principle, i.e., surrendering oneself to
the one God alone: "For, if one goes in search of a religion other than surrendering to God (*al-islam*), it will never be accepted from him, and in the
life to come he shall be among the lost" (Al-i 'Imran 3:85). Commenting on
the verse, Ibn Kathir says that "whoever follows a path other than what God
has ordained, it will not be accepted."[4] Fakhr al-Din al-Razi quotes Abu Muslim as saying that the expression "we surrender ourselves to Him" (*muslimuna
lahu*) means that "we submit to God's command with consent and turn away

from all opposition to Him. This is the quality of those who believe in God and they are the people of peace [*ahl al-silm*]."⁵ Despite the narrow interpretation of some classical and contemporary Muslims, this reading of the verse supports our rendering of *islam* as "surrendering to God."

This emphasis on the unique nature of the Abrahamic tradition underlies Islam's attitude toward other religions. It is by virtue of this linkage that Judaism and Christianity receive more attention in the Islamic sources than any other religion besides, of course, polytheism, which the Qur'an rejects unconditionally. Islam recognizes the reality of other religions but does so with a critical attitude in that all religious communities are called upon to (re)affirm and appropriate the main thrust of Abrahamic monotheism. Any claim to religious belief short of this is denounced as an aberration, metaphysical error, schism, and affront to God.

In what follows, I shall analyze the applications of these general principles and discuss the grounds and limits of tolerance and intolerance toward other religions in the Islamic tradition. The focus will be Judaism and Christianity, leaving aside other religions such as Hinduism and Buddhism for another discussion. I shall claim that, while Islam does not claim a monopoly on belief in God and leading a virtuous life, it sets strict conditions for accepting a faith as a legitimate path that one can follow to reach salvation. The tensions between the oneness and universality of the divine message on the one hand and the multiplicity of human communities on the other will also be discussed. The following verse is the anchor point of our discussion: "Unto every one of you We have appointed a [different] law [*shir'atan*] and way of life [*minhajan*]. And if God had so willed, He could surely have made you all one single community [*ummah wahidah*]: but [He willed it otherwise] in order to test by means of what He has vouchsafed unto you. Vie, then, with one another in doing good works!" (al-Ma'idah 5:48; see also Hud 11:118). I shall discuss the extent to which the call for "vying for the common good" can form the basis of an Islamic notion of religious tolerance.

Universal Revelation and Abrahamic Ecumenism

The Qur'an presents revelation (*wahy, kitab*) as a universal phenomenon. Whether it talks about the creation of the universe or the stories of the prophets, it refers to revelation as having both historical continuity and claim to universal truth. Revelation is historically universal for God has revealed his message to different societies to remind them of faith and salvation and warn against disbelief: "Verily, We have sent thee with the truth, as a bearer of glad tidings and a warner: for there never was any community [*ummah*] but a warner has [lived and] passed away in its midst" (al-Fatir 35:24). The same principle is stated in another verse: "And for every community there is a messenger [*rasul*]; and only after their messenger has appeared [and delivered his message] is judgment passed on them, in all equity" (Yunus 10:47). In both verses, the word *ummah* is used to refer to different communities to which messengers have been sent.[6] While *ummah* has come to denote specifically the Muslim community in the later Islamic scholarship, it is used in the Qur'an and the Hadith to describe any faith community, whether Jewish, Christian, or Muslim. The word *ummah* is also used for humanity in general (compare al-Baqarah 2:213).

While all revelation comes from God, revelation in the specific sense such as a revealed book originates from what the Qur'an calls the "mother of the book" (*umm al-kitab*). Like all other revelations, the Qur'an originates from this "mother book," which is the "protected tablet" (*lawh mahfuz*) in the divine presence:[7] "Consider this divine book, clear in itself and clearly showing the truth: behold, We have caused it to be a discourse in the Arabic tongue, so that you might encompass it with your reason. And, verily, [originating as it does] in the source, with Us, of all revelation, it is indeed sublime, full of wisdom" (al-Zukhruf 43:2–4). The word *umm*, literally "mother," means origin and source.[8] The word *kitab*, book, in this context refers not to any particular revealed book but to revelation as such. This comprehensive meaning applies to all revelation: "Every age has its revealed book [*kitab*]. God annuls or confirms whatever He wills [of His earlier messages]; for with Him is the source of all revelation [*umm al-kitab*]" (al-Ra'd 13:38–39).

The Qur'an, thus, considers the history of revelation as one and connects the prophets from Adam and Noah to Jesus and Muhammad in a single chain of prophetic tradition. The continuity of divine revelation links different socioreligious communities through the bondage of a common tradition. The following verse, while making a strong case against religious communalism and ethnic nationalism, which was rampant in the pre-Islamic Arabia, points to what really unites different communities:

"O humans! Behold, We have created you all out of a male and a female, and have made you into nations and tribes so that you might come to know one another. Verily, the noblest of you in the sight of God is the one who is most deeply conscious of Him. Behold, God is all-knowing, all-aware."

al-Hujurat 49:13

Commenting on the above verses, Fakhr al-Din al-Razi points out that human beings are born in total equality. They acquire the qualities that distinguish them from others as inferior or superior only "after they come into this world; and the noblest among these qualities are the fear of God [al-taqwa] and closeness [al-qurb] to Him."⁹ All "nations and tribes" are called upon to possess these qualities and honor the primordial covenant they have made with God to worship him alone and "turn their face [i.e., whole being] to God." This "turning toward God" is also the essence of the natural disposition or state according to which God has created human beings:

"And so, set thy face steadfastly towards the [one ever-true] faith [al-din], turning away from all that is false [hanifan], in accordance with the natural disposition [fitrah] which God has instilled into man. No change shall there be in God's creation [khalq]. This is the established true religion [al-din al-qayyim] but most people know it not."

al-Rum 30:30

Two words require our attention here. The word hanif(an), translated by Asad as "turning away from all that is false" and by Pickthall as "upright," is used in the Qur'an twelve times (two times in the plural) and derived from the verb hanafa, which literally means "inclining toward a right state." A hanif is a person who turns toward God as the only deity. In pre-Islamic Arabia, there was a group of people called hanifs, who were neither polytheists nor Jew or Christian. Their theological lineage went back to Abraham, who is mentioned seven times in the twelve verses that have the word hanif in them. Abraham is presented as the perfect example of those who are upright and turn their whole being toward God: "Verily, Abraham was a nation [ummatan] by himself, devoutly obeying God's will, turning away from all that is false [hanifan], and not being of those who ascribe divinity to aught beside God: [for he was always] grateful for the blessings granted by Him who had elected him and guided him onto a straight way" (al-Nahl 16:120–21). Another verse stresses the same link between Abraham and monotheism: "Say: God has spoken the truth: follow, then, the creed [millah] of Abraham, who turned away from all that is false [hanifan], and was not of those who ascribe divinity to aught beside God" (Al-i 'Imran 3:95). Millat Ibrahim, "Abraham's community," represents the transnational community that believes in the pure and simple unity of God in tandem with one's primordial nature. Muslims are urged to be Abraham's community and, thus, go beyond both Judaism and Christianity.¹⁰

In this sense, Abraham does not belong to any of the particular faith traditions: "Abraham was neither a 'Jew' nor a 'Christian,' but was one who turned away from all that is false [hanifan], having surrendered himself unto God [musliman]; and. he was not of those who ascribe partnership to Him [mushrikin]" (Al-i 'Imran 3:67). Commenting on the word hanif, Ibn Kathir describes Abraham as "turning away from polytheism [al-shirk] to faith [al-

iman]."[11] The commentators Jalal al-Din al-Mahalli and Jalal al-Din al-Suyuti interpret it as "turning away from all other religions towards the one firmly established religion" (al-din al-qayyim; compare Qur'an, al-Tawbah 9:36, al-Rum 30:30, al-Mu'min 40:12). It is only when commenting on 3:95 that they use the word *al-Islam*, meaning the religion of Islam.[12] The famous Andalusian commentator Qurtubi concurs: the word *hanif* means "turning away from abhorrent religions [*al-adyan al-makruhah*] towards the true religion of Abraham."[13] In the Qur'anic reading of biblical history, the adjective *hanif* places all prophets including Moses and Jesus in a position beyond any particular religion including Judaism and Christianity. *The Religious Dialogue of Jerusalem*, a ninth-century polemic between a Christian monk and Abd al-Rahman, the supposed amir of Jerusalem, quotes the Muslim interlocutor as saying that "you have accredited Christ with idolatry because Christ was neither Jew nor Christian but *hanif*, surrendered to God (Muslim)."[14]

Another key term that points to the universal nature of belief in God is the word *fitrah*, translated as natural disposition or primordial nature. *Fitrah* is the noun form of the verb *fatara*, which literally means to fashion something in a certain manner. It denotes the specific nature or traits according to which God has created human beings. In a famous hadith of the Prophet narrated by both Bukhari and Muslim, the word *fitrah* is used as the presocial state of humans: "Every child is born in this natural disposition; it is only his parents that later turn him into a 'Jew,' a 'Christian,' or a 'Magian.'" It is important to note that the three religious traditions mentioned here are also the three religions that are considered to be the People of the Book. The Hadith states the same principle outlined in the above verses: while belief in one God (and acting in accord with it) is universal and the revelations are sent to confirm it, it is through the multiplicity of human communities that different theological languages develop and come to form one's religious identity as Jew, Christian, Magian, or Muslim.

In relation to the People of the Book, the Qur'an makes specific references to the Abrahamic tradition and asks Muslims as well as Jews and Christians to recognize and appreciate the underlying unity between their religious faiths. "In matters of faith [*al-din*], He has ordained for you that which He had enjoined upon Noah—and into which We gave thee [O Muhammad] revelation as well as that which We had enjoined upon Abraham, and Moses, and Jesus: Steadfastly uphold the [true] faith, and do not break up your unity therein" (al-Shura 42:13). This is usually interpreted as referring to the doctrine of *tawhid*, unity of God, which is the same doctrine revealed to other prophets before Muhammad.[15] According to al-Razi, the warning about breaking up "your unity" pertains to disunity resulting from worshiping deities other than God.[16] The term *al-din*, translated conventionally as "religion," refers not to any particular religion and certainly not to "institutional religion" but to the essence of *tawhid*. The life of Abraham and his followers is a testimony to the robust monotheism of the Abrahamic faith:

"Indeed, you have had a good example in Abraham and those who followed him, when they said unto their [idolatrous] people: "Verily, we totally dissociate ourselves from you and of all that you worship instead of God: we deny the truth of whatever you believe; and between us and you there has arisen enmity and hatred, to last until such a time as you come to believe in the One God!"

al-Mumtahina 60:4

Since both Judaism and Christianity trace their origin to Abraham, the Qur'an returns to him over and over again and invites Jews and Christians to think of Abraham not within the narrow confines of their respective theologies but in light of what he represents in the history of divine revelations. The Qur'an makes a special note of the disputes among Jews and Christians about Abraham: "O People of the Book! Why do you argue about Abraham, seeing that the Torah and the Gospel were not revealed till [long] after him? Will you not, then, use your reason?" (Al-i 'Imran 3:65). Abraham, whom "God has taken as a sincere friend (al-Nisa 4:125), is the "forefather" (*abikum*) (al-Hajj 22:78) of monotheism and, thus, cannot be appropriated by a particular religion or community. His mission is universal as his legacy: "Behold, the people who have the best claim to Abraham are surely those who follow him—as does this Prophet and all who believe [in him]—and God is near unto the believers" (Al-i 'Imran 3:68). The Qur'an goes even further and describes all prophets after Abraham as neither Jew nor Christian: "Do you claim that Abraham and Ishmael and Isaac and Jacob and their descendants were 'Jews' or 'Christians'?" Say: 'Do you know more than God does? And who could be more wicked than he who suppresses a testimony given to him by God?[17] Yet God is not unmindful of what you do' (al-Baqarah 2:140). According to the Islamic sources, this is a reference to the fact that Judaism and Christianity came into being long after Abraham and other prophets. Their claim to call Abraham Jew or Christian is, therefore, supported neither by scripture nor history.[18]

The figure of Abraham is central not only for the universal proclamation of divine unity but also for Muslims as the youngest members of the Abrahamic tradition. In the following verse, Abraham is presented as the "forefather" of all those who believe in one God and follow his "path" (*millah*):

"And strive hard in God's cause with all the striving that is due to Him: it is He who has elected you [to carry His message], and has laid no hardship on you in [anything that pertains to] religion, [and made you follow] the path [*millah*] of your forefather Abraham. It is He who has named you in bygone times as well as in this [divine writ]—"those who have surrendered themselves to God" [*al-muslimun*], so that the Messenger might bear witness to the truth before you, and that you might bear witness to it before all mankind. Thus, be constant in prayer, and render the purifying dues, and hold fast unto God."

al-Hajj 22:78

This verse establishes an unmistakable link between Abraham and the Prophet of Islam. The Qur'an narrates the story of Abraham to confirm the divinely sanctioned authority of prophet Muhammad as the last messenger. The Prophet's legitimacy is, thus, underlined by linking him to Abraham. Yet the verse also indicates to the newly established Muslim community where they agree and part ways with the followers of the earlier revelations. On the one hand, Abraham unites all monotheist believers since he is the most important figure on whom Jews, Christians, and Muslims can agree. Despite the obvious differences in theological languages and historical narratives, his message of divine unity is essentially the same in the three traditions. On the other hand, Jews and Christians are divided over Abraham, each calling him their own "forefather." The Qur'an seeks to overcome this impasse by declaring Abraham neither Jewish nor Christian but *muslim*, i.e., "he who surrenders himself to God."

This is where the prophet Muhammad joins Abraham, and the Qur'an invites the People of the Book to recognize the continuity between the two. The Prophet of Islam is asked to reassert the essential unity of all revelation but to do so with a sense of compassion and respect:

"Because of this, then, summon [all mankind], and pursue the right course, as thou hast been bidden [by God]; and do not follow their likes and dislikes, but say: 'I believe in whatever revelation God has bestowed from on high; and I am bidden to bring about equity in your mutual views. God is our Sustainer as well as your Sustainer. To us shall be accounted our deeds, and to you, your deeds. Let there be no contention between us and you: God will bring us all together—for with Him is all journeys' end.'"

al-Shura 42:15

While the Qur'an presents Abraham as the unifying father of monotheism and emphasizes the essential unity of the Abrahamic tradition, it also recognizes the multiplicity of "nations and tribes." As we shall see below, this multiplicity is presented as part of God's plan to test different communities in their effort to attain goodness. Yet the tension between the unity of the divine message and the plurality of different communities remains as an issue taken up by the later scholars of Islam. Whether the plurality of human communities is a natural state to be accepted or a state of disorder and confusion to be overcome would occupy the Islamic religious thought up to own day. Those who see plurality as chaos and detrimental to the unity of the community would reject all lenient measures and argue for radical orthodoxy. The Qur'an and the Sunnah, however, present different possibilities, to which we now turn.

Plurality of Human Communities: A Paradox for Religions?

According to the Qur'an, each prophet has been sent to a particular community with a particular language while the essence of that message is the same.[19] The Qur'an accepts the multiplicity of human communities as part of God's creation: "Now had God so willed, He could surely have made them all one single community" (al-Shura 42:8). Multiplicity is presented as contributing to the betterment of human societies whereby different groups, nations, and tribes come to know each other and vie for the common good. "O humans! Behold, We have created you all out of a male and a female, and have made you into nations and tribes so that you might come to know one another" (al-Hujurat 49:13). Underlying all this diversity is the same message embodied in the figure of Abraham: believing in one God and leading a virtuous life.

In addressing the question of plurality, the Qur'an uses the word *ummah* in both the singular and the plural forms. *Ummah* signifies a socioreligious community bound together by a set of common beliefs and principles. Within the pagan cotext of pre-Islamic Arabia, it is contrasted with such communal bonds as family, group, tribe, and nation. All of these associations are based on lineages other than what makes different communities an *ummah*. According to Ibn Qayyim, an *ummah* is "a single group [*sinif wahid*] held together by a single goal [*maqsad wahid*]."[20] The Qur'an says that "all mankind were once but one single community [*ummah wahidah*], and only later did they begin to hold divergent views. And had it not been for a decree that had already gone forth from thy Sustainer, all their differences would indeed have been settled [from the outset]" (Yunus 10:19). The essential unity of humankind has been broken because of the inevitable differences that have arisen among people in the long course of history. The Qur'an does not explain what these differences are, but it is not difficult to see that they pertain primarily to the essential matters of religion and faith.[21] Prophets have been sent to address these differences and invite their communities back to their original faith in one God:

"All mankind were once one single community (*ummah wahidah*).[22] [Then they began to differ] whereupon God raised up the prophets as heralds of glad tidings and as warners, and through them bestowed revelation from on high, setting forth the truth, so that it might decide between people with regard to all on which they had come to hold divergent views."

al-Baqarah 2:213

The plurality of socioreligious communities is accepted as divinely decreed because God has willed to make humanity composed of different "tribes and nations": "And had thy Sustainer so willed, He could surely have made all mankind one single community [*ummah wahidah*]: but [He willed it otherwise, and so] they continue to hold divergent views" (Hud 11:118).

These and similar verses display a constructive ambiguity about the delicate relationship between the plurality of human communities and the differences of opinion about God. It is not clear which comes first and what it implies for the history of religions. Are the differences of opinion a natural result of the existence of different communities or have different communities come about as a result of holding divergent and often conflicting views about God? It is hard to state with any degree of certainty that the Qur'an completely endorses or abhors the plurality of "divergent views" held by different communities. At any rate, unity is not uniformity, and the Qur'an tries to overcome this tension by calling all communities to renew their covenant with God and seek guidance from him. "For, had God so willed, He could surely have made you all one single community; however, He lets go astray him that wills [to go astray], and guides aright him that wills [to be guided]; and you will surely be called to account for all that you ever did" (al-Nahl 16:93).

In another context, the "plurality factor" underlies one's attitude toward other communities. While it is true that God has willed communities to be different, it is also clear that the goal is to regulate plurality in such a way to reach a desirable level of unity. The absence of unity in the sense of religious consensus or social cohesion does not nullify the good deeds of those who believe in God and seek virtue:

"Verily [O you who believe in Me,] this community of yours is one single community, since I am the Sustainer of you all: worship, then, Me [alone]! But men have torn their unity wide asunder, [forgetting that] unto Us they all are bound to return. And yet, whoever does [the least] of righteous deeds and is a believer, his endeavour shall not be disowned: for, behold, We shall record it in his favor."

al-Anbiya 21:92–94

That plurality is not a case for disunity is highlighted in the verses that talk about diverse laws and paths given to different communities. There is no

doubt that Islam, like all other religions, would like to see a unity of believers built around its main pillars. The exclusivist believer sees anything short
of this as an imperfection on the part of the community of believers and even
an affront to God. This is where theologies of intolerance arise and lead to
claims of ownership over religious truth. Oppositional identities based on
narrow interpretations of core religious teachings threaten to replace the universal message of faith traditions. Yet to look for perfect unity in a world of
multiplicity is to mistake the world for something more than what it is. The
following verse sees no contradiction between the oneness of God and the
plurality of ways and paths leading upto Him:

> "Unto every one of you have We appointed a [different] law [shir'atan] and way of life
> [minhajan]. And if God had so willed, He could surely have made you all one single
> community: but [He willed it otherwise] in order to test you by means of what He has
> vouchsafed unto you. Vie, then, with one another in doing good works! Unto God
> you all must return; and then He will make you truly understand all that on which
> you were wont to differ."
>
> al-Maidah 5:48

It is important to note that the word shir'a(tan) is derived from the same
root as the word shari'ah. Even though the word shari'ah has come to mean
Islamic law, it essentially indicates the totality of the moral, spiritual, social,
and legal teachings of Islam (or any religion for that matter). Even if we
understand the shari'ah as law specific to a religion, the above verse adds the
word minhaj(an), implying that the combination of the two gives us a belief
system, a code of ethics, and a way of life. In this context, each socioreligious
community has been given a "clear path in religion to follow."[23] According
to Qurtubi, "God has made the Torah for its people, the Gospel for its people and the Qur'an for its people. This is in regards to laws [shara'i] and rituals ['ibadat]. As for the principle of divine unity (tawhid), there is no disagreement among them."[24] He then quotes Mujahid as saying that "the law
[shari'ah] and the way of life [minhaj] are the religion of Muhmmad; everything else has been abrogated." According to Ibn Kathir, God has certainly
sent different paths and "traditions" [sunan] for people to follow, but all of
them have been abrogated after the coming of Islam.[25] While this is invariably the position of most of the classical Islamic scholars and can be seen as
a clear case of theological exclusivism, it does not appear to have invalidated
the policies of tolerance and accommodation toward other religions and particularly the People of the Book.

This is borne out by the fact that the treatment of the plurality of human
communities in the Qur'an is not merely general or abstract. The Qur'an is

deeply conscious of the presence of Jews and Christians in Mecca and Medina and sees them closer to Muslims than other communities. It is this historical and theological proximity that creates a sense of theological rivalry as to who is best entitled to the legacy of Abraham. A large number of verses talk about specific Jewish and Christian objections against the new revelation and the prophet Muhammad. Even though they focus on specific arguments, they provide general guidelines about Islam's attitude toward the People of the Book. And they display both inclusivist and exclusivist tones.

They contain elements of inclusivism because Islam relates itself to Judaism and Christianity through the figure of Abraham, the story of Noah, the story of creation, and the stories of Solomon, Joseph, Moses, Mary, Jesus, and other prophets who are common to the Bible and the Qur'an. The moral and eschatological teachings of Judaism, Christianity, and Islam can also be included in this category of teachings. The focal point of such verses is the recognition of the truth of the new religion and its prophet by acknowledging their common lineage that goes back to Abraham. Instead of rejecting *in toto* the earlier revelations and the religious communities that subscribe to them, the Qur'an invites them to agree and eventually unite on the fundamental principles of the Abrahamic tradition.

Besides specific theological arguments that contain elements of inclusivism, it should also be mentioned that Islam did not have to quarrel with the People of the Book in the way Christianity did with Judaism. Since Islam was neither the fulfillment of a Judaic or Christian prophecy nor was the prophet Muhammad the messiah, Muslims did not have to contest Jews or Christians on issues specific to the theological traditions of these two communities. Furthermore, there was no ground for a blood libel between Islam on the one hand and Judaism and Christianity on the other. Even though Islam quarreled with these two religions on many theological issues, it started out with recognizing and accepting their existence. Since Islam was ethnically diverse and culturally plural from the very beginning, it did not have any reason to oppose or defame Jews on account of their ethnic identity. In short, Islam did not need to establish itself at the expense of its Judaic or Christian predecessors. This explains to a large extent why there was no demonization of Jews or Christians by Muslims despite the rich literature of intense polemics, bitter arguments, and counterarguments.

Yet, despite the legal and sociopolitical factors that have facilitated the policies of tolerance toward the People of the Book, the Qur'an also contains elements of exclusivism, for it calls itself with a specific name, *Islam*, and invites its followers to be *Muslims*. No religion can be entirely inclusivist because this would destroy the spiritual integrity of any tradition. In this sense, Islam could not have called itself simply the *religion of Abraham*; it had to distinguish itself from the other contenders in a way that would give its followers a nonambiguous sense of allegiance and integrity. This has not prevented the Qur'an from approaching the People of the Book with differing degrees of critical engagement while calling upon them to understand the essential meaning of religious faith.

A good example of this is the treatment of non-Islamic rituals in the Qur'an. Putting aside the polytheistic rituals of the pagan Arabs, which Islam rejects unequivocally, the Qur'an discusses a number of ancient ritual practices and asks what purpose they are meant to serve. In its anthropological analyses of rituals, the Qur'an draws attention to their fundamental meaning and invites non-Muslims to look for what is essential in the Muslim rituals.

I will pick up two examples to illustrate this point. The first example is from the Meccan polytheists. To show that true piety is not to perform blindly certain rituals but to seek proximity to God, the Qur'an refers to the Meccan custom of "entering houses from the rear." The Meccans used to dig up holes and stay in them during the time of pilgrimage. As part of the customary ritual, they also used to enter their houses from the backdoors. When the Meccans asked the prophet Muhammad about the significance of the "new moons" and the time of pilgrimage, he was told to give the following answer: "They will ask thee about the new moons. Say: 'They indicate the periods for [various doings of] mankind, including the pilgrimage'" (al-Baqarah 2:189). While this answer addresses the specific question about the "new moons" (*ahillah*), it shifts the focus from a specific ritual to the general question of what constitutes piety and God-consciousness (*al-taqwa'*), which is the essence of all rituals. The remainder of the verse refers both to a specific ritual during pilgrimage and to the larger meaning of an act deemed to be pious: "However, piety [*al-birr*] does not consist in your entering houses from the rear [as it were] but truly pious is he who is conscious of God. Hence enter houses through their doors, and remain conscious of God, so that you might attain to a happy state" (al-Baqarah 2:189). The verse disapproves of the act of "entering houses from the rear" yet gives no specific reason for it. But it also uses a metaphorical language, for the expression "enter(ing) houses through their doors" has the meaning of doing something properly. *Al-birr*, thus, points to the spiritual meaning of ritual acts and invites the Meccan polytheists as well as the People of the Book to go beyond the narrow perpectives of their respective traditions.

The second example is related to facing the Ka'ba as the direction of prayers. In the early years of the revelation, the prophet Muhammad had instructed Muslims to pray toward Jerusalem while facing the Ka'ba at the same time.[26] While this had certainly gained the favor of the Jews of Mecca and Medina especially against the Christians, it has also led them to boast of the fact that Muslims were facing *their qiblah*. This seems to have caused some concern for the Prophet leading him to pray to God for a new direction of prayer for Muslims: "We have seen thee [O Prophet] often turn thy face towards heaven [for guidance]: and now We shall indeed make thee turn in prayer in a direction which will fulfil thy desire. Turn, then, thy face towards the Inviolable House of Worship [*masjid al-haram*]; and wherever you all may be, turn your faces towards it [in prayer]" (al-Baqarah 2:144).

This change was probably expected because, according to the Qur'an (Al-i 'Imran 3:96), the Ka'ba is the first sanctuary devoted to the worship of God to which Abraham (and his sons) turned (al-Baqarah 2:125–29).[27] The incident appears to have caused a rift between Muslims and certain members of the Jewish and Christian communities in Medina. The Qur'an accuses them of not being sincere in their hardened positions: "And, verily, those who have been given the book aforetime know well that this [commandament] comes in truth from their Sustainer, and God is not unaware of what they do" (al-Baqarah 2:144). The People of the Book are expected to welcome such a change because they know the meaning of praying toward a certain direction: "They unto whom We have given the book aforetime know it as they know their own children: but, behold, some of them knowingly suppress the truth" (al-Baqarah 2:146). The prophet Muhammad is asked to endure any criticism or ridicule that may come from the Arabian Jews and Christians. He is also advised to distinguish his *qibla* from theirs and accept it as a fact:

"... even if thou were to place all evidence before those who have been given the book, they would not follow thy direction of prayer [*qiblah*], and neither mayest thou follow their direction of prayer [*qiblah*], nor even do they follow one another's direction. And if thou shouldst follow their errant views after all the knowledge that has come unto thee, thou wouldst surely be among the evildoers."

al-Baqarah 2:145

The Qur'an addresses the *qibla* incident to give assurances to the Muslim community in Medina on the one hand and draw attention to the futility of taking rituals to be an absolute indicator of piety on the other. Against religious sectarianism, God asks all believers to put aside their petty differences: "... every community faces a direction of its own, of which He is the focal point.[28] Vie, therefore, with one another in doing good works. Wherever you may be, God will gather you all unto Himself: for, verily, God has the

power to will anything" (al-Baqarah 2:148). The expression "every community faces a direction of its own" gives a similar meaning stated in al-Maidah
5:48, quoted above. Just as Muslims accept the *qiblah* of Jews and Christians,
they also should recognize the Muslim *qiblah* as valid for turning toward God
during ritual prayers. The Qur'an chastises those who ridicule the Prophet of
Islam for turning toward Ka'ba after praying toward Jerusalem: "The weak-
minded [or the foolish, *sufaha*] among people will say 'What has turned them
away from the direction of prayer which they have hitherto observed?' Say:
'God's is the east and the west; He guides whom He wills onto a straight way'"
(al-Baqarah 2:142–43).

In these and other verses, the Qur'an warns against the danger of causing friction on the basis of differences in ritual acts. While this is an attempt
to safeguard the newly established Muslim community against the accusations of the Jews and Christians of Medina, it is also a call for transcending
religious and sectarian differences. The following verse makes a strong point
about this:

"True piety [*al-birr*] does not consist in turning your faces towards the east or the
west. But truly pious is he who believes in God, and the Last Day; and the angels, and
revelation, and the prophets; and spends his substance—however much he himself
may cherish it—upon his near of kin, and the orphans, and the needy, and the way-
farer, and the beggars, and for the freeing of human beings from bondage; and is constant in prayer, and renders the purifying dues; and [truly pious are] they who keep
their promises whenever they promise, and are patient in misfortune and hardship
and in time of peril: it is they that have proved themselves true, and it is they, they
who are conscious of God."

al-Baqarah 2:177

The word *al-birr*, translated as virtue and righteousness, signifies a virtuous act conducted with the fear and consciousness of God. The person who
has the *birr* is the person who is in constant vigilance and mindfulness of
God.[29] The Qur'an defines true piety as having full consciousness of God,
believing in his books and prophets, and doing such virtuous acts as praying,
almsgiving, and helping the poor and the needy.[30] Virtue requires constant
vigilance, and the believers are not excepted: "[But as for you, O believers]
never shall you attain to true piety [*al-birr*] unless you spend out of what you
cherish yourselves; and whatever you spend, verily God has full knowledge
thereof" (Al-i 'Imran 3:92). The People of the Book are also reminded: "Do
you enjoin other people to be pious while you forget your own self; and yet
you recite the Book [*al-kitab*]" (al-Baqarah 2:44).

In addressing specific rituals, the Qur'an does not belittle their significance but points to what is essential in them. As later Muslim scholars and especially the Sufis would elaborate, this generic rule holds true for all ritual practices. The Qur'an insists that true piety and goodness (*al-birr*) are the ultimate goal of religious acts and that all communities should seek to attain it. Furthermore, vying for piety and goodness is a solid basis for an ethics of co-existence: ". . . help one another in furthering virtue [*al-birr*] and God-consciousness, and do not help one another in furthering evil and enmity" (al-Mai'dah 5:2).

Religious Tolerance and the People of the Book

There are no other two religions on which the Qur'an spends as much time as on Judaism and Christianity. Given Islam's claim to be the last revelation and completion of the Abrahamic tradition, this should come as no surprise. A large number of verses speak about various Jewish and Christian themes. These Qur'anic conversations concentrate, among others, on three issues. The first is the disputes among Jews and Christians about issues such as Abraham, revelation, salvation, and the hereafter. Some verses describe these disputes as futile, selfish, and ignorant (al-Baqarah 2:111), referring, at the same time, to the stiff opposition of Jewish and Christian leaders to the prophet Muhammad. The second is the political alliances which the Jews and some Christians of Medina had formed with the Meccan polytheists against the newly established Muslim community. The most severe statements in the Qur'an and the Hadith collections against the Jews pertain to this historical fact. The only incident in the history of Islam where a particular group of Jews has been ordered to be killed is related to the violation of a treaty of political alliance between certain Jewish tribes and Muslims in Medina. The third issue is the recognition of the validity of the new revelation and the prophet Muhammad, which remains a difficult issue for Christians up to our own day.

The Qur'an brings up the disputes between Jews and Christians to indicate to them that while claiming to be heirs to the legacy of Abraham, they are engaged in destructive quarrels and petty fights. With such bitter disunity and bickering, they cannot be proper models of what Abraham stood for. The Qur'an seems to imply that the intractable opposition of Jews and Christians of Madina to the prophet Muhammad is similar to their internal disputes and thus cannot serve as a basis for a serious dialogue:

"Furthermore, the Jews assert, 'The Christians have no valid ground for their beliefs,' while the Christians assert, 'The Jews have no valid ground for their beliefs' and both quote the Book! Even thus, like unto what they say, have [always] spoken those who were devoid of knowledge; but it is God who will judge between them on Resurrection Day with regard to all on which they were wont to differ."

al-Baqarah 2:113

Following this line of argumentation, the Qur'an addresses Jews and Christians directly because they are different and more special from the polytheists, Magians, or Zoroastrians. In some cases, they are described as behaving worse than the disbelievers of Mecca. It is usually these verses that Muslim exclusivists take up as a basis for classifying the People of the Book together with the Meccan polytheists. The Qur'an, however, does not fail to make a distinction between those who have completely turned against God and those whose hearts are filled with reverence for God among Jews and Christians. There is also a distinction between those who have betrayed the Prophet and his community and those who have honored their promises. The following verse, for instance, is extremely harsh on the People of the Book:

"Overshadowed by ignominy are they wherever they may be, save [when they bind themselves again] in a bond with God and a bond with men; for they have earned the burden of God's condemnation, and are overshadowed by humiliation: all this [has befallen them] because they persisted in denying the truth of God's messages and in slaying the prophets against all right: all this, because they rebelled [against God], and persisted in transgressing the bounds of what is right."

Al-i 'Imran 3:112

This is followed by another verse which reflects the careful discernment of the Qur'an regarding the People of the Book:

"[But] they are not all alike: among the People of the Book are upright people [ummah], who recite God's messages throughout the night, and prostrate themselves [before Him]. They believe in God and the Last Day, and enjoin the doing of what is right and forbid the doing of what is wrong, and vie with one another in doing good works: and these are among the righteous. And whatever good they do, they shall never be denied the reward thereof: for, God has full knowledge of those who are conscious of Him."

Al-i 'Imran 3:113–15

While the classical commentators usually read this verse as referring to Jews and Christians who converted to Islam, there is no compelling reason that we should accept it as abrogated (mansukh). In fact, it would not make sense to call them the People of the Book if they had already converted to Islam. Such subtle distinctions are not hard to find in the Qur'an. Yet in Maidah 5:82–84, we find a clear favoring of Christians over Jews:

"Thou wilt surely find that, of all people, the most hostile to those who believe [in this divine writ] are the Jews as well as those who are bent on ascribing divinity to aught beside God; and thou wilt surely find that, of all people, they who say 'Behold, we are Christians' come closest to feeling affection for those who believe [in this divine writ]: this is so because there are priests and monks among them, and because these are not given to arrogance. For, when they come to understand what has been bestowed from on high upon this Apostle, thou canst see their eyes overflow with tears, because they recognize something of its truth;[31] [and] they say: 'O our Sustainer! We do believe; make us one, then, with all who bear witness to the truth. And how could we fail to believe in God and in whatever truth has come unto us, when we so fervently desire that our Sustainer count us among the righteous?'"

al-Ma'idah 5:82–84

The "closeness" to which the verse refers is a reference to both the social and political proximity which the Christian communities of the period felt toward Muslims. The famous expedition of a group of companions of the Prophet to the Christian king of Abyssinia and the warm welcome they had received can also be seen as a factor in this clearly favorable description of Christians. As a number of early Muslim historians have noted, Muslims were hoping for the eventual success of the Byzantine Empire over the Persians because the former were Christian.[32] Furthermore, the Christians of Medina had remained loyal to the Medinan Treaty against the Meccans, thus gaining the favor and affinity of Muslims. Commenting on the verse above, Ibn Qayyim quotes al-Zujjaj as saying that Christians are praised for they have been "less inclined towards the Meccans than the Jews."[33]

The harsh assessment of the Jews is, thus, a response to the political alliance of the Jews of Medina with the Meccan polytheists and in violation of the Medinan Treaty to which we referred above. According to the treaty, the Jewish tribes in Medina and Muslims had agreed to defend each other against aggressors, i.e., the Meccans. It is clear that the prophet Muhammad was concerned to secure a strong political alliance with the Jews and Christians of Medina against the Meccans. While the Christians remained mostly loyal to the agreement and did not fight or plot against Muslims, the Meccans were able to get some prominent Jewish leaders on their side in their military campaigns against Muslims.[34] Those who violated the treaty and thus betrayed the Muslim community included not only Jews but also those whom the Qur'an calls the "hypocrites" (al-munafiqun). The Qur'an uses extremely harsh language against them because they claim to be part of the Muslim community while forming alliances with the Meccan polytheists. The Qur'an is so stern on this point that the prophet Muhammad is banned from praying for their soul (see al-Tawbab 9:80).

Even though the Qur'an's harsh treatment of Jewish tribes in Medina has not been lost to the Prophet and his followers, it has not led to an anti-Semitic literature in the Islamic tradition. Since the Jewish communities, unlike Christianity, did not pose a political threat that had, at least by association, the backing of the Byzantine Empire, they were hardly part of political conflicts in later centuries. For both political and theological reasons, the great majority of Muslim polemical works in the medieval period have been directed against Christianity more than Judaism.[35] The sociopolitical and economic structure of Muslim societies has been conducive to a largely successful integration of Jewish communities. As I mentioned above, the Jewish merchants were never ostracized for their profession or prevented from practicing it because the economic system of Muslim societies allowed greater flexibility for international trade and finance. Furthermore, the Jews in the Near East where Muslims came to rule were the indigenous communities of the area, not immigrants as they were in Western Christendom. This has given them a right of property and communal freedom that we do not see in Europe. In fact, this can be compared only to the position of Hindus after India came under Muslim rule. Finally, the ethnic composition of Muslim societies was so diverse that the Jewish communities did not have to stand out as different or "strange."[36]

Even though the Qur'an approaches Christians more favorably than Jews, it does not shy away from criticizing them for introducing a number of "inventions" or "corruption" (*tahrif*) into their religion. As mentioned before, there are many such criticisms, the most important of which concern the nature of Jesus Christ and the Christian claim that he was the son of God. This is not the place to go into a discussion of the place of Jesus in Islam. It suffices to say, however, that the Qur'an and the prophetic tradition reject (compare al-Nisa 4:171–73 and al-Ma'idah 5:72–77) the divinity of Jesus as formulated by the later Christian doctrine. Besides theology, one specific practice for which the Qur'an criticizes the Christians is "monasticism" (*rahbaniyyah*). Christians are praised for their fear and veneration of God but criticized for going to the extreme of inventing a monastic life not enjoined by God:

"And thereupon We caused [other of] Our apostles to follow in their footsteps; and [in the course of time] We caused them to be followed by Jesus, the son of Mary, upon whom We bestowed the Gospel; and in the hearts of those who [truly] followed him We engendered compassion and mercy. But as for monasticism [*rahbaniyyah*]: We did not enjoin it upon them: they invented it themselves out of a desire for God's goodly acceptance. But then, they did not [always] observe it as it ought to have been observed: and so We granted their recompense unto such of them as had [truly] attained to faith, whereas many of them became iniquitous."

al-Hadid 57:27

The classical commentators interpret this verse as pointing to the harsh conditions of early Christians to protect themselves against the persecutions of the Roman rulers. Monasticism (and celibacy, we should add) could be seen as a temporary solution in times of extreme measures but cannot be a general rule for attaining piety because religions are meant to save not just the elect but everyone. It is also important to note that the mainstream Islamic tradition does not posit any intermediaries between God and the ordinary believer. There is no need for a monastic institution to train spiritual leaders to provide religious guidance for the average person. The commentators, thus, take this opportunity to stress that Islam has come to establish a balance (*wasatah*) between worldly indulgence and extreme asceticism. This point is reiterated in the following verse:

"And ordain Thou for us what is good in this world as well as in the life to come: behold, unto Thee have we turned in repentance!" [God] answered: "With My chastisement do I afflict whom I will—but My grace overspreads everything: and so I shall confer it on those who are conscious of Me and spend in charity, and who believe in Our messages those who shall follow the [last] Apostle, the unlettered Prophet whom they shall find described in the Torah that is with them, and [later on] in the Gospel: [the Prophet] who will enjoin upon them the doing of what is right and forbid them the doing of what is wrong, and make lawful to them the good things of life and forbid them the bad things, and lift from them their burdens and the shackles that were upon them [aforetime]. Those, therefore, who shall believe in him, and honour him, and succour him, and follow the light that has been bestowed from on high through him—it is they that shall attain to a happy state."

al-A'raf 7:156–57

While Jews and Christians are usually thought to be the People of the Book, the Qur'an also mentions several other communities as part of the non-Islamic religious traditions under protection. The mention of "Sabians" in the following verse shows that the concept of the People of the Book was set to be flexible and ever-expanding from the very beginning: "Verily, those who have attained to faith, as well as those who follow the Jewish faith, and the Christians, and the Sabians;[37] all who believe in God and the Last Day and do righteous deeds shall have their reward with their Sustainer; and no fear need they have, and neither shall they grieve" (al-Baqarah 2:62).[38]

It is important to note that the status of "no fear" mentioned in the above verse legally refers to the protection of the People of the Book as *ahl al-dhimmah*. While the *dhimmi* status was initially given to Jews, Christians, Sabians, and Zoroastrians, its scope was later extended to include all non-Muslims living under Islam especially in the subcontinent of India.[39] This is exactly what happened in India when Muhammad b. al-Qasim, the first Muslim commander to set foot on Indian soil in the eighth century, compared Hindus to Jews, Christians, and Zoroastrians and declared them as part of the *ahl al-dhimmah*.[40] This decision, which was later sanctioned by the Hanafi jurists, was a momentous event in the development of the Muslim attitude toward the religions of India.

That the People of the Book were accorded a special status is not only attested by the various Qur'anic verses but also recorded in a number of treatises signed by the prophet Muhammad after his migration to Medina in 622. The "Medinan Treatise" (*sahifat al-madina*), also called the "Medinan Constitution," recognizes the Jews of Banu 'Awf, Banu al-Najar, Banu Tha'laba, Banu Harith, and other Jewish tribes as distinct communities: "The Jews of Banu 'Awf are a community [*ummah*] together with Muslims; they have their own religion, properties and lives, and Muslims their own except those who commit injustice and wrongdoing; and they only harm themselves."[41] Another treatise signed with the People of the Book of Najran reads as follows:

"They [People of the Book] shall have the protection of Allah and the promise of Muhammad, the Apostle of Allah, that they shall be secured their lives, property, lands, creed, those absent and those present, their families, their churches, and all that they possess. No bishop or monk shall be displaced from his parish or monastery. No priest shall be forced to abandon his priestly life. No hardships or humiliation shall be imposed on them nor shall their land be occupied by [our] army. Those who seek justice, shall have it: there will be no oppressors nor oppressed."[42]

'Umar ibn al-Khattab, the second caliph of Islam, has given a similar safeguard (*aman*) to the people of Jerusalem when he took the city in 623:

"In the name of God, the Merciful and Compassionate! This is the safeguard granted to the inhabitants of 'Alia [Jerusalem] by the servant of God, 'Umar, commander of the faithful. They are given protection of their persons, their churches, their crosses—whether these are in good state or not—and their cult in general. No constraints will be exercised against them in the matter of religion and no harm will be done to any of them. The inhabitants of 'Alia will have to pay the jizya in the same way as the inhabitants of other towns. It rests with them to expel the Byzantines and robbers from their city. Those among them the latter who wish to remain there will be permitted on condition that they pay the same jizya as the inhabitants of 'Alia."[43]

The poll tax called *jizya* was imposed on *ahl al-dhimmah* as compensation for their protection as well as for their exemption from compulsory military service. Contrary to a common belief, the primary goal of *jizya* was not the "humiliation" of the People of the Book. While most contemporary translations of the Qur'an render the words *wa hum al-saghirun* (al-Tawbah 9:29) as "so that they will be humiliated," Ibn Qayyim al-Jawziyyah, who has written the most extensive work on the People of the Book, reads it as securing the allegiance of the People of the Book to laws pertaining to them (ahkam al-millah). According to Ibn Qayyim, wa hum al-saghirun means making all subjects of the state obey the law and, in the case of the People of the Book, pay the jizya.[44] Despite Ibn Qayyim's relatively lenient position, his teacher, the famous Hanbali scholar Ibn Taymiyya, takes a hard position against non-Muslims and calls for their conversion or submission.[45] Yet, Abu Yusuf, the student of Abu Hanifa, the founder of the Hanafi school of law, advises the Abbasid caliph Harun al-Rashid (d. 803) to "treat with leniency those under the protection of our Prophet Muhammad, and not allow that more than what is due to be taken from them or more than they are able to pay, and that nothing should be confiscated from their properties without legal justification."[46] To substantiate his case, Abu Yusuf narrates a tradition in which the Prophet says that "he who robs a dhimmi or imposes on him more than he can bear will have me as his opponent." Another well-known case is the Prophet's ordering of the execution of a Muslim who had killed a dhimmi. In response to the incident, the Prophet has said that "it is most appropriate that I live up fully to my (promise of) protection."[47]

While these examples show the complexities of Islamic history, the underlying principle behind the attitudes of accommodation is that the overall interests of human beings are served better in peace than in conflict.[48] In dealing with the People of the Book, the prophet Muhammad is instructed to take a special care: "Hence, judge between the followers of earlier revelation in accordance with what God has bestowed from on high" (al-Mai'dah 5:49). Yet he is also warned against the temptation of compromising his mission in order to gain their favor: "And do not follow their errant views; and beware of them, lest they tempt thee away from aught that God has bestowed from on high upon thee. And if they turn away [from His commandments], then know that it is but God's will [thus] to afflict them for some of their sins: for, behold, a great many people are iniquitous indeed" (al-Ma'idah 5:49).

None of these measures would have made sense had they not been complemented by a clear rule about the problem of conversion. It is one thing to say that people are free to choose their religion, but it is another thing to set in place a legal and social system where the principle of religious freedom is applied with relative ease and success. This is what al-Baqarah 2:256 establishes with its proclamation that "there is no compulsion in religion." The verse and the way it states the principle are crucial for understanding the policies of conversion that have developed in early and later Islamic history. Both the overall attitude of the Qur'an and the Prophet toward non-Muslims and the legal injunctions regarding the People of the Book stipulate against forced conversion. Furthermore, the Arabic command form *la ikraha* can be read not only as "there is no compulsion" but also as "there should be no compulsion." The subtle difference between the two is that, while the former implies that the proofs and foundations of Islam are clear and therefore the nonbeliever should accept its truth without difficulty, the latter states that no non-Muslim can be forced to convert even if the proofs are clear to him or her.

Like Christianity, Islam encourages its followers to spread the word and argue with peoples of other faiths "in the best possible way" so that they understand and, it is hoped, embrace the message of Islam. This leads us to yet another tension in Islam between claims to universality and policies of protection and accommodation. Furthermore, some later jurists have claimed that Baqarah 256 has been abrogated by other verses after the conquest of Mecca.[49] According to Qurtubi, Sulayman ibn Musa has defended this argument because "the Prophet of Islam has forced the pagan Arabs into Islam, fought them and refused to accept from them anything but professing the Islamic faith."[50] The second view is that the verse has not been abrogated because it has been sent specifically for the People of the Book. This interpretation is supported by the famous incident, for which Baqarah 256 has been revealed, when Bani Salim b. 'Afw, one of the companions of the Prophet from Medina, had forced his Christian sons to accept Islam.[51] According to Ibn Kathir, the verse is a command "not to force anyone to enter the religion of Islam because it is clear and evident."[52] Another incident cited by Qurtubi involves Umar ibn al-Khattab, the second caliph of Islam, who asks an old Christian woman to embrace Islam. The old lady responds by saying that "I am an old lady and death is nearing me." Upon this answer, Umar reads the verse Baqarah 256 and leaves her.[53]

Fakh al-Din al-Razi opposes compulsion of any kind on intellectual grounds. According to him, not just the People of the Book but no one should be forced to believe because "God has not built faith upon compulsion and pressure but on acceptance and free choice." Even though al-Razi considers this "free will defense" to be the position of the Mutazilites, to whom he is always opposed, he rejects al-Qifal's argument that, since all of the proofs of the true religion have been made clear to the disbeliever, he may be forced to accept it. For al-Razi, compulsion in matters of faith annuls the principle of free will (*taklif*) and goes against God's plan to try people.[54]

The last point I will take up here concerns the verse al-Ma'idah 5:51, which has led many Western students of Islam to claim that the Qur'an advises

Muslims against developing friendly relationship with Jews and Christians. The verse reads as follows: "O you who have attained to faith! Do not take the Jews and the Christians for your *awliya*': they are but *awliya*' of one another. Whoever among you takes them as his *wali* is one of them." The word *awliya*' is the plural of *wali,* which is rendered in most of the English translations of the Qur'an as "friend." According to this intrepretation, the verse reads as "do not take Jews and Christians as friends." Even though the word *wali* means friend in the ordinary sense of the term, in this context, it has the meaning of protector, legal guardian, and ally. This rendering is confirmed by al-Tabari's explanation that the verse 5:51 was revealed during one of the battles (the battle of Badr in 624 or Uhud in 625) that the Muslims in Medina had fought against the Meccans. Under the circumstances of a military campaign, the verse advises the new Muslim community not to form political alliances with non-Muslims if they violate the terms of a treaty they had signed with them.[55] It is important to note that Muslims, Jews, or Christians to whom the verse refers represent not only religious but also sociopolitical communities. The meaning of "ally" or "legal guardian" for *wali/awliya*' makes sense especially in view of Ibn Qayyim's explanation that "whoever forms an alliance with them through a treaty [*'ahd*] is with them in violating the agreement."[56]

Relations with Non-Muslims

The Islamic code of ethics for the treatment of non-Muslims follows the overall principles dicussed so far. As far as the Islamic attitude toward Judaism and Christianity is concerned, there is a delicate balance between treating them with respect and refusing to compromise the essential features of the Abrahamic tradition. Among the non-Muslim communities, the only exception is the Meccan polytheists, which Islam rejects *in toto.* The "sword verses" of the Qur'an that aim at the Meccans are misinterpreted as a declaration of war on all non-Muslims. The fact is that the Qur'an calls upon Muslims to take up arms against the Meccans and explains the reasons in nonambiguous terms:

And fight in God's cause against those who wage war against you, but do not commit aggression—for, verily, God does not love aggressors. And slay them wherever you may come upon them, and drive them away from wherever they drove you away—for oppression [*fitnah*][57] is even worse than killing. And fight not against them near the Inviolable House of Worship unless they fight against you there first; but if they fight against you, slay them: such shall be the recompense of those who deny the truth. But if they desist—behold, God is much-forgiving, a dispenser of grace. Hence, fight against them until there is no more oppression and all worship is devoted to God alone; but if they desist, then all hostility shall cease, save against those who [wilfully] do wrong.

al-Baqarah 2:190–93

According to Ibn Hisham, there are primarily two reasons for Islam's extremely hostile attitude towards the Meccan pagans. The first is the impossibility of reconciling paganism and polytheism with the central Islamic doctrine of divine unity (*tawhid*). Numerous Qur'anic verses and prophetic traditions describe the ignorance and arrogance of Meccan polytheists in vivid detail. Their lack of respect for God and human dignity and such social evils as slavery, infanticide (compare al-Mumtahinah 60:12; al-Takwir 81:8–9), and tribal racism are results of their fundamental theological error: taking partners unto God (*shirk*). The second reason, which Ibn Hisham emphasizes more than the first, is their total denial of the messenger of God and the political plots they created to destroy the new Muslim community. Early Islamic history is filled with incidents of the inhuman treatment of Muhammad and his followers. That the Meccans tried to kill the Prophet of Islam has only added to the sense of outrage and hostility towards them.[58] Abu Hanifah and others have pointed out that the only community that will not receive mercy on the day of judgment are the Meccan polytheists to whom the last Prophet has been sent. According to the majority of the classical commentators, the famous "slay them . . ." verse refers exclusively to pagan Arabs who fought against the Prophet and his followers.[59] While military combat is not completely ruled out but kept as a last resort, war, when it becomes inevitable, has to be conducted under certain restrictions.[60]

That the verses of war are specifically for those who have declared war against Muslims is also confirmed by the verses al-Mumtahinah 60:8–9. It is important to note that the chapter cites two main reasons for taking up arms against the Meccan polytheists: suppression of faith and expulsion from homeland.[61] Both actions were taken against the early Muslim community in Mecca and later in Medina. Muslims are ordered not to take the Meccans as allies or protectors (*awliya'*) and show them any "kindness":

O you who have attained to faith! Do not take My enemies—who are your enemies as well—for your allies, showing them affection even though they are bent on denying whatever truth has come unto you, [and even though] they have driven the Apostle and yourselves away, [only] because you believe in God, your Sustainer! If [it be true that] you have gone forth [from your homes] to strive [*jihad*] in My cause, and out of a longing for My goodly acceptance, [do not take them for your friends,] inclining towards them in secret affection: for I am fully aware of all that you may conceal as well as of all that you do openly. And any of you who does this has already strayed from the right path.

al-Mumtahinah 60:1

The verses bring up the example of Abraham who had a similar experience with his community. Abraham is mentioned to have prayed for his father: "I shall indeed pray for [God's] forgiveness for thee, although I have it not in my power to obtain anything from God in thy behalf" (al-Mumtahinah 60:4). This reminder was presumably meant to give moral support to the first Muslims who were persecuted and expelled from their homeland. In fact, the verses draw attention to the weakness of some among them for their desire to approach the Meccans to protect their children and relatives who were still in Mecca. Yet the Qur'an also warns that the enmity in which they find themselves is not unconditional: "[But] it may well be that God will bring about [mutual] affection between you [O believers] and some of those whom you [now] face as enemies: for, God is all-powerful and God is much-forgiving, a dispenser of grace" (al-Mumtahinah 60:7). These provisions and examples are summed up in the following verse, which lays the ground rules for dealing with non-Muslims in times of war and peace:

"As for such [of the unbelievers] as do not fight against you on account of [your] faith [al-din], and neither drive you forth from your homelands, God does not forbid you to show them kindness and to behave towards them with full equity: for, verily, God loves those who act equitably. God only forbids you to turn in friendship towards such as fight against you because of [your] faith, and drive you forth from your homelands, or aid [others] in driving you forth: and as for those [from among you] who turn towards them in friendship; it is they, they who are truly wrongdoers!"

al-Mumtahinah 60:8–9

According to Ibn al-Qayyim, the verse "permits [rukhsah] to have good relations with those who have not declared war against Muslims and allows kindness towards them even though they may not be allies."[62] Al-Tabari interprets the verse along similar lines: "The most credible view is that the verse refers to people of all kinds of creeds and religions who should be shown kindness and treated equitably. God referred to all those who do not fight the Muslims or drive them from their homes without exception or qualification."[63]

In granting permission to Muslims to fight against the Meccans, the Qur'an stresses that the kind of fight Muslims are allowed to engage is not only for themselves but for all those who believe in God:

"Permission [to fight] is given to those against whom war is being wrongfully waged and, verily, God has indeed the power to succour them—those who have been driven from their homelands against all right for no other reason than their saying. "Our Sustainer is God!" For, if God had not enabled people to defend themselves against one another, [all] monasteries and churches and synagogues and mosques—in [all of] which God's name is abundantly extolled—would surely have been destroyed [ere now]."

al-Hajj 22:39–40

Thus, putting aside the Arab pagans during the time of the Prophet, the Qur'an proposes a number of lenient measures for the treatment of the People of the Book and other non-Muslim communities. One verse states this as follows: "Call thou [all mankind] unto thy Sustainer's path with wisdom and goodly exhortation, and argue with them in the most kindly manner" (al-Nahl 16:125). The Jews and Christians are mentioned specifically as partners of a serious and respectful dialogue:

"And do not argue with the People of the Book otherwise than in a most kindly manner—unless it be such of them as are bent on evildoing and say: "We believe in that which has been bestowed from on high upon us, as well as that which has been bestowed upon you: our God and your God is one and the same, and it is unto Him that We [all] surrender ourselves."

al-'Ankabut 29:46

While we can find divergent policies of tolerance and intolerance in the Islamic religious tradition and social history, the contemporary Muslim world has to confront the challenge of religious pluralism in a way that would avoid the extremes of intolerant exclusivism on the one hand and a rootless pluralism at the expense of all orthodoxy on the other. Reading our foundational texts and history must be guided by a set of principles that would remain true to the spirit of the tradition while having enough suppleness to deal with the current challenges. We can cite countless cases from the military conquests of the Ottomans to the employment of Jewish and Christian professionals in various positions across the Islamic world. We can remind ourselves that Muslim empires have had periods of peace and stability as well as conflict and disorder. There have been many confrontations between Muslim and Christian communities in the Balkans, Asia Minor, or North Africa. There is no doubt that all of these factors have had an impact on the development of the Islamic legal tradition and shaped the framework of socioreligious practices in the Muslim world. The historical and contextual reading of Islamic law is, therefore, indispensable for distinguishing between what the contemporary scholar Taha Jabir Alwani calls the "fiqh of conflict" and the "fiqh of coexistence."[64]

A case in point is the question of apostasy in Islam. The classical jurists have usually ruled that apostasy in Islam is punishable by death. The Qur'an does not mention any penalty for the apostate but warns of divine punishment on the day of judgment (compare al-Baqarah 2:217; al-Ma'idah 5:54). The ruling for death penalty is based on the hadith in which the Prophet says to "kill those who change their religion." At its face value, this is an extremely harsh statement and goes against the principle of free choice in Islam. The hadith, however, makes perfect sense when we understand the context in which it has been said. The hadith refers to changing one's political alliance and betraying the Muslim community especially during times of war. This includes taking arms against the Muslim state. That is why the Hanafi jurists have ruled that women apostates cannot be killed because they are not considered soldiers in the army.[65] Contemporary Muslim scholars have applied this approach and concluded that the classical rulings on the death penalty for apostasy are based on sociohistorical circumstances and do not apply today.[66]

Based on the textual evidence gathered from the Qur'an and prophetic traditions, we can answer William Scott Green's five questions [see chapter 1 of this collection] along the following lines. Other religions and especially Judaism and Christianity play a significant role in Islam. Islam's self-view as the seal of the Abrahamic tradition links it to the Jewish and Christian faiths in a way that we don't find in relation to any other religion. Much of the inter-religious dialogue we find in the sacred sources of Islam is addressed to these religions. Islam acknowledges the plurality of human societies and faith traditions but insists on reaching a common ground between them. As we discussed above, each socioreligious community is recognized as an *ummah*, as potentially legitimate paths to God, but invited to reassert the unity of God and commit themselves to upholding the principles of a virtuous life. Different communities and thus different religious paths exist because God has willed plurality in the world in which we live. This should not be a concern for the believer because the ultimate goal of multiplicity is a noble one: different communities vying for the common good of humanity.

While this is a solid basis for a theology of inclusivism, it does not necessarily lead to moral laxity and social incoherence. Each socioreligious community is bound to have some level of exclusivism theologically, ritually, and socially; otherwise, it would be impossible to maintain the integrity of any religious tradition. Each religious universe must claim to be complete and absolute in itself; otherwise, it cannot fulfill the purpose for which it stands. A genuine culture of tolerance and accommodation is possible only when the principles of respect are observed without compromising the integrity and orthodoxy of a religion. This is in no way far from the infinite mercy that God has written upon himself: "And when those who believe in Our messages come unto thee, say: 'Peace be upon you. Your Sustainer has willed upon Himself the law of grace and mercy—so that if any of you does a bad deed out of ignorance, and thereafter repents and lives righteously, He shall be [found] much-forgiving, a dispenser of grace'" (al-An'am 6:54).

Notes

1. Cf. J. Waardenburg, "World Religions as Seen in the Light of Islam," in *Islam: Past Influence and Present Challenge*, ed. A. T. Welch and P. Cachia (Edinburgh: Edinburgh University Press, 1979), 248–49. See also J. Waardenburg, *Muslims and Others: Relations in Context* (Berlin and New York: Walter de Gruyter, 2003).

2. All translations of Qur'anic verses are from Muhammad Asad's *The Message of the Qur'an*. I have occasionally made some revisions in the translations.

3. Referring to "Come to a word [*kalimah*] common between us and you." On October 13, 2007, 138 Muslim scholars and intellectuals sent a letter to all Christians across the world inviting them to what the Qur'an calls the "common word between us and you." The letter emphasizes the love of God and the love of the neighbor as the two themes uniting Muslims and the People of the Book and particularly the Christians. The letter has been sent to all Christian leaders of the world including the Pope Benedict XVI. The letter follows upon a previous letter called "An Open Letter to the Pope" as a response to the Pope's infamous speech at Regensburg University on September 13, 2006. Since its publication, the Common Word letter has triggered a major debate and hundreds of responses from various Christian leaders and communities. It is also important to note that in modern times the Common Word is the only text or declaration over which such a large and global consensus of Muslims has been formed. Many other Muslim scholars and intellectuals have endorsed the letter since its publication. For the text of the letter, signatories and the responses to it including that of over three-hundred Christian scholars, see the official Web site http://acommonword.com/.

As Fakhr al-Din al-Razi points out, the verse refers to some Christian groups that have had veneration for their clergy to the point of worshiping them. Cf. *al-Tafsir al-Kabir* (Beirut: Dar Ihya al-Turath al-Arabi, 2001), 3:252. Qurtubi makes the same point; cf. Abu Abdullah Muhammad ibn Ahmad al-Ansari al-Qurtubi, *al-Jami' li'l-Ahkam al-Qur'an* (Riyadh: Dar al-'Alam al-Kutub, 2003), 2:106. As I shall discuss below, the Christian tendency to extreme monasticism is criticized in several verses of the Qur'an.

4. Ibn Kathir, *Tafsir* (Beirut: Dar al-Ma'rifah, 2006), 290. According to Mujahid and al-Suddi, this verse was revealed for al-Harith b. Suwayd, the brother of al-Hulas b. Suwayd, one of the companions of the Prophet. Al-Harith was one of the *ansar* (Muslims of Medina); then, he left Islam and joined the Meccans. At that time, this verse was revealed. Upon hearing the verse, al-Harith sent a message to his brother and expressed his regret for leaving Islam and joining the Meccans. Cf. Qurtubi, *al-Jami'*, 2:128.

5. al-Razi, *Tafsir*, 3:282.

6. Cf. ibid., 6:261.

7. Ibid., 9:617.

8. In 3:7, the expression *umm al-kitab* refers to the clearly established and nonallegorical verses of the Qur'an (*ayat muhkamat*). This is contrasted to the allegorical ones (*mutashabihat*), which may create confusion and lead some astray: "Those whose hearts are given to swerving from the truth go after that part of the book [*al-kitab*] which has been expressed in allegory, seeking out [what is bound to create] confusion, and seeking [to arrive at] its final meaning [in an arbitrary manner]; but none save God knows its final meaning." When confronted with such a situation, the believers are asked to follow the example of those "who are deeply rooted in knowledge [who] say: We believe in it; the whole [of the divine book] is from our Sustainer—albeit none takes this to heart save those who are endowed with insight." Only those whose hearts are pure can comprehend the whole of the Qur'anic verses whether allegorical or not because the Qur'an is ultimately a well-protected book: "Behold, it is a truly noble discourse [conveyed unto man] in a well-guarded book (*kitab maknun*) which none but the pure (of heart) can touch" (56:78–79). Fakhr al-Din al-Razi provides an extensive analysis of these points with his usual precision; cf. *Tafsir*, 3:137–148.

9. al-Razi, *Tafsir*, 10:113.

10. Cf. Waardenburg, *Muslims and Others*, 99–101.

11. Ibn Kathir, *Tafsir*, 285.

12. *Tafsir al-jalalayn* (Beirut: Mu'assasat al-Risalah, 1995), 62.

13. Qurtubi, *al-Jami'*, 2:109. cf. also pp. 139–140 where Qurtubi says that "Abraham was called *hanif* because he turned to the religion of God, which is Islam."

14. *The Religious Dialogue of Jerusalem*, in *The Early Christian-Muslim Dialogue: A Collection of Documents from the First Three Islamic Centuries (632–900 A.D.) Translations with Commentary*, ed. N. A. Newman (Hatfield, PA: Interdisciplinary Biblical Research Institute, 1993), 285.

15. Ibn Kathir, *Tafsir*, 1414; *Tafsir al-jalalayn*, 484.

16. al-Razi, *Tafsir*, 9:587.

17. According to M. Asad, this is "a reference to the Biblical prediction of the coming of the Prophet Muhammad, which effectively contradicts the Judaeo-Christian claim that all true prophets, after the Patriarchs, belonged to the children of Israel." M. Asad, *The Message of the Qur'an* (Gibraltar: Dar al-Andalus, 1980), 29.

18. Ibn Kathir, *Tafsir*, 285. This point is reiterated in almost all of the classical commentatries. Cf. Qurtubi, *al-Jami'*, 2:107 where Qurtubi quotes al-Zujjaj as saying that "this is the clearest proof against Jews and Christians. The Torah and the Gospel were revealed after him (Abraham) and the name of these religions is not mentioned in them. But the name Islam is in all the books." Fakhr al-Din al-Razi adds that "the religions brought by prophets cannot be different in principles" (*Tafsir*, 3:254).

19. This is a theme repeated throughout the Qur'an: "Never have We sent forth any apostle otherwise than [with a message] in his own people's tongue" (14:4).

20. Cf. Ibn Qayyim al-Jawziyyah, *Zad al-Masir fi ilm al-tafsir* (Beirut: al-Maktab al-Islami, 2002), 1335.

21. Ibn Qayyim says that they pertain to "matters of religion"; Ibid. 124.

22. Some early scholars interpret this as referring to Adam alone because he is the first man and the source of all later generations. Others, however, insist that it refers to both Adam and Eve. The underlying idea is that we are all children of Adam and Eve. Cf. Qurtubi, *al-Jami'*, 2:30.

23. *Tafsir al-jalalayn*, 116.

24. Qurtubi, *al-Jami'*, 2:211. Cf. al-Razi, *Tafsir*, 4:373, and Muhammad al-Ghazali, *A The-*

matic Commentary on the Qur'an (Herndon, VA: International Institute of Islamic Thought, 2000), 102. See also Ibn Qayyim, *Zad al-Masir*, 388.

25. Ibn Kathir, *Tafsir*, 506.

26. As Fazlur Rahman points out, this was also due to the fact that, while in Mecca, Muslims were not allowed to pray in the Ka'ba. There was no reason for them not to face the Ka'ba when they migrated to Medina. The argument that the change of direction came after the so-called "Jewish-Muslim break out" is, therefore, unsubstantiated. Cf. Fazlur Rahman, *Major Themes of the Qur'an* (Minneapolis: Bibliotheca Islamica, 1989), 147–48.

27. Ibn Qayyim, *Zad al-Masir*, 93.

28. Pickthall translates *wa li-kullin wijhatun huwa muwalliha* as "and each one hath a goal toward which he turneth," interpreting *huwa* as referring to the person who prays, not God to whom one turns in prayers. Yusuf Ali translates as "to each is a goal to which Allah turns him." Other translations give different interpretations. While all these readings are linguistically possible, Asad's rendering of *huwa* as "He," i.e., God, seems to be in keeping with the classical commentaries. *Tafsir Jalalayn* renders *huwa* as "his direction in ritual prayer" and "his Master"; cf. p. 23. Cf. Ibn Qayyim, *Zad al-Masir*, 94.

29. The plural *abrar* refers to those who have attained salvation because of their godly acts. See the references in the Qur'an: 3:193, 197, 56:5, 82:13, 83:18, 22.

30. Ibn Qayyim, *Zad al-Masir*, 102.

31. According to Ibn 'Abbas, the verse is a reference to Najashi, the king of Abysennia. Cf. Ibn Kathir, *Tafsir*, 521. As a Christian king, Najashi had received a delegation of Muslims from Mecca before the migration of the Prophet to Medina and given them asylum, despite the demands of the Meccans for their deportation. See also Ibn Qayyim, *Zad al-Masir*, 401.

32. Cf. al-Ghazali, *A Thematic Commentary*, 111–12.

33. Ibn Qayyim, *Zad al-Masir*, 402.

34. Cf. Ibn Kathir, *Tafsir*, 521.

35. Cf. Waardenburg, *Muslims and Others*, 176. This is not to deny the existence of the relatively rich literature of Jewish-Muslim polemical works. Cf. Camilla Adang, *Muslim Writers on Judaism and the Hebrew Bible: From Ibn Rabban to Ibn Hazm* (Leiden: Brill, 1996), and Moshe Perlmann, "The Medieval Polemics Between Islam and Judaism," in *Religion in a Religious Age*, ed. Solomon dob Goitein, 103–138 (Cambridge, MA: Association for Jewish Studies, 1974).

36. For a well-informed discussion of these points, see Mark Cohen, "Islam and the Jews: Myth, Counter-Myth, History," in *Jews among Muslims: Communities in the Precolonial Middle East*, ed. Sholomo Deshen and Walter P. Zenner, 50–63 (New York: New York University Press, 1996).

37. The exegetical tradition has identified the Sabians in various ways. Imam Shafi'i considers them a Christian group. Cf. Ibn Qayyim, *Ahkam*, 1:92. al-Razi mentions several possibilities: a group from among the Magians; a group that worships angels and prays to the sun; still, a group that worships the stars (a reference to the Sabians of Harran). Cf. al-Razi, *Tafsir*, 1:536. They have also been described as Mandaeans, a Baptist sect of Judeo-Christian origin. The etymology of the word *s-b-'* gives the meaning "baptizing." Cf. "Sabi'a," *Enyclopedia of Islam (2)*, VIII, 675a. For other interpretations, see J. D. McAuliffe, "Exegetical Identification of the Sabiun," *The Muslim World* 72 (1983): 95–106. It is a notorious fact that the Harranians, an obscure religious sect with gnostic inclinations from the Harran region, have identified themselves as Sabians during the time of the Abbasid caliph al-Ma'mun. They have traced their origin back to the prophet Enoch (Idris in the Islamic sources) and claimed

to have been related to the Hermetic tradition. Cf. Seyyed Hossein Nasr, *Science and Civilization in Islam* (Cambridge: Islamic Texts Society, 1987), 31.

38. Another verse makes the same point, but this time criticizes the People of the Book for their obstinacy: "Say: 'O followers of the Book! [*ahl al-kitab*]. You have no valid ground for your beliefs—unless you [truly] observe the Torah and the Gospel, and all that has been bestowed from on high upon you by your Sustainer!' Yet all that has been bestowed from on high upon thee [O Prophet] by thy Sustainer is bound to make many of them yet more stubborn in their overweening arrogance and in their denial of the truth. But sorrow not over people who deny the truth: for, verily, those who have attained to faith [in this divine writ], as well as those who follow the Jewish faith, and the Sabians, and the Christians—all who believe in God and the Last Day and do righteous deeds—no fear need they have, and neither shall they grieve" (al-Ma'idah 5:68–69).

39. There is a consensus on this in the Hanafi and Maliki schools of law as well as some Hanbali scholars. For references in Arabic, see Yohanan Friedmann, *Tolerance and Coercion in Islam: Interfaith Relations in the Muslim Tradition* (Cambridge: Cambridge University Press, 2003), 85–86. For the inclusion of Zoroastrians among the People of the Book, see Friedmann, *Tolerance and Coercion*, 72–76.

40. The incident is recorded in Baladhuri's *Futuh al-buldan*. Cf. Friedmann, *Tolerance and Coercion*, 85.

41. *al-Sirat al-Nabawiyyah li-Ibn Hisham* (Beirut: Dar al-Kutub al-'Ilmiyyah, 2004), 255. The full text of the Medinan Treatise is also published in Muhammad Hamidullah, *Documents sur la Diplomatie a l'Epoque du Prophete et des Khalifes Orthodoxes* (Paris, 1935), 9–14. For an English translation, see Khadduri, *War and Peace*, 206–209.

42. Quoted in Khadduri, *War and Peace in the Law of Islam*, 179. The original text of the Najran treatise is quoted in Abu Yusuf's *Kitab al-kharaj* and Baladhuri's *Futuh al-buldan*.

43. From the Treaty of Capitulation of Jerusalem (633) recorded by al-Tabari, *Tarihk al-rusul wa'l-muluk*, quoted in Youssef Courbage and Philippe Fargues, *Christians and Jews under Islam*, translated from the French by Judy Mabro (London/New York: I. B. Tauris Publishers, 1998), 1. Another treaty of safeguard given to the people of Damascus follows the same rules: "In the name of Allah, the compassionate, the merciful. This is what Khalid ibn al-Walid would grant to the inhabitants of Damascus if he enters therein: he promises to give them security for their lives, property and churches. Their city wall shall not be demolished, neither shall any Moslem be quartered in their houses. Thereunto we give to them the pact of Allah and the protection of His Prophet, the caliphs and the believers. So long as they pay the poll tax, nothing but good shall befall them." Baladhuri, *Futuh al-buldan*, quoted in Philip K. Hitti, *History of the Arabs*, 7th ed. (London: Macmillan and Co. Ltd., 1960), 150.

44. Ibn Qayyim, *Ahkam ahl al-dhimmah*, 1:24. For the amount of *jizya* and the treatment of Jews and Christians in Islamic history, see my "Islam and Peace: A Survey of the Sources of Peace in the Islamic Tradition," *Islamic Studies* 44, no. 3 (2005): 327–62.

45. Cf. Ibn Taymiyyah, *al-Siyasat al-Shar'iyyah* (Beirut: Dar al-Rawi, 2000), 127–28.

46. Khadduri, *War and Peace*, 85.

47. Quoted in Friedmann, *Tolerance and Coercion,* 40.

48. Contemporary applications of this can be followed from the growing literature on Islam, nonviolence, and conflict-resolution. For an overview, see Muhammad Abu-Nimer, "Framework for Nonviolence and Peacebuilding in Islam," in *Contemporary Islam: Dynamic, not Static*, ed. A. Aziz Said, M. Abu-Nimer, and M. Sharify-Funk, 131–172 (London/New York: Routledge, 2006).

49. Cf. Ibn Qayyim, *Zad al-Masir*, 157.

50. Qurtubi, *al-Jami'*, 2:280.

51. Ibn Kathir, *Tafsir*, 239–40.

52. Ibid., 239.

53. Qurtubi, *al-Jami'*, 2:280.

54. Al-Razi, *Tafsir*, 3:15.

55. For an analysis of this point, see David Dakake, "The Myth of a Militant Islam," in *Islam, Fundamentalism and the Betrayal of Tradition*, ed. Joseph Lumbard (Bloomington, IN: World Wisdom, 2004), 5–8.

56. Ibn Qayyim, *Zad al-Masir*, 390.

57. The word *fitnah* has a wide range of meanings: trial, calamity, disorder, civil strife, sedition, and even persecution in the particular verse above.

58. Cf. *al-Sirat al-Nabawiyyah li-Ibn Hisham*, 332

59. For full references, see Dakake, "The Myth of a Militant Islam," 9–11.

60. For "just war" (*jus ad bellum*) and conditions of war (*jus in bello*), see my "Islam and Peace," 342–50. Not surprisingly, Osama bin Laden quotes the "slay them . . ." verse in his infamous 1998 fatwa for the "killing of Americans and their allies—civilian and military." For the text of this fatwa and its critique based on the Islamic sources, see Vincenzo Oliveti, *Terror's Source: The Ideology of Wahhabi-Salafism and Its Consequences* (Birmingham, AL: Amadeus Books, 2002).

61. War is also waged to defend the rights of "those who are weak, ill-treated, and oppressed among men, women, and children, whose cry is: 'Our Lord! Rescue us from this town whose people are oppressors'" (al-Nisa 4:75).

62. Ibn al-Qayyim, *Zad al-Masir*, 425. Qurtubi has a similar interpretation; cf. *al-Jami'*, 10:43.

63. Quoted in Taha Jabir al-Alwani, *Towards a Fiqh for Minorities* (London/Washington, DC: The International Institute of Islamic Thought, 2003), 26.

64. Ibid., 11. Numerous studies have been undertaken by contemporary Muslim scholars to address the question of how to engage Islamic law in the face of the contemporary challenges the Muslim world faces. Imam Shatibi's concept of the "purposes of Islamic law" (*maqasid al-shari'ah*), which he has developed in his *al-Muwafaqat*, has been the subject of many studies in recent years. One fine example is Ahmad al-Raysuni, *Imam Shatibi's Theory of the Higher Objectives and Intents of Islamic Law*, trans. Nancy Roberts (London/Washington, DC: The International Institute of Islamic Thought, 2005). Taha Jabir al-Alwani has dealt with the sources and development of Islamic jurisprudence in his *Source Methodology in Islamic Jurisprudence*, 3rd ed., trans. and ed. Yusuf Talal Delorenzo and Anas al-Shaykh Ali (London/Washington, DC: The International Institute of Islamic Thought, 2003). Another contemporary scholar Yusuf al-Qaradawi has adopted a similar point of view in his *Approaching the Sunna: Comprehension and Controversy*, trans. Jamil Qureshi (London/Washington, DC: The International Institute of Islamic Thought, 2006). Other works with a similar approach and scope include Shaykh al-Tahir ibn Ashur, *Maqasid al-Shari'ah al-Islamiyyah* (Tunis: al-Dar al-Tunisiyyah, 1972), and Yusuf al-'Alim, *Maqasid al-Shari'ah* (Herndon, VA: IIIT, 1991).

65. Abu Bakr ibn Sahl al-Sarakhsi, *al-Mabsut* (Istanbul: Cagri Yayinlari, 1983), 10:109.

66. Cf. Taha Jabir al-Alwani, *La ikraha fi'l-din: ishkaliyat al-riddah wa'l-murtaddin min sadr al-islam ila'l-yawm*, 2nd ed. (Cairo/Herndon, VA: IIIT and Maktab al-Shuruq al-Duwaliyyah, 2006).

12

THEOLOGIES OF DIFFERENCE AND
IDEOLOGIES OF INTOLERANCE IN ISLAM

VINCENT J. CORNELL

A Commonality of Faith: Religious Toleration in
Early Muslim Jerusalem

In 1993, a path that led to the road from Jerusalem to Bethlehem near the monastery of Mar Elias was being paved. The path led through an olive grove owned by the Greek Orthodox Patriarchy. In this grove, the paving crew came upon ancient ruins. Under the auspices of the University of Athens, the Orthodox Patriarchy, and the Israel Antiquities Authority, archaeologists conducted three seasons of excavations at the site. What they found were the ruins of an early Christian church called the Kathisma of the Virgin, which commemorated the place where the Virgin Mary rested before giving birth to Jesus in Bethlehem. The Kathisma was a *martyrium* (Gr., "place of witnessing"), a religious structure designed to commemorate a holy person or event. Archaeologists believe that the church was in use from the mid-fifth century CE until some time in the ninth century CE. A large eight-sided building, it measured roughly forty meters along its main east-west axis, and about thirty-five meters on its north-south axis. Its floor plan was similar to but larger than the *martyrium* at Capernaum in Galilee, which was built at approximately the same time to mark the site of the house of St. Peter. The Greek word *kathisma* means "seat" or "chair." This term referred to the stone in the center of the church, which early Christians believed to be the place where the pregnant Virgin Mary rested on her journey to Bethlehem.[1]

Besides being an important early Christian religious site, the Kathisma of the Virgin is important for Islam for two reasons. First, its octagonal shape, large size, general floor plan, and proximity to Jerusalem suggest that it may have been one of the architectural inspirations for the Dome of the Rock. Although Oleg Grabar, the well-known art historian of early Islamic Jerusalem, discounts this possibility, the hypothesis makes sense from a religious point of view.[2] For some time, scholars have suggested that the Dome of the Rock may have been designed on the model of a *martyrium*, both because of its octagonal design and because it commemorates two hierophanies, or manifestations of the sacred. In Jewish tradition, the Rock marks the place on Mount Moriah where the prophet Abraham attempted to sacrifice his son Isaac (Genesis 22:1–19). In Islamic tradition, the Rock marks the site of the Mi'raj or Ascension, where the prophet Muhammad ascended to heaven on the *Buraq*.[3] Both stories, like that of Jacob's dream (Genesis 28:10–22), make of a stone the symbol of an opening onto the supernal, a means of access to the divine realm. For early Christians, because of their belief in Christ's divinity, the same symbolism applied to the stone on which the pregnant Mary rested, as previously mentioned.[4]

Second, the Kathisma of the Virgin is important for Islam because it appears to have been used for worship by both Christians and Muslims at the same time. On the south side of the church, just off the south entrance vestibule, is a *mihrab* or prayer niche that indicates the direction of Mecca. Next to this *mihrab* is a mosaic of three palm trees that was added to the structure in the eighth century CE, in the period of the Umayyad Dynasty. This mosaic commemorates the Qur'anic story of Mary, who sought refuge from her labor pains beneath the trunk of a palm tree (Qur'an 19:23–26). The heavy clusters of dates that hang from the palm trees in the mosaic represent the divine support given to Mary, who trusted in God in her time of need. Less directly, they also symbolize Mary's pregnancy, which promised the coming of Jesus, who in the Qur'an is depicted both as a living Sign of God (*Ayat Allah*, Qur'an 23:50) and as the Messiah of the Jews (*al-Masih*, Qur'an 3:45). Clearly, there was adequate justification for both Christians and Muslims to have worshiped at a place that commemorated the "Seat of the Virgin." The location of the Muslim *mihrab* is separated both from the area around the Rock and from the apse or chapel of the church. This arrangement would have allowed Christians and Muslims to practice their rites at the same time. The Kathisma of the Virgin, thus, offers a prospect that few people could imagine today—Muslims and Christians praying together at the same loca-

tion, each in their own way, in commemoration of similar holy events, despite
the theological differences that divided them.[5]

A similar prospect is offered by the early history of the Al Aqsa Mosque
and the Dome of the Rock in Jerusalem. As suggested above, the Dome of
the Rock is, to all intents and purposes, an Islamic *martyrium* (Ar., *mashhad*).
Like the Kathisma of the Virgin, it is an octagonal building with an ambula-
tory surrounding a stone in the middle. It was built by the Umayyad caliph
'Abd al-Malik ibn Marwan (r. 685–705 CE) to symbolize the prophet Muhammad's ascension to heaven on his Night Journey (*al-Isra'*) from Mecca to Jerusalem and the ascendancy of Islam over Christianity. This latter motive is
attested by the Qur'anic verses around the dome and by inscriptions on two
copper plates over the eastern and southern gates of the sanctuary.[6] However,
while the site of the Dome of the Rock was sacred for both Muslims and Jews,
it was not sacred for Christians.

For early Christians, the top of Mount Moriah was mainly important as
the site of Herod's Temple. To Christian eyes, this was a profaned and debased
reproduction of Solomon's Temple. Far from being sacred, it was reviled
according to the prophecy of Jesus, "I tell you solemnly, not a single stone
will be left on another; everything will be destroyed" (Matthew 24:2). By the
time of the Muslim conquest of Jerusalem in 638 CE, the Temple as a locus
of the divine presence had long been absent from the holy city, along with
the Jews who believed in it. Jews were forbidden to live in Jerusalem after the
second Roman-Jewish war in 135 CE. The city was renamed Aelia Capitolina
and Judea was called Syria Palaestina. These were the names by which Jerusalem and Judea were known to early Muslims. The pre-Islamic Arabic name
for Jerusalem was Iliya (Aelia). Its current name of *al-Quds* ("The Holy") is
more of a description than a proper name. The ascendancy of Christianity
turned Jerusalem into a Christian city but did little or nothing for the Jews.
Even after Rome became a Christian empire, Jews were allowed in Jerusalem
only one day a year. This was on the ninth of Av, the Day of Lamentation,
which commemorated the destruction of the first and second Temples. In 333
CE, the Bordeaux Pilgrim described Jews making pilgrimage to "a rock with
a hole in it . . . They anoint it and tear their clothes, lamenting and sobbing.
And then they go away."[7] The site of the Temple, still marked in the fourth
century by a statue of the Roman emperor Hadrian, was a large empty space.
The sacred focus of the city for Christians was the Church of the Holy Sepulcher. This complex originally consisted of a large basilica called the *Martyrium* erected over the site of Christ's crucifixion and a smaller rotunda called
the *Anastasis*, which marked the site of Christ's resurrection. The message for

Jews was clear: under early Christianity, the only right that they had to Jerusalem was the "right" to recall its loss as God's punishment.[8]

In light of the current enmity between Muslims and Jews, it is important to recall that it was the Muslims—not the Christians—who reopened Jerusalem to Jewish settlement after they occupied the city in 638 CE. Jewish Midrash, composed some sixty years after the building of the Dome of the Rock, hails the Muslims as the initiators of Israel's redemption and praises the Muslim ruler as the builder of the House of the Lord.[9] The Dome of the Rock was built to commemorate the renewal of Solomon's Temple as much as it was built to represent Islam's triumph over Christianity. For the first part of the prophet Muhammad's mission, Muslims faced Jerusalem when they prayed. Even after they turned their prayers toward Mecca, they continued to revere Jerusalem as a sacred city and regarded Solomon's Temple as a sanctuary nearly equivalent to the Ka'ba in Mecca. This was the reason the caliph Umar ibn al-Khattab (r. 634–640 CE) chose to consecrate the site of the Temple with a mosque soon after the Muslim conquest.[10] The Umayyad rulers of Jerusalem added to Umar's act of commemoration by expanding the Al Aqsa Mosque and constructing the Dome of the Rock, the finest surviving example of early Islamic sacred architecture.

An early Muslim history of Jerusalem, *Fada'il al-Bayt al-Muqaddas* (Virtues of the Holy House) by Muhammad ibn Ahmad al-Wasiti (d. after 1019 CE) provides evidence of a religious amity between Muslims and Jews concerning the Al Aqsa Mosque that is difficult to imagine today. Wasiti reports that for eighty years—from the time of the founding of the Al Aqsa Mosque by Umar to the reign of the Umayyad caliph Umar ibn 'Abd al-'Aziz (r. 717–720 CE)—the honor of tending the lamps of the mosque was given specifically to Jews.[11] The Israeli historian Moshe Sharon notes that, in this period, there was no rabbinic prohibition preventing Jews from entering the precincts of the former Temple.[12] Wasiti also reports that rituals perhaps modeled on ancient Temple rites were performed at the Dome of the Rock on Mondays and Thursdays.[13] These rituals involved anointing the rock with a special unguent (as mentioned centuries earlier by the Bordeaux Pilgrim) and purifying the sacred site by burning large amounts of incense. The amount of incense burned in these rituals was so great that its fragrance could be detected in the markets of the city below.[14] Today, hardly anyone would imagine Jews acting as caretakers inside the Al Aqsa Mosque or Muslims anointing the stone inside the Dome of the Rock in the way the Jews did before Islam.

Extra Scriptura: Toleration, Prejudice, and Vernacular Religion

What went wrong? How did we get from Christians and Muslims praying together at the Kathisma of the Virgin to the present confessional wall of separation between Christianity and Islam? The theological issues that separate Islam from Christianity were just as apparent in the Umayyad era as they are today. How did we get from Muslim tolerance of a Jewish presence at the Al Aqsa Mosque to today's demonstrations against Israeli archaeological investigations and repair projects along the boundaries of al-Haram al-Sharif? Part of the answer, of course, is that, in the Umayyad period, the Jewish state of Israel did not exist and the Jews of Palestine lived under a Muslim regime. Furthermore, the Muslim rulers of Jerusalem did not have to contend with Jewish extremists seeking to destroy the Dome of the Rock and rebuild the Temple. Muslims in modern times have also been subjected to significant religious and ideological challenges from evangelical Christianity, secularism, and Western imperialism. However, a subtler yet equally important problem can be found in the current ideologization of the Islamic faith and the intolerance of ideologically driven Muslims. The image of Islamic intolerance has caused Muslims to be regarded as the most uncivil members of global civil society. Today, both Islam and Muslims are in danger of global marginalization. To avoid being marginalized further, Muslims must be willing to confront their prejudices constructively. An important step in this process is to recognize that the dislike of Muslims for Jews is not primordial and that the ambivalence of Muslims toward Christians was not just a product of the Crusades. The modalities of Muslim intolerance inhabit theological, cultural, and ideological discourses whose roots penetrate deeply into the premodern Islamic past.

However, one should not make the mistake of essentializing Muslim attitudes by assuming that the roots of Islamic intolerance are mainly scriptural. Although Muslims frequently draw on scripture for inspiration, one cannot cite scripture alone to determine whether their faith is tolerant or intolerant. Scriptural texts are not sufficient evidence for generalization about any religious attitude. Sacred scriptures—whether they are the Torah, the Qur'an, or the Christian Gospels—are ambivalent in their depictions of the religious other. Human beings—believers—turn them into tolerant or intolerant texts. Faith may be universal, but the details of one's faith are constructed out of many different materials. The same can be said of religious behavior. Actions taken in response to scripture are interpretive statements. At times, such statements may even express attitudes that contradict official discourses.

Anthropologists of religion have used the term *vernacular religion* to describe culturally localized responses to scriptural teachings. Much like vernacular languages, "vernacular" religious discourses are juxtaposed to "standard" or official religious discourses that cut across social or geographical boundaries or locales.[15] In effect, vernacular religious discourses are socially embodied exegeses of sacred scriptures. As embodied exegetical "texts," they are just as significant in their own right as the teachings of theologians and, in fact, may even be more influential. One cannot claim that vernacular expressions of Islam are not "real Islam" just because they disagree with official or standard interpretations of scripture. Islamic faith is defined by Islam in practice, regardless of whether or not one agrees with the practices in question. Whether Islam in a particular context is tolerant or intolerant depends more on what people make of scripture than on the actual wording of scripture itself. The archaeological evidence of Muslims and Christians sharing the same sacred space for prayer at the Kathisma Church and the textual evidence of a Jewish presence at the Al Aqsa Mosque remind us of this fact.

As a form of revealed scripture, the Qur'an is neither essentially tolerant nor essentially intolerant. Its ethical critiques of Jews (but for the most part not of Judaism) and its theological critiques of Christianity express a particular vision of the truth, without regard for liberal notions of fairness. As with other revelatory texts, believers must relate the teachings of the Qur'an to specific and highly localized situations and contexts. The Umayyad officials that ordered a *mihrab* to be built in the Kathisma Church as a token of respect for the Virgin Mary and the "Rightly-Guided Caliphs" that honored the Jews by asking them to tend the lamps of the Al Aqsa Mosque acted according to their best understanding of the Islamic faith. As practicing Muslims, they were aware of the same Qur'anic verses that Muslim extremists now use to justify intolerant attitudes toward other faiths. The idea that either the "problem" or the "solution" of a particular faith can be found primarily in its scriptures is not a historical proposition. Rather, it is a premise of religious fundamentalism and must be recognized as such.

Muslim scholars recognized the influence of vernacular religion on interfaith relations long before the modern era. Over 1,100 years ago, the Abbasid essayist and theologian Abu 'Uthman al-Jahiz (d. 869 CE) attributed the Muslim preference for Christians over Jews to culture and physical proximity rather than to theology. Although Jewish theology is much closer to Islam than Christianity, this made little difference to Muslims. According to Jahiz,

The Jews were the neighbors of the Muslims in Medina and other places, and (as is well known) the enmity of neighbors is as violent and abiding as the hostility that arises among relatives. Man indeed hates the one whom he knows, turns against the one whom he sees, opposes the one whom he resembles, and becomes observant of the faults of those with whom he mingles; the greater the love and intimacy, the greater the hatred and estrangement. The Christians, however, because of their remoteness from Mecca and Medina, did not have to put up with religious controversies, and did not have occasion to stir up trouble, and be involved in war. That was the first cause of our dislike of the Jews, and our partiality toward the Christians.[16]

Although Jahiz privileges what we today would call "cultural" reasons for religious intolerance, he does not ignore scriptural arguments for intolerance. "Another circumstance . . . is the wrong interpretation given by the masses to the following Qur'anic verse: 'Thou wilt surely find that the strongest in enmity against those who believe are the Jews and the idolaters; and thou wilt find the nearest in love to those who believe to be those who say: We are Christians'" (Qur'an 5:85).[17] Despite the apparent pro-Christian and anti-Jewish sentiment in this verse, Jahiz claims that the pro-Christian interpretation given to it by Muslims was due to extraneous influences and not to the text itself. These nonscriptural influences included the respect of Arab Muslims for the Arab Christian tradition of kingship and the apparent influence of Greek philosophy on Christian thought. In an ironic reversal of modern stereotypes, Jahiz portrays the Muslims as the true heirs to the Greek intellectual tradition, the Christians as pseudo-Hellenic imitators, and the Jews as religious fundamentalists. "The cause for the lack of science among the Jews lies in the fact that the Jews consider philosophic speculation to be unbelief, and Kalam theology an innovation leading to doubt."[18]

The fact that Jahiz's Muslims look much like today's Jews and that his Jews look much like today's Muslims adds strength to the argument that extrascriptural religious vernaculars count as much as scripture in determining the tolerance of one's faith. Jahiz's essay also reminds us that the "classical sources" of religion referred to by William Scott Green in the first chapter of this volume must include more than just sacred texts. To avoid privileging fundamentalist notions of scripture, contemporary scholars of interfaith relations must expand the concept of "classical" sources to include both standard scriptures and vernacular religious texts, including some that may have been regarded by official opinion as heretical. It is important to remember in this regard that the Greek root of the word *heresy* means "choice." Choice in religious interpretation is foreclosed by both orthodoxy and fundamentalism. When the interpretation of one's faith is constrained by authoritarian structures and discourses, one's faith becomes, to paraphrase Oscar Wilde, the faith of other people. "Their thoughts are someone else's opinions, their lives a mimicry, their passions a quotation."[19] If the intolerance of faith is to be transformed into tolerance, new choices must be made about the interpretation of scripture. For this reason, the search for resources of toleration in world religions cannot end with some non-Christian version of the Protestant doctrine of *sola scriptura*. This is not to say that tradition is unimportant, however. Muslims cannot claim that a tolerant Islam is doctrinally authentic without drawing on traditional resources from their past. However, if these resources are to represent the full range of Islamic tradition, they cannot be limited to scripture alone or to an artificially imposed set of commentaries.

In the search for resources of toleration, it is important to examine what Green calls the "doctrinal fault lines" of Islam that have led Muslims to resist the notion of a shared faith with other religions. However, it is also important to recognize that religion in practice often goes its own way, in spite of official texts and doctrines. The vernacular Islam revealed by the archaeology of the Kathisma Church and the early history of the Al Aqsa Mosque is just as important as the scriptural reasoning of scholars for mapping out the full range of Islamic attitudes toward the religious other. Thus, not only must the notion of classical sources of religion extend beyond works of scripture, theology, and exegesis, but it must also extend to legal texts and even to archaeological evidence. As the essay by Jahiz indicates, scripture often provides little more than *post hoc* arguments for tolerance or intolerance. Instead, the most significant sources of such attitudes may depend on extrascriptural factors.

E *Lege Scriptura*: Legal Exegesis as a Religious Vernacular

In Islam, the relationship between scripture and practice is doubly problematical because Muslims use two sets of scriptures, although they officially acknowledge only one. The official scripture of Islam is the Qur'an, the revealed word of God. Muslim liberals have often sought to separate the discourse of the Qur'an from other traditional Islamic discourses, assuming that one can find in the Qur'an resources for toleration that were overlooked by previous scholars. This is a justifiable hermeneutical strategy, but, if it is used, an argument must be made for it. To privilege the Qur'an means to limit the second scripture of Islam, the Hadith of the prophet Muhammad, to an exhortative or explanatory role and not to regard it automatically as a precedent for doctrine or practice. One can justify this stance by arguing that the Hadith should not be used as a binding precedent, either because much of it contains internal contradictions or because its oral transmission may have been inaccurate.[20] However, taking this position means going against the majority of Muslim opinion, which considers the Hadith the textual basis of the Sunna, and hence nearly equivalent to the Qur'an in truth-value. This concept of Qur'an–Sunna equivalence is the basis of the Shari'a. Since Sunna is most often equated by Muslims with the Hadith, Qur'an-Hadith correspondence provides the de facto scriptural foundation for the legal science of *usul al-fiqh* (sources of jurisprudence) and the theological science of *usul al-din* (sources of religion).

Historically, this notion of Qur'an-Hadith correspondence was attributed to the early juridical theorist Muhammad ibn Idris al-Shafi'i (d. 820 CE). In his *Risala*, or treatise on Islamic jurisprudence, Shafi'i saw no contradiction between the Qur'an and the Sunna as embodied in the Hadith. "Everything [in the Sunna of the Prophet] is a clear explanation or proof (*bayan*) of the Book of God."[21] The concept of *bayan* was used in medieval Islamic legal and theological reasoning to denote a deductive proof or unequivocal demonstration (also called *burhan*), the kind of proof that is true because of the structure of its propositions. Thus, by saying that the Sunna provided the *bayan* for the Qur'an, Shafi'i implied that the truth-value of the Sunna was equivalent to the truth-value of the Qur'an. When applied to the process of discovering a rule of law (*hukm*) in the Qur'an, the logic of *bayan* was supposed to provide a definitive interpretation for key concepts, as in the following example.

In the Qur'an, Sura 9 (*Surat al-Tawba*, the Sura of Repentance) is the most problematical sura with respect to religious tolerance. This sura contains the following verse, which often has been seen as promoting violence against unbelievers: "When the sacred months are over, kill (*fa-aqtulu*) the *mushrikin* wherever you find them. Seize them, besiege them, and lie in ambush everywhere for them. However, if they repent, maintain the prayer, and pay the *zakat* tax, then let them go their way. Verily Allah is the Forgiving, the Merciful" (Qur'an, 9:5, my translation). The key term in this verse is *mushrikin* since the *mushrikin* are the subjects of the verse's rulings. But how is one to understand the meaning of this term in practice? The word *mushrikin* is the direct object accusative form of the Arabic term *mushrikun*, which means "those who assign partners [to God]." In this verse, the Muslims are exhorted to fight the *mushrikun* until they repent, establish regular prayers, and pay the *zakat* or alms tax. The Qur'an makes it clear in other verses that these religious practices are required only of Muslims. Thus, one is led to conclude that the *mushrikun* must accept Islam as their new religion if they want the Muslims to stop fighting them. At this point, the Sunna becomes relevant to determining the precise meaning of this term. The Hadith and other traditions state that in the time of the Prophet, the conversion of unbelievers was required only of polytheists (with certain exceptions), but it was not required of Christians and Jews. Thus, with regard to the rule of law (*hukm*) contained in Qur'an 9:5, it can be demonstrated conclusively that the word *mushrikin* refers to the polytheists alone. This type of exegesis by deductive reasoning and supported by tradition is what Shafi'i meant by *bayan*. According to Shafi'i's theory of jurisprudence, all applications of *usul al-fiqh* and *usul al-din* should be based on this practice. However, it is not possible to do so in all situations.

Formal opinions of religious law in Islam (sing., *fatwa*) tend to follow a rhetorical structure similar to what in U.S. law schools is known as IRAC—issue, rule of law, argument, and conclusion. Shafi'i, like other Muslim jurists, was aware that most legal reasoning involves inductive proofs (*dalil*) rather than the deductive proofs required for *bayan*. Whereas deductive logic provides a definitive answer to a problem, inductive logic suggests only a probable answer. Jurists are forced to resort to inductive logic because the *ratio decidendi* that determines a rule of law is usually not as clear-cut as in the example given in the previous paragraph. Thus, although Shafi'i saw *bayan* as the ideal form of scriptural reasoning, he realized that it could not always be utilized in practice. Since inductive reasoning determines probability but not fact, there are valid grounds for dissenting opinions. This is the reason that, when Shafi'i equated juridical consensus (*ijma'*) with *bayan* in the *Risala*, he insisted that this consensus be unanimous. Similarly, the IRAC method of legal reasoning in American law schools tends to work best when the rule of law in a case is clear. Disagreements enter the picture when the rule of law is difficult to ascertain. In the case of rules that pertain to the religious other, inductive reasoning must be used whenever key terms are ambivalent. In such cases, the rules of law discovered by jurists may vary considerably because the definitions on which they are based are subject to different interpretations.

A classic example of this problem can be found in the difference of opinion between Sunni and Imami Shiite Muslims concerning the ritual pollution of unbelievers. The Qur'anic verse that deals with this question also comes from sura 9, *Surat al-Tawba*. "O you who believe! Verily the *mushrikun* are ritually impure (*najasun*), so do not let them approach the Sacred Mosque [of Mecca] after this year of theirs is over" (Qur'an 9:28). The historical context (*asbab al-nuzul*) of this verse refers to a truce that existed for a time between the prophet Muhammad's community in Medina and the polytheists of Mecca. This context suggests that the term *mushrikun* in this verse most likely applies only to polytheists, as it did in Qur'an 9:5. However, unlike in verse 9:5, there is no qualifying statement within the verse to indicate conclusively that the polytheists alone are intended. In situations like this, Muslim jurists are first supposed to look for guidance in finding the rule of law in other Qur'anic verses. For example, the Qur'an states that those who say, "Allah is the Messiah, the Son of Mary" (Qur'an 5:72) or "Allah is one of three" (Qur'an 5:72), have rejected [God's teachings] (*la qad kafara*). The Arabic verb *kafara* (to reject) is the root of the noun *kafir*, which means "unbeliever." Therefore, it is reasonable to conclude that, if Christians believe in the Trinity and the divinity of Jesus and if, according to the Qur'an, these ideas constitute unbelief (*kufr*), then Christians must be considered unbelievers (*kuffar*). Furthermore, since it is already known that the polytheists (*mushrikun*) mentioned in verse 9:28 are unbelievers (*kuffar*), then Christianity may be seen as analogous to polytheism and Christians may be considered analogous to polytheists.[22] Does this mean with regard to Qur'an 9:28 that Christians should also be considered ritually impure, as are polytheists? And if Christians are ritually impure, then what about Jews?

The disagreement over the ritual impurity of unbelievers in Sunni and Shiite exegesis illustrates the subjectivity of finding a rule of law through inductive reasoning and provides a further example of Jahiz's point about the intertextuality of scripture and culture. Whereas Sunni jurists were ambivalent about this question, Imami Shiite jurists tended to apply the term *mushrikun* to Christians, Jews, and polytheists indiscriminately. This led them to consider all types of unbelievers unclean. For example, the noted Shiite jurist Muhammad Baqir al-Majlisi (d. 1699 CE) states in his legal compendium *Bihar al-Anwar* (Seas of Light), "The majority of our scholars hold that the meaning of the term *mushrikun* includes both worshipers of idols and Jews and Christians, for these last are polytheists as well."[23]

Majlisi divided ritual uncleanliness into two types: spiritual uncleanliness (*al-najasa al-ma'nawiyya*) and legal uncleanliness (*al-najasa al-shar'iyya*). The origins of Christian and Jewish uncleanliness were spiritual in nature, and reflected, in Majlisi's words, "the filth of their insides and the evil of their beliefs" (*khubth batinihim wa su' i'tiqadihim*).[24] For Majlisi, spiritual or theological filth implied moral filth and moral filth implied bodily filth. However, Majlisi was not content to limit the dirtiness of Christians and Jews just to the insides of their bodies. He also extended the concept of spiritual filth to the things that Christians and Jews touched, such as their food. In practice, this led some Shiite Muslims to treat unbelievers (and also, at times, Sunni Muslims) as untouchables since their touch might necessitate ritual ablution or the discarding of utensils they used when eating food. This type of vernacular exegesis was readily accepted in the lands of Iran and India, regions that were noted for strict concepts of ritual pollution before the coming of Islam. In this way, legal reasoning by inductive logic became an enabling factor for a culturally biased limitation of toleration based on scriptural precepts.

However, treating Christians and Jews as untouchables created an exegetical problem with respect to the text of the Qur'an. Extending the concept of impurity to food prepared by the People of the Book appears to contradict a verse of the Qur'an that states, "The food of those who have been given the Book is lawful for you and your food is lawful for them" (Qur'an 5:5). In getting around this contradiction, Majlisi tries to explain away the problematical verse by rationalizing its context. He concludes that it applies only to former Jews and Christians but not to present-day Jews and Christians because the inner filth of contemporary Jews and Christians has been increased through their alteration (tahrif) of God's word. Following Shafi'i's logic of equating the truth-value of the Qur'an with the truth-value of the Sunna (Shiite scholars like Majlisi often used Shafi'i's principles without acknowledging him as their source), he also cites the Hadith accounts from the Prophet and the Shiite Imams that confirm the principle of the ritual separation of religious communities. "Do not partake of the ritual slaughter of a Jew and do not eat from their vessels." "One may not perform ablutions with the leftover water of a Jew, a Christian, a bastard, a polytheist, or anyone who opposes Islam."[25] It seems to have mattered little to Majlisi that such traditions had questionable origins.

In contrast to the separatist position taken by Majlisi, the Sunni approach to this problem was more nuanced. A Moroccan proverb states, "Eat a Jew's food but sleep in a Christian's bed." As an example of vernacular exegesis, this piece of common folk wisdom is comparable to Majlisi's legal analysis since it attempts to adduce practical rules of behavior from ambiguous Qur'anic verses. Scriptural exegesis should not be seen as the province only of scholars. Even Shafi'i regarded consensus on religious issues as a matter for the Muslim community as a whole and not just for jurists. The Moroccan proverb attempts to adduce a rule of law in the Qur'anic verse about the food of the People of the Book by separating the People of the Book into those who keep dietary rules similar to Muslims (the Jews) from those who do not (the Christians). Thus, Moroccan Muslims are enjoined to eat the food of Jews and avoid the food of Christians. The proverb also reflects Jahiz's argument about cultural bias, in which Muslims regarded Christians as culturally superior to Jews and, hence, cleaner in their habits. This is most likely the reason that Moroccan Muslims are enjoined to sleep in a Christian's bed. Finally, the proverb reflects the Sunni juridical consensus on purity, which does not define creedal filth intrinsically as Majlisi does but rather associates Christian and Jewish uncleanliness with the practical problem of their ignorance of Islamic purification laws. Consequently, the vernacular interpretation of Moroccan Sunnis, based as it is on a pragmatically cultural exegesis of the Qur'an, provides a better resource for toleration than the legalistic but still vernacular interpretation of the Imami Shiite jurist Majlisi, in which cultural prejudices are masked by ideological arguments and juridical casuistry. In the context of day-to-day existence, it is much easier to interact with a non-Muslim neighbor whose uncleanliness is nonintrinsic than with one whose intrinsic uncleanliness extends from his inner faith to the outside of his body. Furthermore, the Sunni notion of nonintrinsic uncleanliness makes it much easier for a Muslim man to marry a woman of the People of the Book, which is allowed in the same Qur'anic verse (5:5) that grants Muslims permission to eat their food.[26]

The foregoing discussion of Shiite and Sunni differences of opinion about the impurity of unbelievers once again demonstrates that a meaningful investigation of the "doctrinal fault lines" of religion must include all vernacular sources of religious opinion, whether they are scriptural, legal, historical, or even literary or proverbial. In the reality of practice, scriptural and legal rulings about the religious other often become literary tropes whose original logic is lost in translation. Majlisi's attempt to circumvent the rule of law in Qur'an 5:5 by asserting that a contemporary person of the Book is not the same type of person of the Book that God meant in his revelation proves that legal exegesis is not substantially different from other forms of vernacular exegesis. Thus, legal exegesis should also be seen as a form of vernacular exegesis, except that it appears in a different hermeneutical register.[27]

For many Muslims, the idea that the interpretation of religious texts may legitimately occur in different vernacular registers runs counter to their notion of "standard" tradition. In actual practice, however, tradition is itself created through vernacular interpretations of scripture. Like other forms of exegesis, vernacular interpretation is a two-edged sword. In practice, it can work both for and against the interest of religious tolerance. The propensity of religiously based legal systems to draw conceptual boundaries around communities of faith works against the liberal notion of inclusiveness that motivates the search for interreligious understanding. If Islam is, in fact, all about the Shari'a, as some modern Muslims assert, then it would behoove Muslims to recognize that our notions of the Shari'a are constructed through an ongoing process of vernacular interpretation. The paradox of the Shari'a is that, although the Shari'a expresses God's will, the details of his will can only become known through vernacular discourses in different hermeneutical registers.

The Ideological Vernacular

However, one should not confuse vernacular exegeses of the Qur'an with individual or idiosyncratic interpretations. Vernacular interpretations also constitute traditions. As Adam B. Seligman has pointed out, premodern believers tended to adhere to religions as members of communities, rather than as individuals.[28] To convert from one religion to another was to change one's communal allegiance for another, an act that Muslim jurists saw not only as apostasy but also as treason. The communal nature of religious identity provided the rationale for jurists such as Majlisi to take on the role of scriptural exegete along with systematic theologians. By its very nature, the juridical approach to religion reinforces communal identities and makes it harder to give voice to dissenting opinions. For this reason, to assume, as many Muslims do, that the Shari'a and the Islamic jurisprudential tradition contain all of the answers to the problems of modern Muslim societies is to engage in a form of de facto fundamentalism that is potentially as dangerous as that of *sola scriptura*. Elsewhere, I have characterized this ideological view of juridical Islam as Shari'a fundamentalism, a form of fundamentalism that reifies the Shari'a as the expression of the divine will in the same way that scriptural fundamentalism reifies the rulings contained in scripture.[29]

A key point about Shari'a fundamentalism is that it makes little difference whether one's political orientation is moderate or extreme. In either case, the boundaries of normative religion are set communally, thus privileging the majority over the minority. Shari'a fundamentalism also creates a barrier against the notion of toleration because, as Seligman says, "Tolerance is a virtue that has everything to do with boundaries and with margins."[30] When the boundary maintenance function of theology is reified, tradition becomes traditionalism. When the boundary maintenance function of the law is reified, the law may be transformed into a communalistic ideology that veers dangerously close to totalitarianism. People whose beliefs or practices place them outside the ideological boundaries of such a system may find themselves marginalized, ostracized, or worse. This has recently been the case, for example, with the Sufis, whose teachings are often suppressed or relegated to marginal status by Islamist political movements. When Shari'a fundamentalism is buttressed by a reified theology, religious minorities may find themselves caught in a cat's cradle of juridical and cultural restrictions that are justified by divine authority.

This threat is exacerbated by the fact that the religion of Islam has an ideological aspect whose roots lie in the Qur'an itself. Unlike Christianity,

Qur'anic theology does not depend for its truth-value primarily on the historicity of its revelation. Instead, Qur'anic theology depends as much on logical arguments as it does on history and relies, in particular, on the *bayan*-type of deductive proof identified by Imam Shafi'i. This type of logic can be seen in the famous "no compulsion in religion" verse of the Qur'an that is often used by Muslims to demonstrate the tolerance of Islam. "There is no compulsion in religion. Right guidance is conclusively distinguished from falsehood (*qad tabayyana al-rushdu min al-ghayy*). Whoever rejects false deities (*faman yakfuru bi-l-taghut*) and believes in Allah has grasped the Firm Bond that never breaks. God hears and knows all things" (Qur'an 2:256, my translation). The literal meaning of this verse is not an argument for tolerance. Rather, it argues that there is no need for compulsion in religion because the truth is evident for all to see. This point is stressed by the phrase, *qad tabayyana*, which comes from the same Arabic root as *bayan*. Thus, the rational course for the human being is to reject (*kafara bi-*) what is plainly false and to believe (*amana bi-*) what is plainly true: namely, the truth of God's word as expressed in the Qur'an. This argument is supported in the Qur'an by other verses, such as the following: "Say: Truth has come and falsehood has vanished. Verily, falsehood always vanishes" (Qur'an 17:81, my translation).

The ideological nature of the Qur'anic message gave rise to vernacular approaches to religious difference in Islam that were analogous to the Soviet doctrine that held that those who did not believe in Communism were irrational or insane. Even today, many Muslims believe that anyone who learns about Islam but rejects its teachings is either irrational or willfully disobedient. This belief helped contribute to a contradictory policy of "theological negation, political toleration, and practical limitation" toward religious minorities that was similar to what Robert Chazen has described as the attitude of medieval Christians toward Jews.[31]

The persistence of unbelief, even among those who are politically tolerated such as Christians and Jews, continues to pose a theological and moral dilemma for many Muslims. This has been the case even in the most tolerant Muslim communities, such as the Ismailis. Among the Ismailis, the contradiction of "what is" versus "what should be" was resolved through the theological doctrine of fulfillment. According to this doctrine, Islam, as the most recent historical religion, was seen as the fulfillment of its predecessors. This can be observed in the early Ismaili doctrinal work *Kitab al-'alim wa al-ghulam* (Book of the Teacher and the Student) by Ja'far ibn Mansur al-Yaman (d. 914–915 CE). At first glance, this text evokes what appears to be a pluralistic view of religion: "The [revealed] books are many and all of them 'are from what is with God' (Qur'an 2:189)."[32] However, the text goes on to assert that, even though all of the revealed scriptures are theoretically "from what is with God," the Qur'an "is clearer in its way of proceeding, since it has replaced what was before it, and nothing has come after it to replace it."[33] Far from advocating a pluralistic approach to religion, the early Ismailis saw Islam as both fulfilling and superseding the previous revelations of God's Word. Although the doctrine of fulfillment led to a relatively liberal policy of religious tolerance on the part of Ismaili regimes such as the Fatimid Dynasty of Egypt, the doctrine of supersession allowed the Fatimid caliph al-Hakim to destroy the Church of the Holy Sepulcher in Jerusalem in 1009 CE. Although the Muslims eventually rebuilt the church in the middle of the eleventh century, this act provided the *causus belli* for the Crusades.

The ideological nature of the Qur'anic approach to ultimate truth placed non-Muslim minorities in a difficult position. On the one hand, they had to be tolerated by the state as People of the Book because this was mandated both by the Qur'an and by the precedent of the prophet Muhammad. On the other hand, the same texts that mandated tolerance for religious minorities also implied that their difference of opinion with Islam was the result of theological deviation, moral backsliding, or a deficit of reason. This ambiguity led to contradictory pendulum swings of acceptance and rejection such as those described above. An eloquent evocation of the theological dilemma faced by non-Muslim minorities can be found in a recently discovered manuscript from the Biblioteca de El Escorial in Spain. Around the middle of the fourteenth century CE, a Jewish subject of the Muslim kingdom of Granada wrote a request in verse for a *fatwa* from the legal scholars of the city.[34] This request was unusual in that it was theological rather than legal in nature and posed the following question: If an unbeliever has the right to follow his own beliefs and not accept Islam as his religion, how can he be condemned for his choice theologically?

> Oh scholars of religion, a *dhimmi* of your religion[35]
> Is perplexed. So guide him with the clearest proof:
>
> If my Lord has decreed, in your opinion, my unbelief
> But then does not accept it of me, what is my recourse?
>
> He decrees my misguidance and says, "Be satisfied with your fate."
> But how am I to be satisfied with that which leads to my damnation?
>
> He curses me and then shuts the door against me. Is there any
> Way out at all for me? Show me the outcome!

For if, oh people, I was satisfied with my fate,
Then my Lord would not be pleased with my evil calamity.

How am I to be satisfied with what does not please my Master?
Thus, I am perplexed. So guide me to the solution of my perplexity.

If my Lord wills my unbelief as a matter of destiny,
How can I be disobedient in following his will?

Do I even have the choice of going against his ruling?
By God, cure my malady with clear arguments!

The respondent to this request was Abu Sa'id Faraj ibn Lubb (d. 1381), a noted Imam, preacher, and *mufti* (jurisconsult) of Granada.[36] His answer is framed in theological rather than legal terms and is written as a discourse on destiny (*qada*) and fate (*qadar*) from the standpoint of Ash'arite theology. According to Ibn Lubb, the petitioner does not understand the true theological relationship between predestination (*al-jabriyya*) and free will (*al-qadariyya*) in Islam. He responds to the questions posed by the Jew primarily in terms of moral theology, employing the legal concept of personal responsibility (*taklif*) and the theological concept of acquired responsibility (*kasb*). He dismisses the key question of the Jew, "Do I even have the choice of going against [God's] ruling?" as mere sophistry. This is because, according to the tenets of Ash'arism, moral responsibility is a combination of divine will and human choice. Since the will of God and the choice of the human being are both made known at the time an action is performed, the Jew cannot claim that he is a helpless puppet in the hands of God. When it comes to moral and theological choices, what the human being chooses and what God decides for him are the same (f. 152v).

Professor Hayat Kara of Mohammed v University in Rabat, Morocco, who discovered the Jew's poem and Ibn Lubb's response, sees this exchange of views as a rare example of medieval interreligious dialogue. If this is the case, it is certainly not an interreligious dialogue in the way that this subject is understood today. On neither side is there any hint of pluralism or even much understanding of the other's doctrines. Neither party admits more than a grudging tolerance of the other. The Jew, ignoring the nuances of Islamic theology, says in effect: "Your religion has condemned me as an infidel. Your fatalism tells you that I am an infidel because God has willed it. Since the decision to condemn me has already been made, I have no recourse against it and cannot change God's will. Therefore, do not criticize me. To you your religion and to me mine." Ibn Lubb replies in effect: "Your pretended helplessness before the will of God is only sophistry and hypocrisy. In reality, what God has willed for you is what you have chosen for yourself. The responsibility for your unbelief is yours, not God's." What is perhaps most striking about this exchange is how Ibn Lubb and the Jew talk past each other but never actually talk to each other. For the Jew, the assertion of Islamic predestination is a pretext to justify allegiance to the religion of Israel. For Ibn Lubb, the Jew is just another unbeliever, who is destined for divine punishment like all other unbelievers. In fact, Ibn Lubb is so far from understanding the actual nature of Jewish monotheism that he likens the Jew's defense of his unbelief to that of Abu Lahab, the pagan uncle of the prophet Muhammad who refused to accept Islam (Qur'an sura 111).[37] For Ibn Lubb, real faith means only one thing: faith in Islam as brought by the prophet Muhammad and interpreted by Maliki jurists like himself.

Toward a Religious Vernacular of Tolerance

T. M. Scanlon has observed that tolerance is a puzzling attitude because it occupies an intermediate space between wholehearted acceptance and unrestrained opposition. Although the practice of tolerance is usually seen as a better alternative than sectarian violence, it falls short as an ideal solution to the problem of difference. In practice, its indeterminacy often leads tolerance to be regarded as a second-best alternative, "a way of dealing with attitudes that we would be better off without but that are, unfortunately, ineliminable."[38] As we have seen from the examples discussed in this chapter, Scanlon's critical view of tolerance as a second-best alternative corresponds closely to the traditional notion of religious tolerance in Islam. In this, Islam is in no way unique, nor was Islam less tolerant than Christianity or Judaism. A further problem with scripturally based arguments for tolerance is that scriptural texts tend to reflect the ambiguity of theoretical discussions of the subject. This is the reason it is meaningless to speak about "Islamic," "Christian," or "Jewish" approaches to tolerance according to scripture or similarly normative texts alone. Ultimately, tolerance is a matter of practice. As such, the expression of tolerance is an expression of vernacular religion.

This being said, it is important to recognize that global interreligious discourse often demands more than tolerance can give. According to Seyyed Hossein Nasr, "The essential problem that the study of religion poses is how to preserve religious truth, traditional orthodoxy, the dogmatic theological structures of one's own tradition, and yet gain knowledge of other traditions and accept them as spiritually valid ways and roads to God."[39] What Nasr is talking about in this statement is not a vision of religious tolerance per se but a postliberal notion of pluralism. With very few exceptions, pluralism has not been an alternative taken by Muslims when dealing with other religions. Even the Sufis, who, like the early Ismailis, often expressed the most open-minded attitudes toward other religious communities, usually espoused doctrines of fulfillment rather than pluralism.

In a previously published article, I asserted, following the Andalusian Sufi Muhyiddin Ibn 'Arabi (d. 1240 CE), that the Qur'an affirms the God-given human rights of life, dignity, and freedom of choice. It is the responsibility of the believing Muslim to observe these rights according to the moral duty of mercy and the moral obligation of justice.[40] This Qur'anic concept of rights and duties constitutes the most cogent argument for religious tolerance in Islam. However, to grant a Jew or a Christian the right to practice her religion is not necessarily to say that one must also accept the religion of the other as a spiritually valid approach to God. On the contrary, it is sufficient under the concept of tolerance merely to accord religious minorities the legal right to practice their beliefs without overt restriction, while at the same time strongly disagreeing about the tenets and foundations of such beliefs.

However, if the adherents of different religions are to live together as more than just rival groups competing over the same territory, our tolerance for each other must go further. As Scanlon reiterates, a more robust form of tolerance must express recognition of common membership in society that goes deeper than our conflicts, "a recognition of others as being just as entitled as we are to contribute to the definition of our society."[41] Attaining this goal is the task of constructive theology and interreligious dialogue. However, in order to be successful, certain demands of this process must be acknowledged. In the context of Islam, such demands would imply, first, the rejection of fundamentalism in favor of the vernacular flexibility of actual historical traditions. Second, this process would require the development of a notion of identity (whether local or global) that transcends the boundaries of confessional communities. Within the context of Islamic thought, fully to implement such a postliberal vision of pluralism would also require a positive act of innovation in service of the greater good—what Hanafi jurists called *istihsan istithna'i*—that goes beyond the guidance of premodern precedents. However, even the most liberally minded Muslims might hesitate before taking such a step because it would imply not only a legal innovation but a theological departure from tradition as well. Will Muslims be able to conceive of a cosmopolitan world of plural religious perspectives as conforming to God's will? At this point, only God knows what the answer will be.

Notes

1. For a description of the Kathisma Church, see Hershel Shanks, "Where Mary Rested: Recovering the Kathisma," *Biblical Archaeology Review* 32, no. 6 (November–December 2006): 44–51. Shanks' contention that the church was turned into a mosque in the Umayyad period is contradicted by the floor plan of the structure. The location of the Muslim *mihrab* on the south side of the Kathisma Church and the narrowness of the space behind it make it unsuitable for congregational prayers. Clearly, this space was meant for Muslim pilgrims to perform canonical prayers individually as well as the supererogatory prayers that are part of the rites of visitation (*ziyara*) at holy places.

2. Grabar describes the Kathisma of the Virgin as "an octagon some 13 meters wide around a largely empty area with a rocky outcrop in the center." This gives the impression that the church is small in size, which is contradicted by the measurements of the floor plan in Shanks' article. Unfortunately, I have not been able to see the site myself since it has been covered up to preserve the ruins. Because the event commemorated by the church is not mentioned in the Gospels, Grabar believes that the Kathisma Church was a *martyrium* of only minor importance. This assumption, plus certain variations in the floor plan of the structure, led him to conclude that it was not a likely model for the Dome of the Rock. See Oleg Grabar, *The Dome of the Rock* (Cambridge, MA, and London: Belknap Press of Harvard University Press, 2006), 104–106.

3. The Qur'an (17:1) only refers to the Night Journey of the prophet Muhammad between *al-Masjid al-Haram* in Mecca and *al-Masjid al-Aqsa* in Jerusalem. The story of the Mi'raj or Ascension comes from the Hadith traditions and the *Sira*, biographical accounts of the Prophet that were circulated after his death. For a synopsis of the most famous of these ascension accounts, see Martin Lings, *Muhammad: His Life Based on the Earliest Sources* (Cambridge: The Islamic Texts Society, 1983), 101–104. The Church of the Ascension of Christ on the Mount of Olives in Jerusalem is also an octagonal *martyrium* and may have provided an additional inspiration for the Dome of the Rock.

4. As mentioned above, the legend of where the Virgin Mary rested does not appear in the synoptic Gospels. While the Gospel of Luke (2:1–6) tells of Mary and Joseph's journey from Nazareth to Bethlehem, it does not mention the event commemorated by the Kathisma Church. Grabar (*The Dome of the Rock*, 104) states that the Kathisma of the Virgin was constructed by Juvenal, the first patriarch of Jerusalem, to commemorate apocryphal traditions of Mary's stopping on the way to Bethlehem and her stopping with the infant Jesus on the flight from Judea to Egypt.

5. It is likely that Muslims in the Umayyad period believed that the Kathisma of the Virgin marked the place where Mary found refuge under the palm tree in the Qur'anic account of her pregnancy. Although this hypothesis is suggested by the location of the palm-tree mosaic next to the *mihrab*, there is yet no conclusive evidence to prove this assertion.

6. Moshe Sharon, "Islam on the Temple Mount," *Biblical Archaeology Review* 32, no. 4 (July–August 2006): 42; the full text of this article covers pp. 36–47 and 68. The most important recent works on Islamic Jerusalem and the Dome of the Rock are Oleg Grabar, *The Shape of the Holy: Early Islamic Jerusalem* (Princeton, NJ: Princeton University Press, 1996), and Grabar, *The Dome of the Rock.*

7. Sharon, "Islam on the Temple Mount," 42.

8. A good discussion of the early Christian view of the Temple and the Jews can be found

in James Carroll, *Constantine's Sword: The Church and the Jews* (Boston and New York: Houghton Mifflin, 2001). See especially the chapter, "Destroy This Temple," 100–122. The Emperor Constantine dedicated the Holy Sepulcher complex in 335 CE. The Martyrium of the Holy Sepulcher was the first *martyrium* in Jerusalem and existed through part of the Islamic period, until 1009 CE, when the Holy Sepulcher complex was destroyed by the Fatimid caliph al-Hakim. This provided the pretext for the First Crusade, which occurred nearly a century later. As a religious and political statement, the Dome of the Rock, built as it was on the Temple Mount and above the Christian holy sites, was clearly intended to symbolize the supersession of Islam over both Judaism and Christianity.

9. Sharon, "Islam on the Temple Mount," 44.

10. According to the historian and traditionist Abu Bakr Muhammad al-Wasiti (d. after 1019), the site where the Al Aqsa mosque was to be built was pointed out to the Calph Umar by Ka'b al-Ahbar, a Jewish convert to Islam. See Abu Bakr Muhammad ibn Ahmad al-Wasiti, *Fada'il al-Bayt al-Muqaddas*, ed. Isaac Hasson (Jerusalem: Institute of Asian and African Studies, the Hebrew University of Jerusalem, 1977), 45–46.

11. Ibid., 43–44; other accounts claim that Jews tended the lamps of the Al Aqsa Mosque until the time of the Umayyad caliph 'Abd al-Malik (r. 685–705 CE), the builder of the Dome of the Rock. See ibid., 44, n. 1.

12. Sharon, "Islam on the Temple Mount," 46; Sharon notes that the first mention of the prohibition of Jews entering the Temple precincts dates from 1488 CE, in a letter sent from Jerusalem by Rabbi Obadia da Bartinoro.

13. Mondays and Thursdays are the days of the "Fast of David," which is mentioned in Islamic Hadith collections. These rites may have commemorated the foundation of Jerusalem by David and the foundation of the Temple by Solomon. Pious Muslims still fast on Mondays and Thursdays in commemoration of this tradition.

14. Wasiti, *Fada'il al-Bayt al-Muqaddas*, 82–83.

15. On the concept of vernacular religion, see, for example, Joyce Burkhalter Flueckiger, *In Amma's Healing Room: Gender and Vernacular Islam in South India* (Bloomington and Indianapolis: Indiana University Press, 2006), 2.

16. Joshua Finkel, "A Risala of al-Jahiz," *Journal of the American Oriental Society* 64 (1905): 323.

17. Ibid., 324.

18. Ibid., 326.

19. Wilde's original quotation begins with the words, "Most people are other people." See Amartya Sen, *Identity and Violence: The Illusion of Destiny* (New York and London: W. W. Norton & Company, 2006), xv.

20. A more moderate position would be to say that only Hadith accounts supported by multiple chains of transmission in each generation (*ahadith mutawatira*) should be used as binding precedent. This was the opinion of Ibn Tumart (d. 1143 CE), the founder of the Almohad movement of North Africa. See Vincent J. Cornell, "Understanding Is the Mother of Ability: Responsibility and Action in the Doctrine of Ibn Tumart," *Studia Islamica*, Paris, Fasc. LXVI (1987): 71–103.

21. Muhammad ibn Idris al-Shafi'i, *al-Risala fi Usul al-Fiqh: Treatise on the Foundations of Islamic Jurisprudence*, trans. Majid Khadduri (Cambridge: The Islamic Texts Society, 1987; reprint of 1961 first edition), 76.

22. This last conclusion is inductive rather than deductive because other verses not men-

tioned in the present discussion call it into question. Furthermore, it is highly problematical with regard to its potential consequences for interfaith relations. Nevertheless, the same conclusion has been drawn by a wide variety of official and unofficial exegetes within Islam, including Usama bin Laden.

23. Cited in Ze'ev Maghen, "Strangers and Brothers: The Ritual Status of Unbelievers in Islamic Jurisprudence," *Medieval Encounters: Jewish, Christian, and Muslim Culture in Confluence and Dialogue* 12, no. 2 (2006): 180.

24. Ibid., 181.

25. Ibid., 183–186.

26. See ibid., 214–215.

27. I am grateful to Dr. Adam Sabra of the University of Georgia for this insight.

28. Adam B. Seligman, *Modest Claims: Dialogues and Essays on Tolerance and Tradition* (Notre Dame, IN: Notre Dame University Press, 2004), 153–155.

29. See Vincent J. Cornell, "Reasons Public and Divine: Shari'a Fundamentalism, Liberal Democracy, and the Epistemological Crisis of Islam," in *Islam in Theory: Essays in Comparative Religious Studies*, ed. Richard C. Martin and Carl W. Ernst (Chapel Hill: University of North Carolina Press, forthcoming).

30. Seligman, *Modest Claims*, 155.

31. Robert Chazen, *European Jewry and the First Crusade* (Berkeley and Los Angeles: University of California Press, 1987), 28–29, cited in Carroll, *Constantine's Sword*, 233.

32. James W. Morris, ed. and trans., *The Master and the Disciple: An Early Islamic Spiritual Dialogue* (London and New York: I. B. Tauris and the Institute of Ismaili Studies, 2001), 76; Arabic text, 12.

33. Ibid, 77: "If people acted according to what is in the first book, it would lead them toward the second. And if they acted in accordance with the second, that would lead them toward the third, until in the end they came to act according to the latest of the books. For it is more deserving than what came before it" (Arabic text, 12). Compare this statement with that of the nineteenth-century Christian missionary and Indologist J. N. Farquhar: "It is our belief that the living Christ will sanctify and make complete the religious thought of India. For centuries her saints have been longing for him, and her thinkers, not least the thinkers of the Vedanta, have been thinking this thought." Harry Oldmeadow, *Journeys East: 20th-Century Western Encounters with Eastern Religious Traditions* (Bloomington, IN: World Wisdom Books, 2004), 217.

34. Biblioteca de El Escorial, Spain (ms. number 1810, ff. 147–155v). I am grateful to Professor Hayat Kara of Université Mohammed V, Rabat, Morocco, for editing this *fatwa* and sharing it with me.

35. The phrase, "a *dhimmi* of your religion," is a pun. The Arabic verb *dhamma*, the root of *dhimmi*, means "to blame." Thus, the phrase *dhimmiyu dinikum* used in the poem can mean both "a non-Muslim whom your religion protects" and "one whom your religion blames."

36. For a biography of Ibn Lubb see Ahmad Baba al-Timbukti, *Nayl al-ibtihaj bi-tatriz al-Dibaj*, ed. 'Abd al-Majid al-Harama (Tripoli, Libya: 1989), 357–360.

37. Folio 155v; the text of sura 111 reads: "Perish the hand of Abu Lahab, perish! Neither his wealth nor what he has earned (*ma kasaba*) will enrich him. He will be plunged into blazing fire and his wife, who will carry the wood, will have on her neck a collar of palm-fiber." The phrase "what he has earned" (*ma kasaba*) is used as a pun by Ibn Lubb. It refers to the Ash'arite doctrine of moral responsibility (*kasb*), which forms the linchpin of his argument.

38. T. M. Scanlon, "The Difficulty of Tolerance," in *Secularism and Its Critics*, ed. Rajeev Bhargava (New Delhi: Oxford University Press, 1998), 54–55.

39. Seyyed Hossein Nasr, *Sufi Essays*, 127, cited in Oldmeadow, *Journeys East*, 223.

40. See Vincent J. Cornell, "Practical Sufism: An Akbarian Foundation for a Liberal Theology of Difference," *Journal of the Muhyiddin Ibn 'Arabi Society* 36 (2004): 59–84.

41. Scanlon, "The Difficulty of Tolerance," 61.

13

THEOLOGICAL FOUNDATIONS OF
RELIGIOUS TOLERANCE IN ISLAM

A Qur'anic Perspective

ISMAIL ACAR

'Adi bin Hatim narrates: When [the Qur'anic verse 2:187] *was revealed: Eat and drink 'until the white thread appears to you, distinct from the black thread,' I took two (hair) strings, one black and the other white, and kept them under my pillow and went on looking at them throughout the night but could not make anything out of it. So, the next morning I went to Allah's Apostle and told him the whole story. He explained to me, "That verse means the darkness of the night and the whiteness of the dawn."*[1]

It has become commonplace in the field of Islamic studies to read the Qur'an as a text that does not admit a very high degree of "tolerance" (*al-tasāmuh*) for non-Islamic points of view, religious and otherwise. And given the arguments of many modern and classical commentators, this common view is not without its merits. It is certainly true that, if one focuses on some historical applications—or seeming lack thereof—of tolerance in traditional Islam and Muslim societies with a contemporary approach without regarding its context, it could be easy to conclude that the Qur'an is a text that does not admit of a palpable level of tolerance. Further, one cannot argue with the fact that the word *al-tasāmuh* itself does not appear in the Qur'an. However, as to this last point, it may be possible to read the Qur'an as a highly nuanced text that, as a whole, actually encourages its readers to be tolerant toward members of other faiths, especially monotheistic religions.

I hold that the common readings of the Qur'an as a text that prescribes a doctrine of intolerance are deeply influenced by the contextual situations of its readers. Readers invariably bring to the text—consciously or unconsciously—many of the prejudices and preconceptions of their given context; and, when a person examines the Qur'an with even a single prejudice, he or she may find something appropriate for his purpose that is not part of the Qur'anic order.[2] In other words, while the Qur'an as a sacred text does speak through its readers, different readers may assume different meanings from the same text. And although these various understandings create a number of diverse perspectives on the text, it gives every reader the specific meaning he or she is looking for. This type of approach to the Qur'an is one of the big challenges for scholars who work on the sacred text. To deal with this challenge, I will examine a series of comments on and interpretations of related verses to religious tolerance made by different scholars in various contexts and circumstances.

The Qur'anic text is more tolerant than what many modern and classical commentators tend to concede. Religious tolerance—"the capacity to live with different religious traditions from one's own"[3]—can be found in the Qur'an when we examine its scripture in a manner that avoids, as much as possible, bringing in preconceived ideas. I will discuss the Qur'anic verses related to religious tolerance in three subjects: salvation, religious diversity, and fighting to see how the Qur'an treats these subjects and how scholars of the Qur'an understand them.

With respect to salvation, I will focus on the Qur'anic verse 2:62 to discuss different meanings of same phrase by Muslim scholars. The phrase *innalladhīna āmanū*, which is placed at the beginning of this verse before mentioning Jews, Christians, and Sabians, basically means those who believe or those who submit themselves to God: Muslims. *Innalladhīna āmanū* appears in the Qur'an more than one hundred times in different chapters, but no one discusses its meanings as he or she does regarding this verse. Many commentators interpret the phrase in 2:62 as misbelievers, hypocrites (*munafiqūn*), while they interpret other occurrences literally: Muslim. Do they want to exclude the possibility of salvation for other three groups—Jews, Christians, and Sabians—by modifying the plain meaning of the phrase?

Salvation of "Others"

According to Islamic theology, only God has the ultimate knowledge of and power over human salvation. He knows who the real believers are and who the unbelievers are. For Muslims, there is no way to attain or to possess this ultimate knowledge of the saved and the damned, of who will be the ultimate residents of paradise and hell (ashāb al-nār wa ashāb al-jannah). This information remains unknown to humans until the day of judgment; only on that day will people see who will go to paradise or hell. Moreover, there is no guarantee of salvation even for Muslims; salvation is possible for them, but it is not entirely assured. Because of this belief, Muslims fear their unknown end, while, at the same time, they have a strong hope in the mercy of God (bayn al-khawf wa al-rajā). But if salvation is not automatically guaranteed for Muslims, what, then, about the people outside of Islamic belief?

Islamic scholars are divided on the issue of whether non-Muslims can attain salvation. On the one hand, Kahled Abou Fadl extends the possibility of salvation to members of other faiths: "Although, the Qur'an clearly claims that Islam is the divine truth, and demands belief in Muhammad as a final messenger in a long line of Abrahamic prophets, it does not completely exclude the possibility that there might be other paths to salvation."[4] Abou Fadl also legitimates this conclusion based on his reading of verse 2:62.[5] However, many Muslim scholars of the Qur'an do not agree with him. They argue, "No one should conclude from this verse that for the eternal salvation [it] is not compulsory to believe in the Prophet Muhammad."[6] Below we will examine in detail the verse cited by Fadl and the scholarly debate surrounding it.

In Qur'anic verse 2:62, four groups of people (Muslims, Jews, Christians, and Sabians[7]) are mentioned side by side, and it is said that whoever truly trusts in God and the hereafter and does good deeds will not have fear and sorrow. This verse proffers the possibility of salvation for those of other faiths:

> Those who believe (in the Qur'an), and those who follow the Jewish (scriptures), and the Christians and the Sabians—any who believe in Allah and the Last Day, and work righteousness, shall have their reward with their Lord; on them shall be no fear, nor shall they grieve.
>
> Qur'an 2:62[8]

This statement evokes very diverse approaches among the commentators of the Qur'an from both classical and modern periods. There is no consensus on the meaning and the judgment of the verse. While classical commentators modify the literal meaning and also use abrogation theory to reject the possibility of salvation for Jews, Christians, and members of other faiths, contemporary Muslim scholars take a more open approach to this verse in terms of tolerance. They accept the literal meaning, maintaining that all of the groups mentioned in the verse hold an equal position.

A major point of contention in this verse is the phrase at the beginning, *innalladhīna āmanū*, which literally means "those who believe" and refers to Muslims. Despite this, many classical commentators go beyond the literal meaning and interpret *innalladhīna āmanū* as "hypocrites," although some classical commentators and modern scholars also interpret it as referring to Muslims. These two different approaches to the same text and phrase create different theological conclusions of the possibility of salvation for other faiths.

One of the contemporary Qur'an translators, Marmaduke Picthall, holds the formulation of "those who believe" to refer to Muslims. He also adds parenthetical comments to the same phrase of similar verses 22:17 and 5:59 "(who believe in the Revelation of Prophet Muhammad)." By adding these comments, Picthall puts the four groups together in regard to their status before God. Muhammad Asad and Yusuf Ali make "those who believe" clearer than does Picthall: they connect the believers directly to the Qur'an. Muhammad Shakir merely cites "those who believe" without any additional comment.[9]

As mentioned previously, contemporary Qur'anic scholars translate the verse as it is: they do not add anything beyond the literal meaning. Also, they do not embed any judgment in their translations about the future of different members of faith on the day of judgment. However, the majority of classical commentators do not count the four groups of faith along the same line and reject the possibility of salvation for other faiths. They either interpret verse 2:62 against plain meaning or use the abrogation theory to eliminate the literal meaning; they modify the meaning of the verse.

Al-Tabarī narrates the journey of Salman al-Farisī, a non-Arab companion of the Prophet, from slavery to freedom. Salman asks Muhammad about the people who live outside the Muslim community of Medina, believe in one God and the hereafter, and seek the new prophet among people but have not accepted the prophet Muhammad as a messenger yet. Muhammad gives a negative response about their salvation, and then Salman becomes sad. After a while, verse 2:62 is revealed to the Prophet Muhammad. According to al-Tabarī, this verse openly declares that other followers of the religions mentioned within the verse have a chance of eternal salvation on certain conditions. However, he does not hesitate to use abrogation theory in his later comments.

As is common for al-Ṭabarī, he cites many opinions on one particular subject. He mentions another comment from Ibn Abbas on verse 2:62 that states: "[The] possibility of salvation in this verse was covering Jews, Christians, and Sabians before the revelation of verse 3:85. This last verse affirms that: 'Whoever seeks a religion other than Islam, it will never be accepted from him, and in the hereafter he will be among the losers.'" Al-Ṭabarī concludes that this verse abrogates the judgment of verse 2:62,[10] eliminating the possibility of salvation for other monotheistic members by abrogation theory (nashk). However, classical period commentators produced the abrogation theory to reconcile so-called contradictions in the sacred text. It is not an order of Qur'anic verses or Hadith texts; it is a production of Muslim scholars in the early centuries of Islam. Moreover, they do not have a consensus on abrogated verses and the abrogation theory, which was and is a debatable issue.[11]

Al-Zamakhsharī considers the meaning of "those who believe" at the beginning of verse 2:62 as "hypocrites" (munafiqūn), those who believe only through their tongues and not from the heart. Also, he adds another comment on the second similar phrase of the same verse (man āmana bi Allahi), stating that "[he] who believes in God" refers to a person who converts to Islam from Judaism or Christianity or was a Sabian, including hypocrites.[12] Zamakhsharī emphasizes an exclusive approach that believing in God and the Last Day and doing good deeds makes sense only within Islam. Otherwise, there will be no chance for salvation in the hereafter.

Commentator al-Razī interprets the statement "those who believe" as true believers among Christians before the prophethood of Muhammad, such as Monk Bahira and Waraqah b. Nawfal. Razī adds a controversial interpretation to this part of the verse, as he says that these believers may refer to the hypocrites also. Besides this interpretation, he mentions a much broader approach from Sufyan al-Savrī: "The first statement of the verse those who believe represent the true believers in the past, before Islamic era, and the second phrase walladhīna hādū[13] represents the true believers in the future, after Islam."[14]

Another commentator, Baydawī, proclaims that "those who believe" with just their tongues are hypocrites. However, Baydawī's comment on the second formulation of "those who believe in God" in 2:62 is different; he interprets "believer" as a person who believes in God and the prophet Muhammad. This interpretation describes the first step of becoming a Muslim, so the news is good only for Muslims on the day of judgment.[15] Baydawī does not give any leeway for believers of other faiths in terms of salvation.

Like al-Ṭabarī, commentator Ibn Kathīr talks about the journey of Salman al-Farisī because of the relation between the revelation of verse 2:62 and

Salman's question. Ibn Kathīr goes beyond the plain meaning of verse 2:62 and makes his comments narrower than the verse itself by appealing to abrogation theory. According to Ibn Kathīr, after Muhammad delivered his message, there was no other way to God. All of the other ways were abrogated at the arrival of Islam. The followers of Moses were acceptable until the coming of Jesus; Christians were acceptable until the advent of Muhammad; after Muhammad, there is only one way, and that is the way of Muhammad and his message. Muhammad is the last one in this chain of prophets: there will be none after him. But since no one's idea about Jesus and Moses would be accepted by God because of verse 3:85, Ibn Kathīr concludes that verse 2:62 was abrogated by verse 3:85; after that abrogation, whoever seeks a religion other than Islam will be lost in the hereafter.[16]

Commentator Tabarsī tells of different possibilities for the believers, Jews, Christians, and Sabians together. He mentions the disagreement among Muslim scholars about the description of these four groups in the verse. He states that the second phrase "who believes in God" refers to Jews, Christians, and Sabians but may also refer to Muslims. By contrast to many other scholars, Tabarsī interprets the first statement of "those who believe" as possibly referring to Muslims, and he does not believe it refers to hypocrites as many other classical commentators do. Accepting that this verse was abrogated by verse 3:85, he does not consider the four groups as being on equal footing.[17] Tabarsī, thus, interprets the abrogation of verse 2:62 in a manner similar to Tabarī.

As seen above, the various classical approaches to the two phrases in the Qur'anic text 2:62, "those who believe" and "who believes in God," hold different opinions on the possibility of salvation for "others" (Jews, Christians, and other monotheistic religions). In addition to this interpretative approach, another obstacle has been the theory of abrogation, as the majority of the classical commentators state that verse 3:85 abrogates verse 2:62. Now let's turn to what later commentators say about verse 2:62.

According to the nineteenth-century commentator Shawkanī, the phrase of "those who believe" refers to hypocrites because hypocrites are mentioned along with Jews, Christians, and Sabians. He argues that the second formulation in the same verse "who believes in God" refers to people who believe in Muhammad. Trusting Muhammad is the faith (iman) that the angel Gabriel told the Prophet in a certain conversation. The angel Gabriel put forth the meaning of faith to the Muslim believers: it is believing in God, his angels, his books, his messengers, and the Last Day. So, according to Shawkanī, without having Muslim faith, doing "good deeds" does not make sense.[18] Doing good deeds without believing in the Muslim faith will not save an individual on the day of judgment since good deeds without a valid faith are not worth anything before God. Shawkanī goes beyond the literal meaning of this verse. He makes comments with a broad viewpoint of Islamic traditional background.

Another nineteenth-century commentator, Alusī, says that two types of believers (mu'min) are mentioned in verse 2:62, each different from the other. As Sufyan al-Savrī says, the first formulation of this verse refers to the people who believe only with their tongues and without their hearts; they are hypocrites. Thus, the second statement covers all sincere Muslims, the hypocrites who repented, and the Jews and Christians who died before the corruption of their religion. He comments that the Sabians are the people who were on the righteous path but who died before the appearance of Muhammad.[19]

Twentieth-century Qur'anic scholar Muhammad Abduh interprets the phrase of 2:62, "those who believe," as those Muslims who believe in Muhammad and his message here in the world and will follow the Prophet in the day of judgment. He accepts Muslims and other believers who are mentioned in this verse in the same line. He thinks that Muslims, Jews, Christians, and Sabians are clear in terms of their followers. He interprets the second formulation in the same verse, "who believes in God," as a substitution from the first expression of believers. Abduh considers both groups of believers in this verse as Muslims. He does not differentiate between the meaning of those who believe and who believe in God as many classical commentators do. Abduh place Muslims, Jews, Christians, and Sabians in the same position before God, if they have sound belief in God and the hereafter and do good deeds. He explains his idea in terms of justice: "God does not change his attitude towards his creatures. He is the source of justice, the Just al-Adl, gives his mercy to all creatures with this features. No one can stop him from doing that."[20] Abduh has a broader point of view than classical commentators on the possibility of salvation for "other believers" because of the principle of God's justice and mercy.

According to mainstream Islamic theology, no one—including Muslims —is guaranteed salvation in the other world without the mercy of God. The mercy of God is the key term for salvation; if God extends his mercy through Jews, Christians, and Sabians because of their accurate belief and good deeds, no one can prevent this mercy. According to verse 2:62, divine mercy will work with sound belief and good deeds, regardless of the entity in this world. However, in the Qur'an, God asks Muslims to follow the last messenger Muhammad.[21] This is the will of God for Muslims. For Muslims, there is no chance to reject the prophecy of Muhammad: bearing witness to the prophet Muhammad is one of the creeds. However, we are discussing non-Muslims who follow what verse 2:62 says. Another Qur'anic verse, 3:64, calls Jews and Christians to a shared point: "Say: 'O People of the Book! come to common terms as between us and you: That we worship none but Allah.'" This underlines the importance of belief in the oneness of God. Muhammad also emphasizes that believing in God consequently brings eternal salvation.

A few Hadith narrations state that a sound belief eventually leads to paradise: "Who says 'there is no god, but God' as a last word in this World he enters the Paradise."[22] Abu Dhar narrates:

Allah's Apostle said, "Someone came to me from my Lord and gave me the news (or good tidings) that if any of my followers dies worshiping none (in any way) along with Allah, he will enter Paradise." I asked, "Even if he committed illegal sexual intercourse (adultery) and theft?" He replied, "Even if he committed illegal sexual intercourse (adultery) and theft."[23]

It is interesting that commentators do not comment on the verse, which we mentioned above, with these hadiths of the prophet Muhammad in mind.

Believers, Jews, Christians, and other pious followers, who really believe in God and the day of resurrection and who do good works in the world will have no fear in the other world and have their reward from God. This is the message for everybody from the last revelation: the Qur'an. Two points are crucial here: believing in oneness of God and in the hereafter is the first one, and the second one is doing good deeds in this world. Belief and practice should coexist in a life of a person who would like to have a consequent hope for salvation. These two aspects are main reasons for the creation of human beings by God, and those who obey these two basic rules will have the possibility of salvation.[24] If a Muslim keeps in his mind that salvation would be possible with the mercy of God for other monotheistic believers, he would act more tolerantly toward other followers in a diverse community.

Tolerant Acts in Diverse Communities

Although the Qur'an claims that Islam is the last version of monotheism, it accepts other religious groups as different entities of humanity. The Qur'an describes itself as a guidance book: "This is the Book; in it is guidance sure, without doubt, to those who fear Allah" (2:2).[25] It also encourages its believers to ask guidance from God: "Guide us the straight way the way of those upon whom Thou hast bestowed Thy blessings, not of those who have been condemned [by Thee], nor of those who go astray" (1:6-7). In this verse, the Qur'an asserts that there are a correct path and incorrect paths.[26] The Qur'an calls people to its correct path without ignoring "others." It criticizes them, but it does not force them to believe Qur'anic teachings. The Qur'an declares its message but leaves the decision to individuals.

If the Qur'an had ever required anybody to force absolute belief on other faith groups, it would have so instructed the prophet Muhammad. However, the Qur'an tells Muhammad that he is only the messenger of God's truth. "And so, [O Prophet,] exhort them; thy task is only to exhort" (88:21). He has no authority to make people believe. The following verse makes his position on calling clearer: "Thou canst not compel them [to believe]" (88:22). The Prophet is required to tell the message in an appropriate way, but he must let people choose. According to the Qur'an, only the individual has a right to choose his path; nobody makes him believe or deny. When Muhammad wished to convert somebody from the Meccan elites to Islam, for example, God revealed to him that "[v]erily, thou canst not guide aright everyone whom thou lowest: but it is God who guides him that wills [to be guided]" (28:56). Even Muhammad has no power to convert people to Islam. Therefore, Muslims should accept other faith members as they are.

The Qur'an asserts that diversity is part of the divine intent and purpose in creation:[27] "O men! Behold, we have created you all out of a male and a female, and have made you into nations and tribes, so that you might come to know one another" (49:13). This verse implies that God wished to create humanity in diverse communities; and "If God had willed, He could surely have made you all one single community: but [He willed it otherwise] in order to test you" (5:48). These two verses openly support an ethnical diversity and tolerance among different communities. Moreover, the Qur'an does not only accept but even expects the reality of difference and diversity within human society. "To each of you God has prescribed a Law and a Way. . . . God's purpose is to test you in what he has given each of you" (5:48).

In such a diverse community, the Qur'an advises its pious followers for peace: "For, [true] servants of the Most Gracious are [only] they who walk gently on earth, and who, whenever the foolish address them reply with [words of] peace" (25:63). This verse implies an active support of peace in a tolerant way. Instead of involving a struggle or clash, the Qur'an asks the pious Muslim to accept tolerance as a basic principle. "And [know that true servants of God are only] those who never bear witness to what is false, and [who], whenever they pass by [people engaged in] frivolity, pass on with dignity" (25:72). These righteous believers need to keep away from vain talks. "And, whenever they heard frivolous talk, having turned away from it and said: 'unto us shall be accounted our deeds, and unto you, your deeds. Peace be upon you—[but] we do not seek out such as are ignorant [of the meaning of right and wrong]'" (28:55).

According to these verses, Muslims are supposed to be appreciative of different groups of people in their daily lives. For their religious purposes, Muslims should follow the most tolerant way while they preach Islam. We see this obligation in the following verse, wherein God tells his messenger Muhammad, "Call thou [all mankind] unto thy Sustainer's path with wisdom and goodly exhortation, and argue with them in the most kindly manner" (16:125). In addition to this order, when God sent his messengers Moses and Aaron to the pharaoh who claimed to possess divinity, God commanded them to behave tolerantly and speak softly: "But speak unto him in a mild manner" (20:44), even though the pharaoh claims that "I am your Lord All-Highest!"[28] (79:24). God asks his messenger to approach even tyranny with tolerance because he created all humanity with dignity: "We have conferred dignity on the children of Adam" (17:70). Therefore, every human being should be considered with honor, regardless of his or her beliefs.

The Qur'an even recommends tolerance with infidels and prohibits any violence unless their aim is to overthrow Muslim community: "Make due allowance for man's nature, and enjoin the doing of what is right; and leave alone all those who choose to remain ignorant" (7:199). Also, there is a whole chapter that explains how to deal with unbelievers in terms of religious tolerance:

> "Say: 'O you who deny the truth!
> 'I do not worship that which you worship,
> 'and neither do you worship that which I worship!
> 'And I will not worship that which you have [ever] worshiped,
> 'and neither will you [ever] worship that which I worship.
> 'Unto you, your moral law, and unto me, mine!'"
>
> (Qur'an 109:1–6)

This chapter openly declares that everybody has his own way in terms of religion.[29] Moreover, the Qur'an commands Muslims not to insult those who worship other gods since they may insult God through ignorance. "If [it] had been Allah's plan, they would not have been taken false gods; we did not make you to watch over their doings, nor you set over them to dispose of their affairs" (6:107–108). Besides all of this, compulsion is forbidden by the Qur'anic verse 2:256: "There is no compulsion in religion." The last verse tells the core value of Qur'anic tolerance for every other group.

It is almost impossible to find any Qur'anic basis or justification for treating believers of other religions intolerantly; however, if a person would like to find the prejudice against the Qur'anic text, he may find evidence sufficient to support his claim. This evidence could be views taken out of context or those purposely set against the general message of the Qur'an. The Qur'an was revealed gradually, so it is better to consider it as a whole. However, the chronological order of Qur'anic verses may produce a suitable approach for commentators who would like to apply the abrogation theory in a verse or a group of verses that do not fit the idea in their mind. Ibn Hazm informs that there are 114 verses that speak of tolerance in early Islam, but all were abrogated by the sword verse (aya al-sayf): "Slay the idolaters wherever you find them" (9:5).[30]

All of the verses that currently exist in the Qur'an have meaning for Muslims; it is not reasonable to say that the verses related to tolerance, diversity, and peace are abrogated by one later verse. Verses related to fighting should be interpreted with the verses related to tolerance because the abrogation issue does not supersede the Qur'anic verses. Abrogation is merely a method of interpreting the Qur'an, and it should remain at that level.[31]

The Doctrine of Fighting

Generally speaking, fighting for the way of God (jihad) should be done in a defensive way, not offensive: "And fight in God's cause against those who wage war against you, but do not commit aggression—for, verily, God does not love aggressors" (Qur'an 2:190). When we interpret this verse with the verses related to religious tolerance, it appears that the Muslim community is asked to defend itself against offenders. This statement, however, is not a permission to offend non-Muslims because of their beliefs; only self-defense (in the widest sense of the word) makes war permissible for Muslims. Also, this verse notifies Muslims not to exceed the limits of justice even in defending their position.

Moreover, according to verses 2:192–193 and verse 8:39 (quoted below), if the offender wants to cease fighting or to surrender, Muslims should accept that offer: "And slay them wherever you may come upon them, and drive them away from wherever they drove you away—for oppression is even worse than killing" (2:191). The command of this verse—"slay them wherever you may come upon them"—is valid only within the context of hostilities already in progress, on the understanding that "those who wage war against you" are the aggressors or oppressors (a war of liberation being a war "in God's cause").[32]

Verse 2:191 does not encourage Muslims to take the offensive toward other groups of believers without reason. However, one of the first organized troops

of the prophet Muhammad attacked a caravan while the caravan was traveling to its destination. The Qur'an records the following verses in relation to
this incident:

"Fighting is prescribed for you, and ye dislike it. . . . Say: 'Fighting therein is a grave
(offence); but graver is it in the sight of Allah to prevent access to the path of Allah,
to deny Him, to prevent access to the Sacred Mosque, and drive out its members.'
Tumult and oppression are worse than slaughter. Nor will they cease fighting you
until they turn you back from your faith if they can."

Qur'an 216–218

It is important that the verses should be interpreted according to their context.
At that time, the prophet Muhammad had sent his companions to check on
the Meccan caravan—not to fight them. However, a small group of his army,
eight Muslim troops, killed one of the traders and captured the caravan's property. It was neither a Qur'anic order nor the Prophet's order to capture the
caravan. Also, Muslims had no trade agreement with Meccans at that time.
But the outcome of the act by the Muslim army did not fit in with the general
Qur'anic view. In this verse, we see an interesting comparison between the current misbehavior by Muslims and previous violence by Meccans; the oppression and tumult are worse than killing people. So, the Muslim army killed a
trader without a declared war; this verse and the incident are suitable clues for
a reader who wants to find something against tolerance in the Qur'an.

Another verse tells something more about fighting for the way of God:

And fight them on until there is no more tumult or oppression, and there prevail justice and faith in Allah altogether and everywhere; but if they cease, verily Allah doth
see all that they do.

Qur'an 8:39[33]

As explained in many other verses as well, this verse orders Muslims to fight
against "tumult or oppression" and not simply against another belief and religion. This is a temporary order to eliminate tumult and oppression; if there
is no oppression, then Muslims should seek cease and peace. However, some
consider this Qur'anic verse as solid evidence to fight against nonbelievers in
order to make them obey the regulations of Muslim rulers. They do not consider the condition so much as they focus on the order of fight.

Ibn Taymiyya holds that it is a duty to wage war on the unbelievers simply because they are unbelievers, even if there is no oppression to the community. He supports his statement with a hadith: "I am commanded to fight
with men till they testify that there is no god but Allah."[34] He re-establishes
this classical point of view within a political context: he emphasizes that the

main function of an Islamic state is to maintain order through coercion, but coercion exercised in a correct way, i.e., by enforcing God's law.[35] This kind of understanding creates an intolerant approach among Muslims toward other faith members.

One of the contemporary commentators, Sayyid Qutb, interprets verse 8:39 with a similar approach; the ultimate goal of an Islamic state is to establish the "Sovereignty of God" all over the world. But his comment does not fit well with the rest of the Qur'an and creates a problematic perspective toward other members of faith in terms of administrative issue. "Sovereignty of God" according to whom? Which group of Muslims? Or which legal or theological school does "Sovereignty of God" refer to?[36] On the contrary, there is no claim in the Qur'an to make the entire world Muslim.[37] The Qur'an clearly states that "[n]ot all people believe (like Muslims)" (12:106).

According to verse 8:39, one of the legitimate causes of a war is the institution of freedom of religion and the alleviation of obstacles that separate the individual from God:

If, as human beings, we have a responsibility on this front, then it is the responsibility to alleviate those obstacles. But, if a state has guaranteed freedom of religion and conscience under the laws and constitution within the supremacy of law, there then will be no pressure on the people to choose a certain religion.[38]

The Qur'an allows for war to prevent anarchy, but it does not sanctify war undertaken in order to compel people of other religions to convert to Islam or to bring the whole world under Islamic sovereignty (Dar al-Islam).[39] In order to see the general aim of the Qur'anic verses, looking at the context is very useful. For example, the following verse seems to encourage Muslims to fight against the People of the Book, Jews and Christians:

Fight those who believe not in Allah nor the Last Day, nor hold that forbidden which hath been forbidden by Allah and His Messenger, nor acknowledge the religion of Truth, (even if they are) of the People of the Book, until they pay the Jizya with willing submission, and feel themselves subdued.

Qur'an 9:29

This verse was revealed to Muhammad when the Byzantine Empire entered into an agreement with the Gassanid Christians to eliminate the new Medinan State of Islam. Muhammad and his companions considered this verse under warfare conditions. Therefore, when taken in its historical context, the verse does not assert that it is reasonable to open war against the People of the Book just because of their belief. They are not considered unbelievers; the Qur'an gives them the status of People of the Book.

Believing in the oneness of God and believing in the last day are the key issues in Islamic faith. If a single person accepts both, then, he is excluded from fighting and probably will attain salvation on the day of judgment depending on his deeds. Thus, verse 9:29 should be interpreted in its context; in the same chapter (9:1–4), the conditions of the fight are laid out. When all possibilities of agreement and treaty have been exhausted and all diplomatic relations have been sundered, then the war is considered according to verse 9:29. Otherwise, verse 9:4 declares, "Do not kill those of the pagan with whom you made an agreement." Moreover, verse 9:6 orders that the pagans who seek refuge or protection should be excluded from the fighting: "And if any of those who ascribe divinity to aught beside God seeks thy protection 'grant him protection, so that he might [be able to] hear the word of God [from thee]; and thereupon convey him to a place where he can feel secure.'"

It is obvious that the Qur'an has very limited tolerance against paganism (*shirk*) and atheism (*kufr*) as compared with other monotheistic beliefs: Judaism, Christianity, and the Sabians. However, this partial tolerance against paganism and atheism does not represent the whole doctrine of Qur'anic tolerance. A Qur'anic approach should be understood in its context and within its aim. In order to see this fractional Qur'anic approach, we need to consider all Qur'anic verses. Otherwise, there could be an interpretation that the Qur'an does not approve.

Conclusion

The Qur'an's main aim is to guide its followers along the straight path: the way of God. It encourages believers to be on the way to God in the form of the last revelation. Verse 2:62 of the Qur'an technically attaches salvation to two conditions: believing in one God and in the day of judgment and performing good deeds. Classical commentators have modified their readings of this verse in a number of ways because of their circumstances. They have managed to remove the salvation of others only by the help of abrogation theory. Contemporary commentators, who have a more diverse community experience than did commentators of previous centuries, interpret this verse in a pluralistic way as it is stated literally in the text. Reading the verse both pluralistically and contextually has been gaining ground among contemporary Muslim scholars. Both methods will create more tolerant meanings in the Qur'anic text.

There are more than a hundred verses in the Qur'an asking Muslims to act tolerantly toward other religious communities and not to force them to convert. These verses order Muslims to expand their religious tolerance in order to be good Muslims before God. However, abrogation theory works against the tolerance espoused by the Qur'an. It is not reasonable to view all tolerance verses as being abrogated by fighting verses. Abrogation doctrine is a production of early commentators of the Qur'an; it is only a theory, not a command of verse or hadith. Classical commentators formulated the abrogation theory to solve so-called contradictions among verses. Therefore, abrogation is a scholarly production for Qur'anic interpretation by a certain group of scholars in early Islam.

The Qur'an has a more tolerant approach to previous monotheistic religions—Judaism, Christianity, and Sabianism—in comparison to other faiths. It is totally against paganism and atheism and barely accepts pagans and atheists in Muslim communities. Moreover, verses related to fighting can give a sense of intolerance to prejudiced readers in an isolated reading. These verses are also part of the Qur'an and should be considered alongside other Qur'anic verses.

Notes

1. Muhammad Muhsin Khan, *The Translation of the Meanings of Sahih al-Bukhari* (Lahore: Kazi, 1983), 3:77.

2. Khawarij, the bloodiest group in Islamic formative history, established an extreme theory of violence in their interpretation of Qur'anic verses, 5:44, 45, 47–49; 12:40, 67; 13:41; and 40:20. For more information, see Elie Adib Salem, *Political Theory and Institutions of the Khawarij* (Baltimore, MD: Johns Hopkins Press, 1956).

3. The United Nations Educational, Scientific and Cultural Organization (UNESCO) describes tolerance in the following way: "It means that one is free to adhere to one's own convictions and accepts that others adhere to theirs. . . . It also means that one's views are not be imposed on others" (http://www.un-documents.net/dpt.htm [12/18/06]).

4. Khaled Abou Fadl, *The Place of Tolerance in Islam* (Boston: Beacon Press, 2002), 17.

5. Verse 5:59 states the same basic idea with some slight variation.

6. Ali Unal, *The Qur'an: with Annotated Interpretation in Modern English* (Somerset, NJ: The Light, 2006), 44.

7. Sabians, or in the original transliteration Sābi'ūn, are followers of any monotheistic religion rather than the "People of the Book" (Jews and Christians). In verse 5:69 of the Qur'an, Sabians are also mentioned as one of other monotheistic religions between Judaism and Christianity.

8. The translations of Qur'anic verses are from Abdullah Yusuf Ali, *The Meaning of the Holy Qur'an* (New York: Tahrike Tarsile Qur'an, Inc., 2004); and Muhammad Asad, *The Message of the Qur'an* (Watsonville, CA: The Book Foundation, 2003). In addition, I sometimes revised the translation.

9. See for each translation verse 2:62.

10. Muhammad b. Jarīr al-Tabarī, *Jāmi'u al-bayān an ta'vīli āy al-Qur'ān* (Cairo: Dār al-Ma'ārif, 1950), 2:143–155.

11. See for details, John Burton, "The Exegesis of Q. 2:106 and the Islamic Theories of 'naskh: mā nansakh min āya aw nansahā na'ti bi khairin minhā aw mithlihā,'" *Bulletin of the School of Oriental and African Studies* 48, no. 3 (1985): 452–469; and A. Rippin, "Al-Zuhrī, 'Naskh al-Qur'ān' and the Problem of Early 'Tafsīr' Texts," *Bulletin of the School of Oriental and African Studies* 47, no. 1 (1984): 22–43.

12. Mahmūd b. 'Umar Zamakhsharī, *al-Kashshāf an haqāiq ghawāmid al-tanzīl al-Qur'ān al-Karīm* (Beirut: Dār al-Kitāb al-Arabī, 1947), 1:146.

13. This phrase is usually translated "those who follow the Jewish faith"; it basically refers to Jewish people, not to Muslims.

14. Fakhr al-Dīn Rāzi, *al-Tafsīr al-Kabīr* (Cairo: al-Matba'ah al-Bahīyah al-Misrīyah, 1934–1962), 3:103–105.

15. al-Qādī al-Baydawī, *Anwār al-tanzīl* (Istanbul: s.n., 1868–1869), 3:352.

16. Ismail b. Omar Ibn Kathīr, *Tafsīr al-Qur'ān al-Azīm* (Jīzah: Mu'assasat Qurtrubah, 2000), 1:430–434.

17. Abū al-Fadl ibn al-Hasan Al-Tabarsī, *Tafsīr Jawāmi' al-jāmi'* (Qum: al-Mu'assasah, 1997) 1:111

18. Muhammad b. Alī b. Muhammad Al-Shawkānī, *Fath al-Qadīr: al-jāmi bayna fannay al-riwāyah wa-al-dirāyah min ilm al-tafsīr* (al-Mansūrah: Dār al-Wafā', 1994), 1:156-158.

19. Mahmūd ibn Abd Allah al-Alusī, *Rūh al-Maānī fī tafsīr al-Qur'ān al-Azīm* (Cairo: Mu'assasat al-Halabī lil-Nashr wa al-Tawzī', 1960), 1:381–384.

20. Muhammad Abduh, *Tafsīr al-Qur'an al-hakīm al-mushtahir bi-ism Tafsīr al-Manār* (Cairo: Dār al-Manār, 1906–1935), 1:333–339.

21. Qur'an 3:31: "Say [O Prophet]: 'If you love God, follow me, [and] God will love you and forgive you your sins; for God is much-forgiving, a dispenser of grace.'"

22. Badr al-Dīn al-'Aynī, *Sharh Sunan Abī Dāwud* (Riyad: Maktabat al-Rushd, 1999), 6:351.

23. Bukharī, *Sahīh al- Bukharī*, Janāiz, 23.

24. Chapter 103 in the Qur'an also emphasizes these two aspects, belief and good deeds, for salvation.

25. For more details, see Qur'anic verses, 3:138; 7:52; 27:1, 76; 17:9–10; 10:57; 31:1; 39:23; 41:44; 45:11, 20.

26. Interestingly, verse 29:69 states many ways to God instead of one straight path: "But as for those who strive hard in Our cause—We shall most certainly guide them onto paths that lead unto Us. . . ."

27. Al Fadl, *Tolerance in Islam*, 16.

28. In Islamic theology, speculating a partner to God, *shirk*, is the most grievous sin, one that will not be forgiven. See Qur'anic verses 25:68 and 6:151.

29. Unfortunately, some commentators who do not want to see Qur'anic tolerance toward nonbelievers apply abrogation theory.

30. Ibn Hazm al-Andalusi, *Al-Nāsikh wal-Mansukh* (Beirut: Dar al-Kutub al-'Ilmiyyah, 1986), 12–21.

31. Abdulaziz Sachedina, "The Qur'an and Other Religions," in *The Cambridge Companion to The Qur'an*, ed. Jane Dammen McAuliffe (New York: Cambridge University Press, 2006), 301.

32. M. Shakir translates the formulation "*wa lā ta'daddū*" of this verse: "but begin not hostilities." M. H. Shakir, *Translation of the Holy Qur'an* (Elmhurst, NY: Tahrike Tarsile Qur'an Inc., 1983).

33. This verse can be found with a slight variation: "And fight them on until there is no more Tumult or oppression, and there prevail justice and faith in Allah; but if they cease, Let there be no hostility except to those who practice oppression" (2:193).

34. Abū Dāwud, *Sunan,* Zakāh, 1.

35. Amhed ibn 'Abd al-Halīm Ibn Taymiyyah, *al-Siyāsa al-Shar'iyya* (Riyad: al-Vuzara al-Shuūn al-Islamī, 1997), 168–78.

36. Sayyid Qutb, *Fī Zilāl al-Qur'ān* (Beirut: Dār al-Shuruūq, 1973–1974), 3:399–403.

37. Ali Bulac, "Jihad," in *Terror and Suicide Attacks: An Islamic Perspective*, ed. Ergun Capan (Somerset, NJ: The Light, 2004), 56.

38. Ibid., 57.

39. Ismail Bayraktar, "The Juxtaposition of Islam and Violence," in *Muslim Citizens of the Globalized World: Contributions of the Gulen Movement*, ed. Robert A. Hund-Yuksel and A. Aslandogan (Somerset, NJ: The Light & IID Press, 2006), 115.

PART 7

BUDDHISM AND HINDUISM

14

TOWARD A BUDDHIST
POLICY OF TOLERANCE

The Case of King Ashoka

KRISTIN SCHEIBLE

Historically, India has been a land characterized by diversity. Twenty-three languages are currently recognized as being "official," and there are hundreds of other regional dialects in use. All major religions are present and active; and, even within the dominant, monolithically monikered "Hinduism," a plethora of gods and goddesses shares the attention of disparate communities' varieties of practices. This rampant diversity, however, does not indicate some innate inclination toward tolerance, as one can readily perceive upon review of the major movements of India's people along religious lines through history (for example, amid the independence movement of the last century, the unification of a populace against continued colonial oppression, and the violent partition of the country occurred along religious lines).

On July 22, 1947, shortly before India won its independence, the *dhammacakra*, or wheel of law, replaced the preindependence symbol of the spinning wheel. While the spinning wheel had humbly represented local industry and gumption, the icon of the *dharma* wheel conjures an illustrious history of native achievement, religious and political. *Dhamma* is variously conceived as morality, order, law, righteousness, and religion, in both private and public dimensions. Here we see that the bifurcation of policy and religion rampant in modern discourse doesn't work in the premodern understanding of

317

the term *dhamma*. In Buddhism, *dhamma* takes on an additional valence as a term referring to the content and form of the Buddha's teachings.[1] As such a multivalent term, *dhamma* predates the formal rise of Buddhism and is a concept shared with other pan-Indic religious traditions. The meaning of this iconic wheel in the Buddhist sense is fairly clear; the wheel of *dhamma* was turned by the Buddha Gotama as he began to teach his understanding of the ways things are, his *dhamma*. His first postenlightenment sermon, the utterance that would initiate the phenomenon now summarized by the term *Buddhism*, was entitled *Dhammacakkhapavattanasutta*, "the Turning of the Wheel of Dharma Sutra."

As a symbol, the wheel is multivalent insofar as meaning has accreted through levels of usage and interpretation. Significantly, the stylized wheel at the core of the Indian flag hints at the Buddhist origins of the symbol, but it simultaneously invokes metonymically the extraordinary reign of the most celebrated native monarch, Ashoka Maurya, the third ruler of the Mauryan Dynasty who rose to power in 268 BCE. In controlling his vast kingdom, Ashoka had pronouncements carved into boulders and pillars that would carry his policy far and wide. The wheel represented on the current Indian flag is the same symbol that adorns several of the Ashokan pillars that have been discovered over the landscape, and it represents the wheel of *dhamma* (Sanskrit: *dharma*), specifically as wielded by this dharmic ruler. This resonant symbol marks Ashoka's rule as a decidedly Buddhist one.

Throughout history, Ashoka has loomed large in pan-Asian Buddhist narrative literature, such as the *Ashokavadana*, *Divyavadana*, *Dipavamsa*, and *Mahavamsa*. His story—his rise to power and relationship to Buddhism—is preserved in various literary sources, all with their own sectarian roots and agendas. The Sri Lankan texts that first turned my attention toward the tolerant character of Ashoka most decidedly reflect the nascent historiographical impetus of a particular sect of Buddhists gathered at the Mahavihara monastic complex in Anuradhapura several hundred years after Ashoka would have reigned in India. It is within these texts that Ashoka has been linked to the missionary intention and expansion of the Buddhist *sangha* (community of monks and nuns).[2] While these early Pali *vamsa* (historical) texts may be considered classical sources, they are also literary sources, compilations and redactions of earlier materials that put forth the biases of the compiling community of monks writing generations after Ashoka's reign.[3] These wishful histories are quick to embrace the symbolic capital of Ashoka, the greatest Buddhist monarch, and his story is refracted through the lens of their mitigating agendas. We could choose to read the *vamsas* as a source of tolerance—or intolerance—but we would need to be very careful about the distortion that comes through refraction. Instead, there is an available source to which we now turn, directly connected to the legendary king himself: his own epigraphical proclamations, inscriptions that are scattered across India in the form of rock and pillar edicts.[4]

Are the Ashokan edicts a "classical source" for the study of early Buddhism? They are extracanonical and are of a different genre altogether from the copious scriptural and commentarial literature in the Buddhist tradition. The edicts are not singularly religious in character; they are the public, politically charged statements of a king rather than the proclamations or revelations issued by the *sangha*. And yet it is within these edicts that Ashoka clearly defines a policy of tolerance, based on what can be interpreted as applied Buddhist ethics. Ashoka espoused the cultivation of both private and public manifestations of morality, what he called *dhamma,* marked by tolerance and respect for all life. Indologist Romila Thapar concurs:

It was in the conception of this policy, seen in the context of Mauryan India, that the true achievement of Ashoka lay. He did not see *Dhamma* as piety resulting from good deeds inspired by formal religious beliefs, but as an emphasis on social responsibility.[5]

Because his policy of *dhamma* exceeded sectarian boundaries and expressly evoked social responsibility, Ashoka may be seen as an exemplar of tolerance in early Buddhism. The edicts are an invaluable source for the tradition precisely because they are writ in stone, committing the policies of the past to a form that remains unchanged (although some of our examples have been damaged by weather and other elements) and can be more or less dated with confidence.

Ashoka as an Ethical Buddhist Exemplar

Ashoka is heralded across the Buddhist world as the paramount Buddhist monarch, even a *cakkavattin* (Sanskrit: *cakravartin*), literally "wheel-turner" but usually translated as "world conquering monarch."[6] One predominant narrative in the later Buddhist literature explains that he underwent a conversion experience spurred by intense feelings of remorse after his murderous military campaign in the Kalinga country in the eighth year of his reign.[7] The Pali *vamsas*, on the other hand, do not corroborate this singular conversion experience, nor do they mention the Kalinga war. Turning to our epigraphical sources, here the Maski Rock Edict, we see an explicit acknowledgment of Ashoka's Buddhist identity:

For more than two and a half years, I have been a lay disciple [*upasaka*] of the Buddha. More than a year ago, I visited the Sangha, and since then I have been energetic in my efforts.[8]

Ashoka was energetic enough in his religious practice to position himself as an authority in correct practice. He issued a proclamation as to what texts the religious professionals in the *sangha* ought to be reading:

King Priyadarshi of Magadha conveys his greetings to the Sangha and wishes them good health and prosperity. You know, Reverend Sirs, the extent of my reverence for and faith in the Buddha, the Dharma, and the Sangha. Whatever the Lord Buddha has said, Reverend Sirs, is of course well said. But it is proper for me to enumerate the texts which express true Dharma and which may make it everlasting.[9]

Ashoka then enumerates several texts. In this Bhabra Rock Edict, it is clear that Ashoka is Buddhist, familiar with and extolling several texts as important for monastic men and women to study. He also explicitly proclaims his faith in the three jewels (Buddha, *dhamma*, and *sangha*),[10] although it is also clear that the audience for this edict was a monastic rather than secular one, as it is explicitly addressed to the *sangha*. Seeing here the self-proclaimed Buddhist leaning of Ashoka, we can thus use his edicts, explicative as they are of his policy of *dhamma*, as a case study for the examination of a particular policy of tolerance in early Buddhism.

As we will see, Ashoka publicly proclaimed an explicit, legal policy of tolerance, so that the behaviors and hearts of his diverse subjects might grow to understand and appreciate the profundity and practicality of *dhamma*.[11] From what we can glean from the edicts, his policy of tolerance represents both a heartfelt urge to better his society as well as a sagacious political maneuver to maintain authority over a religiously diverse polity.

William Scott Green, in the first essay in this collection, sets an agenda with five important questions to ascertain the sources of tolerance in our varied traditions. Taking the Ashokan edicts as my source, I answer his prompt in this way:

(1) The role of other religions as represented in the Ashokan edicts is to act as morally uplifting and edifying conversation partners as well as fields of merit, fit recipients of respect and support, to further one's personal moral evolution on his own chosen religious path.

(2) Different religions are not merely endured but duly acknowledged and considered religiously constructive. Other religions are treated both generically (in general statements regarding "men of all faiths") and differentiated (in references to specific communities, such as the Buddhist *sangha*, Nirgranthas [Jains], and Brahman and Ajivika ascetics).

(3) The edicts simply assume the existence and persistence of other religions as a natural fact. Other religions are not seen as errors, accidents, or the consequence of evil, but instead as a constructive part of reality that comprise a morally productive society.

(4) In Ashoka's edicts, there is explicit tolerance of other religions along political and philosophical lines, which does not reflect the latent intolerance in the canonical texts in stories of ridicule aimed at the Buddha's would-be challengers. Simultaneously, for Ashoka, there is intolerance toward aberrations of practice and belief within a given religious order, especially within his own Buddhist *sangha*.

(5) Ashoka's expression of tolerance directly correlates with the historical, political, and behavioral aspects of the diversity of his kingdom. Likewise, the intolerance indicated for disrupters of the Buddhist *sangha* correlates with historical, theological, and behavioral factors. Ashoka's choices regarding tolerance and intolerance stem from his ethical agenda and are manifest in his policies. For Ashoka, true tolerance is the outward expression of inward moral development (*dhamma*), and an explicit policy of tolerance provides a framework for concomitant ethics to surface. The representation of *dhamma* by a turning wheel underscores the active nature of this policy.

1. The Role of Other Religions in the Ashokan Edicts

The narrative literature of early Buddhism illustrates that, at time of the Buddha in the fifth or sixth century BCE, there were several independent contractors on the spiritual front. In several stories, various charismatic teachers and ascetics meet with the Buddha and argue, debate, and compete for the attention and patronage of potential devotees or disciples. Meanwhile, the brahmanical tradition is envisioned as ceremony-laden and socially unfair and an incomplete path out of *samsara*.[12] The role of other religions represented in the canon, or *Tipitaka* (Sanskrit: *Tripitaka*), is that of a straw man to the Buddha's superior teaching. Other traditions are not entirely rejected, but the closer they appear to be to the Buddha's eremitic tradition, the more competition there is for resources (kingly patronage) and followers, the more they are ridiculed through narrative.

The edicts, on the other hand, presume the existence and indeed viability of various religions. A plurality of religions is seen as a natural consequence of the diversity of human sentiment, and the edicts suggest that other religions have value as conversation partners rather than theological competitors as depicted in the *Tipitaka* narratives. With the rise of Ashoka over two hundred years after the *parinibbana*[13] of the Buddha, we see the religions that arose in the theological foment of the fifth and sixth centuries BCE fully routinized after the passing of their various charismatic founders. In Ashoka's society, even single families seem accepting of diversity. Ashoka's own grandfather Candragupta, the founder of the Mauryan Dynasty and unifier of the sixteen *mahajanapadas* (separate countries) under one kingdom, is thought to have renounced and become a Jain late in life, while Ashoka's father Bindusara may have aligned with the Ajivika sect.

For Ashoka, other faiths have inherent self-worth as well as occupy a crucial role as a mirror to reflect and amplify one's own faith. "The faiths of others all deserve to be honored for one reason or another. By honoring them, one exalts one's own faith and at the same time performs a service to the faith of others."[14] As we will see in the next section, the role of other religions represented in the Ashokan edicts is to act as edifying conversation partners and appropriate recipients of respect and support in one's religious practice.

2. Treatment of Other Religions in the Ashokan Edicts

Ashoka rose to power in a period of religious diversity not unlike that of the Buddha's era a couple of centuries before him and not that unlike the religious scenario today. Ashoka began his reign as a power-hungry conqueror, called Candashoka (Ashoka the Terrible) in the narrative literature, a moniker earned for his rampant destructive behavior in the Kalinga conquest and in the murders of his ninety-nine brothers. But he was remorseful for his bad behavior and discovered the *dhamma*; his conversion rendered him Dhammashoka (Ashoka of the *Dhamma* or "Righteous Ashoka"). It appears that, at the time, religious affiliation was a matter of some degree of choice, if Ashoka's family history and the account of his own conversion to Buddhism are to be believed.

In light of this environment of flux and diverse faiths and practices, it is interesting to consider the medium Ashoka chose for his pronouncements. Pillars function in a certain way on the landscape; they generally proclaim in a not-so-subtle fashion one's conquest or dominion over the land below. Ashoka's rock and pillar edicts appear at the boundaries of his kingdom, as far away as Girnar in the west, Jaugada in the east, Taksasila and Kandahar in the northwest, and Brahmagiri in the south. They are located on trade routes and within the environs of Buddhist monasteries. They are written in a *prakrit* (Magadhi), usually in the Brahmi script (but there are examples of other regionally salient scripts, such as Greek and Aramaic in the northwest). The fact that regional linguistic variations occur suggests that these were intended to be read by local audiences, and not merely erected to fulfill some ceremonial function. There are even inscriptions within secluded meditation caves in the Barabar Hills, some of which were dedicated for use by

Ajivika ascetics rather than Ashoka's own community of Buddhists. This is evidence that Ashoka followed his own dictum to support alternate religious orders. Edicts proclaim a certain kind of social welfare, including the building of rest houses and wells along roads, and there is archaeological evidence that Ashoka practiced what he preached.[15]

The edict that most directly addresses the topic of tolerance is from Kalinga, the area where his brutal military campaign purportedly had been the catalyst for his acceptance of Buddhism. Rock Edict XII reads as follows:

King Priyadarshi honors all faiths, members of religious orders and laymen alike, with gifts and various marks of esteem. Yet he does not value either gifts or honors as much as growth in the qualities essential to religion in men of all faiths. This growth may take many forms, but its root is in guarding one's speech to avoid extolling one's own faith and disparaging the faith of others improperly or, when the occasion is appropriate, immoderately. The faiths of others all deserve to be honored for one reason or another. By honoring them, one exalts one's own faith and at the same time performs a service to the faith of others. By acting otherwise, one injures one's own faith and also does disservice to that of others. For if a man extols his own faith and disparages another because of devotion to his own and because he wants to glorify it, he seriously injures his own faith. Therefore concord[16] alone is commendable, for through concord men may learn and respect the conception of Dharma accepted by others. King Priyadarshi desires men of all faiths to know each other's doctrines and to acquire sound doctrines. Those who are attached to their particular faiths should be told that King Priyadarshi does not value gifts or honors as much as growth in the qualities essential to religion in men of all faiths. Many officials [dhamma mahamatras] are assigned to tasks bearing on this purpose—the officers in charge of spreading Dharma, the superintendents of women in the royal household, the inspectors of cattle and pasture lands, and other officials. The objective of these measures is the promotion of each man's particular faith and the glorification of Dharma.[17]

Within the corpus of the Ashokan edicts, therefore, we see that other religions are not only endured but are actively embraced as religiously constitutive. Furthermore, there is a simple message of tolerance conveyed that many religious views can share a space and engage in dialogue and mutual respect.

While not at all dismissed, within the edicts, the other religions are treated rather generically, lumped together under the umbrella term of "all faiths." The different sects, in fact, shared a common lexicon and some cosmological and philosophical points. However, Ashoka likely would have been alert to the subtle distinctions among the various sects prevalent in his day considering the variety of religious leanings in his own family. There may be an embedded argument for the superiority of his own faith and "glorification of the dhamma" in this edict, in spite of its ostensible focus on genuine tolerance. The general use of "other faiths" may have been a rhetorical device

whereby Ashoka distinguishes his Buddhist faith as a morally weighty counterpart to all other variant faiths combined. Additionally, despite the commonalities among these "other" religious traditions, the very existence of this
edict may provide evidence for sectarian tension. Perhaps a strain of intolerance provoked this proclamation by Ashoka; we may never know.

In some instances, the various faiths are specified within an edict. However, the specific communities are named as beneficiaries of the guidance
and care of Ashoka's own missionary officers, presupposing a hegemonic
relationship over the "other" faiths. In Pillar Edict VII, for example, Ashoka
announces the appointment of "officers charged with the spread of Dharma,
called *Dharma-mahamatras*." Under the guise of care and tolerance, Ashoka
intends to spread the *dhamma*, even when they are charged with looking
"after the affairs" of others:

My officers charged with the spread of Dharma are occupied with various kinds of
services beneficial to ascetics and householders, and they are empowered to concern
themselves with all sects. I have ordered some of them to look after the affairs of the
Sangha [the Buddhist religious orders], some to take care of the Brahman and Ajivika
ascetics, some to work among the Nirgranthas [the Jaina monks], and some among
the various other religious sects. Different officials are thus assigned specifically to
the affairs of different religions, but my officers for spreading Dharma are occupied
with all sects.[18]

3. How the Ashokan Edicts Account for the Existence and Persistence of Other Religions as a Constructive Part of Reality

The *suttas*[19] show that, at time of the Buddha, many seekers, not just the Buddha, were in search of Truth. Other religions were conceived as more or less
effective means to the same end. They were not considered the consequence
of evil forces, only the natural efflorescence of humanity's search for the truth,
the many paths reflective of the many sensibilities of men. Aside from brahmanical *shruti* (revelation) literature, the religions themselves were understood
to be human constructs. Most were shepherded by a charismatic teacher figure. The Buddha himself was such a charismatic teacher, who chose to share
his observations of the truth with humanity.

Many have observed that the Buddha's core teaching of the Four Noble
Truths represents a physician's course of observation, attribution of a cause,
diagnosis/prognosis, and prescription of a cure.[20] This is an overly simplistic
rendering of the Buddha's *dhamma*, but it illustrates the observant and didac-
tic nature of the *dhamma*, and the need for a primed and able doctor-figure to
administer or perpetuate it.

In Ashoka's use of the term, there is a presumption that *dhamma* simply is a fundamental, underlying, even unifying principle that all religions share. With the right oversight (from his *mahamatras*), people of all faiths can be oriented to the *dhamma* as a most common denominator, a unifying ethical structure. This sentiment is echoed in many contemporary inclusive- and pluralism-minded theologians, even in Gandhi's writings, that "all religions are true" insofar as true means revealing of Truth (capital "T") rather than valid or right.[21]

In the edicts, the existence of other faiths is understood as a simple truth, each being a constructive part of reality. They are certainly not evidence of evil at play in the world. This explains what may be anachronistically perceived as an inclusivist or even pluralist tone in Rock Edict XII; the other faiths were not a challenge to Ashoka's own faith, and he even went so far as to admonish the attempt to overtly proselytize others. That said, the omnipresence of his religious ministers suggests at least a subtle attempt at effecting conversions and more likely an exertion of authoritative control over others.

4. Which Teachings within the Ashokan Edicts Justify Tolerance of Other Religions, and Which Justify Intolerance?

Buddhism is not a monolith, nor was it at the time of Ashoka. There must have been some room in the *sangha* for divergent views of other religions, if not philosophically, then practically. However, even though the edicts are issued over the course of a couple of decades, Ashoka's tolerant attitude remains fairly consistent. What does evolve within his relatively consistent vision, however, is a developing intolerant attitude toward wayward or disruptive monks and nuns within the *sangha* itself. Perhaps he has a more generous outlook toward the Buddhist laity and participants (virtuosi and lay) of other faiths than he has of the Buddhist *sangha*. Not all of the edicts proclaim tolerance. In fact, a vehemently intolerant attitude is directed toward the *sangha* itself.

Even though Ashoka seems most concerned with matters of personal conviction and virtue, the communal and behavioral aspect of Buddhist practice becomes a point of contention in what is known as the schism edict. Here presented within the Sarnath Pillar Edict, we see that any monk or nun who "disrupts the Sangha" is to be expelled from residing in the community of monks or nuns (*anabasasi*) and shunned, even forced to wear white robes in lieu of the saffron robes of the monk in good standing:

... No one shall disrupt the Sangha. If a monk or nun disrupts the Sangha, he or she shall be required to put on a white robe and to live in non-residence. This edict should be published both in the Sangha of the monks and in the Sangha of the nuns. . . . Place one copy of this edict in the cloister of the vihara; give another copy to the lay disciples. . . .[22]

The edicts of Ashoka are essentially nondoctrinal, as they are issued from the king rather than from the *sangha*. As such, they do not adequately reflect doctrinal fault lines that, in fact, may have existed. They do, however, reflect the practical divide between the heightened expectations for a member of the *sangha* and the laity. There may be explicit tolerance for other faiths, but there is little tolerance for any faith poorly executed/practiced, especially by the Buddhist monks who are expected to be the pinnacle of Buddhist propriety and moral edification. The example of intolerance is directed internally at the community of monks is particular to practical rather than theological concerns and includes the request for assistance by the laity in enforcement.

5. The Historical, Political, and Behavioral Factors That Correlate with the Expression of Tolerance in the Ashokan Edicts and How We May Explain the Choices Ashoka Made

Ashoka's expression of tolerance directly correlates with the historical, political, and behavioral aspects underlying the diversity of his kingdom. Likewise, the intolerance he chooses to unleash upon disrupters within the Buddhist *sangha* also correlates with historical, theological, and behavioral factors. Ashoka's choices regarding tolerance and intolerance are directly informed by his ethical agenda. These choices are made public and manifest in his policies. True tolerance for Ashoka is the secondary, outward expression of the prerequisite and more fundamental inward moral development (*dhamma*). To ensure that his people could rise to his expectations for behavior and ethics, his explicit policy of tolerance provides the structure within which the right ethics of tolerance could be cultivated.

Historically speaking, Ashoka's *dhamma* agenda, or policy of tolerance, responds to the diversity of his polity. Politically, Ashoka was able to keep a disparate and vast polity more or less unified, partly because of his communication with and express concern for the far reaches of his domain. Behaviorally, he literally wrote his objectives in stone so that they might outlast him:

This edict on Dharma has been inscribed in order that it may endure and be followed as long as [my] sons and great-grandsons [shall reign and] as long as the sun and moon [shall shine]. . . . This edict on morality should be engraved wherever stone pillars or stone slabs are available, in order that it may endure forever.[23]

Dhamma is the foundation of Ashoka's public and private agendas, his policy and his religious outlook. For Ashoka, *dhamma* is a fundamentally ethical and universally accessible principle. Romila Thapar observes, "Moving away at one level from the usual hegemony of imperial systems, he was nevertheless endorsing a process equally important to imperial needs, namely, acculturation. This he sought to encourage through a policy of persuasive assimilation in which conforming to the ethical ideals of *dhamma* was encouraged."[24] For Ashoka, his *dhamma* was the vehicle for social welfare, as we see in the results of his alignment with *dhamma* manifested in the building of roads, wells, and medical facilities, among other generous acts. But *dhamma* also served political ends, as a universally salient point of discourse promulgated by a savvy and seemingly genuinely earnest king to unify his unwieldy kingdom (in both geographical size and demographic diversity).

While *dhamma* in the Ashokan sense is often referred to as his law or policy—and it was policy—perhaps another sense of our English word *law* is called for. For Ashoka, *dhamma* is a natural law, such as the natural law of gravity or more proper to the Indic context of his day, the law of *karma*. The law of virtue fulfills man's natural inclinations to be tolerant and to be oriented toward good. *Dhamma* just exists, and it is perceived in action (to see *dhamma*, one is good to people, just as to perceive gravity, the apple drops). It is, thus, an egalitarian, universally salient, ethical concept. It sounds idealistic and perhaps overly simplistic, but the idea behind the policy of *dhamma* is that good begets good, and adherence to *dhamma* would, thus, heighten the moral value of Ashoka's people, all his people, regardless of sectarian affiliation or orientation. The intended result of all the resulting good behavior is the goal of any righteous monarch—a kingdom built on a cultivated moral life of his subjects.

Unlike the narrow usage of *dhamma* in the Buddhist texts to mean the teachings (basic and profound) of the Buddha, Ashoka's use of *dhamma* was expansive and, therefore, inclusive in nature. "It is apparent that the principles of *Dhamma* were acceptable to people belonging to any religious sect. . . . Of the basic principles, the one on which Ashoka laid most stress and which he repeated frequently was that of toleration. Toleration according to him was of two kinds: a toleration of people themselves and also a toleration of people's beliefs and ideas."[25]

Conclusion

In his keynote address to this collection of essays, William Scott Green frames our project in terms of the ubiquitous diversity of the present day:

Diversity is now a ubiquitous fact of life. . . . For the world's religions, this is an important new condition. Not only do religions imagine one another in doctrine, in principle, and in theory; they now experience and engage one another increasingly in practice. No religion, whatever its doctrine may say, can pretend that it is the only one here, or even that it is the only one succeeding, at least in earthly terms.[26]

Upon reflection, it appears that diversity was a very real condition in the Ashokan landscape. Ashoka confronted the diversity issue and rendered a model policy that was salient and attractive for new territories, border communities, both rural and urban environments, as well as the virtuosi in the Buddhist *sangha*, the laity, and even communities of other faiths.

In spite of the tenor of inclusivity present in Ashoka's idea of *dhamma*, the social landscape of the day was dominated by caste prescriptions and restrictions and concomitant systems of ethics. Buddhism shared a similar lexicon of terms and concepts with several religious movements of its day, including Brahmanism and Jainism, and perhaps a somewhat universal familiarity with the concept *dhamma* provided Ashoka with the ability to cast his policy of tolerance in palatable terms. To some degree, toleration presupposes a power relationship and definite hierarchy between the one in a position of tolerating and the one being tolerated. This was never denied or hidden in the edicts of Ashoka, who was, after all, politically in charge.

Perhaps this classic model for toleration from the ubiquitous diversity of a bygone era can be of use for contemporary dialogue. Of course, the consideration of tolerance must proceed for us without an all-powerful king making pronouncements that are inscribed for public consumption, fixed in stone for posterity. India's continued bursts of violence stemming from religious intolerance illustrates that, in spite of the emblematic wheel of *dhamma* on the flag and the ancient pronouncements of tolerance on pillars and rocks, actions speak louder.

Notes

1. Romila Thapar notes that Greek terms were used to illustrate the universality of the concept of *dhamma*: "The word *dhamma* is translated as *eusebia* meaning 'piety, loyalty, reverence for the gods and for parents.'" Romila Thapar, *Ashoka and the Decline of the Mauryas* (New York: Oxford University Press, 1997), 276.

2. Mahavamsa XII; see *The Mahavamsa*, ed. Wilhelm Geiger (London: Pali Text Society, 1908), and *The Mahāvamsa or The Great Chronicle of Ceylon*, trans. Wilhelm Geiger and Mabel Haynes Bode (London: Pali Text Society, 1912).

3. Pali is related to Sanskrit. The *vamsas* are a genre of literature most often called chronicles or histories, and they interweave accounts of what seem like historically plausible events with retellings of colorful legends and miracles.

4. Jules Bloch, ed. and trans., *Les inscriptions d'Ashoka* (Paris: Les Belles Lettres, 1950); N. A. Nikam and Richard McKeon, ed. and trans., *The Edicts of Ashoka* (Chicago: University of Chicago Press, 1959).

5. Romila Thapar, "Asoka and Buddhism," *Past and Present* 18 (November 1960): 45.

6. This characterization is beyond our scope. On the attribution (perhaps anachronistic) of *cakkavattin*, see Stanley Jeyaraja Tambiah, *World Conqueror and World Renouncer* (Cambridge: Cambridge University Press, 1976); A.L. Basham, "Ashoka and Buddhism: A Reexamination," *Journal of the International Association of Buddhist* Studies 5 (1982): 1; F. Kern, *Ashoka* (Bern: Francke Verlag, 1956); Romila Thapar, *Ashoka and the Decline of the Mauryas* (New York: Oxford University Press, 1997), 146.

7. From Rock Edict XIII, the Kalinga conquest would be dated about 259 BCE. Ashoka's characterization of his "conversion," the salient passages of this edict, read as follows:

> The Kalinga country was conquered by King Priyadarshi, Beloved of the Gods, [in] the eighth year of his reign. One hundred fifty thousand persons were carried away captive, one hundred thousand were slain, and many times that number died. Immediately after the Kalingas had been conquered, King Priyadarshi became intensely devoted to the study of Dharma, to the love of Dharma, and to the inculcation of Dharma. The Beloved of the Gods, conqueror of the Kalingas, is moved to remorse now. For he has felt profound sorrow and regret. . . . King Priyadarshi considers moral conquest [that is, conquest by Dharma, *Dharma-vijaya*] the most important conquest. . . .

See Nikam and McKeon, 27–29.

8. Maski Rock Edict in Nikam and McKeon, 66; Bloch, 145–46.

9. Bhabra Rock Edict, Nikam and McKeon, 66–67; Bloch, 154.

10. This tripartite formulation is also known as the triple refuge and is as close as the Buddhist tradition comes to a creedal formulation.

11. Ashoka reflects on the process of tuning his people into the *dhamma* in Pillar Edict VII: "The people can be induced to advance in Dharma by only two means, by moral prescriptions and by meditation. Of the two, moral prescriptions are of little consequence, but meditation is of great importance. The moral prescriptions I have promulgated include rules making certain animals inviolable, and many others. But even in the case of abstention from injuring and from killing living creatures, it is by meditation that people have progressed in Dharma most." See Nikam and McKeon, 40.

12. *Samsara* is a pan-Indic concept that refers to this world and the ongoing cycle of birth-life-death it entails.

13. *Parinibbana* (Sanskrit: *parinirvana*) is the death and ultimate cessation, the "snuffing-out" of the Buddha.

14. Nikam and McKeon, 51–52.

15. See Dilip K. Chakrabarti, "Buddhist Sites across South Asia as Influenced by Political and Economic Forces," *Buddhist Archaeology* 27, no. 2 (October 1995): 196–97. This was a special volume of *World Archaeology*.

16. The term *samavayo* literally means "coming together" and thus may refer more to a religious dialogue than to a concordance of beliefs or to peace.

17. Nikam and McKeon, 51–52. Also see J. Bloch, *Les Inscriptions d'Ashoka* (Paris: Les Belles Lettres, 1950), 121.

18. Nikam and McKeon, 34–35.

19. Sanskrit: *sutra*, the "sermons" of the Buddha contained in the *Tipitaka*.

20. The Four Noble Truths are, briefly: 1. All life is dis-ease; 2. There is a cause to the dis-ease (craving and clinging against the inevitability of flux); 3. There is an end to dis-ease; 4. The way to the end is following the Noble Eightfold Path (a series of right behaviors).

21. See Mohandas K. Gandhi, *All Religions Are True* (Bombay: Bharatiya Vidya Bhavan, 1962).

22. Nikam and McKeon, 68.

23. Pillar Edict VII, Nikam and McKeon, 35–36.

24. Thapar, *Ashoka and the Decline of the Mauryas*, 309.

25. Thapar, "Ashoka and Buddhism,": 49.

26. William Scott Green, this volume, p. 3.

15

A POLICY OF INTOLERANCE

The Case of Sinhala Buddhist Nationalism

BRADLEY S. CLOUGH

In their long history as members of a religion spread across the continent of Asia and in their more recent history as members of the fastest-growing religious groups in Europe and North America, Buddhists have shown remarkably little intolerance of people of other ethnicities and/or religions. But to make such an assertion count, we must define what is meant by "intolerance." To not tolerate something is to find it unacceptable and unallowable. For members of a religion to practice intolerance, they, therefore, must be actively involved in trying to suppress others' ways of life or prevent others' ways of life from being carried out.

Buddhist Critiques of Other Religions and Assertions of Superiority

With respect to other people's religions, Buddhism's various forms have generally been quite tolerant, according to this definition. In looking at the spread and establishment of various forms of Buddhism across Asia, we find few wars of conquest, forced conversion campaigns, or policies of persecution. Instead, we find Buddhism repeatedly coexisting with or assimilating indigenous religious traditions. The common pattern has been for Buddhism to absorb animistic or theistic elements. This is usually accompanied by a narrative of the Buddha or another great Buddhist master winning over a country's spirits and gods by making them "protectors of the *dharma*." Acknowledging the existence of spirits or gods is largely in keeping with the Buddhist worldview, which includes powerful deities and other benevolent and malevolent spiritual forces. Thus, we have Sri Lankan Buddhists worshiping their *devas*, Burmese Buddhists propitiating their *nats*, and a Tibetan Buddhist pantheon that includes scores of deities not found in the Indian Buddhist world from which so many Tibetan Buddhist traditions descended. Perhaps the most telling example comes from Japan where, not long after Buddhism's inception there, one could find images of *bodhisattvas* on the grounds of the shrines of Japan's indigenous Shinto religion and shrines to the Shinto *kami* on the grounds of Buddhist temples. *Kami* were seen as counterparts of *bodhisattvas* and vice versa. By medieval times, the concept of *honji-suijaku*, borrowed from China, pervaded Japanese religion. According to this theory, Shinto *kami* were the "manifest traces" (*suijaku*) of the "original substance" (*honji*) of particular Buddhas and *bodhisattvas*.[1]

Despite occasional monkish censure of the worship of spirits or gods, the Buddhist division of religious practices into those that are "worldly" (Sanskrit: *laukika*) and those that are supermundane (Sanskrit: *lokottara*) has made accommodation easy. The spirits and gods may be worshiped in order to improve one's condition in this world, for such beings do have power over the state of the world; but when it comes to ultimate matters of a better rebirth and release from suffering, only Buddhist practices are deemed efficacious.

Furthermore, the earliest extant Buddhist scriptures repeatedly present the Buddha as one who discovers, analyzes, and observes, and whose doctrine is experientially verifiable (Pali: *ehipassaka*, literally "come and seeable"). Being this kind of religious seeker and teacher stands the Buddha in contrast with any divinely chosen receiver and authoritative giver of religious law, whose doctrine is to be unquestioningly obeyed.[2] Thus, the Buddha and his teaching yield tolerance because they leave open the possibility of others discovering aspects of truth or whole truth for themselves.[3] Indeed, Buddhism posits this possibility in the person of the "solitary Buddha" (Sanskrit: *pratyekabuddha*) who discovers the truth that liberates from suffering without previously having heard a Buddha's teaching.[4]

As far as its attitude toward other religions is concerned, Buddhism has typically adopted a position of what K. N. Jayatilleke has called "critical tolerance."[5] It has developed critiques of what it sees as typical religious worldviews, but it does not go as far as to say that people should not be allowed to pursue them, and, in some cases, it regards other religions as putting forth at least partially true understandings of reality. A typical example comes from the *Sandaka Sutta*, in which the Buddha details four doctrines that are not conducive to the holy life (Pali: *abrahmacariyavasa*) and four doctrines that hold some truth but are ultimately "unsatisfactory" (Pali: *anassasikam*). The former four are: (1) materialism—there is only one physical existence; (2) any doctrine that encourages immoral actions; (3) any doctrine that denies free will and moral responsibility; and (4) any doctrine that teaches that there is an inevitable end to suffering, regardless of the nature of one's actions. The latter four teach commendable doctrines like life after death (in the Buddhist context this means rebirth), moral free will and responsibility, and the non inevitability of suffering's end, unless religiously profitable measures are taken. These doctrines, however, lack a reliable foundation because they are based on one or more of the following: (1) the omniscience of its founder; (2) revelation or tradition; (3) logical and metaphysical speculation; and (4) pragmatic skepticism or agnosticism.[6]

While the former set of doctrines most closely apply to religious philosophies of the Buddha's own environment, it is easier to take the latter set and apply them to other world religions, a few of which do claim the omniscience of their founder and many of which are based on revelation and tradition and engage at least occasionally in logical or metaphysical speculation. As indicated above, the Buddha's concern seems to be in distinguishing what he called "evidenced faith" (Pali: *akaravati saddha*) from what he considered "baseless faith" (Pali: *amulika saddha*). The Buddha's positions in this area are reinforced in his oft-cited "Sermon to the Kalamas" (Kalama Sutta[7]), in which the Buddha advocates that no teaching be followed merely on the grounds of tradition or repeated hearings, scripture, logical conjecture, predisposition to an idea, and the apparent ability and status of the teacher. Rather, the basis for accepting a teaching should be that, when it is undertaken and carried out, it leads to results that are of religious profit—namely, well-being and happiness—and praised by the wise.

The claims of the brahmanical religion of the Buddha's day that the brahman class was a religiously superior one whose members' sacrificial rituals were beneficial, were also dismissed as baseless and unverifiable by personal experience. Of these claims, the Buddha said that no Brahman was in a position to say, "I see this; I know this."[8]

Furthermore, if we look at the Buddhist stance on an all-powerful God who is the uncaused Creator of everything, we see that it is dismissive of a cardinal belief of Judaism, Christianity, Islam, and the monotheistic strains of Hinduism.[9] Based on the fundamental doctrine of *pratitya-samutpada* (Sanskrit), which holds that every phenomenon always arises in dependence upon some related previous condition, Buddhist philosophers have maintained that it is impossible for any cause to exist that is not also an effect, brought about by something else. Thus, the idea of God as a self-abiding, uncaused First Cause is a contradiction in terms, logically inconsistent and unverifiable.[10] From its beginnings, Buddhism has acknowledged a divine ruler of the universe or king of the gods, but the texts portray him as deluding other gods and beings (and even himself!),[11] that, because his power is greater and life is longer than other beings, he must have created his own power and, therefore, all things.[12] Lastly, Buddhism maintains that belief in such a God leads to ethical degradation. They have maintained that if someone thinks that God takes care of all matters, it is easy for that person either to regard personal deeds as predestined by God or to believe that God forgives all actions, right or wrong. In either case, one does not take responsibility for one's own deeds.[13]

While one cannot say, as was shown at the outset, that Buddhists have been atheists, these positions and others like them show us that Buddhism has thought of itself as a religion superior to any one that was theistically *centered*. This was clearly articulated by that most influential of Japanese Buddhist masters Kukai (774–835 CE) who, in his famous ranking of religious systems, relegated theistically oriented traditions like Hinduism and religious Taoism to the lowly stage of the "fearless infant." This was stage three in Kukai's ten-tiered system. Stages four to ten were assigned to different forms of Buddhism. Thus, any form of Buddhism is said to be superior to any non-Buddhist religion.[14]

Yet, however sharp doctrinal critiques of other forms of religious thought and practice have been and however much Buddhists have distanced their supposedly superior means to liberation from suffering from others' means, they have not in themselves typically produced policies of intolerance. But in looking for Buddhist intolerance, we cannot simply look to scriptures and expect to find any direct correlation with specific Buddhist behaviors. Here we would do well to heed Stanley Tambiah's words that,

> The canonical texts of Buddhism . . . are complex and rich in meaning . . . capable of different levels of interpretation. . . . Any perspective that naively assumes that there are certain unambiguous prescriptions and value orientations in Buddhism from which can be deduced behavioral correlates that bear an intrinsic and inherent relation to the religion is inaccurate, usually misguided, and sometimes pernicious.[15]

To find Buddhist intolerance, then, we must look instead to the local and the particular, and, in doing, so we discover history revealing that, in modern times especially, some Buddhists or Buddhist-led governments have been actively intolerant; that is, they have sought to prevent others from freely practicing their religion or from otherwise carrying out their way of life in a manner in which they enjoyed the same rights and privileges as Buddhists. So what factors do produce Buddhist policies of intolerance? It will be my thesis here that a much more totalizing discourse than typical doctrinal expression is required, a discourse that closely ties religion to politics, ethnic or national identity, and land in a way that leads to completely hegemonic (or almost completely hegemonic) claims. I will argue that this certainly has been the case with respect to one well-known case of Buddhist intolerance in recent times, that being the intolerance that has stemmed from Sinhala Buddhist chauvinism and nationalism in Sri Lanka. This chapter will attempt to trace the development of this form of Buddhist intolerance and identify the factors that have contributed to it.

Roots of a Buddhist Policy of Intolerance: Lankan Chronicle Literature

Outside of its strictly canonical writings, Sinhala Buddhism has produced a large literature of officially noncanonical historical chronicles that, nevertheless, have enjoyed authority and influence that equal and often outstrip that of even the most well-known scriptures in its official canon. Sinhala Buddhism has produced many such chronicles, with the most well known and influential being the *Mahavamsa* or "Great Lineage," produced in the fifth century CE by Lanka's leading monastic community.[16] Attesting to the central place of the *Mahavamsa* in the lives of Sinhala Buddhists, Steven Kemper has written:

The *Mahavamsa* occupies the same position in Sinhala society that the *Ramayana* holds in Indian society. People know the tradition before they know that they know it. As children, they hear shreds and patches of the tradition recited, they see temple paintings evoking it, or they follow cartoons in Sinhala newspapers representing the lives of righteous kings. As they grow older, they discover that there is an historical chronicle from which the episodes derive.[17]

Scholars have long recognized that the *Mahavamsa* and other chronicles are much more than straightforward retellings of historical events. Heinz Bechert has said of the chronicle tradition that,

The origin of historical literature in Ceylon . . . was an intentional act of political relevance. Its object was the propagation of a concept of national identity clearly connected with religious tradition, i.e., the identity of Sinhalese Buddhists. . . . Without the impact of this idea, the remarkable continuity of the cultural as well as of the political traditions in spite of vicissitudes in the history of the island would be impossible.[18]

Gananath Obeyesekere has remarked that the roots of Sinhala Buddhist violence and intolerance toward others are in its historical, rather than in its doctrinal, writings,[19] and indeed, as Bechert suggests above, the chronicles are highly polemical works. In them, myth is argument, pushing for an understanding of Lankan history that is thorough in its Sinhala Buddhist triumphalism. The *vamsas* or "lineages" that chronicles like the *Dipavamsa*, *Mahavamsa*, *Culavamsa*, *Buddhavamsa*, and *Thupavamsa*[20] narrate are genealogies of Sinhalese Buddhist kings who protect the land's asserted pure Buddhist heritage by patronizing the *sasana* or Buddhist religion and fighting off the Tamil people, who are largely portrayed as outsiders, interlopers, invaders, and usurpers. Furthermore, the chronicles are ideological, emphasizing above all the unbreakable unity of polity, ethnicity, land, and religion. It should be acknowledged at this point that the chronicles are complex texts with multiple layers of meaning. Nevertheless, while recognizing that cultural artifacts are rarely if ever single discourses, but are rather universes of discourses in which different ones contend with and play off each other,[21] there is no denying the long-lasting influence of this particular totalizing discourse of the chronicles. And as we will see in a moment when we look at examples from the chronicles, the chronicles also function to separate Lanka's Sinhalas from its Tamils, to demonize these Tamils, to assert that the land has a sacred destiny that is wholly Buddhist, and that, therefore, only Sinhala kings have the right to rule, in order to protect this holy legacy.

The chronicles' myth of origin of the Sinhala people tells of their progenitor, Prince Vijaya, journeying from his homeland in north India to the island where he, along with his seven hundred male cohorts, encounter *yakkhas* or demons, whom they slaughter. Vijaya goes on to establish a new order there and founds various settlements throughout Lanka. He is made king, takes an Indian princess as his queen, and begins the "great lineage" of Sinhala kings in the land. Bruce Kapferer, in his analysis of the chronicles' myths, has remarked that, as ideologies, they are filled with the meaning of the times in which they are *written* (my emphasis).[22] I would argue, as we will see throughout this investigation, that the myths are filled with the meanings of the times in which they are *read*. This can be seen in the Sinhalas' increasing emphasis, especially in modern times, on their self-identity as "Aryans" from north India, as opposed to "Damilas," whom Sinhalas almost invariably interpret as South Indian Dravidian Tamils. Thus, the place of origin of the queen, which suggests that she was from south India and, therefore, that the Sinhala people of Lanka are of mixed ancestry, is usually glossed over in later readings that assert the "pure Aryan" stock of the Sinhalas.

Even more important in the establishment of Sinhala Buddhist chauvinism and eventual nationalism are the chronicles' tellings of the Buddha's visits to Lanka. As in the Vijaya myth, the Buddha on his first visit finds the island overrun with *yakkha* demons, whom the Buddha judges too inferior to receive his *dhamma* (Sanskrit: *dharma*). The Buddha's mission, the chronicles tell, is to purify and consecrate Lanka so that it may realize his prophetic vision of it as the future *dhammadipa* or "island of the [Buddhist] doctrine,"[23] where "his teachings will shine in glory."[24] A noteworthy feature of the Buddha's conquest of Lanka and his preparation of it as a "fit dwelling for men"[25] to practice and protect Buddhist *dhamma* is the violent nature of his defeat of the demons. Unlike the earlier canonical portrayals of how the Buddha subdues opponents with pacification, in the chronicles he strikes fear in the demons, visiting terrible storms and darkness upon them.[26]

On two subsequent visits to Lanka, the Buddha further clears the ground for the future establishment of the *dhamma* by overcoming other nonhuman inhabitants, again by forceful means. With these forces out of the way, the Buddha predicts that the island will now become the *dhammadipa* in the hands of the descendants of Vijaya, who lands on the island on the very day of the Buddha's final passing into nirvana.[27] Moving ahead in the chronicles' account, King Asoka ensures the buddhacization of Lanka, prefigured but yet to be actualized in the Buddha's visits, when he sends his monk son Mahinda and his nun daughter Sanghamitta to establish the *sangha* or Buddhist monastic community there. Mahinda meets the then-current Sinhala ruler, King Devanampiyatissa, who converts and provides the necessary support for Asoka's offspring to spread the *dharma* throughout the island and for the monks to be "lords upon the island."[28]

As we will see, the *dhammadipa* concept powerfully informs Sinhala Buddhist chauvinism and nationalism in the modern and contemporary periods, often feeding intolerance toward any perceived outsiders who might threaten the land's special Buddhist mission. What the *dhammadipa* concept has meant to so many Sinhalas over history is perhaps most succinctly summarized in this passage from the thirteenth-century chronicle, the *Pujavaliya*:

The island of Lanka belongs to the Buddha himself; it is a like a treasury filled with the Three Gems. Therefore, the residence of wrong-believers on this island will never be permanent, just as the residence of the demons of old was not permanent. Even if a non-Buddhist ruled Lanka by force [for] a while, it is the particular power of the Buddha that his lineage will not be established. Therefore Lanka is only suitable for Buddhist kings; it is certain that their lineages will be established.[29]

The *Mahavamsa* has functioned as a charter for how Sinhala Buddhists—especially the monks and kings, but the laity as well—should act in order to maintain their political, ethnic, geographic, and religious heritage; and it has provided a rationale for why it is good and meritorious to do so. No narrative has contributed more to this charter and rationale as they are understood by Sinhala Buddhist chauvinists than the victory of the Sinhala king Dutthagamani (Sinhala: Dutugemenu) over the Tamil king Elara, purported to have taken place in the mid-second century BCE. This legend is filled with Buddhist triumphal significance. Elara is portrayed as a usurping outsider who threatens the destiny of Lanka as the preserve of Buddhism, having taken over the north of the island and the capital at Anuradhapura, sacralized by Mahinda's planting of a bodhi tree sapling there and the enshrining of Buddha relics in the great stupa built there. Dutthagamani brings five hundred monks with him for blessings and protection in the final battle against Elara, which he declares is being fought "to bring glory to the doctrine."[30] But beyond this declaration, Dutthagamani commits a *saccikiriya* or "act of truth"—a noble declaration that is fulfilled if the wish it expresses is true. Dutthagamani's *saccikriya* is that, if he is fighting the battle not for sovereignty but for establishing the Buddha's religion forever, "may the armour . . . of my soldiers take the color of fire."[31] This is fulfilled, as he wins a decisive battle over the mighty Elara, who had not ceded power for fifteen years.

Alice Greenwald has observed that, if we look for thematic continuity between the *Mahavamsa*'s stories of the Buddha and Dutthagamani's conquests, the Tamils defeated by Dutthagamani become the typological equivalent of the demon *yakkhas*.[32] The evil nature of the Tamils is something that the chronicle tradition builds upon over the centuries, as Sinhala Buddhist chauvinism solidified and moved toward the modern Sinhala Buddhist nationalism that will be our main focus. Bruce Kapferer notes that, while the Elara of the *Mahavamsa* possesses some noble traits, a thirteenth-century chronicle, the *Pujavilaya*, portrays him as the unrighteous destroyer of monasteries, and a seventeenth-century chronicle, the *Rajavilaya*, equates his armies with the hordes of Mara, the demonic opponents of the Buddha. Kapferer maintains that the association of the Tamils with such evil is not simply ethnic prejudice or racist intolerance; it carries the additional metaphorical load of that which is demonic, outside, and subordinate. Furthermore, the Tamils in these narratives are not just a separate category of people, to be subjugated and discriminated against. They are "threateningly evil, striking at the very core of Sinhala Buddhist identity and existence."[33]

Kapferer's points are well taken, but surely an equally insidious contribution to Sinhalese Buddhist intolerance toward the mostly Hindu Tamils can be found as far back as the *Mahavamsa* itself. Like Asoka, Dutthagamani in the aftermath of his great conquest is filled with remorse at thousands of opponents who have gone to their deaths. But the outcomes of the Asoka and Dutthagamani stories are quite different. Like Asoka, Dutthagamani is able to make peace with himself, but it is at the consolation of eight *arahant* monks who come to comfort him, assuring him that, in the end, he has only killed one-and-a-half people, one who was a full convert and another who was a partial convert to Buddhism.[34] As for the thousands of other Tamils, the *Mahavamsa* says, "Unbelievers and men of evil life were the rest, not more to be esteemed than beasts. But as for you, you will bring glory to the religion of the Buddha in many ways. Therefore cast away care from your heart, O ruler of men."[35] Here we see one of the most fundamental moral principles of Buddhist doctrine—that of nonviolence (*ahimsa*)—overturned. And as Heinz Bechert has noted, this also signals the elimination in Sri Lanka of the Asokan program of tolerant, pluralist coexistence, and its replacement with an ideology that justifies any action in the defense of the sovereignty of one ethnic or national group (in this case the Sinhalas) and protection and sustenance of a single religion (in this case Buddhism).[36]

We have seen presented in the *Mahavamsa*, then, and in the other chronicle texts a kind of manifest destiny in which the Sinhala people are to conquer, unite, and rule the island of Lanka for the preservation and glory of the Buddhist religion. The texts supply the material that has fueled an ideology that unites one group of people with territory and religion and that sets up an alien group as threateningly opposed to this destiny and union.

Anagarika Dharmapala and the Makings of Sinhala Buddhist Intolerance

In making the leap from a fifth-century source to examine how Buddhist intolerance has manifested itself in a revivalist and nationalist movement that arose little over a century ago, some of Jacob Neusner's observations about the role and function of tradition are particularly salient. Neusner says that tradition is:

[s]omething . . . from the past which is made contemporary and transmitted because of its intense contemporaneity. Tradition imposes a dynamic relationship . . . between the remote past, with its authority based on a myth . . . and the remote future, with its power vested in the capacity to continue to vivify . . . a received legacy.[37]

Neusner continues:

> The point and purpose of tradition are not to pass on historical facts but both to create and interpret contemporary reality, to intervene in history. The interest in the past arises solely because of its paradigmatic value. . . . The past is not dead, is not past, specifically because it is paradigmatic.

The person most responsible for bringing the past—as it is told in the mytho-history of the chronicles—to the present is Anagarika Dharmapala, the architect of modern Sinhala Buddhist chauvinism and nationalism. Much has been written about the leading, central role that Dharmapala played in the revival of Buddhism and the promotion of Sinhala Buddhist nationalism.[38] Thus, our purpose here will not be to rehearse all of his programs and accomplishments; rather, it will be to focus on his rhetoric as it pertains to the formation of intolerant attitudes that later translated into intolerant action. Richard Gombrich and Gananath Obeyesekere have noted that one of the hallmarks of Dharmapala's Buddhist discourse was his abandonment of Buddhism's traditionally irenic treatment of other religions for a polemical stance[39] and that his politicization of Buddhism involved castigating all the non-Sinhala communities of Sri Lanka.[40] Indeed, despite his espousal of the superiority of Buddhism over other religions on the grounds of its historical record of nonviolence and nonpersecution, Dharmapala's thoughts on non-Buddhists laid the ideological framework for later discrimination and violence against other groups in the country, especially the Tamils, Hindu and Muslim alike. This occurred because of the powerful nature of Dharmapala's rhetoric and the widespread influence he had.

But before we turn to Dharmapala's expressions of intolerance, expressions that became part and parcel of the Sinhala Buddhist nationalism that he more than anyone else created, it is important to see how he perpetuated the notion of Lanka as the special preserve of the *dhamma* and thus revivified the chronicles' received legacy and made the past paradigmatic, to use Neusner's language. In his writings and speeches, Dharmapala frequently drew on the *Mahavamsa*'s myth of origins and invariably spoke of Sinhala culture as a "purely Aryan and purely religious civilization," that was never truly conquered by either "filthy pagan Tamils" or "European vandals," thus leaving the Sinhalas untainted by any "slave or savage blood."[41] He often waxed nostalgically about Lanka's uninterrupted twenty-two centuries of glorious civilization, begun when Asoka's son Mahinda promulgated the "humane religion," such that "Lanka, the pearl of the Indian ocean, the resplendent jewel, became the future repository of the pure dharma of the Tathagata."[42] One particular lengthy piece, titled "Buddhism, Past and Present," is basically a retelling of the chronicles' narrative of Sinhala Buddhist triumphalism but with some stinging embellishments added by Dharmapala. Through writings and speeches like these, Dharmapala reintroduced the chronicles' worldview to a wide Sinhala audience and strongly reinforced their demonizing of the Tamil other. According to Dharmapala's version of the *Mahavamsa*'s story of Sinhala origins, the "Yakkhus" [sic] whom the purely Aryan scion Vijaya conquered upon his arrival in Lanka, were a Dravidian tribe.[43] His version of Dutthagamani's truth act, victory, and consolation closely follows the *Mahavamsa*'s telling, although he goes beyond it in singling out the Tamil king Elara for particularly harsh reprobation, describing him as "fiercely antagonistic to Buddhism" and a destroyer of the holy monuments in sacred Anuradhapura, who committed his reign to full suspension of all religious activities.[44] Speaking of future warring Sinhala kings, they always took "sons of the Buddha" with them against the Tamils, showing that, like Dutthagamani, they fought purely in the spirit of religion. As for those Tamil kings who did rule part of the land at various points in history, Dharmapala issues a blanket condemnation that they all "made every effort to destroy the religion of the Buddha."[45] But in Dharmapala's version of history, their power and efforts were short lived, and, thus, Buddhism in Lanka became "the religion of the conqueror . . . completely identified with the racial individuality of the [Sinhala] people."[46] These Sinhalas were a race, Dharmapala continued, "free from foreign influences, untainted by alien customs, with the words of the Buddha as their guiding light. . . . Such was the glorious period of Buddhism in Ceylon in the days when the foreigner was not in the land."[47]

We find in Dharmapala's discourse a sharpening of the totalizing idea that to be Lankan is to be Sinhala and that to be Sinhala is to be Buddhist. He encourages a return to an imagined Sinhala civilization that, in his word, is "untainted" by any non-Buddhist influence or ways of life. But as we saw just above, a direct demonization against the Tamils was also perpetrated. They are clearly portrayed as a people whose presence in the country is most unwelcome, if not intolerable.

So, Dharmapala not only affirmed a particular Sinhala Buddhist identity but opposed it to other identities. As with the later Sinhala Buddhist chauvinism and nationalism that have been the offspring of Dharmapala, ethnic groups more than religions are the target of intolerance. But Dharmapala's vituperations did not spare religious groups either. Furthermore, just as he essentialized Sinhalas as invariably Buddhist, he regarded Tamils as essentially Hindu (but sometimes Muslim as well). Regarding Hindus, he often expressed an ambivalent attitude,[48] though this attitude did not prevent him from sometimes denouncing them outright. His mixed feelings stemmed from his conception that Buddhism and Hinduism were both religions of Aryan heritage, and his affections for India in general led him often to wish that Buddhism would soon return there to coexist in amity with Hinduism. But peaceful coexistence only went so far with him. In his tireless campaigning for the restoration of the Mahabodhi Stupa complex in Bodhgaya, he could not tolerate its control by those whom he called the "heads of the Hindu fakir establishment,"[49] the Shiva-worshiping lineage of priests who committed the atrocity of disfiguring some Buddha images into the "monstrous figures" of the Puranic pantheon.[50] Speaking of this pantheon, Dharmapala derisively commented that Hindus "suffer from a plethora of muddle headed deities," whose devotees "annex any god that comes their way" and who foolishly treat gods like people who will become angry if not fed.[51] In comparison with the Sinhalas and people of other Buddhist countries whose religion bestowed an enlightened intelligence upon them, the Hindus were mostly cast into dark ignorance, a condition that had much to do with the knowledge contained within the religion they profess.[52] From Dharmapala's perspective, Hinduism had much to benefit from Buddhism, and in his earliest writings, we find him wondering why Hindu theologians would abandon and attack a religion that rests on peace, love, and mercy, and, in so doing, destroy the very foundation that Buddhism gave their own Hindu religion.[53] Furthermore, he refused to conceive that perhaps Hinduism's greatest thinker, Shankara, could have ever opposed the Buddhists, as popular tradition says he did; instead Shankara's most likely targets were the "vulgar sects of Vaishnavas and Saivas."[54]

Of course, his country was inhabited not only by Hindus but by Christians and Muslims as well, and neither of these groups was spared Dharmapala's fierce condemnations. In the spirit of Sinhala Buddhist revivalism, Christianity, as the religion of the colonizers, was subject to strong attacks, and the country's Sinhala and Burgher Christians were mostly guilty by association with the imperialists and missionaries. Even Sinhalas who were Christians were seen as aliens, as is evidenced by writings from the late-nineteenth century that saw Sinhala Christian members of the government's Legislative Council as "sworn enemies"[55] unrepresentative of the Sinhala community, being followers of "a hostile faith . . . unfitted to act for Buddhists."[56]

Dharmapala judged Christianity on the fruits he saw it producing and the conduct of its exponents. He said that virtue in a religion is in its potentiality to bring peace and blessings on its followers, and he saw little of this in Christian history, which had produced much bloodshed, ignorance, and craven sensuality under the control of a decadent papal empire that had kept Europe in a state of wretched penury and hygienic darkness. And the admirable ethical teachings of Christ—which are a "hotch potch of Judaism, Brahmanism and Buddhism" in Dharmapala's eyes—exist only in the minds of theologians but are not lived-out examples among "ecclesiastical imbeciles" who are the religion's representatives.[57]

Speaking theologically, Dharmapala often expressed incredulity that "the more polite and cultured peoples of Aryan descent" could ever accept the God of Christianity, an ever-wrathful anthropomorphic deity of mythology. A God who loves the blood of his own son to appease his own anger for sins committed by others could not possibly be considered by thoughtful people to be possessed of love and forgiveness. Every "savage race" has its own totem deity, and the deity presented to Asiatic Aryans by Westerners could never win the respect of "cultured races" whose ancestors lived long before the introduction of the terrible concept of an angry god with the power to torture people in eternal damnation.[58] These comments make it clear that it was intolerable to Dharmapala that many of his fellow Sinhalas had converted to Christianity. This was nothing less than utterly ruinous, for "monotheistic peoples have always deteriorated when they are not inspired by fanaticism and hatred. Like religion like people."[59]

As for Muslims, they, like Christians, were assessed by the criteria of a history that Dharmapala selectively and often unrepresentatively constructed. According to Dharmapala's historical assessment, the Muslims, an "inhuman, barbarous race"[60] not only destroyed Buddhism in India[61] but erased the purity of Aryan India.[62] And as with Chrisitianity, its presence in the country could only be a corrupting one, for, wherever Islam established itself, "bigotry, intolerance, and persecution . . . worked heavily."[63] Speaking in the late-nineteenth and early-twentieth centuries, a time when sizeable numbers of Muslim merchants were coming to the island to settle and trade, Dharmapala struck fear in his fellow Sinhala Buddhists by making it clear what, in his mind, Islamic civilization brought with it. He spoke frequently about how lands from Persia to India saw their "centers of learning become centers of brigandage," utterly destroyed by a "barbarous foe who recognized neither art, literature, nor aesthetic beauty."[64] The worst case was that of India, where Buddhism was completely eliminated by violent invasion, forcing lay Buddhists to become Muslims by the millions.[65]

In the case of the country's still relatively small Muslim minority, Dharmapala's damning words, which include speeches and writings that accused Muslim merchants of economically exploiting the Sinhalas, translated into intolerant action all too readily and horribly, as many Sinhala organized and carried out systematic riots against the Muslims in 1915. In the eyes of the British authorities at least, Dharmapala and the sentiments he stirred up had more than a little to do with this. Immediately following the 1915 riots, he was found guilty of incitement and was interned for five years. When we see the words of Dharmapala, we can understand why this occurred; their rhetoric about the unwelcome foreign interloper threatening the island's true inhabitants is markedly Mahavamsaic in style and force:

The Mohammedans, an alien people . . . by Shylockian methods become prosperous like Jews. The Sinhalese [are] sons of the soil, whose ancestors for 2385 years have shed rivers of blood to keep the country free from alien invaders. . . . The alien South Indian Mohammedan comes to Ceylon, sees the neglected villager . . . and the result is that the Mohammedan thrives and the sons of the soil go to the wall.[66]

In Dharmapala's world as in the world of the chronicles, all non-Sinhalese people are aliens who threaten the ethnic and religious purity of Lanka as *dhammadipa*. Dharmapala's words were strong enough to incite persecution against one of the supposedly alien groups. We will see that, as Sri Lanka entered into its period of independence in the mid-twentieth century, other voices would take up Dharmapala's battle cry against another one of these groups.

Dharmapala's Sons: The "Political Monks"

This other group is, of course, the Tamil population of Lanka, made up mostly of Hindus but also including a small percentage of Muslims. The bloody conflict between some Tamil factions, most notably the separatist Liberation Tigers of Tamil Eelam (LTTE) and the armed forces of a government dominated by leaders elected by the country's Buddhist majority has been going on for over nearly twenty-five years now and is the most well-known manifestation of Sinhala-Tamil tensions, frequently making news headlines around the world. We will treat this period in the final section of this chapter, but our task here will be to see how Buddhist forces in mid-twentieth century Lankan politics fomented policies of discrimination against the Tamils, these policies being the main cause of Lanka's conflict. As Stanley Tambiah has pointed out and H. L. Seneviratne[67] has richly detailed, Dharmapala's activist legacy was inherited by two distinctly different monastic groups. What took place in the first half of the twentieth century and has come to a head in the past fifty years of Sinhala Buddhist and Tamil conflict is a rift between Buddhist revivalist monks of two variant stripes. One, originally associated with the Vidyodara monastic university, has focused mostly on economic and social reform in its activism and otherwise remained free from political involvement, emphasizing the Buddhist principles of detachment, restraint, and moral cultivation. The other group, originally associated with the Vidyalankara monastic university, has moved to make the *sangha* or monastic authorities a major force in the country's politics, where they could push their agenda of forming a Buddhist state. In this latter movement, one can see the wish to fulfill the *Mahavamsa*'s promotion of Buddhist monks as "lords upon the island." This group, who became known as the "political monks," have revived the ideology of the chronicles and Dharmapala by largely occupying itself with promoting the unity of the Sinhala language, ethnicity, Buddhist religion, and state, and by paying little to no attention to the concerns of Lanka's minority groups. Like the chronicles and Dharmapala, the political monks pay attention to these minorities only to the extent that they see them as obstacles to achieving their goals.

Two major figures stand out in the rise of the political monks. The first is Bhikkhu Walpola Rahula, whose work *Bhiksuvage Urumaya* (Sinhala) or *The Heritage of the Bhikkhu* (the title of its English translation)[68] provided the charter that justified the monks' involvement in political affairs. Rahula brought all of his considerable skills of scholarship to the composition of this work, drawing on a wealth of examples of monastic participation in politics in Lanka's history. But, as Stanley Tambiah has significantly noted, almost all of the evidence that he supplies is drawn from the mytho-historical *Mahavamsa* and other chronicles.[69] The politically engaged monks are "custodians of freedom," who, on every occasion of danger to both country and religion, come forth to protect them. And in a comment that would chillingly resonate with the events of the recent Sinhala-Tamil conflict, Rahula boldly declares the following about the history of monks' participation in political and military affairs: "The religio-patriotism . . . assumed such overpowering proportions that both the *bhikkhu* and layman considered that even killing people in order to liberate the religion and country was not a heinous crime."[70] Along similar lines, Rahula, commenting on the episode from the *Mahavamsa* where the *arahant* monks assure King Dutthagamani that he should not be troubled by the thousands whom he killed because all of them were inhuman, except for two who showed allegiance to Buddhism, states that *responsible* (my emphasis) monks and layfolk have regarded the monks' response as acceptable because they recognize that when it comes to the matter of "freedom and uplift of the religion and country . . . the destruction of human beings for that purpose was not a very grave crime."[71]

Besides Rahula, the other source for the polical monks' Buddhist chauvinism and nationalism were the writings of Bhikkhu Yakkaduve Pragnarama. H. L. Seneviratne's work has already provided us with a full analysis of Yakkaduve's work,[72] so it will suffice here to summarize Seneviratne's findings, as they pertain to our subject matter. Seneviratne shows that Yakkaduve's writings are preoccupied with "country, nation, and religion," a usage that Seneviratne traces to Dharmapala but could be traced, I think, back to the earliest chronicles. "Country" to Yakkuduve meant the territory of Lanka, "nation" meant the Sinhala ethnic group, and "religion" meant Buddhism.[73] So, once again, we are given the equation that to be Lankan is to be Sinhala, and that to be Sinhala is to be Buddhist. Yakkuduve, in calling the Tamils "illegal immigrants,"[74] leaves little doubt that this was what he meant.

Another major event from this era that raised Sinhala Buddhist nationalist feelings to fever pitch was the issuing of a national report, composed by a committee of leading monastic chiefs and lay scholars, entitled *The Betrayal of Buddhism*. The chronicles' portrayal of history looms very large again, especially in the report's introduction, which tells of a beleaguered history of Sinhala Buddhism, "the special treasure of the isle." Buddhism is presented as being in constant danger of destruction, mostly by a steady stream of Tamil but later colonial invaders and of being in a condition of steady decline ever since the period of the "three great kings," namely, Devanampiyatissa, Dutthagamani, and Parakramabahu I (the latter is credited with establishing Lanka's second age of Sinhala Buddhist dominion, the Polonnaruwa period).

The report made two proposals to revive Buddhism, both of which the newly independent government adopted. The first was the establishment of what was called the Buddha Sasana Council, to which may be entrusted all the previous prerogatives of Buddhist kings.[75] This is a remarkable move of returning to the established pattern of the chronicles, in which Buddhist kings are portrayed as constantly collaborating with the *sangha* to regulate and protect the religion. It also was clearly a boost to the political monks' agenda. The second measure was to withdraw grants in aid to Christian mission schools and to take over all assisted schools by the state.[76] This motion effectively put an end to the allowance of Christian education and, thus, can be regarded as a decidedly intolerant measure. Unlike Christian schools, Buddhist schools had little to fear because they were confident, especially with the establishment of the Buddha Sasana Council, that government policy would favor the transmission of Buddhist values.[77]

In fact, the Buddhist activists of the 1950s moved to go beyond even these measures, pushing for special affirmative action on behalf of Buddhism and the *sangha* in future state action. This would have the effect of excluding all other religious groups from special favored treatment.[78] The 1950s was a time when Sinhala Buddhist nationalists felt emboldened to make such demands that would ensure greater advantages for their people and a diminishing of any perceived advantages held by the country's other groups, especially the Tamils. What was called for was greater representation in government than that for Tamils, and more places in the universities than available to Tamils, thus giving Sinhalas much better job opportunities. They also advocated Sinhala only as the official language of the state, thus giving Sinhalas great advantage in civil-service examinations and thus a much larger number of postings to civil-service positions. The political monks were at the forefront of campaigning for these measures; especially effective was a group called the Eksath Bhikkhu Peramuna (United Monks' Front); the influence of this group and their followers basically ensured the election of S.W.R.D. Bandaranaike to the presidency in 1956; they guaranteed widespread support as long as he promised to implement their agenda, which he did. When Tamils staged a nonviolent sit-in in protest of these discriminatory measures at the capital in Colombo, many Sinhalas responded with brutal riots in which many lives were lost. The message through all the events of 1956 was clear: equal rights for Tamils was intolerable. Interestingly, Bandaranaike began to feel otherwise, and together with a leading Tamil politician, he put together the Bandaranaike-Chelvanayagam Pact, which proposed to accept Tamil as a national language and create a system of regional councils that would have given Tamils greater representation in government. The reaction by the United Monks Front and other powerful monk-led groups like the Sri Lanka Maha Sangha Sabha (Sri Lanka Great Buddhist Community Party) could not have been more strongly oppositional. The attitude of Sinhala Buddhist nationalists is perhaps best summarized by these words from an article composed by a monk in 1957:

Buddhism has always been a tolerant religion. There are examples of extreme tolerance amidst several challenges. Although tolerance is advocated, at this time of emergency when it is attacked in various ways, Buddhists cannot be tolerant. . . . Buddhists have to fight to save their lives.[79]

The monks and their political cohorts who were opposed to the positions of the Bandaranaike government on the status of Tamils also exploited the chronicles' narratives to put pressure on it. Buddhist monks and laity alike used these narratives to argue for the defense of the Sinhalas and their religion against the Tamils, who continued to be viewed as an unacceptable threat to the very survival of Buddhism.[80] Encapsulating their attitude are the following words from a monk opposed to Bandaranaike's attempts to treat the

Tamil minority equally. This monk attacked a comparison likening the leader to Dutthagamani. Unlike Bandaranaike, the monk said, "Dutugemunu[81] conquered by the sword and united the land without dividing it among our enemies and established Sinhala and Buddhism as the state language and religion."[82] No small amount of revisionist history is added to the Mahavamsaic model here. There is no suggestion in the *Mahavamsa* that any language or religion was made the official one of the "state," as anachronistically imagined here.

The monk pressure groups, along with their lay sponsors and allies, would prove to be the final destroyers of the pact, protesting vehemently against "surrendering" to Tamil demands. They staged a sit-in near the prime minister's home and refused to move until the pact was rescinded. After many unsuccessful attempts to get the monks to disband, Bandaranaike gave in and withdrew the pact.[83]

One would have thought that this would have appeased Sinhala Buddhist nationalists (and eventually, come the 1960s and 1970s, they would be so), but great anger arose again in response to another round of Tamil disobedience, this time in the form of strikes against government workers in 1958.[84] Tragically, more riots broke out, and more lives were lost. What is also worth knowing here is the enduring power of the chronicles' worldview to incite. Just weeks before the riots of 1958, a monk writing in the political monks' mouthpiece publication, *Bauddha Peramuna*, sounded something akin to a Mahavamsaic declaration of war:

When Dutugemenu was preparing for battle [against the Tamils], there were many monks who disrobed to join the army. . . . When Mahinda II was attempting to battle against [Tamil-occupied] Ruhuna Province, he first met with monks to justify his actions.[85]

What is striking here is the clear incitement to violent action and approval of violent action itself by those held to be the paragons of Buddhist virtues like *ahimsa* (non-harming)—the Buddhist monks. Commenting on this same statement, Tessa Bartholomeusz keenly points out "the fusion of the Tamil to the enemy of the country and of Buddhism in this expression of demonization and war."[86] She also notes how this rhetorical denunciation of the Tamil articulates the notion that history repeats itself,[87] and I would add that it is the chronicles' worldview that fosters this notion.

1983–the Present: The Sinhala-Tamil Civil War

The agenda and triumph of the political monks and their followers in the 1940s and 1950s ushered in a new level of militant political Buddhist intolerance that would not accept the full participation and inclusion of minorities—especially the Tamil Hindus—in the educational, economic, and political spheres. While a relatively peaceful situation held during the 1960s and the better part of the 1970s, the government's intolerant and discriminatory policies were bound to force concerted opposition at some point; and, indeed, since 1983, the country has been torn apart by a terrible civil conflict that has taken a tragic toll on all sides. This piece is not the place to explore the many complexities of this war, which has included much Tamil- as well as Sinhala-initiated violence, especially on the part of the separatist and terrorist organization known as the Liberation Tigers of Tamil Eelam. And it must be acknowledged that many Sinhala Buddhists, along with members of other ethnic and religious groups, have endeavored to introduce and promote a peace process. That said, it must also be acknowledged that Stanley Tambiah is correct when he states that the dominant form that Sinhala Buddhism has taken today is a "militant, populist, fetishized form . . . emptied of much of its normative and humane ethic," which has functioned as part of a "homogenizing national identity" and which sanctions and instigates violence.[88] Our task in this last section will be to look at government statements and actions, as well as those of other nationalist and chauvinist Sinhala Buddhist parties and individuals that have been most responsible for maintaining a Buddhist policy of intolerance in Sri Lanka.

Beginning with Bandaranaike's time in office, the governments of Sri Lanka, like the kings as portrayed in the chronicles, have regarded themselves as protectors of Buddhism and have risen to power by appealing to the country's Buddhist majority, pledging to support both the Buddhist religion and the Sinhala Buddhist people in the face of other groups—especially the Tamil Hindus—who are perceived as threats to this cause. In the 1980s and 1990s, the United National Party (UNP) governments under J. R. Jayawardene and R. Premadasa have emphasized even more the government's responsibility to protect the *Buddha-sasana* or institution of Buddhism.[89]

Jayawardene believed that the country's Buddhist heritage (the vision of which, as we have seen, was produced mostly by the chronicles) provided a mandate for the government to rule and protect the land, the Sinhala people, and the Buddhist establishment.[90] Soon after he was elected in 1977, the first year that saw Sinhala-Tamil riots since the late 1950s, Jayawardene declared that his government would create a "Dharmic" (Sinhala: *dharmista*) society, by which he pointedly meant that his government would be based on the principles that Buddhist kings used in ancient days, according to the chronicles. Indeed, one of the country's most prominent monastic leaders immediately linked Dutthagamani's precedence and authority to Jayawardene's administration:

Prince Dutugemunu appointed fourteen Buddhist monks as heads of administration . . . on all dharmista principles . . . after the historic defeat of Elara. Similarly, our Dharmista Prime Minister Mr. J. R. Jayawardene with his cabinet would certainly bring peace and harmony to Sri Lankans.[91]

For his part, Jayawardene consciously adopted the paradigm of the righteous king as he coped with growing Sinhala-Tamil tensions in the early 1980s. Tessa Bartholomeusz has pointed out that, like the *Mahavamsa's* treatment of Dutthagamani, he contextualized his right to pursue war within the framework of the Dharma:

I feel you cannot attain Nirvana by killing people [but] . . . you cannot sit while a snake comes and bites you. You must deal with that snake. . . . The state [has the right] to exercise violence to protect its citizens.[92]

Jayawardene frequently made speeches that sounded as if they were taken right off the pages of the *Mahavamsa* or a Dharmapala rant. In one speech, he claimed that his government aimed "at building a new society on the foundations of the principles of Dharma. We have a duty to protect the Buddha and to pledge that every possible action would be taken to develop it."[93]

Like Dutthagamani, Jayawardene was willing to fight against the Tamils in what he considered a just war to promote Buddhism.[94] Tessa Bartholomeusz reminds us that it is worth remembering here the *Mahavamsa's* view of the non-Buddhist *damilas* or Tamils: they are nonhuman. "In the context of the war in Sri Lanka," she continues, "the ramifications of Jayawardene's views are disturbing to say the least."[95] Drawing on images of righteous kings from the *Mahavamsa*, Jayawardene defended the use of violence in his regime:

I cannot follow that [precept of not killing any living being] because my duty is laid down in the Constitution. . . . Sri Sangabo wanted to follow Buddhism fully after he became king, so he released all the prisoners. . . . And they started robbing and killing people. . . . There was big turmoil and the people forced him to resign. . . . I am not going to be like that, I want to govern this country, I was elected to govern.[96]

When the violence that Jayawardene expected, if not invited, broke out in the 1983 riots that began the war that now nears its twenty-fifth year, what was remarkable about the government's reactions was not its attention to the unprecedented number of deaths on the Tamil side, but its concern that Sri Lanka not be divided.[97] And the concern was not so much that different communities or regions in the country would be divided but that some portion of Sinhala Buddhist hegemony and primacy would be taken away. Take, for example, the following words from one government official:

... there are certain unalterable facts. The problems begin when we seek to change the unalterable facts. The first is that ... Sri Lanka is one. The Sinhala people ... and people of many other communities will never, never, allow the division of this country. To put it simply, so long as there is one Sinhala man remaining on the soil of Lanka, there will be one person to oppose this division. The second unalterable fact is something which we Sinhala people ... have a duty to explain to our compatriots from other communities. The Sinhala people ... have an important place in this country ... they have a special place here. For example, in protecting the Buddhist religion. ... But while this has been so, it is also a fact that other communities have lived in Lanka. ... We must look forward to a Sri Lanka which is *the indisputable home* (my emphasis) of the Sinhala people and *also the home* (my emphasis) of other people. ...[98]

As is clear here, the implication is that Sri Lanka is inherently and rightfully a Sinhala Buddhist state. What is suggested in other government statements is that the Tamils, given the grave threat that they pose, have only themselves to blame for the wrath of the Sinhalas. Again, appealing to that seemingly inexhaustible moment from the storied past, we find the then-current Minister of Finance and Planning speaking along these lines:

The Sinhala race ... has lived more than 2,500 years on this island. We have faced more dangerous and severe threats in the past if we look back at history. ... Elara, a Dravidian king, ruled this country for forty years. The King Dutugemunu emerged ... and defeated Elara at war. ... With all these foreign threats ... our culture was saved. ... We will never allow the country to be divided.[99]

This equation of the present conflict with the Tamils and the famous defeat of Elara is troubling in what it implies, for, as we can recall, those Tamils killed by Dutthagamani and his forces were justified on the basis of their being "not more than beasts."

As for R. Premadasa, who governed into the 1990s, he even more than Jayawardene believed that politics should be infused with Buddhism.[100] He quite consciously modeled himself after the Buddhist kings as portrayed in the chronicles, defenders of the faith who did not hesitate to use violence when they felt it was necessary to protect the Dharma from the perceived threats from other peoples, especially the Tamils. He exercised very strong control over both the Ministry of Defense and his newly founded (1990) Ministry of the Buddha Sasana.[101] It was clear that these two departments were not seen by Premadasa as entirely separate ones with different aims, as one might otherwise guess, given Buddhism's heavy emphasis on nonviolence. Premadasa also, following the model of the *Mahavamsa*'s kings, set up a Supreme Council of Buddhist Leaders to advise him.[102] This extended even further the primacy of Buddhism over other religions in the country. Under Premadasa's rule the dominant form of Buddhism became even more chauvinist, violent, and nationalist.[103] The legitimacy of this brand of Buddhism was used by Premadasa as a rationale for attacking opponents.[104] For example, Premadasa attacked the nongovernmental agency (NGO) known as Shramadana Sarvodaya, a movement based on Buddhist ethical and Gandhian principles, as an enemy of the nation for joining with Tamils in peace marches.[105]

It is telling of the prevailing mood among the Sinhalas during Premadasa's time in office that songs composed by the militant monk Elle Gunavamsa, a staunch supporter of Premadasa's government, became widely popular, selling in large quantities.[106] To provide an idea of what messages the songs conveyed, here are some of the lyrics from one of his songs, titled "Memory for the Soldier":

> My brave, brilliant soldier son,
> Leaving to defend the motherland;
> That act of merit is enough
> To reach nirvana in a future life . . .
>
> We'll shed the last drop of blood
> To defend the land which gave us birth;
> We will, like lions, conjure
> Before our enemy our skill.
> Where is a country without a nation,
> A nation without a country, where?
>
> O Heroes battlefield bound,
> Brothers, weapons in hand,
> Soldiers of Dutugemunu
> Reborn in my motherland.
>
> It's not to be king that I bear my weapons,
> I defend my lands as Gautama's son.
> Country, religion, race are my triple gems.
> Children, I make tomorrow in your name.
> For us Sinhalas, to be born and die,
> Where's another except this earth.
>
> The sword is pulled from the sheath;
> It is not put back unless smeared with blood.

This is the way of the the Sinhala of old,
Who vanquished the foe.
Son, you must know how it was.[107]

As H. L. Seneviratne has noted, what is most striking here is the connection between images of violence with those of religion and worship.[108] Whereas Jayawardene was willing to commit to violence but acknowledged that it was no path to *nirvana*, Gunavamsa says that violence, which, after all, is done in defense of the "motherland" and all it represents, earns the soldier enough merit to gain it eventually. Seneviratne has said that this is the equivalent of the *Mahavamsa*'s conception of killing nonbelievers with impunity. Here, however, it goes beyond impunity to a promise of the religion's *summum bonum*. The soldiers are said to be Dutthagamani's very own, reborn. And in armed defense of the Sinhala motherland, they are branded as no less than the Buddha's own sons. The Buddha's teaching and his community have been replaced in the formula of the three gems with country, religion, and race. Most disturbing of all, "the way of the Sinhala of old" is not that of Buddhism's central ethic of nonviolence but is that of those who do not put their swords back in their sheaths until they are covered with blood.

As Sri Lanka's Sinhala-Tamil conflict moves into the twenty-first century, we find that a policy of intolerance has continued, as none of the Tamil's demands for equal rights, opportunities, and representation have been granted by the Sinhala-dominated government. The causes for the conflict's ongoing nature are complex, with no insignificant cause being the continued acts of extreme terrorism by the separatist Liberation Tigers of Tamil Eelam. Be that as it may, the majority of Tamils want nothing more than equality, and it seems apparent that the policy of intolerance will not change until the totalizing discourse of one nation protecting one people and one religion loses its power. Are there any signs of this in the most recent years? It would seem there are not too many. While only a minority of Sinhala Buddhist nationalists argue that they are the only true inheritors of the island, this minority is ever-present in the background of the conflict, and it sets the tone for the country's political discourse. And while a larger majority argue that anyone can live in Sri Lanka, the majority still maintain that this situation can only remain as long as the Sinhala Buddhists enjoy linguistic, economic, religious, and cultural hegemony.[109]

But perhaps the surest sign of the Sinhala Buddhist policy of intolerance surviving is the continued use of the chronicles' mytho-history to legitimize it. In speaking of this power of myth, Bruce Kapferer has said,

> Where human beings recognize the argument of mythic reality as corresponding to their own personal constitutions—their orientation within and movement through reality—so myth gathers force and can come to be seen as embodying ultimate truth. Myths so enlivened . . . can become imbued with commanding power, binding human actors to the logical movement of its scheme.[110]

Indeed, the story of Dutthagamani's defeat of Elara continues to be used to legitimize the dominance of Sinhala Buddhists over the Tamils. And as Oddvar Hollup has observed, the reactivation of this mytho-historical charter indeed has been used to interpret present conditions, mobilizing the masses and directing their anger and violence against the Tamils.[111] Drawing on the chronicles' legends, Sinhala Buddhist chauvinist-nationalists continue to see themselves as a unified body in opposition to a monolithic Tamil community, with the two locked together in an ongoing cosmic drama. Recently, the Venerable Sobhita Thera, a monastic leader of the Mavbima Surakime Vyaparaya or "Movement for the Protection of the Motherland" and a proponent of "finishing the war"—as he euphemistically puts it—with the Tamils, portrayed the General Anuruddha Ratwatte, the architect of the government's present strategy for fighting Tamil opponents, as a modern-day Dutugemenu.[112]

While it is monks like Venerable Sobhita Thera who usually promote the *Mahavamsa* as the normative history of the country, it is the laity as much as the *sangha* that, to paraphrase Kapferer, links mythic reality with their own personal constitutions. As this is so, perhaps it is fitting to give the last word to a leading contemporary Sinhala Buddhist layperson. Professor Abaya Aryasinghe is General Secretary of Sinhala Maha Sammata Bhumiputra Pakshaya or "Sinhala Universal Approved Sons of the Soil Party," a ten-thousand-member organization whose stated raison d'etre is separating authentic Sri Lankans from illegitimate ones. That is why "the party is not ready to accept Tamil members," he explains.[113] According to Aryasinghe, the destiny of Sri Lanka is to be *Sinhala dwipa* or the "island of the Sinhalas." To support this conclusion, he points to the *Mahavamsa*'s placing of the Sinhalas as the land's earliest human inhabitants. As for Dutugemenu, he represents the hope that Sri Lanka once again may be victorious over "foreign" elements. But this does not mean, Aryasinghe hastens to add, that contemporary foreigners like Tamil Hindus, Moorish and Tamil Muslims, and Burgher Christians need to be killed. Rather they should assimilate; they should learn to speak Sinhala and become Buddhist. Then, the use of violence becomes unnecessary. Unless, that is, the "foreigners become rebellious." In that case, "quashing them with weapons does become necessary."[114]

Conclusion

What contributes to a Buddhist policy of intolerance? To draw any conclusions regarding this, one would have to look for commonalities in all of the particular cases of Buddhist intolerance in history. Such a project lies outside the course of this chapter. What can be said about this particular case is that what has yielded a policy of intolerance has been a totalizing discourse that closely ties religion to politics, ethnic and national identity, and land in a way that has led to completely hegemonic claims. When these factors are combined, it is hard to imagine intolerance not being bred among a society's dominant group. In the case of Sinhala Buddhists, we have a case of religion, country, ethnicity, and nationality being linked not only in modern discourse with the strong rhetoric of Anagarika Dharmapala and the political monks, but a discourse that has been built up in its long-standing tradition of mytho-historical chronicles, the earliest of which dates to the fourth century CE and the latest of which goes up to the eighteenth century CE. This forms a powerful tradition indeed, and it goes a significant way in explaining why Sinhala discrimination against the Tamil coinhabitants of Lanka has proven so intractable.

Notes

1. H. Byron Earhart, *Japanese Religion: Unity and Diversity* (Belmont, CA: Wadsworth Publishing Company, 1982), 108.

2. Harold Coward, *Pluralism in the World Religions: A Short Introduction* (Oxford: Oneworld, 2000), 129.

3. Ibid.

4. It must be acknowledged, however, that what the *pratyekabuddha* is said to discover is identical to what Buddhas teach.

5. K. N. Jayatilleke, *The Buddhist Attitude to Other Religions* (Kandy, Sri Lanka: Buddhist Publication Society, 1975).

6. *Majjhima Nikaya* 76 (i. 514–521).

7. *Anguttara Nikaya* 3:65/i. 18ff.

8. *Canki Sutta* (Majjhima Nikaya 95).

9. The Buddhist position was, in fact, developed in response to the assertions of theistic Hindu opponents in debate.

10. Bradley Clough, "Buddhism," in *God*, ed. Jacob Neusner (Cleveland: Pilgrim Press, 1997), 57.

11. It is always a "he," usually either Brahma or Indra/Sakra.

12. See *Digha Nikaya* 24 and i. 222–223. Also another sutta, the *Mahatitthayatana Sutta* (*Anguttara Nikaya* i. 173–75) identifies as "unsatisfactory"—again in the sense of having an unsound basis—the religious view that all that is felt is due to the creation of God (Pali: *issara-nimmana-hetu*).

13. Clough, "Buddhism," 57.

14. Kukai, "The Precious Key to the Secret Treasury," in *Kukai: Major Works*, ed. and trans. Yoshito S. Hakeda (New York: Columbia University Press, 1972), 157–244.

15. Stanley J. Tambiah, *World Conqueror and World Renouncer: A Study of Buddhism and Polity in Thailand against a Historical Background* (Cambridge: Cambridge University Press, 1976), 402.

16. Other Pali language chronicles besides the *Mahavamsa* include the earlier (fourth-century) *Dipavamsa* ("Lineage of the Island") and the *Culavamsa* ("Minor Lineage," with updated versions going from the twelfth to the eighteenth centuries), the *Mahabodhivamsa* ("Lineage of the Great Awakening," tenth century), the *Thupavamsa* ("Lineage of the Reliquary," twelfth century), and the *Dathavamsa* ("Lineage of the Tooth Relic," thirteenth century). There are also two noteworthy later Sinhala language chronicles, the *Pujavilaya* ("Lineage of Offerings') and the *Rajavilaya* ("Lineage of Kings"), which are from the thirteenth and seventeenth centuries, respectively.

17. Steven Kemper, *The Presence of the Past: Chronicles, Politics, and Culture in Sinhala Life* (Ithaca, NY: Cornell University Press, 1991), 20–21.

18. Heinz Bechert, "The Beginnings of Buddhist Historiography: Mahavamsa and Political Thinking," in *Religion and the Legitimation of Power in Sri Lanka*, ed. Bardwell L. Smith (Chambersburg, PA: Anima Books, 1978), 7.

19. Gananath Obeyesekere, "Buddhism, Nationhood, and Cultural Identity: A Question of Fundamentals," in *Fundamentalisms Comprehended*, ed. Martin E. Marty and R. Scott Appleby (Chicago: University of Chicago Press, 1995), 232.

20. See footnote 16.

21. G. G. Raheja and Ann Grodzins Gold, *Listen to the Heron's Word: Reimagining Gender and Kinship in North India* (Berkeley: University of California Press, 1994), 3, as cited in Tessa Bartholomeusz, *In Defense of Dharma: Just-War Ideology in Buddhist Sri Lanka* (London: Routledge Curzon, 2002), 8.

22. Bruce Kapferer, *Legends of People, Myths of State: Violence, Intolerance, and Political Culture in Sri Lanka and Australia* (Washington, DC: Smithsonian Institution Press, 1998), 81.

23. This is how the term has usually been understood. Recent scholarship has revealed that it originally may well have meant "lamp of the doctrine." Personal communication, Kristin Schnieble, 3/25/07.

24. *Mahavamsa* 1:43.

25. Ibid.

26. *Mahavamsa* 1:24–27.

27. *Mahavamsa* 7.

28. *Mahavamsa* 13 and 14.

29. *Pujavaliya* (Colombo: Jinalankara Press, 1926), 656, as cited and translated in Walpola Rahula, *History of Buddhism in Ceylon* (Colombo: M. D. Gunasena and Company, 1956), 63.

30. *Mahavamsa* 25:2–3.

31. *Mahavamsa* 25:17–18.

32. Alice Greenwald, "The Relic on the Spear: Historiography and the Saga of Dutthagamani," *Religion and the Legitimation of Power in Sri Lanka*, ed. Bardwell L. Smith (Chambersburg, PA: Anima Books, 1978), 22.

33. Kapferer, *Legends of People*, 81–82.

34. The way the text puts it is that one man took the [three Buddhist] refuges and the other took the five [Buddhist] precepts. *Mahavamsa* 25:110.

35. *Mahavamsa* 25:110–11.

36. Bechert, "Beginnings of Buddhist Historiography," 7.

37. Jacob Neusner, "The Study of Religion as the Study of Tradition," *History of Religions* 14 (1975): 193.

38. See chapter 2 of George Bond, *The Buddhist Revival in Sri Lanka: Religious Tradition, Reinterpretation and Response* (Charleston: University of South Carolina Press, 1988); chapter 6 of Richard Gombrich and Gananath Obeyesekere, *Buddhism Transformed: Religious Change in Sri Lanka* (Princeton, NJ: Princeton University Press, 1988); and chapter 2 of H. L. Seneviratne, *The Work of Kings: The New Buddhism in Sri Lanka* (Chicago: University of Chicago Press, 1999).

39. Gombrich and Obeyesekere, *Buddhism Transformed*, 215.

40. Ibid., 213.

41. Anagarika Dharmapala, *Return to Righteousness* (Colombo: Department of Government Printing, 1965), 474, 479, 494, et passim.

42. Ibid., 481.

43. Ibid., 485.

44. Ibid., 488.

45. Ibid., 480.

46. Ibid., 488–89.

47. Ibid., 489.

48. This ambivalence is captured well in his description of India as "an asylum for devout men, devotees, and the religiously mad." Ibid., 823.

49. Ibid., 689.

50. Ibid., 603.

51. Ibid., 402.

52. Ibid., 218–19.

53. Ibid., 791.

54. Ibid., 356.

55. *The Buddhist* 3, no. 16 (April 10, 1891): 128, as quoted in *Buddhist Fundamentalism and Identity in Sri Lanka*, ed. Tessa J. Bartholomeusz and Chandra R. De Silva (Albany: SUNY Press, 1998), 32, n. 96.

56. "Correspondence: To the Editor of The Buddhist," *The Buddhist* 1, no. 6 (1889): 47, as quoted in Bartholomeusz and De Silva, *Buddhist Fundamentalism*, 32, n. 96.

57. Here I am paraphrasing and combining three separate statements by Dharmapala. Dharmapala, *Return to Righteousness*, 419, 464, and 798.

58. Ibid., 408–409.

59. Ibid., 419.

60. Ibid., 207.

61. Throughout his writings, Dharmapala roundly denies all theories concerning the demise of Buddhism, placing all blame on "invading Muslim hordes." Ibid., 394 et passim.

62. Ibid., 394.

63. Ibid., 352.

64. Ibid., 471.

65. Ibid.

66. Ibid., 540.

67. Stanley J. Tambiah, *Sri Lanka: Ethnic Fratricide and the Dismantling of Democracy* (Chicago: University of Chicago Press, 1986), 83; and H. L. Seneviratne, *The Work of Kings: The*

New Buddhism in Sri Lanka (Chicago: University of Chicago Press, 1999), chapters 3 and 4.

68. Walpola Rahula, *The Heritage of the Bhikkhu* (New York: Grove Press, 1974).

69. Stanley J. Tambiah, *Buddhism Betrayed? Religion, Politics, and Violence in Sri Lanka* (Chicago: University of Chicago Press, 1992), 27–28.

70. Rahula, 21, as quoted in Tambiah, *Buddhism Betrayed?* 28.

71. Ibid., 22.

72. Seneviratne, *The Work of Kings*, 149–61.

73. Ibid., 159.

74. Ibid.

75. Tambiah, *Buddhism Betrayed?* 34.

76. Ibid., 34–35.

77. Ibid., 35.

78. Ibid.

79. "Buddhist Tolerance," *Bauddha Peramuna*, April 27, 1957, as quoted in Bartholomeusz, *In Defense of Dharma*, 77.

80. Bartholomeusz, *In Defense of Dharma*, 12.

81. This is Sinhala for Dutthagamani.

82. *Bauddha Peramuna*, September 21, 1957, 2, as quoted in Bartholomeusz, *In Defense of Dharma*, 13.

83. Stanley J. Tambiah, "Buddhism, Politics, and Violence in Sri Lanka," in *Fundamentalisms and the State*, ed. Martin E. Marty and R. Scott Appleby (Chicago: University of Chicago Press, 1996), 599.

84. Ibid.

85. Hewapitagedera Piyananda, "The Country Was Always Protected by the Monks," *Bauddha Peramuna*, May 3, 1958, as quoted in Batholomeusz, *In Defense of Dharma*, 82.

86. Bartholomeusz, *In Defense of Dharma*, 82.

87. Ibid.

88. Tambiah, *Buddhism Betrayed?* 92.

89. George Bond, "Conflicts of Identity and Interpretation in Buddhism: The Clash between the Sarvodaya Shramadana Movement and the Government of President Premadasa," in Bartholomeusz and De Silva, eds., *Buddhist Fundamentalism*, 41.

90. Ibid., 41–42.

91. Venerable Pandita Dampelle Gurusiri, "Help Premier Usher in a Dharmista Society," *The Daily News*, September 6, 1977, as quoted in Bartholomeusz, *In Defense of Dharma*, 61.

92. "Revolutions of Violence Not for Me," *The Daily News*, January 25, 1990, as quoted in Bartholomeusz, *In Defense of Dharma*, 61.

93. Quoted in D. Little, *Sri Lanka: The Invention of Enmity* (Washington, D.C.: 1994), 79

94. Bartholomeusz, *In Defense of Dharma*, 65.

95. Ibid.

96. Quoted in J. van der Horst, *Who Is He, What Is He Doing: Religious Rhetoric and Performances in Sri Lanka during R. Premadasa's Presidency (1989–1993)* (Amsterdam: VU University Press), 134.

97. Elizabeth Nissan, "Some Thoughts on Sinhalese Justifications for the Violence," in *Sri Lanka in Change and Crisis*, ed. J. Manor (London: Croom Helm, 1984), 176.

98. L. Athulamudai, as quoted in Nissan, "Some Thoughts on Sinhalese Justifications," 181–82.

99. Ronnie de Mel, quoted in "Government Will Never Allow Division of the Country," *The Island*, August 26, 1983, as quoted in Tessa Batholomeusz, *In Defense of Dharma*, 95.

100. Bond, "Conflicts of Identity," 42.

101. Ibid., 42–43.

102. Chandra De Silva, "The Plurality of Buddhist Fundamentalism: An Inquiry into Views among Buddhist Monks in Sri Lanka," in Bartholomeusz and De Silva, *Buddhist Fundamentalism*, 60. De Silva further notes (61) that the political strength of those who believe protection of Buddhism over other religions is a special obligation of the Sri Lankan state was seen in certain similar acts by the recent president Chandrika Kumaratunga, who, despite being a longtime promoter of a secular approach to politics, gave official constitutional status to the Supreme Council of Buddhist Leaders for the first time in 1997, a year that also saw her newly proposed constitution officially "give Buddhism the foremost place" among religions.

103. Bond, "Conflicts of Identity," 44.

104. Ibid., 48.

105. Ibid.

106. Seneviratne, *The Work of Kings*, 244–45.

107. Translated and quoted in ibid., 272–74.

108. Ibid., 245.

109. Bartholomeusz and De Silva, *Buddhist Fundamentalism*, 2–3.

110. Kapferer, *The Presence of the Past*, 46–47.

111. Oddvar Hollup, "The Impact of Land Reforms, Rural Images, and Nationalist Ideology on Plantation Tamils," in Bartholomeusz and De Silva, *Buddhist Fundamentalism*, 76.

112. "Princely Warrior Not for Polls," *The Sunday Leader*, August 2, 1998, as cited in Bartholomeusz, *In Defense of Dharma*, 38.

113. Quoted in Bartholomeusz, *In Defense of Dharma*, 116.

114. Quoted in ibid., 114–15.

16

TOLERANCE AND HIERARCHY

Accommodating Multiple Religious Paths in Hinduism

RICHARD H. DAVIS

The Politics of Hindu Tolerance

"I am proud to belong to a religion," proclaimed Swami Vivekananda, spokesman for the Hindu religion, to a large audience at the 1893 World's Parliament of Religion in Chicago, "which has taught the world both tolerance and universal acceptance. We believe not only in universal tolerance, but we accept all religions as true." In this respect, the swami suggested, Hinduism was superior to the other great world religions as exemplar and instructor. Vivekananda went on to cite how India had in the past sheltered Jews and Zoroastrians fleeing persecution by adherents of other faiths and then quoted a hymn he had recited as a child: "As the different streams having their sources in different paths which men take through different tendencies, various though they appear, crooked or straight, all lead to Thee" (Vivekananda 1893). Later in his opening speech, he also cited a well-known verse from the *Bhagavad Gita*, in which the god Krishna says, "Whosoever comes to Me, through whatsoever form, I reach him; all men are struggling through paths which in the end lead to me."

Four decades later, writing from prison to his daughter, Jawaharlal Nehru picked up the same theme of exceptional Indian tolerance. "It is curious and rather wonderful to compare other countries with India in the matter of treat-ment of different religions. In most places, and especially in Europe, you will find, in the past, intolerance and persecution of all who do not profess the offi-cial faith." Nehru noted the Inquisition and the burning of witches as histori-cal examples of European persecution of other religious beliefs and practices. "But in India," he goes on, "in olden times there was almost full tolerance" (Nehru 1942, 98). Nehru did not pretend to be a spokesman for Hinduism, but, as an ardent Indian nationalist leader imprisoned many times by the British rulers, he was eager to impart to his daughter Indira the "splendid past [of India] of which we may be proud and think with pleasure" (Nehru 1942, 4). As India's first prime minister from 1947 through 1964, Nehru would later preside over the emergence of the Indian republic as a secular state, in which the state would remain neutral in relation to the various religious communi-ties who populate India. His daughter Indira Gandhi would largely maintain that secular policy when she herself was prime minister from 1966 to 1977 and again from 1980 to 1984.

In the past two decades since Indira Gandhi's assassination, questions concerning the "tolerance" of Hinduism have become a political issue of pub-lic debate in India. Some have asserted, along with Vivekananda, that Hindu-ism is a uniquely tolerant religion. Like Nehru, they have juxtaposed claims that Hindus have been especially accepting of other religions throughout his-tory with assertions that the Abrahamic religions, chiefly Christianity and Islam, exhibit a history of religious intolerance, to point to the superior value of Hinduism.

Hindu society has been the meeting point as well as the melting pot of as many spir-itual visions as the human psyche is capable of springing up spontaneously. It has been a willing and welcoming platform for as many seers, sages, saints, and mystics as has responded to the deeper stirrings in the human soul. It has been a repository of as many metaphysical points of view as human reason can render in human language. And it has been a vast laboratory for as many cultural, social, economic, and political experiments as human nature in its widest range can carry out and cope with.

Goel 1993, 4–5

Ironically, in contemporary India, those who have most fervently cele-brated Hindu tolerance have been the Hindu nationalists who, at the same time, most loudly attack the Muslim and Christian communities of India and seek to transform India from a secular state into a Hindu nation. Sita Ram Goel, the author of the encomium of Hindu society's tolerance above, has also written that Hindus should understand Islam as "an imperialist ide-ology of terrorism and genocide masquerading as a religion, in fact as the only true religion" (Goel 1993, vi). Goel has compiled lists of Hindu temples allegedly destroyed in the past by Muslim conquerors and iconoclasts to support his view (Goel 1990, 1993). In response, secular historians have persuasively questioned his methods and sources for these lists (Eaton 2000).

Others have questioned claims of Hindu tolerance on historical grounds. They have pointed to past acts of Hindu intolerance and persecution directed at adherents of other faiths, such as the Saiva pogrom of Jains in early medieval south India, as counterexamples. In the complexity of social history, no civilization is entirely free from episodes of intolerance based on or rationalized upon religious grounds. Some have accused Hindu nationalists, with their accusations of Christian and Islamic intolerance, of "semiticizing" Hinduism. In their eagerness to right historical wrongs, secularist opponents argue, Hindu nationalists may be introducing into Hinduism exactly the kind of doctrinal unanimity and animosity toward other religions that they have ascribed to and derogated in religions other than Hinduism (Panikkar 2002). These opponents of Hindu nationalism juxtapose the tolerance built into the "secularism" of the Indian constitution with the intolerance they say is inherent in any attempt to impose religion in the public sphere. But in India, "secularism" is itself a contested term.

Tolerance and a Scale of Religious Forms

In this chapter, I do not aim to resolve debates over tolerance and secularism within current Indian discourse. Rather, I intend to look back to classical and medieval Hindu texts to see how they deal with the question of religious tolerance. My concern is not with the historical actions of Hindu agents of the past (which have been, as everywhere, decidedly mixed) but with ideological visions embedded within Hindu texts. However, before I discuss any Hindu work, I need to refine my terms. In Sanskrit, the lingua franca of classical and early medieval India, we will find no single word that can adequately translate our term *tolerance*. We need to consider first just what we mean by *tolerance* in English.

The earliest usage of the English word *tolerance*, the *Oxford English Dictionary* informs us, dates back to the fifteenth century. At that time the word denoted "the action or practice of enduring or sustaining pain or hardship; the power or capacity of enduring." Deriving from this sense are several technical usages in sciences that involve an entity's ability to survive or flourish despite some detrimental condition either external, as a tree may tolerate shade or drought, or internal, as an animal organism may tolerate a parasite.

By the sixteenth century, *tolerance* had also gained a more political meaning: "the action of allowing; license, permission granted by authority." Here some sovereign or other authority allows practices that depart from the norm or the desirable, as a form of implicit license, as Queen Elizabeth I could have, but did not, permit the practices of the Puritans. It should be noted here that tolerance is the prerogative of those with relative power over others. We do not tend to speak of the Puritans' tolerance of Queen Elizabeth, just as we do not think of a parasite tolerating its host organism.

Subsequently, *tolerance* takes on the broader sense in English usage of a disposition: "the disposition to be patient with or indulgent to the opinions and practices of others; freedom from bigotry or undue severity in judging the conduct of others; forbearance; catholicity of spirit." Here we can recognize the way in which we adopt the term in contemporary usage to questions of religious tolerance. The defining phrase "catholicity of spirit" conveys an attitude of liberality and universality. It indicates willingness on the part of adherents of one religion to acknowledge other religions and to allow for their legitimacy as alternative religious formations. This is the basis for Nehru's observation of a history of Indian tolerance of multiple religious practices. At times, it may extend further, to an acceptance of other religions as offering their adherents valuable or equal paths to spiritual attainment, however that may be defined. This latter sense is what Vivekananda had in mind when he spoke of accepting "all religions as true" and quoted the hymn with its metaphor of all streams ultimately leading to a single divine destination.

I want to identify one characteristic rhetorical strategy by which proponents of various religious viewpoints in Hindu texts have spoken about and addressed themselves to other religious perspectives and practices. This rhetoric involves recognition of multiple religious paths, first of all, and inclusion and provisional acceptance of those paths. Yet it also involves an evaluation and critical ranking of those paths against some common criteria. These texts, then, seek to construct what Ronald Inden, following R. G. Collingwood, has called a "scale of forms" (Inden 2000, 11, 50–51) Others have called this rhetorical practice "inclusivism," "englobement," or "encapsulation" (Halbfass 1995, Biardeau 1994, Embree 1993). It enables Hindu religious groups to tolerate a myriad of other forms of religious thought and practice, both "Hindu" and non-Hindu, while also maintaining or seeking to establish a superior status for their own.

No term in classical Indian discourse denotes what we understand as "religion." Three terms, however, offer useful approximations: *dharma* (duty, morality, a code of proper conduct), *darsana* (viewpoint, philosophical school of thought), and *marga* (route, religious path). In classical and medieval India, a scale of religious forms was grounded on an awareness that each individual religious aspirant began from his or her own distinct situation. That is, most Hindu texts accepted that religious paths (*marga*) are relative to the points of view (*darsana*) and moral responsibilities (*dharma*) of practitioners, whose individual circumstances may make one or another course of action more appropriate in their particular situations. This contextual awareness took into account, first of all, the particular social group (*varna*) and stage of life (*asrama*), as well as the gender, of the person. Treatises on *dharma*, or codes of proper religious conduct, would specify obligations and responsibilities in terms of conduct according to one's social class and stage of life (*varnasramadharma*). This could also extend more broadly to the social and political setting. Proper conduct might vary during periods of distress (*apaddharma*), such as that brought on by family disruption or political unrest. And still more broadly, many texts spoke of different temporal eras making various religious practices more or less suitable. During a period of greatly diminished virtue, such as the Kali-era in which we currently live, simpler forms of practice are acceptable and advisable.

> There is one set of Laws for men in the Krta Age, another in the Treta, still another in the Dvapara, and a different set in the Kali, in keeping with the shortening taking place in each Age. Ascetic toil, they say, is supreme in the Krta Age; knowledge in the Treta; sacrifice in the Dvarpara; and gift-giving alone in the Kali.
>
> Olivelle 2004, 1.85–86

The linguist and poet A. K. Ramanujan has called this Indic orientation "context-sensitivity" and proposed that we view this as part of a distinctive "Indian way of thinking" (Ramanujan 1989).

Throughout history, Hindus often do appear to have taken a remarkably relaxed view of the religious practices of others. They accept, as Sly Stone put it in a different setting, "different strokes for different folks." This recognition of the relativity of context, however, does not mean that Hindu texts adopt a position of equanimity toward all religious paths. In fact, Hindus have historically put much effort and debate into specifying the most efficient path to attain the best or highest end (*sreyas*). To return to Vivekananda's metaphor, Hindu teachers may tolerate and accept all streams as ultimately leading to the same ocean, but they also observe that some are crooked and others are straight and that some are more suitable to follow than others, depending on the place from which one sets out.

In order to illustrate this particular Hindu form of *critical tolerance*, I would like to look at two sets of teachings. The first is the well-known classical-period discourse that Krishna delivers to Arjuna on the battlefield of Kuruksetra, preserved in the *Bhagavad Gita*. The second is the medieval group of treatises that define Saiva Siddhanta as a Hindu school of knowledge and practice, in relation to other existing Indic religious orders. In both cases, I will show how the texts construct scales of forms, by which their audiences may assess and evaluate a complex religious environment. Both provide a way to comprehend and accept multiple religious practices as suitable and efficacious for their practitioners, while, at the same time, they articulate arguments for what they consider to be superior paths to the highest ends.

Krishna's Scale of Religious Forms

We begin with a classical Indian text that is often spoken of as the "Bible of Hinduism." Although the *Bhagavad Gita* is undoubtedly an important and influential work within the history of Hindu traditions, the biblical designation is a serious misnomer. It never had the status of a broadly accepted "Bible," nor does it speak to a unitary "Hinduism." At the time of its composition in the early centuries CE, northern India was a highly diverse religious environment, full of spirited and contentious disagreement over fundamental questions. Debates between the various groups we now commonly label as "Hindu" and others identified as Buddhist, Jain, Ajivaka, and many others circulated throughout elite circles. The virtue of the *Bhagavad Gita*, for our purposes, is that it sought in relatively succinct form to engage many of the existing religious ideologies and practices of its Indian setting.

The *Bhagavad Gita* is itself situated in a much larger text, the epic poem *Mahabharata*, which relates the story of a cataclysmic war between two sets of cousins, the Pandavas and the Kauravas, for control of a central Indian kingdom. At the onset of the eighteen-day battle, the foremost warrior on the Pandava side, Arjuna, develops profound doubts about the course of actions he is about to pursue. How can it be virtuous, he wonders, to make war on those he esteems as family (*kula*): cousins, grandfathers, and teachers? He asks his charioteer, Krishna, to drive his chariot out between the two contending sides on the battlefield to survey the battle arrays. There he wilts with physical tremors and threatens to abandon the war. Krishna responds to Arjuna's qualms with a series of arguments intended to persuade Arjuna that he should fight.

Krishna's lengthy battlefield sermon on action begins with questions of proper conduct (*dharma*), but, subsequently, it turns to other broader topics that have to do with action in general and with religious action as the most important form of action. Krishna advises Arjuna that his duty as a warrior (*ksatriya-dharma*) to fight in a just war outweighs his obligations to family (*kula-dharma*). However, Krishna is not just concerned with the question of which aspect of dharmic responsibility has priority. He also seeks to explain how worldly actions, even ones like fighting in a war, can be just as efficacious, religiously, as the renunciation of action. During the period when the *Bhagavad Gita* was composed, adherents of the teachings of the Buddha and Mahavira the Jina, as well as orthodox brahmanic ascetics, contended that the preeminent route to reaching the highest spiritual goals was to abandon worldly life, in order to avoid what they considered the "bondage" of worldly desires and actions. Krishna asserts that, if one can renounce one's attachment to the fruits of one's actions and undertake action on the basis of *dharma* in a mental state of equanimity, one avoids the bondage of action.

However, Arjuna is not entirely assured by Krishna's argument. "With quite contradictory words you seem to confuse my own insight," he complains, then demands of Krishna, "Therefore tell me definitely which is the course by which I will attain to the supreme good (*sreyas*)" (Van Buitenen 1981, 3.2). Arjuna's confusion directly reflects the religious situation of the period in which the *Bhagavad Gita* was composed. Many religious teachers and groups competed with contradictory claims as to what was the best path to religious attainments. There were orthodox sacrificers, brahmanic renouncers of various sorts, yogic ascetics, heterodox groups like Buddhists and Jains, and worshipers of various new gods. There were debates about the relative efficacy of action versus knowledge, debates over the necessity of renunciation or the value of worldly life. There were philosophical monists, dualists, pluralists, theists, agnostics, and atheists. Even among one type of practice, there were countless variations. Krishna lists some of the ways religious seekers were practicing the central ritual of sacrifice (*yajna*).

There are yogins who regard sacrifice as directed to deities; others offer up sacrifice by sacrificing into the fire that is *brahman*. Others offer the senses of hearing and so forth into the fire of restraint, while others offer the objects of sound, etc., into the fires of the senses. Others again offer up all the actions of the senses and those of the vital faculties into the wisdom-kindled fire of the yoga of self-restraint. There are sacrificers who offer with substances, others with austerities, others with yoga, others with knowledge and Vedic study—ascetics all and strict in their vows. Some sacrifice *prana* into *apana* and *apana* into *prana*, blocking the passage of *prana* and *apana* as they practice breath control. Others limit their meals and offer *pranas* into *pranas*.

Van Buitenen 1981, 4.25–30

Among this welter of competing claims, views, and paths, Arjuna's request was simple: how is one to know the best route to the *sreyas*, the highest state?

At this point in the conversation, Krishna begins gradually to reveal his divine nature to Arjuna. At the same time, he offers a guide to the perplexed. Before granting a vision of his full awesome, all-encompassing divine form to Arjuna, Krishna reviews the various systems of religious thought and practice available in India of the time and evaluates their efficacy. A key to his interpretive method can be found in the following statement:

> There have been many who, rid of passions, fears, and angers, and made pure by the austerities of insight, have immersed themselves in me, resorted to me, and become of one being with me. I share in them in the manner in which they turn to me; for in all their various ways men do follow my trail, Partha.

> Van Buitenen 1981, 4.10–11

The second sentence here, one should note, is the same passage that Vivekananda quoted (using a different translation) in his 1893 speech. However, in the context of his larger argument Krishna's position here is considerably more nuanced than the statement of universal tolerance and religious equality Vivekananda found in it. In fact, Krishna makes several points. First, he recognizes that other persons in the past have attained the highest state, usually termed *moksa* or *nirvana*. They have done so through methods that have rid them of the forces and obstacles that had previously bound them. However, the highest state they achieved may not have been exactly what they anticipated. Krishna claims it is to be "immersed" in Krishna himself. In other words, Krishna redefines *moksa* in terms of participation in the being of himself, as God. And finally, he asserts, all the methods that humans follow devoutly and rigorously lead ultimately to Krishna. They are said to be efficacious insofar as they involve disinterested action. In the end, this yields a simple criterion for assessing other religious paths: how direct they are in leading one toward Krishna.

Let us take one example of Krishna's critical tolerance. The existing practices of yoga were adeptly summarized by Patanjali in the *Yogasutras*, a text roughly contemporary with the *Bhagavad Gita* (Miller 1995). In that text, Patanjali outlined yoga as a set of non-theistic practices based largely on the philosophical premises of the dualistic Samkhya school. In the *Bhagavad Gita* Krishna reviews these practices and presents them to Arjuna as efficacious.

> Let the yogin yoke himself at all times, while remaining in retreat, solitary, in control of his thoughts, without expectations and without encumbrances. Let him set up for himself a firm stool in a pure spot, neither too high nor too low, with a cover

of cloth, deerskin, or *kusa* grass. As he sits on his seat, let him pinpoint his mind, so that the workings of mind and senses are under control, and yoke himself to yoga for the cleansing of his self. Holding body, head, and neck straight and immobile, let him steadily gaze at the tip of his nose, without looking anywhere else. Serene, fearless, faithful to his vow of chastity, and restraining his thinking, let him sit yoked. . . .

So far Krishna might be offering a direct restatement of the *Yogasutras*. Covering key steps in Patanjali's eightfold practice, Krishna recommends finding a comfortable seated position (*asana*) in an isolated place, control of breath (*pranayama*), and withdrawal of senses from the exterior world (*pratyahara*), leading to a concentrated one-pointedness of mind (*dharana*). Yet now he adds what Norvin Hein (1983) has termed his "modifying addendum":

. . . his thought on me, his intention focused on me. When he thus yokes himself continuously, the yogin of restrained thought attains to the peace that lies in me, beyond *nirvana*.

Van Buitenen 1981, 6.10–15

Krishna here inserts his theistic self into the previously nontheistic practice of yoga, as both the subject of contemplation and as the end to which yoga leads its practitioner. He provisionally accepts yoga as an effective path (*marga*) but one that may be made still more direct and efficacious when it is allied with a recognition and contemplation of Krishna's own divine nature.

At the conclusion of his review of yogic practices, Krishna introduces a new term. He speaks of one who "shares" in Krishna's divine being. "He who shares in me as living in all creatures and thus becomes one with me, he is a yogin who, however he moves, moves in me" (6.31). The term is *bhakti*, most often translated as "devotion," but also connoting the sense of "sharing" (as Van Buitenen's translation renders it) or "participating" in God's being (Prentiss 1999, 17–24). *Bhakti* is the most effective form of yoga, Krishna tells Arjuna, and recommends that he follow this path.

The yogin surpasses the ascetics (*tapasvin*), surpasses even the sages who know (*jnanin*), surpasses the workers who merely act (*karmin*). Therefore, Arjuna, become a yogin. Him I deem the most accomplished man of yoga among all yogins who shares (*bhajate*) in me in good faith, with his inner self absorbed in me.

Van Buitenen 1981, 6.46–47

All these existing religious methods—asceticism (*tapas*), metaphysical knowledge (*jnana*), and ritual action (*karma*)—are judged as valuable for those who practice them; but, for Arjuna, Krishna emphasizes, the most efficacious path is that of a devotee, a *bhakta*. Here is Krishna's scale of religious forms, in its most succinct formulation.

Later, Krishna returns to the discussion of sacrifice and adds his modifying addendum to that practice as well.

Even they who in good faith devote themselves to other deities really offer up their sacrifices to me alone, Kaunteya, be it without proper rite. For I am the recipient of all sacrifices and their master, though they do not really recognize me and therefore slip. To the Gods go they who are avowed to the Gods, to the ancestors (*pitr*) go they who are avowed to the ancestors, to the ghouls (*bhuta*) go those who are avowed to the ghouls, to me go they who sacrifice to me.

Van Buitenen 1981, 9.23–25

Krishna acknowledges sacrifice as an effective ritual action, even when the sacrifice is offered to some other god than himself, since the sacrificial offering will ultimately reach Krishna as the Supreme Lord. However, the lack of recognition involved in sacrificing to some other figure, whether it be another deity, an ancestor-spirit, or a powerful semidivine *bhuta*, leads those sacrificers on a detour in their course toward the highest end. The sacrifice that is offered straight to Krishna, of course, follows the most direct route.

Krishna's emphasis on selfless and devotional action leads him to declare that *bhakti* is a method that is open to all. It is not limited according to one's ability to offer material resources for sacrifice.

If one disciplined soul offers to me with love a leaf, a flower, fruit, or water, I accept this offering of love from him. Whatever you do, or eat, or offer, or give, or mortify, Kaunteya, make it an offering to me, and I shall undo the bonds of *karman*, the good and evil fruits. . . . I am equable to all creatures, no one is hateful to me or dear—but those who share me with love are in me and I am in them.

Van Buitenen 1981, 9.26–30

Here Van Buitenen renders *bhakti* first as "love" and subsequently also as "share." Krishna's universal equanimity extends to all. "Even people of low origins, women, *vaisyas*, nay *sudras*, go the highest course if they rely on me" (9.33). It is not restricted on the basis of gender or class origin, he specifies, nor is limited to those who have observed righteous conduct (*dharma*) in the past. "Even a hardened criminal who loves me and none other is to be deemed a saint, for he has the right conviction; he soon becomes Law-minded and finds peace forever" (9.30–31).

Within the context of his argument, Krishna values *bhakti* directed toward himself as the Supreme Being most highly for three principal reasons. First, *bhakti* does not involve any particular action or type of conduct but rather focuses on the inner attitude or mental state of the actor. Any religious activity or worldly action can be done with an attitude of *bhakti*. Thus, it does not require renunciation. Arjuna can even fight his upcoming battle, without sin or bondage, if he does so in a mental state of *bhakti*. Second, the inner mental attitude of *bhakti* is available to all: women, low castes, and even evil-doing persons can practice this path. Thus, it avoids the kinds of restrictions on religious practice and attainment found both in the Vedic sacrificial tradition and in renunciatory orders like the Buddhists and Jains. Third, *bhakti* helps solve the problem of disinterested action that worried Arjuna earlier in Krishna's discourse. Krishna argued that the important thing is to act without attachment to the fruit of one's action but recognized that this requires the discipline and training normally found only among yogis and renunciants. *Bhakti* offers a less difficult means of achieving that equanimity. If one devotes all actions to Krishna and makes Krishna the fruit of all one's actions, one can take one's own self-interested ends out of the equation of action.

Krishna's teaching to Arjuna on the battlefield, recorded in the *Bhagavad Gita*, articulates a position of critical tolerance. On the one hand, Krishna appears to accept all existing practices within the crowded religious environment of classical India. That is, he views all of them as acceptable and as having something of value to offer their adherents. Schools of thought and practice that fall outside of the boundaries of "Hinduism" (as they were later constructed), such as Buddhism, Jainism, and other heterodox groups, are accepted in this regard just as much as ones that are faithful to supposed Hindu criteria. Even persons who make sacrifices to lowly "ghouls" are doing something of worth, in Krishna's provisional opinion. However, his summaries and commentaries on other religious forms are not without an overarching agenda. Through rhetorical strategies like the "modifying addendum" and the scale of religious forms, Krishna can frame other knowledges as less complete and other practices as less direct than the new practice of *bhakti* that he promotes as being the most comprehensive and most efficacious way of attaining the highest goal.

Siva's Scale of Religious Forms

Let us now go forward several centuries, to the early medieval period in India, roughly 700–1200 CE, and consider the position of Saiva Siddhanta, a major order of worshipers of the god Siva. They defined themselves as a distinct school of thought and practice in a large genre of texts consisting of Agamas, which are presented as the direct teachings of Siva himself, and Paddhatis, ancillary texts by human authors.

In his study of one important Saiva Siddhanta text, the Indologist Heinrich Von Stietencron has argued, "Saivism is conceived of as an independent religion, and not as part or sect of any larger entity which we might call Hinduism" (1995, 53). This is a valuable perspective. It stresses the religious variety of early medieval India and reminds us that there was at that time no overarching category such as "Hinduism" by which the worshipers of Siva might include themselves with votaries of Visnu and the Goddess, Advaita Vedantin monists and Dvaita dualists, and practitioners of any number of other schools of thought and practice, as members of a unitary religious community. In my view, however, Von Steitencron's use of the term *religion* here reifies the Saiva Siddhanta school in ways not suitable to the manner in which they defined themselves vis-a-vis other religious schools of thought and practice of their time and place. I will argue that it is more apt to consider the rhetoric by which Saiva Siddhanta locates itself as a form of critical tolerance, including and ranking all religious groups within a scale of forms. They do not view themselves as a distinct, bounded, and separate "religion," so much as a more complete or perfected (*siddhanta*) form of a broadly shared religious outlook.

According to Saiva Siddhanta, the central task for the human being, and indeed for all conscious living creatures, is to attain liberation (*moksa*), a final state of complete freedom in which one's soul becomes like Siva himself. To do so, one must employ the twin powers of consciousness—the power of knowledge (*jnanasakti*) and the power of action (*kriyasakti*)—which are latent in every conscious being. One must exercise these powers in a coordinated effort to remove bondage, which the Saivas understand in terms of three types of fetters (*pasa*). The powers of consciousness are inherently all-powerful, but they are inhibited and constrained in all bound creatures by the fetters. To remove the fetters requires the grace of Siva (exercised in part through his teachings in the Agamas), and it also requires directed human effort on the part of the one who aspires to liberation. Therefore, Saiva Siddhanta evaluates itself and other religious teachings and practices in terms of their respective abilities to enlighten and empower, and thereby to enable humans to gain fuller access to their inhering powers of consciousness.

For Saiva Siddhanta, various forms of knowledge differ hierarchically. They may be more or less comprehensive in their scope and offer more or less illumination. Of the many knowledge systems in the world, sciences like medicine and astronomy are adapted to useful but limited worldly affairs, while other systems of thought like Buddhism and Vaisnavism aim at comprehending the fundamental organization of the cosmos and enabling one to act most effectively in accord with this structure. Of all bodies of knowledge, the Saiva Siddhantins claim, the system taught by Siva in the Agamas is the highest and most complete form, for three main reasons: its authorship, its appropriate audience, and its illuminating power.

The Agamas come originally from the mouth of Siva, as we have seen, and since Siva is defined as an omniscient being, they are considered to be infallible. Many other Indic systems of knowledge like Buddhism and Samkhya trace themselves back to a human originator, and humans are, according to Saiva Siddhanta, necessarily limited in their knowledge. The distinction between divine revelation and human fallibility is a common argument in religious polemics, of course. The Saivas add one new wrinkle, however, that enables them to articulate a more complex hierarchy among religious revelations. According to Saiva teachings, the highest form of Siva is one called Sadasiva, the "eternal Siva." This form of Siva is envisioned as a being with five faces, four of them facing in the four cardinal directions and the fifth an upraised and "subtle" face. Of these faces, the fifth upraised face, known as Isana, is considered the highest. The Agamas tell us that Siva has transmitted different teachings from his different faces. From his four cardinal faces, he taught such forms of knowledge as astronomy, the Nyaya school of logic, Vedic teachings, Tantric schools, and lesser forms of Saiva knowledge. However, the teachings central to Saiva Siddhanta, namely, the Agamas, were emitted by Siva's highest upraised face (Davis 1991, 29).

Siva intends the Saiva Siddhanta teachings for the most highly qualified persons, those most able to exercise their powers of knowledge. For others, say the Agamas, Siva teaches other systems of knowledge more congenial to their lesser abilities. Of course, when one's fetters begin to "ripen" and one's powers of knowledge become more powerful, the knowledge of Saiva Siddhanta will come to be recognized as the most suitable one. This is because it is more comprehensive and illuminating.

This knowledge is authoritative because, while it elucidates matters accessible to other systems, it also enables the comprehension of matters to which these systems do not give access. As it is said, "A science which enables the comprehension of unknown things as well as known ones is most authoritative."

Mrgendragamavrttidipika, quoted in Davis 1991, 30

Some systems of knowledge like medicine and astronomy deal exclusively with one of the three principal categories (*padartha*) of the cosmos, namely, the material world, which Saivas label *pasa*. Other systems of thought like the Vedas, the Saivas acknowledge, can illuminate matters pertaining to the world and to the soul (*pasu*), the second of the three categories. Only the

Saiva Siddhanta, however, can enable one to know the third fundamental category of the cosmos, Siva (pati). For the Saivas, it is not a matter of right and wrong doctrine but of differing degrees of comprehensiveness within various systems of knowledge.

Systems of knowledge are not simply passive bodies of contents. In the Saiva view, correct knowledge does something: it destroys ignorance by elucidating more fully the true nature of things. This, too, admits of gradation, just as the more powerful rays of light from the sun illuminate things more fully than the relatively weaker light from the full moon. Possessing correct knowledge gives one a greater power of perception. In one Agama, Siva puts it this way: "One should consider the distinction between superior and inferior systems of knowledge like the difference at night between the eyes of a cat and those of a man (Purvakamikagama, quoted in Davis 1991, 30). One who has learned the most comprehensive knowledge taught by Siva in the Saiva Siddhanta Agamas gains the feline ability to see the true nature of things even in a darkened world.

Purposeful action, like knowledge, is a basic capacity of the human soul, and like knowledge, action takes different forms in the world. All may be effective toward some end, but some can be judged as superior to others. Some actions rely on limited worldly knowledge, use instruments of limited efficacy, and aim at accomplishing limited everyday results. Others, by contrast, may be based on more comprehensive knowledge of the cosmos, make use of more powerful means, and aim at attaining more far-reaching results; and these the Saivas judge to be superior actions. For example, an Ayurveda physician attempting to recover the bodily health of his patient bases his treatment on a body of largely empirical knowledge concerning the human organism and treats the patient with dietary and medicinal concoctions that have a therapeutic effect on the patient's body. For some maladies, this is entirely adequate, while, for others, a more penetrating intervention may be needed. A patient suffering from the bite of a poisonous snake requires stronger treatment than Ayurveda offers. In such a case, one must seek out a healer adept in the use of the Garuda-mantra, a special powerful mantra that magically removes snake poison. And to treat the condition of the human soul in its more profound state of bondage, action of a still greater efficacy is needed. In this case, the Agamas insist, only Saiva ritual action is able to have a complete and fully liberating effect.

Saiva ritual action is based on the more comprehensive knowledge of the cosmos, as taught by the one being of supreme omniscience, Siva. It makes use of the most efficacious instruments of action, namely, mantras. Therefore, it is bound to lead to superior results. However, Saiva Siddhanta readily concedes, the rituals of other groups are also useful.

Those who are purified through Vedic rituals like the Fire Sacrifice and vows like the Fortnight Fast attain joy in the three worlds. Those who offer a hundred sacrifices to the god Indra gain the abode of Indra.

Matangaparamesvaragama, quoted in Davis 1991, 34

Joy and heavenly abodes are certainly legitimate and worthy goals for attainment. However, they are decidedly inferior in the Saiva scale of values.

However, the place attained by those dedicated to Siva, even when they perform Saiva rituals improperly, cannot be achieved by non-Saivas even with a thousand sacrifices.

Matangaparamesvaragama, quoted in Davis 1991, 34

Unlike Vedic rituals and other religious systems, Saiva ritual action can lead one to final liberation from all worldly bondage (*moksa*). But even here, some Saiva texts also accommodate the claims of other schools, which also claim to enable their practitioners to attain this state of liberation. There are grades of *moksa*, they assert. According to Vedajnana, "there are seven grades of *moksa*," ranging from lesser forms that leave one still somewhat subordinate, to the one highest form that is subtle, transcendent, fully achieved, and completely autonomous (*Saivaparibhasamanjari*, quoted in Davis 1991, 34). Only ritual based on Saiva Siddhanta principles of action leads to that highest form of *moksa*.

Concluding Remarks

The German Indologist Paul Hacker has written of "inclusivism" as a characteristic Indic mode of thought (Halbfass 1995, 10–12). Like Swami Vivekananda, he finds great value in the sense of acceptance and tolerance found within the Hindu traditions historically. For Vivekananda, this implied a "universal tolerance" of Hinduism toward other religions. I agree that Indic religious groups regularly seek ways to accommodate and include the practices and even the deities of other groups and that this has generally led to a relative "catholicity of spirit" among many Hindu schools of thought and practice. Inclusivity is a Hindu resource for tolerance. Yet I agree with Hacker, and against Vivekananda, that inclusivism is not the same as unqualified tolerance. I have argued here that classical and medieval Hindu texts do not express tolerance uncritically.

In a medieval Hindu temple, we may see many images of all the various gods, who find their places within the larger temple complex and receive worship from those devoted to them. In any given temple, however, only one deity can stand at the center of the sanctum sanctorum as the principal recipient of worship. So, too, I have tried to show in looking at two important sources that the rhetoric of inclusivism does not preclude hierarchy. Surveying the range of religious options in their complex religious situations, classical and medieval Hindu texts characteristically convey their visions in the form of a scale of forms. This hierarchizing viewpoint allows for the provisional validity of many religious viewpoints, but it reserves a highest validity for one particular perspective.

Speaking to a still more varied international audience at the 1893 World Parliament of Religions, Vivekananda looked back to the generous inclusivism of texts like the *Bhagavad Gita* but largely ignored their critical evaluation. In so doing, he laid the foundation for a modern Hindu conception of itself as uniquely tolerant among world religions. If we wish to amend Swami Vivekananda's statement that Hindus "accept all religions as true" to make it cohere more closely to historical texts like the *Bhagavad Gita* and the Saiva Siddhanta positions that we have reviewed here, we would have to give it a modifying addendum. Krishna in the *Bhagavad Gita* and Siva in the Saiva Agamas instruct Hindus to accept all religions as true and valid for those who believe and practice them; but, at the same time, they hold that one religious viewpoint is still truer and more efficacious than the rest.

References

Biardeau, Madeleine. 1994. *Hinduism: The anthropology of a civilization*. Trans. Richard Nice. French Studies on South Asian Culture and Society. New York: Oxford University Press.

Davis, Richard H. 1991. *Ritual in an oscillating universe: Worshiping Siva in medieval India*. Princeton, NJ: Princeton University Press.

Eaton, Richard M. 2000. Temple desecration and Indo-Muslim states. In *Beyond Turk and Hindu: Shaping Indo-Muslim identity in premodern India*. Ed. David Gilmartin and Bruce B. Lawrence, Gainesville: University Press of Florida.

Embree, Ainslie T. 1993. *Utopias in Conflict: Religion and nationalism in modern India*. Comparative studies in religion and society. Berkeley: University of California Press.

Goel, Sita Ram. 1993. *Hindu temples: What happened to them*. Vol. II: The Islamic evidence. New Delhi: Voice of India.

————. 1990. Let the mute witnesses speak. In *Hindu temples: What happened to them (a preliminary survey)*. Ed. Arun Shourie et al., 62–181. New Delhi: Voice of India.

Halbfass, Wilhelm. 1995. *Philology and confrontation: Paul Hacker on traditional and modern Vedanta*. Albany: State University of New York Press.

Hein, Norvin. 1983. Hindu formulas for the facilitation of change. In *Traditions in contact and change: Select proceedings of the XIVth congress of the International Association for the History of Religions*. Ed. Peter Slater and Donald Wiebe, 39–52. Waterloo, Ont.: Wilfred Laurier University Press.

Inden, Ronald B. 2000. *Querying the medieval: Texts and the history of practices in South Asia*. New York: Oxford University Press.

Miller, Barbara Stoler. 1995. *Yoga: Discipline of freedom*. Berkeley: University of California Press.

Nehru, Jawaharlal. 1942. *Glimpses of world history*. New York: The John Day Company.

Olivelle, Patrick. 2004. *The law code of Manu*. World's classics. Oxford: Oxford University Press.

Panikkar, K. N. 2002. *An agenda for cultural action, and other essays*. New Delhi: Three Essays.

Prentiss, Karen Pechilis. 1999. *The embodiment of bhakti*. New York: Oxford University Press.

Ramanujan, A. K. 1989. Is there an Indian way of thinking? An informal essay. In *The collected essays of A. K. Ramanujan*. Ed. Vinay Dharwadker, 34–51. New Delhi: Oxford University Press.

Van Buitenen, J. A. B. 1981. *The Bhagavadgita in the Mahabharata*. Chicago: University of Chicago Press.

Vivekananda, Swami. 1893. Response to welcome. *Swami Vivekananda's Chicago addresses*. Accessed 29 May 2007 <http://www.caip.rutgers.edu/~kanth/jwz/mbm/sv/address1.html>.

Von Stietencron, Heinrich. 1995. Religious configurations in pre-Muslim India and the modern concept of Hinduism. In *Representing Hinduism: The construction of religious traditions and national identity*. Ed. Vasudha Dalmia and Heinrich Von Stietencron, 51–81. New Delhi: Sage Publications.

CONTRIBUTORS

ISMAIL ACAR received his Ph.D. in Islamic Law from Dokuz Eylul University in Turkey in 1999. He is currently visiting assistant professor of religion at Bard College. Prior to working at Bard, he was visiting scholar of Christian-Muslim relations at the Lutheran School of Theology at Chicago and visiting scholar of Islam at the Center for Near Eastern Studies at UCLA. He is currently working on a project titled, "First Period of Christian-Muslim Relations in Both Historical and Theological Perspectives."

ALAN J. AVERY-PECK is Kraft-Hiatt Professor of Judaic Studies and chair of the Department of Religious Studies at the College of the Holy Cross, Worcester, Massachusetts. Specializing in Jewish history and religion in the first six centuries CE, he is, most recently a co-author and editor of *The Encyclopaedia of Judaism* (2nd edition in 4 vols., Brill, 2005) and *The Mishnah in Contemporary Perspective*, part 2 (Brill, 2006). He is also editor of the journal *The Review of Rabbinic Judaism*.

ROBERT M. BERCHMAN is professor of philosophy and religious studies, Dowling College, and Senior Fellow Institute of Advanced Theology, Bard College. He has published numerous books and articles in the fields of history of philosophy and history of religions, among them *Porphyry against the Christians* (Brill Academic Publishers, 2005). He has also served as an editor for *The Dictionary of Religious and Philosophical Writings in Late Antiquity* (Brill Academic Publishers, 2007); co-edited with John F. Finamore, *Plato Redividus: A History of Platonism* (University Press of the South, 2005); and co-edited with John F. Finamore, *Metaphysical Patterns in Platonism* (University Press of the South, 2007).

BRUCE CHILTON is Bernard Iddings Bell professor of religion, executive director of the Institute of Advanced Theology, and chaplain at Bard College. An ordained priest, he received his Ph.D. from Cambridge University. He is an expert on the New Testament and early Judaism and the author of many scholarly articles and books.

BRADLEY S. CLOUGH occupies the Abdulhadi H. Taher Chair in Comparative Religion at The American University in Cairo. He has previously taught at Columbia University, Sarah Laurence College, Bard College, and Antioch College's Buddhist Studies Abroad Program in India. He does research on the history of Buddhist thought and practice in South Asia. Currently, he is working on a study and translation of the 2nd century CE Sanskrit epic poem on the life of the Buddha, Asvaghosa's *Buddhacarita*.

VINCENT J. CORNELL is Asa Griggs Candler Professor of Middle East and Islamic Studies at Emory University. From 2000 to 2006, he was professor of History and director of the King Fahd Center for Middle East and Islamic Studies at the University of Arkansas. From 1991 to 2000, he taught at Duke University. His published works include thirty articles, a five-volume set, and three books. His interests cover the entire spectrum of Islamic thought from Sufism to theology and Islamic law. He is currently working on projects on Islamic ethics and moral theology in conjunction with the Shalom Hartmann Institute in Jerusalem and the Elijah Interfaith Institute. For the past five years, he has been a key participant in the Building Bridges Seminars hosted by the Archbishop of Canterbury.

KEVIN CORRIGAN is professor of the Liberal Arts in the Graduate Institute of the Liberal Arts at Emory University. His recent books are *Plotinus' Theory of Matter-Evil and the Question of Substance: Plato, Aristotle and Alexander of Aphrodisias* (Peeters, 1996); *Reading Plotinus: A Practical Guide to Neoplatonism* (Purdue, 2004); and, with Elena Glazov-Corrigan, *Plato's Dialectic at Play: Structure, Argument, and Myth in the Symposium* (Penn State, 2004). He has written many articles ranging over the history of philosophical and religious thought from the Pre-Socratics, Plato, and Aristotle, through Patristics, late antiquity and medieval thought, to Whitehead, Bergson, Levinas, and Derrida in contemporary thought.

RICHARD H. DAVIS is professor of Religion and Asian Studies at Bard College. He is author of *Ritual in an Oscillating Universe: Worshiping Siva in Medieval India* (Princeton, 1991) and *Lives of Indian Images* (Princeton, 1997). He is the winner of the 1999 A. K. Coomaraswamy Award from the Association for Asian Studies. He has also edited two volumes, *Images, Miracles, and Authority in Asian Religious Traditions* (1998) and *Picturing the Nation: Iconographies of Modern India* (2006). Currently, he is completing work on a translation of a twelfth-century Sanskrit ritual text, the *Mahotsavavidhi of Aghorasiva*, and starting work on a cultural history of early India.

CAROLYN DEWALD taught for many years at the University of Southern California and is now professor of History and Classics at Bard College. She has written extensively on Herodotus, including the introduction and notes to the Oxford World's Classics translation (1998) and is co-editor with John Marincola of the *Cambridge Companion to Herodotus* (2006). She is the author of *Thucydides' War Narrative: A Structural Study* (2006) and is currently co-editing with Rosaria Munson a commentary on Herodotus I for the Cambridge Greek and Latin Classics series.

WILLIAM SCOTT GREEN teaches religion at the University of Miami, where he also is senior vice provost and dean of Undergraduate Education, and a senior fellow of the Miller Center for Contemporary Judaic Studies. He has written extensively on ancient Judaism and higher education. Most recently, he is co-editor, with Jacob Neusner and Bruce Chilton, of *Historical Knowledge in Biblical Antiquity* (2006).

DANNY L. JORGENSEN, a sociologist, is professor of Religious Studies at the University of South Florida. Over the past thirty-some years, his research, much of it conducted by way of participant-observation, has focused on the sociology of new religions in the United States. This includes a variety of publications on the Latter-day Saint (Mormon) religion of several varieties, neopaganism and witchcraft, occultism and divination, Scientology, Shakers, and the Ozark Amish.

IBRAHIM KALIN is an assistant professor at Prince Alwaleed bin Talal Center for Muslim-Christian Understanding, Georgetown University. He has published on Islamic philosophy, relations between Islam and the West, and the contemporary Muslim world. He is the author of *Knowledge in Later Islamic Philosophy: Mulla Sadra on the Unification of the Intellect and the Intelligible* (Oxford University Press).

BARUCH A. LEVINE is Skirball Professor, Emeritus, of Bible and Ancient Near Eastern Studies, New York University. Previously on the faculty of Brandeis University, he is also a rabbi. Dr. Levine is author of *JPS Torah Commentary on Leviticus* (1989) and of the *Anchor Bible Commentary on Numbers*, 2 vols. (1993, 2000), as well as numerous publications in ancient Semitic epigraphy, history, and religion, some in Hebrew.

JACOB NEUSNER is a Distinguished Service professor of the history and theology of Judaism and senior fellow of the Institute of Advanced Theology at Bard College in Annandale-on-Hudson, New York. He received his Ph.D. in religion from Columbia University. The author and editor of hundreds of publications on religion and other topics, he is the only scholar to have served on both the National Endowment for the Humanities and the National Endowment for the

Arts. He is the recipient of numerous honorary degrees, medals, prizes, and academic awards, and resides in Rhinebeck, New York.

WILLIAM REISER, S.J., is a professor in the Department of Religious Studies at the College of the Holy Cross, where he has been teaching theology since 1978. A graduate of Weston Jesuit School of Theology and Vanderbilt University, he has published in the areas of systematic theology and Christian spirituality.

KRISTIN SCHEIBLE is assistant professor of religion at Bard College, where she has taught the last four years. Formerly, she was a lecturer at Brown University and senior teaching fellow at Harvard University. She received her Ph.D. from Harvard University in 2006, with a dissertation examining the ethically transformative power of narrative in the Pali *Mahavamsa*, an important historical source in Theravada Buddhism.

NAME AND SUBJECT INDEX

ANCIENT SOURCES INDEX